# Property Tax Planning

# Property Tax Planning

Seventeenth Edition

by

**Zeeshan Khilji**
Founder and Managing Director, Tax Consulting Group

Bloomsbury Professional
LONDON • DUBLIN • EDINBURGH • NEW YORK • NEW DELHI • SYDNEY

**BLOOMSBURY PROFESSIONAL**

Bloomsbury Publishing Plc

50 Bedford Square, London, WC1B 3DP, UK
1385 Broadway, New York, NY 10018, USA
29 Earlsfort Terrace, Dublin 2, Ireland



**British Library Cataloguing-in-Publication Data**

A catalogue record for this book is available from the British Library.

| | | |
|---|---|---|
| ISBN: | HB: | 978 1 52652 625 0 |
| | ePdf: | 978 1 52652 626 7 |
| | ePub: | 978 1 52652 627 4 |

Typeset by Evolution Design & Digital Ltd (Kent)
Printed and bound by CPI Group (UK) Ltd, Croydon, CR0 4YY

# Preface

There have been a significant number of changes to the treatment of UK property in recent years, both directly to such ownership and to commonly used structures. These changes have a profound impact on the tax treatment of the holding of UK property. Such changes include:

- Significant changes to the treatment of non-resident landlords from 6 April 2019 and 6 April 2020.
- New capital allowances regime, including 'full expensing' from 1 April 2023 and new rules in respect of capital allowance eligibility for plant and machinery for use primarily within a freeport or investment zone tax site following the UK's departure from the EU.
- The Construction Industry Scheme (CIS) rules and HMRC's increasing powers.
- The domestic reverse charge rules for building work.
- Changes to rules relating to withholding tax on payments of interest and royalties following Brexit.
- Changes to the capital gains tax compliance for non-corporate taxpayers disposing of UK land.
- Full implementation of the Corporate Interest Restriction (CIR), including its application to non-resident landlords from 6 April 2020.
- Changes to the conditions for Business Asset Disposal Relief (BADR).

This book also includes reference to the possible impact of the UK's exit from the European Union.

This Seventeenth Edition continues to adopt the popular format of previous editions. Each chapter has been set out as a series of important tax planning opportunities and pitfalls which, for ease of reference, are summarised at the beginning of each chapter by a chart. This arrangement is designed to help the busy reader to use it as a checklist of the points he or she might want to consider. In addition to a practical explanation of the position, relevant cases, statutes and other authorities are quoted to facilitate further reference by the interested reader.

Those familiar with past editions will know that it is divided into four parts. These reflect the four categories of property ownership, viz:

Part A　Property Investors

Part B　Property Dealers and Developers

Part C　Trading Premises

Part D　Private Residences

Each category has its own particular topics which are dealt with in the chapters in that part – although there are some cases where the same topic is relevant to more than one category. To avoid too much duplication, certain points cross-refer to other parts of the book where the same topic is covered in detail.

The book is intended to assist the following:

- *Individuals and companies owning property*

  Investors, dealers/developers, trading organisations and owners of private residences. These companies and individuals would welcome a book which provides them with ideas which they could in turn 'bounce' off their professional advisers.

- *Practising accountants*

  The book can assist the busy accountant in keeping abreast of the latest in property tax planning opportunities.

- *Tax practitioners*

  The book provides a useful compendium of tax planning points in property situations for the tax practitioner's reference.

- *Other professionals*

  Solicitors, surveyors, estate agents and bankers involved in property situations often need to be aware of the tax aspects of situations they encounter, without necessarily having to sift through technical detail.

I would like to thank Tim Mallon of Mallon Tax for proofreading the chapters, and Jane Deeks of Deeks VAT Consultancy and Phoebe Hindlet of MJS Tax for their input into updating the VAT and capital allowances chapters respectively.

Whilst every effort has been made to ensure the accuracy of the contents of this book, neither the author nor the publisher can accept any responsibility for a loss arising to anyone relying on the information contained herein. Indeed, specific professional advice on possible tax implications should always be sought in relation to any proposed transaction or situation.

The law is stated as at 31 December 2023.

Zeshan Khilji, Tax Consulting Group
January 2024

# Contents

# Table of Cases

## J



## K



## L



## M



## N



## O

# Table of Statutes

# Table of Statutory Instruments

# Table of HMRC and Other Materials

# Abbreviations

| | |
|---|---|
| ABA | Agricultural Buildings Allowance |
| AIA | Annual Investment Allowance |
| ANGIE | Adjusted Net Group Interest Expense |
| ATED | Annual Tax on Enveloped Dwellings |
| BADR | Business asset disposal relief |
| CAA | Capital Allowances Act |
| CFC | Controlled Foreign Company |
| CGS | Capital Goods Scheme |
| CGT | Capital Gains Tax |
| CIR | Corporate Interest Restriction |
| CIS | Construction Industry Scheme |
| CIV | Collective Investment Vehicle |
| CNR | Centre for Non-Residents (within HMRC) |
| CPI | Consumer Price Index |
| CTA | Corporation Tax Act |
| EBITDA | Earnings Before Interest Tax Depreciation and Amortisation |
| ECAs | Enhanced Capital Allowances |
| EIS | Enterprise Investment Scheme |
| ETPL | Energy Technology Production List |
| FA | Finance Act |
| FA (No 2) Act | Finance (No 2) Act |
| FRS | Financial Reporting Standard |
| GAAP | Generally Accepted Accounting Practice |
| HMRC | Her Majesty's Revenue and Customs |
| IBA | Industrial Buildings Allowance |
| IHTA | Inheritance Tax Act |
| IM | Inspectors' Manual |
| IR | Inland Revenue (known as HM Revenue and Customs – which also incorporates the former HM Customs & Excise) |
| ITEPA | Income Tax (Earnings and Pensions) Act |
| ITTOIA | Income Tax (Trading and Other Income) Act |

| | |
|---|---|
| ITA | Income Tax Act |
| KIC | Knowledge-Intensive Companies |
| Para | Paragraph |
| NRB | Nil Rate Band |
| NRCGT | Non-Resident Capital Gains Tax |
| OMV | Open Market Value |
| QNGIE | Qualifying Net Group Interest Expense |
| QPP | Qualifying Private Placement |
| REIT | Real Estate Investment Trust |
| RI | Revenue Interpretation |
| S | Section |
| SBAs | Structures and Buildings Allowances |
| Sch | Schedule |
| SEIS | Seed EIS |
| SDLT | Stamp Duty Land Tax |
| SI | Statutory Instrument |
| SLS | Syndicated Loan Scheme |
| SP | HMRC Statement of Practice |
| SSCD | Simon's Special Commissioners' Decisions |
| STC | Simon's Tax Cases |
| TA | Income and Corporation Taxes Act |
| TC | Tax Cases |
| TCGA | Taxation of Chargeable Gains Act |
| TIOPA | Taxation (International and Other Provisions) Act |
| TMA | Taxes Management Act |
| TOGC | Transfer of a Business as a Going Concern |
| VATA | Value Added Tax Act |
| VATTR | Value Added Tax Tribunals Reports |

*Part A*

# Property Investors

*Chapter 1*

# Acquisition of a property through a non-UK resident company

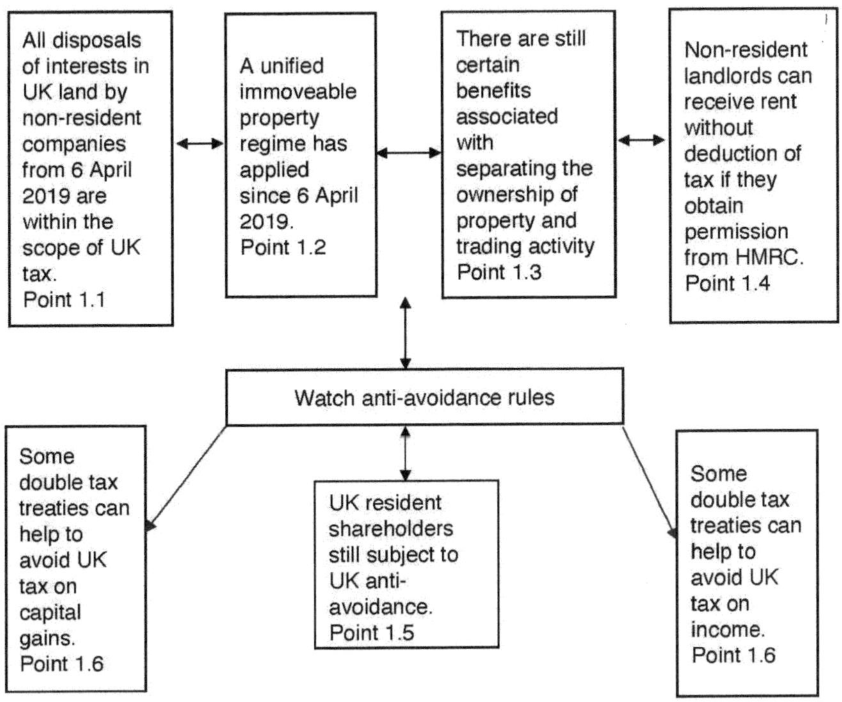

# 1 ACQUISITION OF A PROPERTY THROUGH A NON-UK RESIDENT COMPANY

**Point 1.1:** ***Prior to 6 April 2019, subject to limited exceptions a company resident outside the UK was a useful vehicle for the ownership of commercial investment property in the UK, since capital gains on sale could be realised free of UK tax. However, from 6 April 2019, all disposals of interests in UK land (including commercial property) by non-resident companies are within the scope of UK tax.***

The non-resident capital gains tax (CGT) regime was rewritten and extended to cover both non-residential UK property and indirect disposals of UK property with effect from 6 April 2019, meaning all disposals of interests in UK land by non-resident persons (including companies) are within the scope of UK tax from this date *(Finance Act 2019, s 13, Sch 1 paras 1, 2; TCGA 1992, ss 1A, 1C and 1D)*.

For companies, non-resident capital gains resulting from disposals of UK land are subject to corporation tax from 6 April 2019, rather than CGT, which was the case under the pre 6 April 2019 rules.

An interest in UK land is defined very broadly and includes any 'estate, interest, right or power in or over land' sited in the UK as well as the benefit of an obligation, restriction or condition affecting the value of such an interest *(TCGA 1992, Sch 1B, para 4)*.

Before April 2020, non-resident companies were subject to income tax on rental income arising from UK land at a flat rate of 20%. However, from 6 April 2020, non-resident companies are subject to corporation tax rather than income tax on profits from UK land (*FA 2019, s 17, Sch 5; s 5 (2) CTA 2009)*. Certain transitional rules apply for accounting periods which straddle this commencement date.

**Point 1.2:** ***A non-resident company owning residential property in the UK was liable to one of two possible alternative UK tax charges on capital gains arising prior to 6 April 2019. These provisions were abolished from that date and replaced with a unified immoveable property regime.***

The following legislative measures were introduced in respect of UK immovable property for non-resident persons:

- Between 6 April 2013 and 5 April 2019, disposals of high value UK residential property by non-resident companies, partnerships with a corporate member and collective investment schemes were subject to CGT at a rate of 28% where the property was chargeable to the annual tax on enveloped dwellings (ATED-related gains). This regime was repealed for disposals made on or after 6 April 2019. It is important to note that while the ATED-related gains regime has been abolished, the ATED charge itself still applies, where relevant. This is further discussed in Chapter 5.

- Between 6 April 2015 and 5 April 2019, a CGT charge applied more generally to non-UK residents disposing of UK residential property, known as the non-resident capital gains tax (NRCGT) regime. As such, only gains on direct disposals by non-resident persons of UK residential property interests were potentially subject to UK tax. With effect from 6 April 2019, this was extended to commercial property and so all disposals of interests in UK land by non-resident persons (including companies) are within the scope of UK tax from this date.

Any pre-April 2015 element of the gain is not subject to tax. This means that the company will be faced with alternative methods of computation including time apportionment of the gain: applying the April 2015 value as base cost or taking the gain/loss arising over the entire ownership period. The position was quite complex between 6 April 2013 and 5 April 2019, until the annual tax on enveloped dwelling (ATED) related capital gains tax charge existed. This applied to high-value residential properties owned by companies, partnerships with at least one corporate member or collective investment schemes. The tax applied regardless of whether or not the owning entity is tax resident in the UK.

Up to 5 April 2015, 'high value residential properties' meant properties worth more than £2 million and, in determining the chargeable gain, the property's value is rebased at 5 April 2013. From 6 April 2015, the threshold was lowered to £1 million and from 6 April 2016, it was reduced to £500,000. As mentioned above, the rules changed from 6 April 2019. No further ATED-related gains or NRCGT are applicable since this date and such companies are only subject to tax under the immovable property regime thereafter. The ATED related capital gains regime has therefore not been discussed any further in this chapter.

Where there is a disposal of UK land by a non-resident and the asset that is disposed of was held on 5 April 2019, the legislation allows for rebasing to market value at that date (*TCGA 1992, Sch* 4AA, *para 3).*

In the relatively straightforward case of an asset which was not within the charge to CGT prior to 6 April 2019 (eg non-residential land owned by a non-resident), this is achieved by deeming the asset to have been sold and immediately re-acquired on 5 April 2019 at market value. The gain arising is not chargeable to tax. It is possible to elect for rebasing not to apply, but in such a case any loss arising will not be an allowable loss.

If the asset was wholly chargeable to CGT before 6 April 2019 (eg residential land held by a non-UK resident) and was owned on 5 April 2015 (UK land held by a non-resident was not chargeable before that date), rebasing in this case applies by assuming a deemed disposal and re-acquisition at market value on 5 April 2015. There is an option to either elect for rebasing not to apply or to elect for straight-line time apportionment of the gain, with only the post-5 April 2015 proportion being chargeable.

If the asset was only partially chargeable to CGT before 6 April 2019 (eg a property owned by a non-resident that was residential for only part of the pre-6 April 2019 period of ownership) which was owned at 5 April 2015, there are two deemed disposals and reacquisitions, on 5 April 2015 and 5 April 2019 respectively. The earlier (April 2015) disposal is not chargeable to CGT and the gain on the later (April 2019) disposal is not treated as accruing until actual disposal of the asset. It is also possible to elect for re-basing not to apply.

**Point 1.3:** ***There are still certain benefits associated with separating the ownership of property and trading activity, even after the introduction of the new immoveable property legislation from 6 April 2019.***

Where trading premises are to be purchased, the ownership of the property and the trading activity could be separated.

For example, where it is proposed to buy premises for a retail business in the UK, a non-UK resident company could acquire and own the property. A separate company, which may be a UK resident company, could carry on the retail trade. The trader would occupy the premises under a lease from the non-resident owner.

The lease to the trader would be a short lease at a market rental and subject to regular review. In this way, none of the capital appreciation in the property over time would accrue to the UK trading entity.

The main advantage of this arrangement historically would have been the capital gains tax exemption that was available pre-6 April 2019 for gains realised by non-resident investment companies on commercial property. The appropriateness of such a structure must, however, take account of the ultimate exit strategies and the application of the immoveable property legislation from 6 April 2019. Specifically, the disposal of 'land rich' entities from 6 April 2019 will be subject to UK taxation on the increases in value from that date unless an exemption applies. One such exemption is (broadly) that the land is used in a qualifying trade for at least 1 year by the property owner or a connected company and that it is reasonable to assume that the trade will continue following the disposal.

The application of VAT and SDLT on the rental payments would need to be considered.

Where a non-UK landlord is receiving rents on property in the UK, there is potentially a withholding tax issue. This is discussed in Point 1.4 below.

**Point 1.4:** ***Where a UK tenant or agent pays rent to a non-UK-based landlord, tax at source may have to be withheld. This can be avoided by entering into a special arrangement with HMRC.***

Prior to 6 April 2020, non-resident landlord companies were subject to a flat rate of income tax of 20% on the property income. From 6 April 2020, non-UK resident companies are chargeable to corporation tax rather than to income tax on UK rental profits, and so are required to submit corporation tax returns for income arising from this date.

Without special provisions, non-UK resident landlords could avoid the UK tax charge on their rental income. Therefore, non-resident landlord companies are subject to the provisions of the non-resident landlords scheme, which requires income tax to be withheld on the rent, either by the tenant or letting agent as appropriate. If there is a letting agent acting, then the obligation transfers from the tenant to the letting agent. If the agent is responsible for paying any expenses on the property these can be deducted from the income in computing the tax due – providing that the expenses are allowable for tax purposes (*SI 1995/2902, reg 9*).

The landlord can deduct any tax paid by the tenant or agent from any tax due when filing the annual self-assessment tax return in the UK. Overpaid tax can be recovered.

The non-resident corporate landlord can receive the rent without deduction of tax if they obtain permission from HMRC. There are two situations where the tenant or agent need not account for tax to HMRC. These are where:

- a tenant's gross weekly rent is £100 or less; or
- the non-resident landlord obtains HMRC approval to receive the rents with no tax withholding.

Obtaining this approval is a relatively straightforward procedure. It involves the submission of a form (form NR1Li) by the non-resident to HMRC (Personal Tax International (PTI)). If the non-resident landlord is a company, the appropriate application form is NRL2i; if it is a trust, NRL3i. PTI will grant approval where the following applies to the non-resident landlord:

(a) UK tax affairs are up to date; or

(b) the landlord does not expect to be liable to UK tax for the year in which the application is made; or

(c) the landlord has never previously had any UK tax obligations.

Where properties are jointly owned, a separate application needs to be submitted for each non-resident owner.

Any letting agent acting for a non-resident landlord must register with PTI. Registration should be within 30 days of the date the agent became liable to operate the Non-Resident Landlord Scheme. Tax must be paid within 30 days of the quarter dates which for these purposes are 30 June, 30 September, 31 December and 31 March. The agents must also prepare an annual return (form NRLY) detailing all income, expenses and tax deducted. This must be sent to HMRC by 5 July following the end of the tax year. Agents must by the same date provide the landlord with a certificate of tax deducted. They may use form NRL6 for this purpose.

The entitlement for a landlord to receive rents gross and account for any tax annually on a company tax return can be withdrawn. This may happen if HMRC cease to be satisfied that information provided for the application is correct; or it is no longer satisfied that the non-resident landlord will comply with its UK tax obligations; or fails to send information requested. If this happens, the non-resident may have to wait at least two years before being approved to go back to the annual self-assessment basis.

**Point 1.5:** ***Anti-avoidance rules and the need to establish non-resident status create hurdles in the use of non-resident companies.***

Notwithstanding the changes as noted above that apply from 6 April 2019, it may remain important for many structures to continue to be operated in the manner envisaged (ie with central management and control taking place outside the UK). The reasons for this could include the potential application of UK withholding tax on interest payments made by UK resident borrowers.

For UK tax purposes, a foreign company is not resident in the UK if its central management and control is exercised abroad (*De Beers Consolidated Mines Ltd v Howe* (1906) 5 TC 198). A UK incorporated company will always be resident in the UK (*CTA 2009, s 14*) regardless of where it is managed and controlled, subject to the provisions of certain double tax treaties.

An HMRC Statement of Practice (SP 1/90) raises a number of issues in determining 'central management and control' which can be summarised as follows:

(a) Do the directors of the company in fact exercise management and control?

(b) If so, where do they exercise it (which is not necessarily where they meet)?

(c) If not the directors, by whom and where is central management and control exercised?

(SP 1/90)

In practice, there are many non-UK incorporated companies involved in UK activities where their residence is accepted without question as being outside the UK. However, that does not mean that investors in UK property can simply avoid tax here by using an offshore vehicle.

In the first place, HMRC have stated that they will look at such companies 'to see whether there has been an attempt to create the appearance of central management and control in a particular place without the reality'. That could well defeat a situation where local directors in a tax haven location are merely rubber stamping instructions issued by a UK-based individual or company.

For the company to be resident outside the UK, all or most of the directors should ideally be based outside the UK, although HMRC states in its manuals that it is the place from which an individual exercises central management and control that is the relevant factor for locating the residence of a company. The non-UK directors should be active in making business decisions. All major policy decisions must be decided at board meetings outside the UK. These include purchasing and selling the property, issuing instructions to any managing agents in the UK and negotiating any financial arrangements. In addition, agreements relating to the property should be concluded outside the UK.

In the cases of *Wood & Another v Holden* [2006] STC 443 and *News Datacom Limited & Another v Revenue & Customs* (SpC 561), the Court of Appeal and

Special Commissioners respectively found in favour of the taxpayer companies whose overseas tax residence status had been challenged by HMRC. In contrast, a Dutch company lost a non-UK tax residence argument in front of the First-tier Tax Tribunal (*Laerstate BV v HMRC FTT* [2009] UKFTT 209 (TC)). The Tribunal felt in that case that the company's Dutch director was merely acting on the instructions of its UK-based controlling shareholder. These cases serve to emphasise the importance of the need for active involvement by the non-resident directors in the business of the company, and the evidencing of that by company minutes and contemporaneous supporting documentation such as emails and notes of telephone conversations. The case of *Development Securities (No 9) Ltd and others v HMRC* [2017] UKFTT 565 in 2017 found in the favour of HMRC, who were able to successfully contend that the Jersey incorporated entities were, in fact, centrally managed and controlled from the UK and were accordingly UK resident. The Courts found that the Directors of the Jersey incorporated companies were acting upon decisions that had either already been made or upon the instructions on their parent.

Further anti-avoidance provisions may tax shareholders who are resident in the UK (whether or not they are domiciled here) on any income arising in the company (*ITA 2007, s 714* and subsequent sections) if the income arises directly or indirectly from a transfer of assets abroad.

**Point 1.6:** ***Some countries have tax treaties with the UK which prevent HMRC from using anti-avoidance rules to tax UK shareholders on non-trading property gains in overseas companies. UK-based shareholders could invest via companies in these jurisdictions to shelter property gains from UK tax. Certain treaties have been revised and aligned with the immoveable property legislation from 6 April 2019.***

Anti-avoidance provisions can subject UK individual and corporate shareholders to tax on their share of capital gains realised by a closely controlled non-resident company in which they have a sufficiently large interest.

Many countries tax their residents (eg the UK) and/or their citizens (eg the US) on their worldwide income and gains. Most countries also tax, to some extent, income and gains arising within their jurisdictions. Therefore, there is significant scope for double taxation.

Most of the modern treaties to which the UK is party are based on OECD models, which aim to ensure that a resident of a territory which is party to a double tax treaty is only taxed in one state; persons who are resident in both territories are usually treated, for the purposes of applying the provisions of the treaty, as resident in the territory with which they are most closely related under a 'tie-breaker' clause.

Certain tax treaties that the UK has with other countries prevent those provisions from applying to companies resident in those jurisdictions. Prominent examples are Belgium and Luxembourg. In any event, the anti-avoidance rules can still apply where the gain arises from the sale of UK property, rather than the shares in a property holding company. As tax treaties are renegotiated, the protection from those provisions is being removed, as happened with the Netherlands. It is important, therefore, to check the up-to-date position.

On 19 July 2023, the Luxembourg Parliament approved the enforcement of the revised double tax treaty with the UK, which should be implemented in 2024.

The revised Treaty will contain certain significant changes, predominantly in relation to property, such that Luxembourg real estate investors holding indirect interests in UK real estate could now be subject to UK tax on capital gains, in accordance with UK tax rules.

As a result of the new immoveable property rules introduced in 2019, the indirect sale of UK real property could apply to the sale of a company which derives 75% or more of its gross value, directly or indirectly, from UK property (ie a UK property rich company). The existing treaty allocates sole taxing rights to Luxembourg in relation to gains realised on the disposal of indirect sales of UK property. As such, under the existing treaty a Luxembourg resident disposing of a UK property rich company would be subject to Luxembourg tax only (if applicable).

Article 13(2) of the Treaty now allocates taxing rights to the UK or, as applicable, Luxembourg, on the sale of shares deriving more than 50% of their value directly or indirectly from property in the jurisdiction in which the property is located.

The Treaty will not supersede the UK rules (such that the 75% threshold in the definition of UK property rich, still applies). However, the new provisions mean that a Luxembourg resident disposing of a UK property rich company will now be subject to UK tax on the gain (subject to applicable UK exemptions).

Broadly, for this to apply, there is a minimum 25% hold requirement (a substantial indirect interest). The exception to this is if the entity qualifies as a collective investment vehicle and makes an election for an exemption to apply, For the purchaser, buying a company represents a different proposition from buying the property itself. and the purchaser could also avoid SDLT by buying the company. Nevertheless, for residential property, inherent gains may subsist for increases in value from April 2013. Similarly, from 6 April 2019, inherent gains have also needed to be considered in respect of non-residential property as set out above.

**Point 1.7:** ***UK anti-avoidance rules can tax certain income and gains accruing to an offshore company.***

If there is evidence that a property is purchased for reasons other than long-term investment, a gain on sale could be chargeable as trading income or under special provisions relating to certain transactions in land (*ITA 2007, s 752* and subsequent sections and those within the scope of UK income tax and *CTA 2010, s 356OA* and subsequent sections for those within the scope of UK corporation tax).If either of these treatments applies, a company's non-resident status will not afford any exemption from tax. In that connection, the government introduced rules in the *Finance Act 2016* aimed at taxing all profit from developing or dealing in UK sited property. This includes indirect gains, e.g., when shares or units in the property-owning entity are sold.

The rules are aimed at a situation where a number of connected persons act together to carry out development activity that amounts in substance to a single trade of UK property development.

Where the conditions are met the profits or gains of the connected parties will be combined and the person making the disposal will be taxed on the whole amount.

If a relevant contribution is made by an associated party and the profit will already be brought into account as income in calculating profits, for UK corporation tax or income tax purposes there will be no extra profit to assess.

Where an amount is taxed by another jurisdiction unilateral relief may be available and/or an application for the mutual agreement procedure (MAP) may be made.

*Chapter 2*

# Property ownership through a non-UK resident trust

> With effect from 6 April 2019, the unified immoveable property regime also applies to non-resident trusts, to include UK commercial property.
>
> Point 2.1

# 2 PROPERTY OWNERSHIP THROUGH A NON-UK RESIDENT TRUST

**Point 2.1:** ***With effect from 6 April 2019, the unified immoveable property regime also applies to non-resident trusts, to include UK commercial property. Previously, non-domicile individuals based in the UK could benefit from using a non-resident trust for UK commercial property investment***

Gains arising on non-residents in respect of residential property was introduced with effect from 6 April 2015, which was broadened considerably by *FA 2019* under the Non-Resident Capital Gains Tax (NRCGT) provisions to also include interests in UK commercial land. In addition, this also covered significant holdings in 'property-rich' companies. A trust which meets the conditions of a non-UK resident trust is therefore covered by the NRCGT rules.

Further, the UK has anti-avoidance provisions which, in many cases, tax settlors on gains realised within trusts they have created (*TCGA 1992, s 86, Sch 5*) on or after 17 March 1998.

The anti-avoidance legislation applies where any of the following individuals ('defined persons') can benefit under a trust:

(a) the settlor;

(b) the settlor's spouse or civil partner;

(c) any child or step-child of the settlor or of the settlor's spouse or civil partner;

(d) any grandchild or step-grandchild of the settlor or of the settlor's spouse;

(e) any spouse or civil partner of such a child or grandchild;

(f) any company controlled by persons within (a)–(e) above; and

(g) any company associated with a company within (f) above.

If a gain arises in a year, that gain is treated as accruing to the settlor (*TCGA 1992, s 86(4)*). This is so, even if no benefit is actually received.

The gain is calculated as if the trustees were UK resident except that there is no annual exemption. Unused trust capital losses can be deducted (*TCGA 1992, Sch 5, para 1(1), (2)*).

The gains treated as accruing to the settlor can be offset by personal losses and still attract the personal annual exemption.

This tax charge under the anti-avoidance provisions cannot apply where the settlor is domiciled outside the UK. An individual who does not intend to make the UK his or her life-long home may not be domiciled here even if he or she has been living here for some years. Typically, such an individual would have been born outside the UK or have parents of non-UK origin.

Anyone who was able to establish non-domicile status could have potentially avoided tax on UK investment property gains where that person created, and owned the property through, an overseas trust (*TCGA 1992, s 86(1)(c)*). From 6 April 2017, any individual who has been UK tax resident for more than 15 years out of the previous 20 is deemed to be domiciled here. This has application as where a UK domiciled or deemed UK domiciled settlor adds property to a trust; this can 'taint' the trust and therefore bring the individual within the provisions of *TCGA 1992, s 86*.

Where gains on the sale of UK residential property are not taxable on a UK resident individual under the anti-avoidance rules mentioned above, from 6 April 2019, the disposal of both residential and commercial property is fully within the charge to UK tax regardless of the application of the rules referred to above. It should be noted, however, that commercial properties will benefit from a re-basing at this date such that gains that accrue following this only should be brought within the charge to UK tax.

UK resident beneficiaries are taxable on the gains when the beneficiary receives a capital payment from the trust in the UK. This rule has applied since 6 April 2008 where the beneficiary is UK resident but non-UK domiciled. If the capital payment is received offshore and not remitted to the UK, the non-domiciled beneficiary will not be taxed on the gains if they claim to be taxed on the remittance basis. A subsequent remittance of the funds to the UK would give rise to a charge.

A UK domiciled settlor would not be subject to this tax charge if the trust realises the gain at a time when they are no longer UK-resident, provided that at least five complete years elapse between the year in which they cease to be resident and the year in which they resume residence. In that situation, the gain cannot be taxed on them (*TCGA 1992, ss 86(1)(c), 86A*).

The structures noted above do not prevent income tax on income from UK property arising. Anti-avoidance rules on UK source income do not distinguish between domiciled and non-domiciled settlors. Particular care must be taken in connection with the 'Transfer of Assets Abroad' provisions (*ITA 2007, s 720*) and the specific 'Settlement' provisions (*ITTOIA 2005, s 624*).

### *Point 2.2:* For non-resident trusts excluding certain beneficiaries, gains on non-residential property could accrue in the trust free of UK tax until 6 April 2019

If a non-resident trust is created which expressly excludes any of the beneficiaries listed in Point 2.1 above, then it is not caught by the anti-avoidance rules mentioned therein, hence allowing scope to create trusts to benefit other relatives, eg parents, brothers, nieces, great-grandchildren or friend. In these cases, gains on non-residential property could have accrued in the trust free of UK tax until 6 April 2019 and any UK resident beneficiaries taxed as described above on the gains when the beneficiary received any capital payment from the trust.

To take advantage of these arrangements, the settlor must have had to set up the trust out of his or her own funds and without any element of reciprocity. If, for example, Adam gives money to his sister Linda to set up a trust for himself,

Adam (and not Linda) will be treated as the settlor. Similarly, arrangements whereby Adam settles a trust for Linda in reciprocation for her settling a similar-sized trust for him would not work. Adam and Linda would be treated as settlors of their own trusts (*ITTOIA 2005, s 620*).

A gift into settlement is a transfer of value for inheritance tax (IHT) purposes, potentially giving rise to a liability to IHT at a rate of 20% once aggregate gifts exceed the Nil Rate Band (NRB). IHT is, however, beyond the scope of this book.

*Chapter 3A*

# Relief for finance costs incurred by individuals, trustees and non-UK resident investment companies

**Accrued interest on finance to buy, improve or repair property or repay loans for that purpose is deductible against letting income for tax purposes. The position for non-UK resident investment companies also changed from 6 April 2020.**
**Point 3.1**

↓

Surplus interest costs can be carried forward to offset against future letting income.
Point 3.2

↓

To avoid carrying forward unusable losses, it may be better to grant a lease at a premium instead of a sale or assignment.
Point 3.3

↓

Funds can be borrowed from UK and overseas associates but these must be on commercial arm's length terms.
Points 3.4 and 3.5

↓

20% withholding tax deduction but may be reduced or eliminated where the Eurobond exemption applies, there is a double tax agreement or the borrowing is set up as discounted security.
Points 3.6 and 3.7

↓

The introduction of rules for 'alternative finance' has improved tax relief for financing structures which are compliant with Islamic law.
Point 3.8

# 3A RELIEF FOR FINANCE COSTS INCURRED BY INDIVIDUALS, TRUSTEES AND NON-UK RESIDENT INVESTMENT COMPANIES

**Point 3.1:** ***Accrued interest and other finance costs can be deducted from total rental income, although tax relief in respect of residential lettings has been restricted. The position for non-UK resident investment companies changed from 6 April 2020.***

Although HMRC do not regard letting as a trading activity, taxable profits from property letting are computed as if it were a trade (*ITTOIA 2005, s 272(1)*). That means that any finance costs incurred are potentially deductible from total rents received. The deduction is for the accrued costs, calculated in accordance with generally accepted accounting practice (GAAP) (*ITTOIA 2005, s 25*), regardless of when they are actually paid.

The finance must relate to the purchase or improvement (including repairs) of the let property or the repayment of another loan that had been taken out for these purposes. Certain incidental costs of obtaining such finance are also allowable, including situations where the financing is aborted (*ITTOIA 2005, s 58*). Personal borrowings or loans for other purposes or activities would not qualify, even if secured on the let property.

These relatively generous rules will not necessarily apply to finance on residential properties or in the case of properties (commercial and residential) owned by non-resident investment companies. In the July 2015 Budget, the government announced measures to restrict tax relief on residential lettings in order to put a dampener on the buy-to-let housing market. The restriction was phased in from 5 April 2017 when non-corporate landlords were only entitled to offset 75% of their finance costs (including incidental finance costs such as derivative payments and lender fees). The remaining 25% attracted tax relief which was restricted to the basic rate of tax. In the following tax years, the amount deductible progressively reduced to 50%, 25% and finally nil, such that from 2020/2021 onwards, only basic rate tax relief is allowed. Borrowings on commercial property and commercially let holiday lettings (see chapter 10) are not affected by these restrictions. Where finance covers both residential and non-residential property, the related costs need to be apportioned against the respective amounts of income when calculating the restricted relief due.

With effect from 6 April 2020, non-UK resident investment companies are affected by the the introduction of a fixed ratio rule for net interest deductions in excess of £2m – see Point 3.30 in Chapter 3B.

All UK properties let by a landlord are treated as a single business (*ITTOIA 2005, s 264*). If finance costs and other costs exceed that year's total rental income, only the loss attributable to any capital allowances can be offset against the landlord's other income or gains (*ITA 2007, s 120*). Note, however, that since 5 April 2013, there has been an annual cap on the amount of such losses and certain other deductions which can be offset against general income. This cap is the greater of £50,000 or 25% of the individual's income. The surplus costs can, however, be carried forward in full against future income from the letting activity (*ITA 2007, s 118*).

The position becomes further complicated in relation to the restrictions on residential letting finance costs mentioned above. Where finance costs exceed property income, there will be an unrelieved cost element to carry forward but only basic rate income tax relief may be available in a future year even where there is sufficient income to cover both current and brought forward losses.

**Point 3.2:** ***If there are surplus finance costs following a property sale, these can be used against the rental income from a property owned and let subsequently.***

As mentioned in Point 3.1 above, surplus finance costs cannot be offset against other income or gains but they can be offset against future profits from the letting of UK property. Therefore, following a sale of a property, unused past finance costs can be used to shelter tax on income from another property, whether owned at the time or bought subsequently.

HMRC will allow the losses to be carried forward indefinitely whilst the UK letting business is being carried on. However, if the letting business actually ceases, the unused expenses will be forfeited.

This does not mean that losses cannot be carried forward if there is any gap in the letting activity. Where a property is sold but there is the clear intention to carry on a letting business, the costs can be carried forward. Therefore, if there is a gap in time following a sale of a property and, in that period, the investor is actively looking for a replacement investment property, the loss carry-forward should not be affected.

The offset of losses is subject to the restrictions introduced from 2017/2018 in respect of residential property finance costs incurred by non-corporates, referred to in 3.1 above.

Losses will be forfeited if they accrue to a non-resident company which subsequently becomes UK-resident. However, there are provisions that seek to ensure that when non-UK resident investment companies fall within the scope of UK corporation tax on rental income (ie from 6 April 2020) any historical losses accrued under the UK income tax regime should be available to be utilised as UK corporation tax losses.

**Point 3.3:** ***Where finance costs exceed rental profit throughout ownership, tax on a capital gain on sale can be reduced if a short lease can be granted at a premium prior to a sale of the main interest in the property.***

Unrelieved finance costs cannot be offset against a capital gain on investment properties for tax purposes. If there is to be no further rental income from this or any other properties, future relief for these costs will be forfeited.

Where there is the prospect of a capital gain that will be chargeable to UK tax, the tax liability can be reduced if the capital gain were partially converted to income for tax purposes.

This can be achieved by granting a short lease at a premium, with an option for the buyer to buy the main interest at the end of the lease period. For the reasons set out in Point 9.1, such a premium is partly treated as income, depending on the length of the lease involved. The shorter the lease, the higher the proportion of premium treated as income.

---

## Example

Mrs Wiggins owns a freehold commercial property that she lets. The rent is £30,000 per year. Over the past few years, repairs and finance costs have given rise to an accumulated loss of £100,000.

The property is sold in November 2020 for £400,000; this will give Mrs Wiggins a capital gain of £100,000 on which she will pay 20% tax, ie £20,000. (NB the capital gains tax rate on residential property is 18% or 28% depending upon the individual's marginal rate.) Alternatively, Mrs Wiggins offers the prospective buyer a four-year lease for no rent and a premium of £107,000 together with the freehold reversion for £293,000.

As a consequence of this transaction, 94% of the premium of £107,000 – or £100,580 – on grant of the four-year lease will be treated as letting income (see Point 9.1). Against this, the £100,000 losses can be offset, leaving just £580 in charge to income tax.

The capital gain, following the reduction in the capital element of the receipt by £100,580, has now disappeared. No capital gains tax therefore arises.

Mrs Wiggins has, therefore, saved just under £20,000 tax.

There could also be a short-term benefit for a buyer who is using the property for trading premises. The premium rules allow the buyer a trading deduction against taxable profits over each of the four years of the lease of £25,145 (ie £100,580/4 – see Point 27.1).

---

There is exposure, in arrangements such as this, that HMRC might seek to attack the grant of a lease as an artificial step inserted in the transaction under the principle in *Furniss v Dawson* [1984] STC 153. Additionally, *Finance Act 2013* introduced a general anti-abuse rule (the so-called GAAR) to counter tax planning arrangements that are considered to be abusive. The GAAR provisions require HMRC to successfully show that the arrangements cannot reasonably be regarded as a reasonable course of action. This double reasonableness test is intended to set a high threshold in determining whether a particular arrangement is considered to be abusive and therefore liable to counteraction.

Ultimately, the dividing line between arrangements that work and those that do not is a matter for the courts to determine, rather than HMRC. It is essential in such arrangements for there to be commercial or structural features that make the pure tax avoidance aspects less significant. For instance, the lease could be granted to an entity occupying the premises for trading purposes, whilst a separate (but possibly associated) entity buys the reversion for investment purposes.

In some situations, there may be no taxable capital gain. This could be, for instance, where the gain is less than the available annual exemption for the individual or trust. In other cases, there may be unused capital losses. Where the owners are non-UK resident individuals and non-UK companies, they may not be subject to UK tax on capital gains (see Chapter 1). In cases such as this, the conversion of capital into income would not give rise to any benefit. Indeed, it may be preferable to preserve losses in case there is a resumption of letting.

As already indicated, restrictions introduced from 2017/2018 may mean that that surplus finance costs in relation to residential property may only be relievable at the basic rate of income tax.

**Point 3.4:** ***Finance costs are allowable on funds borrowed from associated and connected persons. This includes lenders based abroad.***

Interest is allowable even on a loan from a connected party. Therefore, finance can be obtained from associated individuals (including spouses and relatives) and trust funds.

For the most part, there is no stipulation as to the amount of interest that is allowed, even where it is paid to a non-resident. However, excessive finance costs will be disallowed as not 'wholly and exclusively' for the purposes of the business (*ITTOIA 2005, s 34(1)(a)*). Interest relief can also be denied where the sole or main benefit of incurring the interest is to secure an income tax advantage (*ITA 2007, s 809ZG*).

There is also the possibility that transfer pricing rules may apply to adjust excessive interest to arm's-length rates where one company borrows from a lender with which it has a 'special relationship'. This will typically include situations where one company has a controlling or major interest in the other, or the same third person has such an interest in both companies.

Transfer pricing (see also Chapter 3B and Point 3.5 below) applies also to transactions wholly within the UK. In most cases, however, the transfer pricing rules now no longer apply unless the person receiving the tax advantage ('the advantaged party' – here, the borrowing company) is a 'large enterprise' (see Point 3.20 in Chapter 3B for the definition of 'large enterprise'). Even where they do apply, the 'disadvantaged party' (the lending company, which is receiving the excess interest) can claim exemption from UK taxation on the amount of interest that is disallowed for the borrower.

See also Point 3.5 below, and Points 3.20 and 3.21 in Chapter 3B.

**Point 3.5:** ***The terms of any borrowing must be wholly arm's length to obtain a deduction for related finance costs. Where borrowings are from a foreign associate, the terms should be based on those offered by a reputable third-party lender.***

The UK's transfer pricing rules (*TIOPA 2010, Pt 4*) may apply to limit the allowability of finance costs payable by non-UK resident companies. Transfer pricing applies to non-arm's-length transactions between two persons, one of whom has a controlling or major interest in the other. It does not, therefore, apply to transactions between individuals or to non-business transactions, but can apply to business transactions between an individual and a company or partnership. The rules apply even where both parties are taxable in the UK, but there is an exemption where the advantaged party – the party whose liability to UK tax has been reduced as a result of the transaction – is a small or medium-sized enterprise (SME), unless the other party is located in a tax haven or certain other jurisdictions with which the UK does not have an appropriate double tax treaty. For transactions involving UK companies, see Point 3.4 above, and Points 3.20 and 3.21 in Chapter 3B.

Under the rules, 'excessive' interest payable to an associated lender abroad will be disallowed. This does not just apply to situations where the rate of interest is too high. It also applies where the amount of the loan is greater than would have been supplied by a third party.

In a situation where a third party might normally lend up to, say, 65% of the value of a property on purchase, finance higher than this may be considered excessive. The loan does not have to be between two associates for the rule to apply. Interest will also be disallowed where a third party lends a higher than normal amount on the strength of the security of a guarantee or deposit provided by the borrower's associate. So-called 'back to back' arrangements are, therefore, caught.

If the interest payable under the arrangements is greater than would have applied in an arm's-length transaction, a deduction for the excess will not be allowed. If the entire loan is not on an arm's -length basis – for instance, where a top-up loan is required in addition to a normal secured loan – the whole of the top-up interest can be disallowed, unless it is on the same terms as subordinated debt available from third-party lenders.

Companies which borrow with the direct or indirect assistance of a foreign associate must be prepared to justify the loan arrangements as arm's length. It is advisable to approach a bank or other lender for a loan quote which ignores any security from associates. If a reputable third-party lender can be found which is prepared to take a greater than usual risk, any loan arrangement with an associate which replicates those terms should be acceptable as arm's length. Whilst a number of specialist lenders are now well established in the market for 'top-up' property finance, HMRC may be sceptical of terms apparently quoted by third-party lenders where they feel that these were obtained without any real commitment by the lender at that stage to lend on those terms.

UK property businesses to which the transfer pricing rules apply, for example those undertaken by non-UK resident property investment companies, may be able to apply to HMRC for an advance thin capitalisation agreement (ATCA), where the availability of related-party finance relief has a significant commercial impact on an enterprise's profits or losses. If successful, an ATCA ruling from HMRC can be binding for up to five years (HMRC SP 1/12).

As has already been noted, however, if the advantaged party (here, the borrower paying an excessive interest rate or in receipt of an advantageous loan) is an

SME, the transfer pricing rules are of no application, with three exceptions where:

(a) the lender is located in a tax haven etc;

(b) the borrower is a medium-sized enterprise and HMRC direct that the transfer pricing rules shall apply after an inquiry into the borrower's tax return; or

(c) the borrower irrevocably elects to be subject to the transfer pricing rules.

(*TIOPA 2010, ss 166–168*)

**Point 3.6:** ***If interest is paid to a non-UK resident lender, there is a requirement to deduct income tax at the time of payment unless the loan is from a non-UK source.***

Any person paying interest to a foreign lender on a long-term loan is required to deduct tax at a current rate of 20% unless the loan interest does not have a UK source (*ITA 2007, s 874*).

There is no statutory definition of UK source.

Whether or not interest has a UK source depends on all the facts and on exactly how the transactions are carried out. HMRC consider the most important of factors in deciding whether or not interest has a UK source to be:

- the residence of the debtor and the location of his/her assets. This will influence where the creditor will seek to enforce any judgement following default;
- the place of performance of the contract and the method of payment. Here we are looking at the substantive (not immediate) origin of the funds out of which the interest was paid;
- the competent jurisdiction for legal action and the proper law of contract; and
- the residence of the guarantor and the location of the security for the debt.

(HMRC Savings and Investment Manual SAIM9090).

This list of factors is derived from the leading case on the source of interest, *Westminster Bank Executor and Trustee Company (Channel Islands) Ltd v National Bank of Greece SA* (46 TC 472) and this approach was reinforced by the Court of Appeal in *Ardmore Construction Ltd v Revenue and Customs Commissioners* (2018) EWCA 1438. These cases have confirmed that in applying this multifactorial, fact-sensitive test where different factors give different answers, the question of source should be looked at from a practical, or realistic point of view.

The *Hargreaves Property Holdings v HMRC (2023)* case also reaffirmed certain best practice points and considerations with regards to withholding from yearly interest payments.

Practitioners previously regarded the long-established practice of executing and retaining so-called specialty debt agreements outside the UK as sufficient to ensure that the corresponding interest could be regarded as arising outside the UK. This would involve the debt being evidenced by deed with no UK property used as security. HMRC disputed this practice and took the opportunity in *Finance Act 2013* to introduce blocking legislation. In determining whether interest arises in the UK, no account is to be taken of any deed recording the obligation to pay interest.

Note that, where the withholding of tax is required of the borrower, it is only on payment of the interest. It is quite separate from the tax deductibility of the interest from profit, which is on an accrued – rather than a paid – basis.

Withholding tax will still, in principle, apply even if the interest is not allowable for tax purposes (for instance, where it is disallowable under Point 3.4 above). However, if excess interest is disallowed under the transfer pricing rules (see Point 3.5 above), the recipient of the interest can claim exemption from withholding tax for the excess (*TIOPA 2010, s 187*).

**Point 3.7:** ***Where a deduction of tax might otherwise apply, it can be exempted or reduced under the provisions of a double tax treaty. Exemptions are also available where the interest is short interest, where the quoted Eurobond exemption applies or where discount is payable on the redemption of a deeply discounted security.***

UK withholding tax may be reduced under the provisions of a double tax treaty (DTT). Prior to 1 June 2021, payments of interest and royalties made to EU resident associated companies were also exempt from UK withholding tax, under the UK domestic legislation which gave effect to the EU Interest and Royalties Directive. This legislation is repealed from 1 June 2021, with no exemption from UK withholding taxes on payments to EU associated companies permitted from that date, even in cases where HMRC has previously provided clearance (known as an exemption notice) which extends beyond 1 June 2021. While the changes affect payments made on or after 1 June 2021, anti-forestalling provisions also apply from 3 March 2021 to counteract attempts to put arrangements in place between these dates.

At present, it is also possible to avert a UK withholding requirement where any of the following apply:

- Where the loan is not capable of exceeding 12 months, any interest paid is referred to as 'short' as opposed to 'yearly' interest. Deduction of tax only applies to 'yearly' interest (*ITA 2007, s 874*). Therefore, no tax withholding is necessary on interest on short-term facilities from a foreign lender.
- Where interest arises on a quoted Eurobond, there is a withholding tax exemption (*ITA 2007, s 882*), provided the borrower is a company and it lists the bond on a recognised stock exchange (eg London, Luxembourg or the Channel Islands). For payments of interest made on or after 1 April

2018, the quoted Eurobond exemption above additionally includes securities admitted to trading on a multilateral trading facility (MTF).

Discount payable on the redemption of a deeply discounted security (ie one that is issued at a discount to redemption price) is not regarded as interest for the purposes of the withholding rules. These securities typically have a low or zero interest rate, but the borrower must repay a specific sum over and above the original sum borrowed. However, a First-tier Tribunal case (*Nicholas Pike* TC O1151) considered that a discount may be regarded as interest where debts are redeemable at a premium calculated by reference to a rate of interest. The taxpayer lost his subsequent appeal to the Upper Tribunal, which was heard during May 2013. (See Point 3.28 below for further details regarding deeply discounted securities.)

**Point 3.8:** ***The introduction of rules for 'alternative finance' has enabled tax relief to be obtained for costs incurred in relation to financing structures that are compliant with Islamic law.***

See Point 3.29 in Chapter 3B for an outline of the typical structures that have been accommodated by changes in the UK tax rules introduced since *Finance Act 2005*.

This 'alternative finance arrangements' legislation has subsequently been consolidated into *ITA 2007* for income tax and capital gains tax purposes (*ITA 2007, Pt 10A*).

For alternative finance costs related to residential property lettings, the new restrictions referred to earlier will apply as with conventional finance costs.

*Chapter 3B*

# Finance costs for UK property investment companies or companies within the scope of UK corporation tax

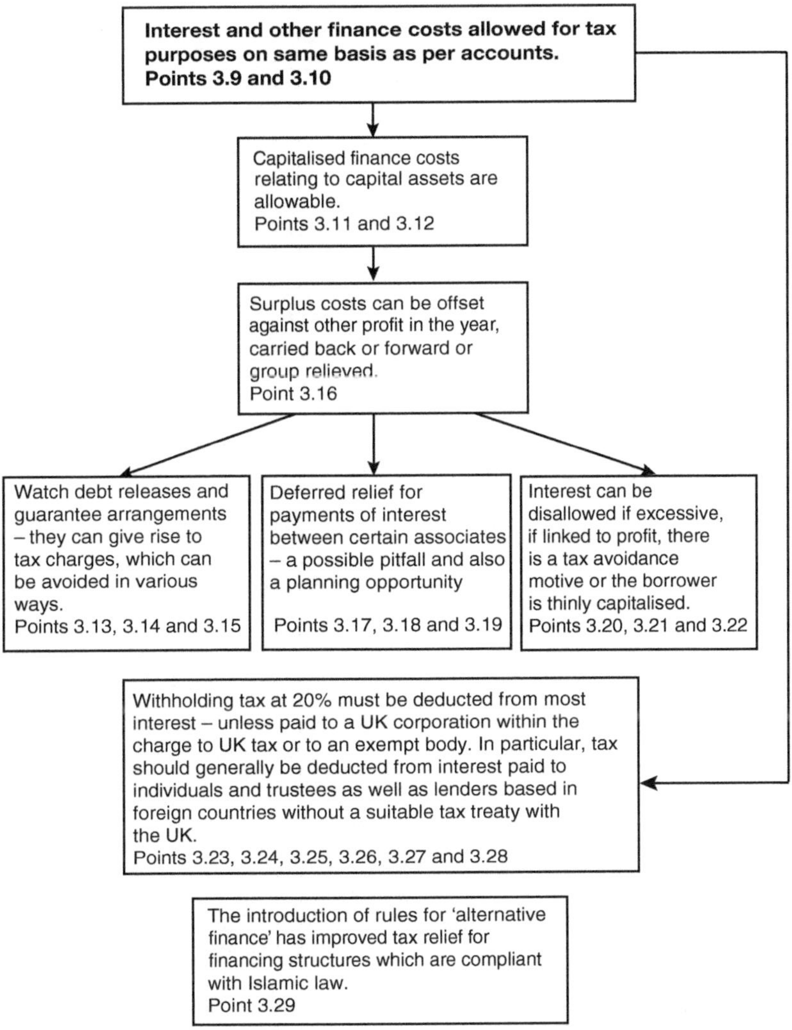

## 3B FINANCE COSTS FOR COMPANIES WITHIN THE SCOPE OF UK CORPORATION TAX ON RENTAL INCOME

**Point 3.9:** ***A company that obtains conventional finance from an unconnected lender for property investment is entitled to a tax deduction for the related finance costs. The deduction for the interest and other costs is normally given on the same basis as they are treated in the accounts.***

Typically, the acquisition of a property by property investors will be financed via debt and it will often be crucial for the buyer to obtain any available tax deductions for the financing costs.

Finance costs are, generally speaking, deductible for tax purposes on the same basis as they are reflected in the accounts (subject to the corporate interest restriction referred to at Point 3.30 below). This applies to:

- interest;
- incidental costs of obtaining finance or repaying a loan; and
- a premium/discount payable on redemption of a loan.

More specifically, a deduction is available for the following:

- discounts (including a variable discount influenced by market conditions);
- premiums;
- costs of obtaining loan finance, including the issue expenses incurred in connection with quoted debt;
- abortive expenditure and expenses incurred in connection with a loan facility which is never drawn;
- termination costs, including any penalty on loan redemption; and
- any other payments made under the terms of a loan, including payments to reimburse a lender's costs.

(*CTA 2009, s 307*)

The general rule on deductibility is subject to the condition that the indebtedness in question is a 'loan relationship'. Loan relationships arise in the following situations:

(a) a money debt resulting from a transaction involving the lending of money;

(b) an instrument issued to represent security for a money debt; or

(c) an instrument issued to represent rights of a creditor in respect of a money debt.

(*CTA 2009, ss 302–303*)

Shares carrying normal distribution rights are excluded from this definition. Unpaid trade debts or outstanding consideration on the purchase of an asset are typically money debts, but they do not usually satisfy the above criteria, and are not loan relationships. However, some aspects of money debts, notably interest, foreign exchange, impairment debits and release credits, can be brought within the loan relationships regime as relevant non-lending relationships. In the case of impairment debits and release credits they would need to arise from transactions where the borrower has claimed a trading or property business deduction.

These specific rules allow tax relief on interest on debts which are not loan relationships (*CTA 2009, Pt 6*), so that the interest is treated in the same way as costs incurred under loan relationships.

In many situations, from a borrower's perspective, there should be no practical difference between the treatment of a debt that is a loan relationship and the treatment of one that is not.

For a property investor, interest on a loan taken out to purchase a rental property is not an allowable expense in arriving at the income taxed as profits from a property business. Instead, the loan interest is treated as a non-trading loan relationship debit under the loan relationship rules (*CTA 2009, s 211*). As a general rule, the tax treatment of finance costs follows the accounting treatment. In most cases, the costs accrued in the borrower's profit and loss account will be deductible for tax purposes (see Point 3.10 below). There are, however, special 'late interest' rules which can apply in particular situations where the borrower and lender are associated (eg in certain cases where the lender is an individual, trustee or non-resident company based in a tax haven). These anti-avoidance measures provide for the deferment of tax relief for accrued and unpaid interest. See Point 3.17 below for further commentary on these rules.

Borrowers will receive relief for any discount payable on 'deeply discounted securities' in a similar way to the rules relating to interest-bearing debt referred to above. There are rules that can defer tax relief until the discount is paid (ie on redemption) where the holder is a participator in the issuer of the security and is a not a UK corporate (eg in certain situations where the holder is an individual, trustee or non-resident company based in a tax haven). See Point 3.17 below for further commentary.

There is the potential to exploit the mismatch if the recipient of the income from the security is not taxable under the loan relationship rules where such persons are non-associated. That person may only be taxed when the income is received. That could be the case with, for example, lenders who are individuals or certain foreign holders of the security. The borrower can still enjoy a tax deduction as the expense accrues.

A company that issues convertible debt can often claim a deduction for interest payable where it represents a reasonable commercial coupon, provided the convertible is either listed on a recognised stock exchange or issued on 'comparable terms' to listed convertible securities. However, if these conditions are not satisfied, the security can be treated as quasi-equity, rather than debt, with the consequence that the interest arising can be recharacterised as a disallowable distribution. This treatment can also apply to interest arising on other types of debts if they are either 'non-commercial securities' or 'special securities' (see Point 3.21 below for further commentary).

**Point 3.10:** ***The deduction is for all the costs reflected in the accounts in accordance with generally accepted accounting practice.***

Most companies will be claiming a deduction for the costs reflected in the income statement (ie profit and loss account) on an amortised cost (ie accruals) basis.

There are a number of ways to accrue expenses. To minimise the scope for creativity, the rules require the basis adopted to be in accordance with generally accepted accounting practice (GAAP), namely UK GAAP, which for most companies will be based on Financial Reporting Standards (FRS) FRS 102 if not FRS 101 or International Financial Reporting Standards (IFRS).

For interest or other expenses of a loan relationship to be recognised under GAAP in determining the borrower's taxable profits, they must be brought into account in the borrower's financial statements, including:

(a) its profit and loss account/income statement;

(b) its statement of recognised gains and losses;

(c) its statement of changes in equity; or

(d) any other statement of items brought into account in computing its profits and losses, except for those items recognised in order to correct a fundamental error

*(CTA 2009, s 308).*

For accounting periods which commenced on or after 1 January 2016, loan relationship profits, gains and losses have been based on debits and credits recognised within the income statement, unless there is an express provision to the contrary elsewhere in the legislation.

A broadly drafted regime anti-avoidance rule was contained within the *Finance (No 2) Act 2015*. These anti-avoidance measures are designed to future-proof the loan relationships rules from tax avoidance planning whilst also facilitating the repeal of existing targeted anti-avoidance rules. The 'follow the accounts' approach means that the actual payment dates of interest, or due and payable dates, do not themselves influence the timing of the deduction – other than for certain connected-party loans (see Point 3.17 below).

Accounting bases that comply with GAAP, such as the amortised cost basis, would similarly apply where there are either stepped or 'balloon' payments of interest. This may mean smaller payments in earlier years and larger amounts later. For the payer and the recipient, the effect of accruing these costs in the accounts over the period of the loan under the amortised cost basis would be to smooth out the payments. This has the effect of recognising a larger tax-allowable expense for the borrower in the early years compared to the actual amount paid. The lender, on the other hand, would be taxed on accelerated income.

This treatment is also relevant for discounted borrowing (see Point 3.28 below).

**Point 3.11:** ***If finance costs are capitalised in the balance sheet, tax relief can still be claimed in that year where the finance is in respect of capital assets.***

The normal rule provides for a deduction for any finance costs that are properly charged to the profit and loss account or, under current rules, other statements.

Where finance costs are included in the value of a fixed asset in the balance sheet, it might be thought that due to there being no interest expense in the accounts, there can be no relief for the interest expense. However, the loan relationship provisions can override the position in this case, such as to still treat the interest costs as loan relationship debits. This is provided that the debit relates to a loan relationship item, is capitalised in accordance with generally accepted accounting practice, and any profit or losses on that asset or liability will not fall to be taken into account for tax purposes (*CTA 2009, s 320*).

Examples would include interest on finance for purchases and construction of investment property or the purchase of shares in a property company.

However, no deduction is allowed in respect of any amounts representing a writing-down of the asset which is attributable to the finance costs or in respect of amortisation or depreciation representing a writing-off of the interest component (*CTA 2009, s 320(5), (6)*). This is to prevent a 'double dip' for any impairment or depreciation provided in respect of the interest element in the cost of the fixed asset.

The finance costs are allowed as if they had been expensed to the profit and loss account in accordance with GAAP (*CTA 2009, s 320(2)*). In the absence of such a provision, capital-related costs in respect of, say, finance for a property or company purchase might not be tax deductible if they are never charged to the profit and loss account.

HMRC regard this treatment for capitalised financing expense as only relevant to costs in relation to a fixed capital asset or project (ie excluding financing costs booked to work-in-progress, for example, in the case of property being developed for resale).

Where interest costs are included within the stock / work-in-progress cost in a company's accounts, there is no corresponding deduction for the interest cost under the loan relationship rules. The deduction instead becomes available when the item of stock is sold and the interest is then debited to the profit and loss account.

**Point 3.12:** ***For those within the scope of UK corporation tax, borrowers funding purchases of investment property or related capital projects, fees should be allocated as far as reasonable to the funding.***

The purchase of investment property – or, indeed, any capital asset – gives rise to costs that may not be deductible from taxable profit. Such costs are of a capital nature and normally cannot be expensed for tax purposes against the profits of this or any other year.

The exception to this rule is funding costs, because the loan relationship rules do not differentiate between capital and revenue items. As indicated above, any capitalised legal or professional fees that are part of the finance exercise can be deducted from taxable income as if they were expensed to the income statement.

It is, therefore, worthwhile liaising with professionals supplying their services in relation to a property acquisition, reconstruction or refurbishment to ensure they allocate an appropriate portion of their fees to the related funding exercise.

Care must, however, be taken as regards the impact of the Corporate Interest Restriction rules.

**Point 3.13:** ***Watch debt releases, as these can generate taxable income.***

In the same way that costs and expenses reflected in the income statement are allowed for tax purposes, so any credits may be taxable.

For the borrower, it will be a rare event to have a credit in the income statement in respect of finance it has received. However, distressed property situations are sometimes addressed by an arrangement between the lender and borrower resulting in the forgiveness of some or all of the debt.

Any credit to a company's income statement as a result of such a release generally gives rise to taxable income if the parties are not connected.

However, this general rule does not apply in a number of corporate rescue or insolvency situations.

Relief is available for a certain debt releases and waivers involving an unconnected borrower. Such releases are tax-free where debt is forgiven as part of a statutory insolvency arrangement (as defined at *CTA 2009, s 1319*). This includes corporate rescues involving a voluntary arrangement under the *Insolvency Act 1986* or a compromise or arrangement with creditors under *Companies Act 2006, Pt 26*, or equivalent foreign proceedings (*CTA 2009, s 322(3)*).

Debt can also be released tax-free where it is capitalised for ordinary share capital of the borrowing company (*CTA 2009, s 322(4)*). See Point 3.14 below.

For releases in the course of an insolvency process, the occasions when a release of the debt is tax-free include situations in which the borrowing company is in:

(a) insolvent liquidation;

(b) insolvent administration;

(c) insolvent administrative receivership;

(d) insolvent provisional liquidation; or

(e) foreign proceedings equivalent to any of these.

(*CTA 2009, s 322(5)*)

Similarly, where a release of debt takes place after connection between the lender and borrower has ceased, by virtue of an insolvency event, the release of the debt is tax-free for the borrower where the lending company is in any of the insolvency situations noted above (*CTA 2009, s 359*).

The legislation does refer to releases (*CTA 2009, ss 322, 359*). An unconnected lender, on the other hand, does not need to release a debt to get tax relief. It is sufficient for this purpose to impair the debt or provide against it as a bad/ doubtful debt.

*Finance (No 2) Act 2015* extended the ambit of corporate rescue relief with effect from 1 January 2015. This applies where the debts of distressed companies are released subject to the condition that that there was a material risk that, in the absence of a release, the borrower would be unable to pay its debts at some time within the next 12 months (*CTA 2009, s 322(5B))*.

When a debt release is contemplated that is not in the course of a formal corporate rescue or insolvency procedure or covered by the new reliefs referred to above, the alternative actions suggested in Points 3.14 and 3.15 below could be adopted where possible. This may also apply to payments under a guarantee by another party (see Point 3.15 below).

Debt releases between connected parties are generally tax neutral under the corporate debt rules, with the consequence that the borrower is not subject to tax on any release credit and the lender does not obtain a deduction for any release debit (*CTA 2009, ss 354, 358*).

There are limited situations where a connected lender can obtain tax relief on distressed debt. These are where:

(a) the lender has become insolvent, but only to the extent that the impairment accrues in the course of the insolvency process (*CTA 2009, s 357*);

(b) connection has ceased, but only to the extent that the impairment did not arise whilst the companies were connected and it accrues in later accounting periods when the companies are no longer connected (*CTA 2009, s 355*); or

(c) the lender becomes connected to the borrower solely as a consequence of the lender releasing the borrower from its liability in consideration of an issue of ordinary shares or an entitlement to such shares (*CTA 2009, s 356*).

There are also limited exceptions to this general rule which can result in the borrower being subject to tax on a connected party debt release where:

(a) there is a deemed release of loan relationship debt (*CTA 2009, ss 361* and *362*) or a release of relevant rights (*CTA 2009, s 358(2)*); or

(b) in scenarios not involving an actual or deemed loan relationship where a release of debt arises which has previously been claimed as an expense of management (*CTA 2009, s 1229*).

See Point 3.17 below for an explanation of 'connected'.

The tax charge on release will similarly not arise where a loan relationship debt liability is novated from one group company to another, with the consequence that the first borrowing company is thereby released from the debt (*CTA 2009, s 340*). The effective release in that situation is ignored. Different rules apply where the transferor company (the original borrower) uses fair-value accounting to account for the loan relationship.

As mentioned in Point 3.10 above, there is a useful relief where an accounting credit arises in a borrower's accounts under GAAP following debt restructuring, involving a substantial modification of the loan terms. A credit is no longer taxed where, without modification, there is the material prospect of insolvency within the following 12 months.

**Point 3.14:** ***A loan that is on the point of being released could be waived, bought back or converted into shares.***

If Farah Limited owes Browns Bank £100,000, any release of that debt by the bank will trigger taxable income of £100,000 in the company, unless the conditions for relief referred to in Point 3.13 above apply.

In particular, the corporate rescue relief (*CTA 2009, s 322(5B)*) will provide a workable business turnaround solution in many cases where a company is in distress but entering into a formal insolvency procedure is neither desirable, nor feasible. This relief will eliminate many of the complications experienced before its introduction (see below), but only where there is a material risk that at some time in the next 12 months the company would be unable to pay its debts. Inevitably, there will be borderline situations where the outcome of such a subjective insolvency assessment remains unclear.

Instead, a commercial solution might be to buy back the impaired debt from the bank. However, a tax charge can also be triggered in this situation or where impaired group debt is acquired by another group member from a bank or other third party. This can deem the debt to have been released, even if no actual release takes place, and results in a tax charge for the borrower, although in some situations this could be averted. Due to perceived abuses, these so-called 'debt buy-back' rules were tightened, with effect from 14 October 2009, to narrow the circumstances where an upfront taxable deemed release could be avoided, and introduce a tax charge for any subsequent release or capitalisation of impaired debts. A deemed release, taxable on the borrower, can also be triggered where debt has been impaired and the lender becomes connected with the borrower. This could arise where one party to a property joint venture buys out the other. These rules were further tightened with effect from 1 December 2011 (to counter a particular scheme) and 27 February 2013 (generally, including targeted anti-avoidance rules) with the relevant measures incorporated into *Finance Act 2012*.

Helpfully, for debt buy-backs, the deemed release rules have been relaxed primarily to accommodate corporate rescue situations.

The buying-in of impaired group debt will no longer be vulnerable to an upfront deemed release charge (under *CTA 2009, s 361*) to the extent that there is (a) a release of the impaired debt within 60 days of the buy-back provided that the acquisition was on arm's-length terms; and (b) before the buy-in there was a material risk that the borrower would be unable to pay its debts at some point within the next 12 months (*CTA 2009, s 361D*). A deemed release charge would still be in point in relation to the remaining face value of the debt that exceeds its carrying value in the borrower's books.

The *Finance (No 2) Act 2015* changes also removed tax charges on a subsequent release or capitalisation of the impaired debts, whilst there would still be a full exclusion from a deemed release tax charge where shares are issued as consideration for the buy-in of impaired debt (in line with *CTA 2009, s 361C*).

A similar corporate rescue exclusion applies to deemed releases where debt has been impaired and the lender becomes connected with the borrower (under *CTA 2009, ss 362* and *362A*).

In any event, the legislation does provide for a way of mitigating the risk of triggering taxable debt releases in case it is not possible to reach a satisfactory insolvency assessment by swapping debt for equity. This can be achieved by capitalising the debt through the issue of ordinary shares with a typically low nominal value. Provided there was no intention at the time of capitalising the debt for Browns Bank to sell the shares to a person connected with Farah Limited for that value, this should not result in triggering taxable income of £100,000 within Farah Limited. The bank should still be in a position to claim a deduction for the loss in value of the debt.

Before the *Finance (No 2) Act 2015* changes noted above, perceived abuses of the tax rules applying to distressed debt situations had resulted in changes to HMRC's approach to the tax treatment of debt equity swap transactions, as well as legislative changes tightening the deemed release rules in the case of debt buy-backs (described above).

HMRC have revised their Corporate Finance Manual guidance in relation to debt equity swaps a number of times. This suggests that the borrower's tax exemption for debts released in consideration of the issue of ordinary shares (or an entitlement to such shares) could be denied where the lender has released debt gratuitously and has no interest in acquiring shares in the borrower. It also indicates that situations where the lender is issued warrants or options over shares might not be tax effective where it is unlikely they would ever be exercised. The ensuing confusion over HMRC's interpretation of these rules has provoked a flood of non-statutory business clearances for transactions involving a debt equity swap. In an attempt to reduce the volume of clearance applications being received, HMRC's debt equity swap guidance was updated and it lists a number of debt restructuring features that HMRC accept as not in themselves casting doubt on the availability of the debt equity swap exemption.

**Point 3.15:** ***Watch for adverse tax consequences for the debtor if a guarantee is about to be called upon.***

Connected party guarantees can be problematic if a guarantee is called upon by the lender. The problem arises because a guarantee is normally called upon when the borrower is unable to meet its obligations. Part and parcel of the guarantee process is that, on payment of the guarantee, the debtor would be released from its indebtedness to the lender. Such releases from third-party lenders can, therefore, give rise to a taxable credit (see Point 3.14 above), unless the reliefs referred to in Point 3.13 apply.

However, where the guarantor stands in the shoes of the lender, by way of subrogation, a taxable release can be avoided since the borrower is not released from its indebtedness. Instead, it would owe the corresponding debt to the guarantor. The fact that the borrower and the guarantor are connected means that any impairment of the receivable by the guarantor will deny it tax relief.

If the guarantee contract does not include a subrogation clause, or subrogation does not happen by the operation of common law, it may be preferable for the guarantor to put the borrower in funds to meet repayments or redeem the debt to mitigate the risks of a taxable release occurring.

In distressed situations, where the lender accepts a reduced amount from the guarantor, a deemed release could inadvertently be triggered if a guarantor acquires the loan receivable at a discount by way of a debt buy-back (see Point 3.14 above).

**Point 3.16:** ***The borrower that has incurred finance costs under a non-trading loan relationship has some flexibility about the manner in which charges are offset. In any case, careful planning will be required to ensure optimal use of the tax deduction.***

It is important to recognise how non-trade loan relationship debits and credits arise and the extent to which they give rise to non-trading loan deficits or profits.

A company can incur non-trading debits in the following ways:

(a) interest payable on finance for non-trade purposes;

(b) bad debts on loans not made in the course of trade;

(c) losses on non-trade related foreign exchange transactions;

(d) payments in respect of derivative financial instruments (eg caps, collars and swaps) entered into for non-trade reasons;

(e) finance and other incidental costs of a non-trade-related loan relationship; or

(f) abortive costs of trying to obtain non-trade-related finance.

Similarly, a company can make profits from its non-trading loan relationships in the following ways:

(a) releases from indebtedness;

(b) reimbursement of finance costs;

(c) non-trade-related foreign exchange gains;

(d) non-trade-related derivative financial instrument receipts and profits; or

(e) deemed releases from indebtedness.

These particular items are relevant when analysing the relief available for net deficits or the manner in which profit may be taxed.

Where a borrower incurs finance costs under a borrowing for non-trading purposes, the finance costs are deductible in several ways. All costs and profits must first be aggregated.

It is possible for a borrower to have surplus profits from its non-trading loan relationships, and these would be taxed as non-trading profits of a company in respect of its loan relationships. Where a net loss ('a non-trading deficit') arises, which should more likely be the case for a borrower, this could be relieved in any one or more of the following ways (up to the total amount of the net loss).

For periods prior to 1 April 2017, the non-trading deficit can be used as follows:

(a) Offset (in whole or in part) against the company's total profits in the same year (*CTA 2009, s 459(1)(a)*). The flexibility to specify categories and amounts of income or gains to offset deficits against means this option can help preserve eg foreign income in charge to tax thus enabling the company to use any foreign tax credit.

(b) Surrender (in whole or in part) as group relief against the total profit of other group companies (*CTA 2010, s 99*).

(c) Carry-back (in whole or in part) against the company's previous year's profits arising from its non-trading loan relationships (*CTA 2009, s 459(1)(b)*). This also includes non-trading foreign exchange and financial instrument profits.

(d) Carry-forward (any remaining deficit) against all non-trading profits and gains as well as any foreign trading profits of the following year (*CTA 2009, s 457*). It is possible to 'skip a year' when carrying the deficit forward, providing a claim is made (*CTA 2009, s 458*). This allows any foreign income against which double tax relief is available to remain in charge, thus not wasting the foreign tax credits.

The above claims, with the exception of a claim to use the deficit in the following year, must be made within two years of the end of the accounting period in which the deficit is incurred. Any claim to use the deficit in a following year must be made not later than two years after the end of the period in question.Where these other options are not used, deficits are carried forward automatically against future non-trading profits of the company.

*Finance (No 2) Act 2017* introduced a reform of the loss carry forward rules for non-trading deficits with the aim being to simplify the rules and provide more flexibility in how losses carried forward can be relieved.

The key changes are the carry forward of non-trading deficits against future total profits (as opposed to solely against non-trading profits) and the carry forward and surrender by way of group relief of losses from previous years that arise after 1 April 2017.

The key legislative provisions are provided in *CTA 2009, ss 463A–463G*. Certain additional tax filing obligations also apply and are set out in *CTA 2010, s 269ZV*.

However, after 1 April 2017, there is a restriction on the amount of profits against which the brought forward losses can be offset. Broadly, groups of companies are subject to a restriction on the offset of carried forward losses to £5m plus 50% of the excess of current year taxable profits (after the offset of current year reliefs) over £5m. Profits under £5m are available for offset in full. This restriction applies to all losses carried forward, both pre 1 April 2017 and post 1 April 2017 losses.

Where a company's accounting period straddles 1 April 2017, the periods before and after 1 April 2017 are treated as two separate accounting periods and profits/ losses are time apportioned or apportioned on a just and reasonable basis where time apportionment would produce an unreasonable result.

**Point 3.17:** ***In some limited situations, where the lender is connected to the borrower and is not subject to UK corporation tax on the full amount of accrued interest, no deduction for accrued interest in a period is available unless the interest is paid within 12 months of the year end.***

The fact that a borrower is connected to a lender does not prevent a deduction for accrued interest. Where the lending, for example, is between UK companies, the treatment is no different for the borrower than if the loan were with an unconnected lender, except that fair-value accounting cannot be used to account for the loan relationship for tax purposes.

However, where there is a connection between the lender and borrower, and the lender is not subject to UK corporation tax on the full amount of accrued interest, in certain circumstances the borrower may not receive a deduction for interest accrued unless it is paid within 12 months of the year end (*CTA 2009, s 372*). In that case, the deduction for tax purposes will be deferred to the accounting period when the interest is paid.

'Connection', in this context, can catch situations involving connected companies, participators in close companies and major interests although their scope was restricted by *FA 2015* due to perceived abuses (see below).

These 'late interest' rules are essentially a set of anti-avoidance measures and seek to prohibit companies from taking advantage of an interest mismatch which could arise if the borrower obtained relief for accrued interest which is not paid for until later, and the lender is either outside the loan relationship rules (and only taxed on that interest when it is received) or is completely outside the UK tax net.

These rules only apply to interest, and not to other charges and financing costs arising in respect of loans.

There are two specific situations where relief could be deferred until the interest is actually paid (although subject to the point above that the interest may still be deductible if the lender is a UK or non-'tax haven'-based foreign company). These are where, at any time in the accounting period:

(a) The borrower is a 'close company' and the lender is a 'participator' in the borrower or an 'associate' of such a participator (*CTA 2009, s 375*).

A close company in this context is, broadly, any company that is under the control of fewer than six 'participators' or any number of directors (*CTA 2010, s 439*). A 'participator' is generally a shareholder, although the term extends to a loan creditor and a person with a right to acquire such a share or interest (*CTA 2010, s 454*). The term 'participator' cannot, however, include certain loan creditors – most notably banks – where they are participators solely by virtue of being a loan creditor (*CTA 2009, s 376(3), CTA 2010 s 453(4)*).

In certain circumstances, even a company fully listed on the Stock Exchange can be close (*CTA 2010, s 446*).

(b) The loan is made by pension trustees, and:

(i) the borrower company is the employer of scheme members;

(ii) the borrower company and the employer are connected; or

(iii) the employer is a company and the borrower company has a major interest in that employer or the employer has a major interest in the borrower company (*CTA 2009, s 378*).

Similar provisions can apply to defer relief for the discount arising on deeply discounted securities issued by close companies (*CTA 2009, s 409*).

As noted in Point 3.20 below, tax relief for interest and discount on loans from connected parties might be restricted under the transfer pricing rules.

**Point 3.18:** ***The fact that a company might not get a tax deduction for interest until it is paid under the connected party rules could previously help in planning to ensure that it falls in a period when the tax relief can be fully exploited.***

As noted in Point 3.17 above, where the borrower is connected with certain lenders, there will be no relief for accrued interest under the loan relationships rules until payment if the interest is paid more than 12 months after the accounting year end. Where the interest is paid late, the borrower is in a similar position to that prevailing before the corporate debt rules when interest in many cases was allowed only on a paid basis.

There are circumstances where that sort of flexibility could have been useful. For instance, a deduction may occur in a year when neither the borrower nor any group company has any profit to offset it against nor are there carry-back opportunities. This would have left the unrelieved costs to be carried forward; these could become stranded or difficult to use in the future.

Deferring payment of interest could crystallise relief in a year when the group could use it. However, as noted in the following example, this is unlikely to have such a practical impact from 1 April 2017 onwards.

## Example 1

Hindes Ltd borrows £1 million from its controlling shareholder, Kenny. Hindes Ltd is loss making. Hindes Ltd has a subsidiary, Clark Ltd, which is also loss making.

In the years to 31 December 2015 and 31 December 2016, Hindes Ltd accrued £90,000 interest to Kenny but this was not paid.

In the year ended 31 December 2017, Hindes Ltd continued to lose money but the subsidiary company, Clark Ltd, had surplus income in excess of £90,000.

If Hindes Ltd pays the year 2015 accrued interest in either the year to 31 December 2015 or the year to 31 December 2016 (ie within 12 months of the year end) Hindes Ltd will receive a deduction on the accrued basis in the year to 31 December 2015. The unrelieved interest will simply be carried forward. An expense in the year ended 31 December 2015 cannot be group relieved in the year to 31 December 2016 against Clark Ltd's income, based on the prevailing law at that time.

On the other hand, if Hindes Ltd delays paying until the year to 31 December 2017, the deduction is allowed on a paid basis in that year. In that year, it can offset these costs by way of group relief against Clark Ltd's income. In practice, from 1 April 2017, this is likely to be of less relevance due to the increased flexibility afforded to corporation tax payers in relation to the transfer of non-current year losses by way of group relief. The corporate interest restrictions will, however, need to be considered together with the £5m loss restriction legislation.

**Point 3.19:** ***The mismatch between the accruals basis of relief under the corporate debt regime and the received basis of taxation for certain lenders offers a cash flow tax planning opportunity.***

Point 3.17 above referred to the situation where the borrower will not be entitled to a tax deduction for interest accrued in a year if the interest is not actually paid within 12 months of the year end (*CTA 2009, s 373*). Instead, the deduction will be allowed in the accounting period when the interest is subsequently paid.

Individuals and trusts are outside the corporate debt regime. Where individuals and trusts are liable to UK tax on interest, it is normally on a received basis.

In many cases, that gives rise to an opportunity to exploit a potential cash flow tax advantage.

**Point 3.20:** ***Foreign investors need to be aware of potential restrictions on tax relief when they are using associated funds to finance UK property acquisitions.***

Tax relief on interest paid to associated lenders may be restricted or disallowed if the interest is excessive or the finance involves a 'top-up' to normal commercial lending. This is particularly relevant where foreign investors are behind purchases of UK investment property.

The transfer pricing rules aim to prevent reductions in UK tax liability as a result of arrangements between associated persons on uncommercial terms (*TIOPA 2010, Pt 4*). The transfer pricing rules apply to transactions wholly between UK persons as well as cross-border situations. However, there can be an exclusion from the transfer pricing rules where the person attempting to derive the UK tax advantage is a small or medium-sized enterprise (SME) (*TIOPA 2010, s 166*).

A small enterprise is one with less than 50 employees and with either an annual turnover not exceeding €10 million or a balance sheet total not exceeding €10 million. A medium-sized enterprise is one with less than 250 employees and with either an annual turnover not exceeding €50 million or a balance sheet total not exceeding €43 million. If a company is a member of a group, these criteria are applied to the group as a whole. It will be seen that the UK-to-UK transfer pricing rules should only apply to relatively few property enterprises.

There are three exceptions to this exclusion of SMEs. The first is where one party to the transaction is resident in a territory with which the UK has no double tax treaty or has a treaty that does not have an appropriate non-discrimination article. Such territories will normally be tax havens.

The second exception generally applies to medium-sized enterprises only. In certain circumstances, when an inquiry is opened into the tax return of a medium-sized enterprise, HMRC can direct that the transfer pricing rules apply (*TIOPA 2010, s 168*). Small enterprises can only be subject to such a notice from HMRC where the affected transactions take place in accounting periods starting on or after 1 April 2013 and involve patents (*TIOPA 2010, s 167A*).

The third exception is where the SME irrevocably elects for the transfer pricing rules to apply to it.

These rules apply to finance transactions where the lender or borrower participates directly or indirectly in the control, management or capital of the other (*TIOPA 2010, s 148*). They bite in the following situations:

(a) where interest payable to the lender exceeds an arm's-length amount or other terms are agreed that would not have been agreed in the absence of the special relationship between the parties;

(b) where the loan is in addition to or greater than a normal loan that a third-party lender would be prepared to make in the circumstances;

(c) where the loan would not have been made at all in the absence of the special relationship.

The provisions aim to correct the loss of UK tax arising from these situations. They do this by treating the transactions as having taken place at arm's length. These rules supplement the recharacterisation of certain interest payments as distributions (CTA 2010, Pt 23) – including situations where the interest is payable to a UK lender (see Point 3.21 below).

Under present transfer pricing restrictions for situations (a) and (b) above, any firm loan offers from established third-party lenders as to how much they would be prepared to lend and on what terms could provide a basis for acceptable associated-party lending. If a third party can state that it would lend, say, 65% of a property's value at, say, 6% interest, then those terms should, in principle, be regarded as commercial if taken up with an associated lender. HMRC are, however, sceptical about indicative third-party loan offers, for example, where there is no intention to pursue the loan application to the stage of obtaining credit committee approval.

Additional security or guarantees available from the prospective borrower's overseas associates cannot influence the third-party's terms. For example, if a third party is prepared to increase its lending from 65% to 75% of the property value because of guarantees from overseas shareholders of the borrower, that extra lending is uncommercial. Related interest would, therefore, be disallowed. This is the case even if it is actually the third party that lends the funds. Similarly, HMRC will look at loans routed through third parties (*TIOPA 2010, s 150*).

The transfer pricing rules explicitly cover situations where a loan is received on favourable terms from a third party because of a guarantee given by a party connected to the borrower, as well as loans from a connected party.

Where any of the following circumstances would have applied in the absence of the special relationship (between the borrower and the guarantor or the borrower and the lender):

(a) the guarantee would not have been provided at all;

(b) a smaller amount would have been guaranteed; or

(c) the consideration for the guarantee would have been greater and other terms would have been less favourable,

any excess interest arising as a result (which could amount to the whole of the interest, if the loan would not have been made at all between independent third parties in the absence of the guarantee, for example) is disallowed (*TIOPA 2010, s 153*).

A possible way around such a problem might be for the foreign associate to provide funds by way of subscription for ordinary or preference shares. That would improve the borrower's balance sheet and increase the security for the lender. This, in turn, may secure a larger commercial loan than would otherwise be available.

On the question of so-called 'safe harbours' for thin capitalisation, HMRC's current commentary includes the following:

> Unlike many jurisdictions, the UK does not operate safe harbours. A safe harbour in this context is a legislative limit on interest deduction by reference to fixed ratios, such as a debt:equity ratio of 3:1 applicable to all company funding. Instead, UK legislation operates by direct reference to OECD principles and guidance, and although UK thin capitilisation agreements use covenants expressed in the form

of debt and earnings based ratios, these ratios are used because they are appropriate to the particular company based on a close analysis of the facts and circumstances of the individual case.

(Extract from INTM516050)

Other HMRC guidance suggests that HMRC are increasingly placing reliance on independent studies to help them assess what they consider to be arm's-length commercial terms in relation to lending. HMRC appear to favour the Department of Land Management at De Montfort University's annual report entitled *The UK Commercial Property Lending Market*, as this report is often used by advisers to benchmark third-party financing terms.

Genuine commercial transactions that, say, a bank has with parties that happen to be connected with each other should not, in principle, be caught by the provisions. For instance, associated entities may use the same organisation for deposit and lending transactions. It may be important to be able to demonstrate that the transactions are not related; HMRC can look through back-to-back transactions, and other similar arrangements involving third parties (*TIOPA 2010, s 150*).

Interest disallowed under the transfer pricing rules is not treated as a distribution (dividend), in contrast to the situations described in Point 3.21 below. Since April 2004, it has also not been necessary to deduct tax at source from payments of disallowed interest if the lender is able to make, and makes, a compensating adjustment (so that, in effect, the lender is taxed as if the disallowed interest had not been paid to it).

UK property investment companies, to which the transfer pricing rules apply, may be able to apply to HMRC for an advance thin capitalisation agreement (ATCA), where the availability of related-party finance relief has a significant commercial impact on the company's profits or losses. If successful, an ATCA ruling from HMRC can be binding for up to five years (HMRC SP 1/12).

### Point 3.21: *The deductibility of loan interest can be restricted if it is regarded as a distribution.*

There are specified situations where interest will be treated as a disallowable distribution by the company rather than a deduction from taxable profit (*CTA 2010, Pt 23*). The disallowance principally arises in the following situations:

(a) Interest payable on so-called 'non-commercial securities', but only to the extent that the interest exceeds a reasonable return for the use of the principal (*CTA 2010, ss 1000(1E), 1005*). This can apply even where the lender is based in the UK and taxable on that interest. 'Reasonable' for this purpose can take into account the lender's commercial rationale, notably risk.

(b) Interest payable on so-called 'special securities' (*CTA 2010, ss 1000(1F), 1015*), except to the extent that interest arising is already disallowed by (a) above, including:

- unlisted convertible debts which are not issued on terms comparable to listed convertibles;
- securities issued otherwise than for new consideration;
- debts with a profit participating, or results dependent coupon (but not if this represents a qualifying alternative finance arrangement, eg under Islamic principles);
- debts connected with shares, eg so-called stapled stock; and
- equity notes, eg where the debt has no fixed repayment date or a term exceeding 50 years.

(c) Interest recharacterised as a distribution under (b) above will not, however, be subject to a disallowance where the lender is a company which is within the charge to corporation tax (*CTA 2010, s 1032*).

The above situations, therefore, will be relevant where the lender is an individual, trustee, foreign company or exempt fund such as a pension fund. If the recipient is an individual or trust, the reclassification of the payment as a distribution would mean that the receipt would be taxed as if it were a dividend, rather than interest, with no withholding obligation arising for the payer (Revenue & Customs Brief 100/09).

**Point 3.22:** ***There are various anti-avoidance provisions which can prevent a deduction for finance costs where a financing transaction has a tax avoidance objective.***

HMRC can deny a deduction for finance costs where the objective of finance concerned involves an 'unallowable' purpose (*CTA 2009, ss 441–442*).

Unallowable purposes include those where the sole or main purpose of being party to a loan relationship or related transaction is tax avoidance. This could be tax avoidance by the borrower, the lender or some other person.

Tax avoidance is sufficiently widely drafted to include any arrangement designed to reduce a company's tax liability and has led to widespread concern. In response to concerns, the Economic Secretary to the Treasury at the time the original legislation was introduced, Mrs Angela Knight, announced that the measure was primarily aimed at artificial avoidance. However, there remains some uncertainty about the scope of the provision. This is, no doubt, deliberate to discourage exploitation.

The provision is arguably similar in scope to the long-established restriction on the allowability of loan interest where tax avoidance is the sole or main motive for the transaction (*CTA 2009, s 443*). As with that section, it may well be sufficient to show a business motive for the borrowing.

The fact that there was also an incidental tax advantage or that the finance could have been structured less tax-efficiently should be irrelevant. On the other hand, routing loans through companies which themselves have no commercial justification for being involved in the loan relationship could be challenged under this provision.

This 'unallowable purpose' test has to be satisfied in each accounting period. It is not enough to show that the loan was taken out originally for an allowable purpose, if its ongoing existence is for an unallowable purpose.

Several cases have shown HMRC's keenness to counter abusive financing arrangements using the unallowable purpose rules.

HMRC were successful in the First-tier Tribunal during 2011 in using these rules to prevent the avoidance of corporation tax in a scheme involving derivative transactions (*Explainaway and others v R&C Commissioners* TC01267).

A subsequent 2012 unallowable purpose First-tier Tribunal case (*AH Field (Holdings) Limited* TC01800) also found in favour of HMRC in relation to transactions involving the taxpayer borrowing to fund a dividend, the proceeds of which were lent back to the company by way of a deeply discounted security.

However, this has not all been one-way traffic. A First-tier case released in 2013 (*Fidex Limited v Commissioners for Her Majesty's Revenue & Customs* TC/2010/08369) found in favour of the taxpayer. In *Fidex*, the favourable tax effects of adopting IFRS were not considered to have an unallowable purpose because the tax advantage accrued in a different accounting period to the change of accounting standards.

*Finance (No 2) Act 2005* introduced the anti-arbitrage rules. In broad terms, this legislation enables HMRC to counteract certain cross-border financing arrangements, involving companies in charge to corporation tax, which use hybrid entities or hybrid instruments to achieve a UK tax advantage (*TIOPA 2010, Pt 6*). An HMRC clearance process enables companies to obtain assurance as to whether their cross-border financing arrangements are regarded as acceptable.

The anti-arbitrage legislation is subject to its own informal clearance process controlled by the arbitrage specialists within Business, Assets & International. However, according to HMRC guidance in INTM595100, where a company has made an arbitrage clearance application alongside an advanced thin capitalisation agreement application, so that the company is asking for a set of transactions to be reviewed from both perspectives, HMRC will endeavour to deal with them in as coordinated a way as it can.

Successive recent *Finance Acts* have also introduced numerous targeted anti-avoidance rules to counter tax avoidance schemes involving financing and group treasury arrangements. These schemes are generally designed to achieve artificial financing deductions or to derecognise financing profits for accounting purposes, so they fall out of the charge to tax.

This anti-avoidance legislation has been added piecemeal, followed notifications of tax avoidance arrangements made to HMRC since the introduction of the disclosure regime during 2004. Where possible, HMRC have supplemented targeted measures with new principles-based legislation, incorporating general anti-avoidance rules, to discourage iterations of tax schemes of this nature (eg so-called 'group mismatch' and 'derecognition' schemes). However, the continuing game of cat and mouse, to identify and then block tax avoidance involving financial instruments, has led to HMRC's proposals to modernise the tax rules for corporate debt and derivatives. Consequentially, a regime anti-avoidance rule has been included in *Finance (No 2) Act 2015* intended to future-proof the corporate debt legislation from abusive tax schemes whilst also facilitating the repeal of various targeted anti-avoidance provisions.

The regime anti-avoidance acts separately from the unallowable purpose rule mentioned above. In broad terms it is intended to counteract avoidance arrangements which result in a loan-related tax advantage for a company (unless intended by Parliament), such as:

- bringing into account a debit or more of a debit than it is entitled to;
- avoiding bringing into account a credit or less of a credit than it should recognise; and
- bringing into account a debit or credit earlier or later than it otherwise would.

A general anti-abuse rule (GAAR) was adopted in *Finance Act 2013*. The GAAR is intended to be targeted narrowly at artificial and abusive tax planning arrangements and operate alongside existing anti-avoidance provisions.

HMRC have substantially revised and expanded their guidance on their approach to whether a loan relationship has an unallowable purpose and the guidance in their Corporate Finance manual has been updated in 2023 following recent court decisions.

For example, the guidance now includes new sections on how 'purpose' is to be determined for the purposes of the application of the rules, how HMRC will assess whether a loan relationship has an unallowable purpose and other examples of the application of the rules.

It could be argued that the new guidance, and decisions in recent cases, will be concerning to taxpayers. The use of UK acquisition vehicles within a group structure, in particular, will need to be carefully analysed. The revised approach makes clear that, even where there is a commercial acquisition, HMRC will seek to challenge such situations in the absence of a clear commercial link between the acquiring company and the target and where the use of a UK vehicle is chosen predominantly due to the availability of loan relationship debits.

There have been a number of recent cases where the application of the unallowable purpose rule has been considered, including *JTI Acquisition Company v HMRC* [2022] UKFTT 166 and *HMRC v BlackRock Holdco 5 LLC* [2022] UKUT 199. Both of these cases involved the use of a UK vehicle as part of a group structure to undertake a commercial third-party acquisition financed by intra-group borrowings. In both cases, it was partly a consideration for the structure used, that there would be the ability to use the loan relationship debits arising in the UK. In both cases, the FTT and the UT decided that in these circumstances it was a 'main purpose' of the loan relationship that the

UK tax advantage arising from the debits should be obtained. This was despite the fact that the tax advantage in these cases was simply the availability of the debits (and the ability to use them within the wider UK group) which arose from the normal operation of the rules where costs of borrowing can be treated as allowable deductions.

The HMRC guidance is valuable as it provides useful insight into HMRC's current thinking with regard to when the unallowable purpose rule could apply to restrict UK tax deductions for interest. The guidance now contains a lengthy section which sets out factors which HMRC will take into account in assessing evidence of a main purpose of tax avoidance.

The guidance sets out that HMRC will seek to gain a full understanding of the factual context and the UK and non-UK tax consequences resulting from any arrangements. They will also assess whether there is a net tax benefit to the group as a whole and a UK tax benefit to the arrangements. HMRC will also seek to understand the commercial purposes of the arrangements. For example, the guidance states that:

> 'if group financing is routed through a UK special purpose vehicle (SPV), earning a margin for the vehicle, the fact that the involvement of the SPV generates this intragroup margin does not contribute to net group commercial (non-tax) benefits. HMRC will wish to understand whether the involvement of the SPV does so in any other way, and if so, to what extent.'
>
> 'Understanding the full factual context will enable case teams to make sense of the picture as a whole, and so more effectively assess the purposes for which the company is party to the loan relationship'.

The guidance also includes a list of factors that may, depending on any particular facts, be relevant in there is a main objective of securing a tax advantage, including:

- the size of the tax advantage, both absolute and in comparison to the commercial benefits;
- the existence, or lack, of net UK tax benefits in wholly UK or cross-border financing arrangements;
- the existence, or lack, of net global tax benefits in cross-border financing arrangements;
- the degree of attention paid to securing the tax advantages (including the existence of substantial fees for tax advice);
- where the borrowing funds activities or investments which are not expected to generate UK tax, either immediately or at all; and
- whether or not the arrangements would have happened, or would have happened in a different way, had the potential for the tax advantage never existed or had ceased to exist in the course of developing the arrangements, that is, 'but for the tax advantage'.

In particular, HMRC consider that if the arrangements would have happened in a simpler way (or not at all) but for the tax advantage, then this is a factor pointing towards securing a tax advantage as a main purpose.

> 'In cross-border financing arrangements, whether or not there is any material net group commercial (non-tax) benefit from involving the UK is often a key point. For instance, if there is a non-UK entity who would from a commercial (non-tax) perspective be the natural entity to borrow to acquire shares in a third party, but instead financing is obtained via the UK because of the tax advantage by way of tax deduction available (perhaps as part of achieving a net global tax benefit), then in many circumstances, having assessed all relevant factors, it is likely there will in fact be a main tax avoidance purpose.'

It is worth noting that the original guidance, based on statements of the Economic Secretary in Hansard when the original legislation was debated, confirmed that the unallowable purpose rule:

> 'will not normally apply where a company borrows to acquire shares in companies, whether in the United Kingdom or overseas, or to pay dividends, provided that the borrowings are not structured in an artificial way. And a similar view is taken as regards borrowings, whether from a third party or intra group, to acquire other business assets whether located in the United Kingdom or overseas.'

HMRC confirm that they still regard this as being consistent with their revised approach and whilst they do not expressly state how, this must presumably be on the basis that arrangements involving UK acquisition vehicles where there is a tax advantage are 'artificial'.

**Point 3.23:** ***There is no requirement to withhold tax from interest payments made to UK banks, building societies and other companies that are within the charge to corporation tax.***

There is no requirement to withhold income tax from any interest payments made by a company within the UK to any qualifying bank (*ITA 2007, s 879*), building society (*ITA 2007, s 880*) or other companies (*ITA 2007, ss 933, 934*) that are within charge to UK corporation tax. As a consequence, UK companies can enter into loan arrangements without the need to deduct tax from any interest payments or comply with the requirement to complete the related quarterly returns to HMRC. Payments may also be made gross to the UK branches of non-resident companies, provided that the company carries on a trade in the UK via a permanent establishment and the interest will form part of its profits chargeable to UK tax.

**Point 3.24:** ***Interest may also be paid to exempt funds without deduction of tax.***

The exception from the withholding requirement on interest paid to UK companies is also extended to payments made to UK bodies that are exempt from tax. Thus, payments to pension funds and charities, among others, may be made without deduction of tax, if the payer is a company or local authority (*ITA 2007, s 936*).

**Point 3.25:** ***The borrowing company should ensure that the lender is a UK company subject to corporation tax or an exempt body before paying interest without tax deduction.***

The exceptions from the tax deduction requirement still leave categories of lenders that could be subject to withholding tax. This might apply to lenders such as individuals and trustees as well as companies not resident in the UK without a trading branch here. Possible changes to income tax rules on interest were the subject of an HMRC consultation exercise during 2012. Following strong representations, the resulting changes to the income tax regime for interest, implemented in *Finance Act 2013*, did not significantly affect the property-related situations typically subject to interest withholding.

The existing exception for interest on short-term borrowings (known as 'short interest') applies where the loan is not capable of exceeding 12 months. Any interest paid on such loans is not subject to any tax deduction requirement. Under the income tax and interest consultation noted above there was a proposal for the distinction between short interest and yearly interest to be removed, but HMRC did not proceed with that.

Another exception is the position mentioned in Point 3.27 below, where certain treaty resident overseas lenders are involved. *Finance Act 2015* introduced an interest-withholding tax exemption for qualifying private placements with effect from 1 January 2016 (*ITA 2007, s 888A*) known as the qualifying private placement exemption (QPP exemption). In March 2018, HMRC published its guidance on the practical application of the QPP exemption in its Savings and Investment Manual. *The Qualifying Private Placement Regulations 2015 (SI 2015/2002)* (the Regulations) came into force on 1 January 2016.

The QPP exemption applies to interest payments on a qualifying private placement (QPP) which is defined as a security which:

(a) represents a loan relationship (as defined in *CTA 2009, Pt 5*) to which a company is a party as debtor (ie the QPP exemption is not available where the debtor is not a company);

(b) is not listed on a recognised stock exchange (in this case, the Quoted Eurobond exemption should usually apply); and

(c) meets additional conditions specified by Treasury regulations (currently being the Regulations).

Borrowers need to have a reasonable belief that the lender is subject to UK corporation tax, an exempt body or otherwise not subject to any withholding before making interest payments gross. Alternatively, under current rules, they will need to be sure that the interest is short interest or that Point 3.27 below is relevant. It may be prudent to obtain a confirmation from the lender's professional advisers to this effect before paying interest.

**Point 3.26:** ***Where an individual borrows to lend to a company, he or she needs to take into account the cash flow shortfall.***

Non-corporate lenders should be mindful of the cash flow effect of the tax deduction requirement. Where an individual borrows from a bank personally and on-lends to a company, his or her interest payments will have to be made gross to the bank. Unless extra interest is charged on the loan on to the company, there will be a shortfall as between the interest net of 20% tax received from the company and the gross interest payable to the bank.

As far as the paying company is concerned, the timing of interest payments subject to deduction of tax at source can secure a cash flow advantage. In that connection, the tax must be accounted for to HMRC no later than 14 days after the end of a return quarter. Return quarters end on 31 December, 31 March, 30 June and 30 September. Where a company's year end does not coincide with one of these dates, its accounting date will form the end of a fifth return period.

It is easy to see that paying the interest at the beginning of the following return quarter is better than paying at the end of the previous quarter.

---

## Example 3

Adams Limited pays interest on its loan from Joshua on 30 June. 20% tax must be withheld from the payment and sent to HMRC by 14 July.

If Adams Limited pays the interest one day later – ie 1 July – the tax does not need to be paid over until 14 October – ie three months later.

---

Note that, as mentioned in Point 3.19 above, there is a restriction on the personal tax relief available to individuals for interest and certain other deductions. This imposes an annual cap on the total available reliefs of the higher of £50,000 or 25% of an individual's income.

**Point 3.27:** ***Tax must be withheld from annual interest payments made abroad subject to certain exceptions.***

The general rule is that interest payments made to a foreign lender must be subject to a deduction of income tax, currently at a rate of 20%. This tax must be accounted for to HMRC in the same way as other withholding situations already referred to.

Many double tax treaties provide for reduced rates of withholding tax on cross-border payments of interest.

Prior to 1 June 2021, payments of interest made to EU resident associated companies were also exempt from UK withholding tax, under the EU Interest and Royalties Directive. This legislation was abolished from 1 June 2021, with no exemption from UK withholding taxes on payments to EU associated companies permitted from that date, even in cases where HMRC has previously provided clearance.

DTAs typically require the recipient to be the beneficial owner of the interest. This is unlikely to be the case where a third jurisdiction has been inserted in the financing arrangements with a view to obtaining a double tax treaty benefit.

The reduced or nil withholding cannot apply unless and until the borrower has received express authorisation from HMRC. The overseas company has to apply to HMRC using a form certified in their country of residence. This process, often referred to as the 'certified claim method', can result in delays of months and must be repeated for each loan made by an overseas lender. Once approved in that jurisdiction, the form is forwarded to the UK authorities, who issue the formal authorisation to the borrower.

Since that procedure can take several months and has proved cumbersome, a new scheme was introduced from September 2010 which can be used where certain corporate lenders are involved. Under this, the lender can apply to HMRC for a Double Taxation Treaty Passport ('Passport'). HMRC will issue this Passport if they are satisfied that the lender is properly resident in a jurisdiction with a tax treaty with the UK that has a debt-claims article. Once this Passport is issued, the lender will be added to an HMRC database, and any corporate borrower subsequently borrowing from that lender should be able to formally apply for a direction from HMRC that the lower or nil treaty withholding rate can be applied.

Since overseas lenders will rarely be prepared to suffer a tax deduction from the interest payments, the borrower will need to act quickly to obtain the appropriate tax treaty authorisation once a loan is entered into.

In certain situations, the syndicated loan scheme (SLS) can enable a UK company borrower to pay interest without deducting withholding tax pending approval of treaty claims. SLS only applies in cases involving unconnected company lenders providing syndicated loans. However, borrowers are not obliged to adhere to a SLS authorisation, and they may be reluctant to do so where there is doubt that a lender's treaty claim could fail and the borrower is exposed to a 'grossing up' risk.

Where a payment is made gross prior to clearance being obtained from HMRC and clearance is subsequently given, an obligation to withhold the income tax and account for it to HMRC remains enforceable in relation to any payments made before the clearance was granted. Further, late payment interest will be charged by HMRC on the outstanding withholding tax obligation from the due date (normally 14 days after the quarter in which the yearly interest was paid) until payment.

Prior to 4 May 2023, HMRC did not apply late payment interest charge where UK source interest was paid to a person taxable in an EU Member State. However, with effect from 4 May 2023, this concessionary treatment was stopped; it is now possible for the payer to subsequently apply to HMRC to reclaim the withholding tax. However, there is no relief or discharge from the late payment interest charged on the payer.

Short interest is not currently subject to withholding (Point 3.25 above).

**Point 3.28:** ***Other ways to avoid tax withholding are to structure the loans as non-UK source or to structure the return on the loans as discount on a deeply discounted security or to list the debt on a recognised stock exchange.***

Where a favourable double tax treaty or other exemption does not apply, a borrower may find that a lender still expects to receive the gross interest and thus the borrower will have to bear the cost of any tax withheld. In that situation, the borrower should explore the possibility of siting the loan outside the UK. Interest on a non-UK sourced loan is not subject to UK withholding.

The following factors should ensure that a loan is sited outside the UK and that there are no withholding requirements:

(a) the borrower is resident abroad;

(b) the interest is paid abroad;

(c) the nature and location of the security is abroad;

(d) the interest is paid from foreign funds; and

(e) the debt is subject to foreign law.

It is arguable whether the fact that the majority of the above conditions apply will be sufficient to site a debt abroad. HMRC do not necessarily take that view and they regard the most important factors, in deciding whether or not a loan is UK sited, to be the residence of the borrower and location of its assets (HMRC Savings and Investment Manual SAIM9090). See also Point 3.6.

Where the borrower is UK-resident, there was a view that it might help if the loan was established as a 'specialty debt'. This involved having the loan agreement drawn up and executed under seal outside the UK and subject to foreign law. The debt was then treated as situated where the document was physically kept. The view was that, as long as the document was abroad, so was the debt. HMRC did not accept this argument, but acknowledged that the position was unclear. To put the matter beyond doubt *Finance Act 2013* amended the interest withholding tax legislation so that the location of specialty debt documentation is now disregarded in determining whether interest has a UK source. This measure formed part of the HMRC consultation regarding changes to income tax rules on interest. However, payments made by a UK branch to its non-UK resident company may be made without deduction of tax where the branch is liable to corporation tax and not exempt under a treaty.

*In Perrin v Revenue and Customs Comrs* (TC 03363) [2014] UKFTT 223 (TC), interest paid by a taxpayer to an Isle of Man recipient arose in the UK and was therefore subject to a deduction for UK tax under *ITA 2007, s 874*.

Another scenario where interest withholding tax would not apply is by structuring a debt as a deeply discounted security or series of such securities. Discounts are not, in law, interest, although discounts other than discounts in deeply discounted securities are regarded as interest for income tax purposes (*ITTOIA 2005, s 381*).

A First-tier Tribunal case, *Nicholas Pike* (TC 01151), was released during May 2011. The case was also then heard in the Upper-tier Tribunal in 2013

([2013] UKUT 0225 (TCC)). This concerned an income tax avoidance scheme involving a debt with relatively unusual features that was intended to represent a deeply discounted security. The case was not directly related to withholding tax, but nonetheless it was held that a debt issued at par and redeemable at a premium was not a deeply discounted security (ie the redemption premium represented interest rather than discount). This was because the redemption premium was calculated by reference to a fixed annual percentage of the debt principal which accrued on a daily basis. Based on this case, which the taxpayer lost on appeal to the Upper Tribunal, it would be inadvisable for the drafting of any deeply discounted securities to define the discount by reference to a rate of return for issue price of the debt or for it to incorporate uncommercial terms.

Another exemption from the withholding requirements applies where interest is paid in relation to a debt which qualifies as a quoted Eurobond (*ITA 2007, s 882*). This would cover a debt listed on a recognised stock exchange (*ITA 2007, ss 987, 1005*). Accordingly, where a UK company borrows from, say, an overseas entity, it may be possible for that debt to be issued in the form of loan notes which have been admitted to the official list of, for instance, the International Stock Exchange, before any interest is paid on the debt. HMRC issued guidance on this matter during April 2008 outlining that, for the Eurobond exemption to apply, the debt must be both listed on a recognised stock exchange and admitted to trading on that exchange (HMRC Revenue & Customs Brief 21/08).

The quoted Eurobond exemption was another issue forming part of the HMRC consultation regarding possible changes to income tax rules on interest. HMRC believed that this exemption was being abused by companies listing intra-group debts on stock exchanges, such as the Channel Islands, where, it appeared, there was no substantial or regular trading of the bonds.

HMRC's view was that these bonds were normally issued with the intention of circumventing withholding obligations, rather than raising third-party finance. However, following strong representations, HMRC decided that no steps were to be taken to narrow the quoted Eurobond exemption.

**Point 3.29:** ***The introduction of rules for 'alternative finance' has enabled tax relief to be obtained for costs incurred in relation to financing structures which are compliant with Islamic law.***

The government introduced measures in *FA 2005* and subsequent *Finance Acts* that were largely aimed at establishing the UK as a pre-eminent location for the growing volume of transactions which are structured to comply with Islamic Sharia law. For accounting periods commencing on or after 1 April 2009, these measures have been consolidated into *CTA 2009, ss 501–521*. For income tax purposes, with effect from 6 April 2010 these measures have been consolidated into *ITA 2007, Pt 10A*.

There are a number of areas where commercial transactions undertaken by Muslims are expected to comply with religious and ethical precepts. These cover, amongst other things, the lending of money. In particular, the charging of interest by lenders is prohibited, and arrangements for the provision of finance need to involve a return other than the payment of interest.

As a consequence, finance structures have evolved and continue to evolve which are compliant with Islamic law. Typically, these have taken a number of forms, for instance:

- Diminishing Musharaka (diminishing shared ownership arrangements) – Musharaka more generally involve the financing party entering into a form of partnership arrangement with the commercial owner of the property. A profit share is secured by the financing partner that would be comparable to a finance return in a more conventional lending arrangement. Typically, the return paid by the commercial owner to the financing party is in the form of rent. Property financing structures generally involve a diminishing Musharaka arrangement. Under this, the initial ownership of the asset is held between the two parties according to the contribution to the finance. The finance party's share then diminishes over the specified period as payments are made by the commercial owner, who as a consequence, progressively acquires a greater share of the property until it is fully owned at the end of the finance period.
- Mudaraba/Wakala (deposit arrangements/profit share agency arrangements) – As a form of investment limited partnership, these are variations on the above arrangement which involve the finance party advancing funds for the acquisition of the property in return for a share of profits (or losses) arising.
- Murabaha (purchase and resale arrangements) – This has some similarities to a finance lease. The financing party actually buys the asset in question or a commodity readily convertible into cash and on-sells it to the commercial venturing party at a mark-up and on deferred terms which again give rise to a similar level of return that a conventional lender might expect.
- Sukuk (investment bond arrangements) – This is a form of securitisation. A security, or Sukuk, is issued by a special purpose vehicle which would typically buy the property and let it to the commercial owner. Often, the Sukuk vehicle will acquire the property in a sale and leaseback arrangement. As with Musharaka, the owner pays a return in the form of rent. This in turn is distributed by the SPV to its Sukuk holders as a profit distribution.

As the global Islamic community has become more influential in commercial transactions in the UK in recent years, there has been an increasing interest in these alternative finance structures. With that, there has been the growing recognition that our tax rules would not necessarily accommodate a tax deduction, even though a similar level of costs in a conventional finance arrangement would be tax deductible.

One particular problem has been the nature of the payments. As they are expressly not interest payments, it has been difficult to find a basis in the UK tax code for their deductibility. In the absence of relieving legislation, where a company makes Mudaraba or Wakala payments as profit shares, these would be generally treated as distributions and disallowed (*CTA 2010, Pt 23*). Other problems can arise with Murabaha payments, given that what otherwise would be annual costs of finance are presented as a series of payments for the asset, probably totalling more than that asset's market price.

Even with Musharaka and Sukuk transactions, where the payments are in the form of rent, there might ordinarily be a tax deductibility problem if the annual payments are greater than the normal commercial rent.

A further issue arises with non-UK based financing parties, as involvement in a Mudaraba or Wakala arrangement could result in that party having a taxable activity in the UK.

With these concerns in mind, the government introduced a series of provisions, initially in *FA 2005*, to enable tax relief to be available in circumstances where that previously may not have been the case.

To come within the new rules, the arrangements in question must involve a financial institution, which should include one of the following:

(a) a bank (within *CTA 2010, s 1120*);

(b) a building society;

(c) a wholly owned subsidiary of a bank or building society;

(d) a person licensed under the *Consumer Credit Act 1974* to carry on credit or hire business;

(e) a bond-issuer in relation to any bond assets which are rights under purchase and resale arrangements, diminishing shared ownership arrangements or profit share agency arrangements;

(f) a person authorised in a jurisdiction other than the UK to receive deposits or repayable funds from the public and to grant credits for its own account;

(g) a UK-regulated insurance company; or

(h) a person authorised outside the UK to undertake insurance business.

(*CTA 2009, s 502*)

The alternative finance provisions specify that, providing the return, profit share or mark-up (as the case may be) reflects a reasonable arm's-length finance return, the payment can be allowed for tax relief purposes.

In the case of a situation where a 'turn' is made in the form of a mark-up on goods purchased from the financing party, the part payments for the goods each year are treated as principal with interest and the allowable element computed accordingly (*CTA 2009, s 503*).

With regard to the profit-sharing, Mudaraba style deposit arrangements, the provisions switch off the distribution rules in *CTA 2010, Pt 23* from preventing a tax deduction (*CTA 2010, s 1019*).

The SDLT rules were amended to ensure there was not a double charge to SDLT as ownership of a property changed progressively under the diminishing Musharaka or Murabaha style arrangements.

In the case of a Sukuk type investment bond, to the extent that the return enjoyed by investors is on a par with a commercial return for the provision of funds, the return is then assessed on the bond holders in the same way as interest would be, and allowed to the payer on a similar basis. Changes to SDLT, chargeable gains and capital allowances rules have also facilitated the economic viability of land asset-based Sukuk securities (*FA 2009, Sch 61*).

The modification of pre-existing rules has gone a long way to assisting with the tax effectiveness of these various arrangements. There remain areas, however, where the strict tax position is still unhelpful. For instance, the structure can fall outside the alternative financing reliefs where the financing party does not satisfy the tax definition of financial institution, or the financing party has an interest in the future income or capital growth of the property. This has been a feature of the partnership-style arrangements.

Also, no special rules exist for VAT. Accordingly, the financing party in a Sharia-compliant structure may be treated as principal or part principal in a property transaction for VAT purposes, and thus have to consider different VAT consequences to a conventional lender.

Although the primary focus of these relatively new rules is to legislate for the tax deductibility of costs in these financing transactions, there is no reference to Islamic law in the legislation or to the terms referred to above. The government has deliberately sought to ensure that such rules should not be specific to any particular religious group or community. As a consequence, the tax treatment is available for any commercial arrangements that adopt these structures in preference to a conventional financing scenario.

**Point 3.30:** ***The introduction of a corporate interest restriction in April 2017 will have a significant impact for all corporate property investors.***

The Corporate Interest Restriction rules came into force with effect from 1 April 2017 and were introduced in line with Action 4 of BEPS, issued by the OECD, which aims to prevent companies from obtaining excessive tax relief for net interest and similar financing costs. The provisions apply to corporation tax payers and therefore apply to non-resident landlords from 6 April 2020.

The rules apply to a 'worldwide group' headed by a corporate entity including any subsidiaries, broadly as defined under International Accounting Standards. There are a number of tests that must be met in order to determine the identity of the worldwide group, as set out in TIOPA 2010, s 473, namely:

(a) A worldwide group includes the ultimate parent and each consolidated subsidiary.

(b) An ultimate parent is a company that is either not a member of an IAS group (as defined below), or is a member of an IAS group but is not consolidated by any other company within that group.

(c) Under International Accounting Standards, an entity is part of a 'group' if it is controlled by another entity (known as the parent).

Control is defined as the power to govern the financial and operating policies of an entity so as to obtain benefits from its activities. Control is presumed when the parent acquires more than half of the voting rights of the entity. It should be noted that control may still be acquired even when less than one half of the voting rights are owned.

The CIR applies to 'tax interest expense'. This is the term used in the legislation to include a wide range of interest and interest-like transactions such as:

- most loan relationship debits;
- some derivative contract debits; and
- the finance cost element of certain arrangements or transactions involving finance leasing, debt factoring or service concession arrangements.

Under the CIR rules, the amount of interest that is deductible for a group may potentially be restricted.

A group's interest capacity is the higher of a £2 million de minimis (pro-rated for short / long periods) (but split between UK corporation taxpayers only) and the below interest allowance.

An interest allowance will be calculated under either a Fixed Ratio (30% of 'tax-EBITDA') or Group Ratio (worldwide group's ratio of third party interest to 'tax-EBITDA').

Under the Fixed Ratio rule, a group's interest capacity will be limited to the lower of:

(a) 30% of tax-EBITDA, or

(b) The Fixed Ratio debt cap, being the Adjusted Net Group Interest Expense ("ANGIE") plus any excess debt cap from the prior period.

The ANGIE is based on the net group-interest expense of the group for the period of account, with specific upwards and downwards adjustments. A specific adjustment is for the treatment of capitalised interest (unless an election is made to follow the accounting recognition).

Under the Group Ratio rule, a group's interest capacity will be limited to the lower of:

(a) The Group Ratio percentage as applied to the Group-EBITDA, or

(b) The Group Ratio debt cap, being the Qualifying Net Group Interest Expense ('QNGIE').

The Group Ratio percentage is calculated as the QNGIE divided by Group-EBITDA. The QNGIE is based on the ANGIE with specific downward adjustments, including related party loans, and amounts arising on perpetual and long-dated instruments.

Any interest costs that are disallowed (by virtue of being in excess of the interest allowance) can be carried forward for the subsequent five years and 'reactivated' in future periods should the group have excess interest capacity.

Similarly, an excess interest capacity can also be carried forward to future accounting periods and used to increase the interest allowance.

If the aggregate UK net tax-interest expense of the group is below £2 million, the CIR will not generally apply. Broadly speaking, this will be the case where the group's deductible interest expense in the UK exceeds the group's taxable interest income in the UK by no more than £2 million (*TIOPA 2010, s 373*).

Assuming a 4% interest rate, this would mean that a group could borrow £50 million of net debt before the CIR rules could apply. This assumes no finance lease interest or any other items comprised in the full definition of tax-interest expense. Most small and medium-sized groups are unlikely to be affected by the CIR regime.

A number of additional compliance requirements must be met in order to allocate any disallowances within the group, and to ensure excess interest capacity or interest costs disallowed can be carried forward to future periods.

Certain exemptions / elections can be made albeit the impact of these must be carefully reviewed given that some are irrevocable for a fixed period.

## Point 3.31: *Hybrid and other mismatches*

The UK hybrid mismatch rules require that adjustments are made to corporation computations to counteract situations where there would otherwise be a:

(a) deduction/non-inclusion mismatch; or

(b) double-deduction mismatch.

A deduction/non-inclusion mismatch arises when a tax deduction for a payment is obtained without there being a corresponding amount of taxable income arising to another entity. This includes unreasonably long delays between the obtaining a deduction and the arising of a taxable receipt. A double-deduction mismatch occurs when tax deductions are available to two entities (or to the same entity for two taxes) in relation to just one payment.

The provisions apply from 1 January 2017 for those within the scope of corporation tax. Accordingly, non-resident landlords will fall within the scope of the provisions from 6 April 2020 (from which time such companies cease to be within the scope of UK income tax and will be within the scope of UK corporation tax).

The scope (and indeed complexity) of the provisions should not be underestimated and may technically apply in a number of wide-ranging scenarios. Particular difficulties may also apply when reviewing structures and financing arrangements involving entities such as US LLCs.

*Chapter 4*

# Repairs, renewals and improvements

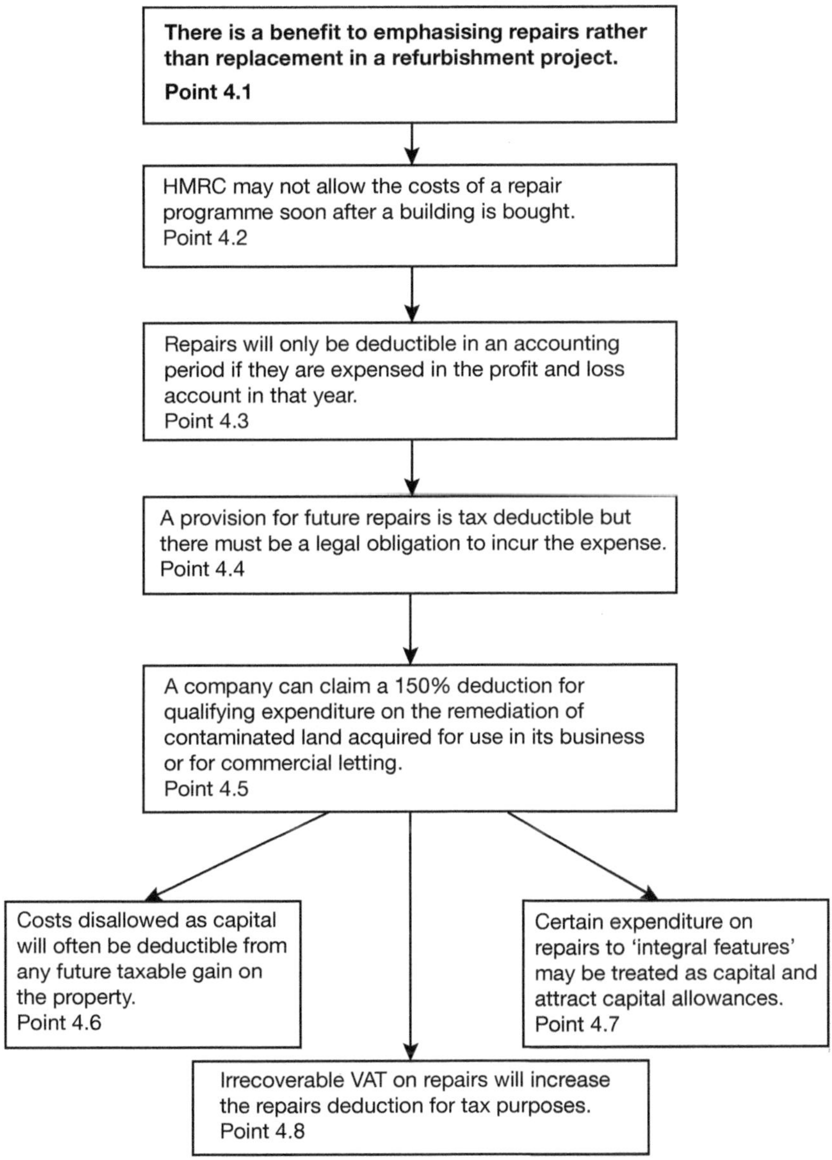

# 4 REPAIRS, RENEWALS AND IMPROVEMENTS

**Point 4.1:** ***A landlord contemplating an expenditure programme can influence the deductibility of amounts spent by placing the emphasis more on repairs than improvements.***

Where substantial refurbishment or redecoration is carried out, the related expenditure may not be fully deductible against rental income for tax purposes. To be allowable, such expenditure must be in respect of repairs or maintenance rather than improvements.

The distinction between repairs and improvements can give rise to problems. The courts have distinguished between repairs, which are allowable, and renewals, which are not.

Judicial decisions on this suggest that the restoration or replacement of part of an asset is a repair. The replacement of an entire asset is a renewal (see *O'Grady v Bullcroft Main Collieries Ltd* (1932) 17 TC 93 and *Jones (Samuel) & Co (Devondale) Ltd v IRC* (1951) 32 TC 513).

It is not easy to determine whether there has been a replacement of the whole asset or just part of it. Within the building there are a number of assets which make up the whole. A possible approach might be:

(a) For assets within a building, such as lifts or heating systems, the initial installation and subsequent complete replacement are renewals. If the system is overhauled or parts replaced, then that is a repair (*Lurcott v Wakely & Wheeler* [1911] 1 KB 905).

(b) If there is no separate asset, the test is whether the work performed enhances the asset as a whole. A new roof, for instance, could improve the building and would then be a capital item. The stripping down and repair of an entire roof on the other hand should still qualify as a revenue expense.

If an old building is repaired using modern materials, that is a repair. In one case, the old wooden oak floors of a 400-year old building were replaced much more cheaply and effectively by a concrete floor covered with terrazzo tiling. In the same case, steel joists encased in oak replaced wood lintels. The High Court upheld the Commissioners' decision that these were repairs and not improvements (*Conn v Robins Bros Ltd* (1966) 43 TC 266).

HM Revenue and Customs guidance on repairs and renewals is in the Business Income Manual from BIM 46900 onwards. This is worth reading to ascertain how HMRC approach the distinction between allowable deductions from income and disallowable capital expenditure. For instance, it reiterates its position that replacing a part is a repair to the larger asset, whereas replacing the whole asset is not a repair, and is not an allowable deduction for tax purposes because it is capital expenditure.

The manuals also give examples showing that where modern materials are used to replace older materials (eg steel girders replacing wooden beams), that may still constitute a repair if the floor/structure is still being used in the same way. There may be a different conclusion if there are enhancements such as greater usable area or load bearing capacity.

The manuals similarly deal with changing technology indicating that where something is replaced by its modern equivalent, that may well constitute an allowable repair and not an improvement (which would be disallowed as capital). Specific examples of repairs given include double glazing replacing single glazing.

In June 2013, the First-tier Tribunal ruled in the favour of a taxpayer company that had claimed as repairs the cost of reinstating an area within an industrial estate which, after 40 years, was in a poor state. The work involved resurfacing, re-siting a car park, re-routing of cabling, and the diversion of a carriageway. The Tribunal ruled that the estate was one asset and the work was all required to put it back into its fully serviceable state (*Hopegar Properties* TC2734).

A landlord might well review any proposed refurbishment programme to see whether repairs rather than improvements could be carried out. Furthermore, where both repairs and improvements are included in a work specification at the outset, a quantity surveyor could be asked to identify the related costs separately. General costs can then be allocated between them. In the absence of such a split, it is likely that the builders' invoices would not contain sufficient detail to support a revenue deduction for an appropriate part of the costs.

Since 1 April 2008 for companies subject to UK corporation tax and 5 April 2008 for other UK taxpayers, certain replacement expenditure on integral features has been treated as capital expenditure eligible for capital allowances rather than a 100% write-off as a repairs expense (see Point 4.7 below).

**Point 4.2:** ***If there is a large repairs cost soon after a building is bought, HMRC are likely to treat this cost as capital and not allow a deduction from taxable income.***

Expenditure is not deductible from taxable income if it formed part of the acquisition cost of the property. Furthermore, if a property is purchased in a dilapidated state, restoration expenditure will be treated as part of the capital cost of the property (*Law Shipping Co Ltd v IRC* (1923) 12 TC 621 and *Jackson v Laskers Home Furnishers Ltd* (1956) 37 TC 69).

To obtain a deduction for the repairs, it is necessary to establish that a building was commercially habitable without carrying out the repairs. The best evidence of this would be if the repairs did not take place until quite a while after occupation commenced (see *Odeon Associated Theatres Ltd v Jones* (1971) 48 TC 257).

**Point 4.3:** ***There may be no deduction for repairs expenditure if it has not been reflected in the profit and loss statement of the investment activity. Therefore, repairs which are 'capitalised' in the accounts are likely to be disallowed.***

The rules determining how a profit from a property investment activity is taxed now closely follow the accounting treatment. This, in turn, is determined by normal accounting principles as applied also to trading activities (*CTA 2009, s 210* for companies, and *ITTOIA 2005, s 272(2)* for non-corporate landlords). It does not matter whether the investor is a company, individual, partnership or trust.

HMRC will regard the profit and loss account of the entity as showing the proper measure of profit and loss for tax purposes on the premise that it is prepared in accordance with generally accepted accounting principles. Subject to that, HMRC will be reluctant to see an adjustment to profit for expenditure which it was not considered appropriate to include in the profit and loss account in the first instance. Instead, a deduction should be available for tax purposes as the asset is written down in value in the accounts. On the other hand, there will be no deduction for items that are specifically disallowable such as depreciation/ amortisation, entertaining or capital expenses.

In view of this, there is a clear conflict between maximising profit for accounts purposes and minimising profit for tax purposes. In either case, of course, the objective must be subservient to the proper treatment of the item to ensure that the accounts give a true and fair statement of the position.

**Point 4.4:** ***A deduction is available for a repairs provision, providing that there is a contractual obligation to undertake the expenditure and the repairs are specific.***

It had been assumed in the past that provisions for repairs were not tax deductible. HMRC's position on this was successfully challenged when the owner of a department store sought a deduction for a provision for refurbishment costs to be incurred in accordance with a feasibility report (*Jenners Princes Street (Edinburgh) Ltd v IRC* [1998] STC (SCD) 196). As the store was about to undertake the specific and detailed work set out in the feasibility report, the Special Commissioners felt that was sufficient to say that the funds had been 'expended' in an accounting sense.

In another case on the allowability of future costs, a firm of solicitors was held entitled to deduct for tax purposes the future rent commitment on its business premises (*Herbert Smith v Honour* [1999] STC 173).

Since these cases, UK GAAP has been restated in Section 21 of FRS 102. This makes it clear that a provision should be recognised where there is a present obligation (either legal or constructive) as a result of a past event and where a transfer of economic benefits is probable to settle the obligation and the obligation can be reliably measured. Provisions are measured at the best estimate of the amount required to settle the obligation at the reporting date and should take into account the time value of money where material. The provision is then adjusted at each reporting date. HMRC will not allow a provision for tax purposes if it does not satisfy Section 21 of FRS 102 (or, if appropriate, its international equivalent, IAS 37).

HMRC's present position is as set out in Business Income Manual BIM46510. In this, it is stated that an accounts provision will be allowable for tax only if:

(a) it is in respect of allowable revenue expenditure;

(b) it is in accordance with GAAP;

(c) it does not conflict with any specific statutory tax rule; and

(d) it is estimated with sufficient accuracy.

The message is that a provision for repairs can attract tax relief in a year, as the law currently appears to stand, even though monies are not paid out until a future period. This should be the case where there is a specific programme of work to be undertaken and a legal commitment to incur the expenditure.

**Point 4.5:** ***Companies can obtain deductions of 150% on qualifying expenditure on cleaning up contaminated land they acquire for their own trading purposes or for commercial letting.***

A company incurring 'qualifying land remediation expenditure' qualifies for a deduction of 150%. Qualifying land remediation expenditure encompasses direct land remediation costs, professional expenses and any internal time costs of the company's personnel.

The company must acquire the land for the purposes of its trade or for commercial letting and, from 1 April 2009, have a 'major interest' in the land. A major interest includes a freehold or leasehold interest of more than seven years unexpired. If all or part of it is contaminated, and the contamination is not due to any action or inaction on the company's own part, or on the part of any connected party, certain types of expenditure on remedying the contamination qualify for the relief.

The expenditure must satisfy five conditions to qualify, as follows:

(a) the land in question must be in such a condition that harm of a defined environmental nature (injuring the health of living organisms, interference with ecological systems etc) is being caused or may potentially be caused or that pollution of controlled waters is being or is likely to be caused;

(b) the expenditure must be undertaken directly by the company or on its behalf and consist of works, steps or operations designed to prevent, minimise, mitigate or remedy the harm or pollution;

(c) in the case of in-house costs, it must be incurred on employee costs or the cost of materials. There is no relief for the cost of support staff or items eligible for capital allowances;

(d) it must not be partly or wholly funded by any grants or subsidies nor must the cost of it, in fact, be borne directly or indirectly by a third party. This restriction might be a problem if there is a specific discount negotiated with a seller to reflect the remediation costs; and

(e) the expenditure must be of a kind that would not have been incurred if the land had not been contaminated.

Provided that the above conditions are met, the company can opt to claim a deduction of 150% of the expenditure when computing its taxable profits (either of the trade for the purposes of which the land was acquired or of the commercial letting business in which the land is being used) for the accounting period in which the expenditure is incurred. If, in that period, the company makes a loss that is unrelieved, it may instead claim a tax credit equal to 24% of the smaller of the loss and 150% of the qualifying expenditure. A loss is unrelieved to the extent that it has not been, and could not be, used to offset other profits of the same period or previous periods or as part of a group-relief claim.

The relief is only available to corporate taxpayers. Income taxpayers will not be able to claim the deduction.

Changes to the legislation removed land remediation relief after 1 April 2009 in relation to certain natural substances that will no longer be deemed to be 'contaminating substances'. However, the clearance of arsenic, radon and Japanese knotweed does qualify for relief (companies may make retrospective claims on costs incurred since May 2001 on Japanese knotweed clearance).

It is worth noting that a property investment company that incurs such costs can elect to claim a tax deduction for these, even though they may be included in the balance sheet cost of the property. A company which holds the property as trading stock, on the other hand, can only get the deduction when the stock is sold.

The credit is not treated as taxable income of the company and can be applied against any corporation tax liability the company may have, or be claimed as a repayment.

**Point 4.6:** ***If expenses are disallowed by HMRC on the grounds that they represent improvements, ensure that these costs are included in the capital cost of the property when computing any future chargeable gains.***

If refurbishment or related expenditure (including any irrecoverable VAT thereon) is disallowed as capital, it is important to keep a note of these amounts. They should form part of the CGT base cost of the property as enhancement expenditure, assuming the related improvements are reflected in the state or nature of the property when sold (*TCGA 1992, s 38(1)(b)*).

These expenses will reduce any subsequent capital gain arising or augment a capital loss.

**Point 4.7:** ***Expenditure on replacing part of an integral feature may not be tax deductible as repairs, although it may attract capital allowances.***

Since April 2008, expenditure on the replacement of part of an item of plant which qualifies as an integral feature is treated as capital expenditure and thus not tax deductible if the cost is more than 50% of the cost of replacing the whole asset (*CAA 2001, s 33B*).

Where less than 50% of the replacement cost is incurred, the expenditure can be treated as revenue and tax deductible unless further expenditure is incurred on the same asset within 12 months.

The key issue will be to identify the entirety of the asset concerned, since it is this against which the 50% is measured. In other words, is it possible to identify a number of individual assets which together comprise the whole integral feature. For example, consider what individual items make up the entirety of the water heating system. Provided that the replacement cost is less than 50% of the whole, then a tax deduction should be available. HMRC have confirmed that they view a boiler as part of the larger water system rather than the asset in its entirety.

Where expenditure falls under this category, capital allowances at a 'special' rate of 6% per annum (8% prior to April 2019) should instead be available – see Point 6.5 regarding capital allowances on integral features.

The interaction between the rules for plant classified as integral features and repairs to plant eligible for the special rate makes correct classification of expenditure even more important. Whilst repairs totalling more than 50% of the cost to replace a lift would not be tax deductible in the year they are incurred, those same repairs to a hoist would entitle the taxpayer to a full revenue deduction.

**Point 4.8:** ***Remember that irrecoverable VAT will attract a tax deduction.***

Where VAT on repairs expenditure is irrecoverable, the non-recoverable VAT will be a deductible expense for income and corporation tax purposes.

*Chapter 5*

# Stamp duty land tax

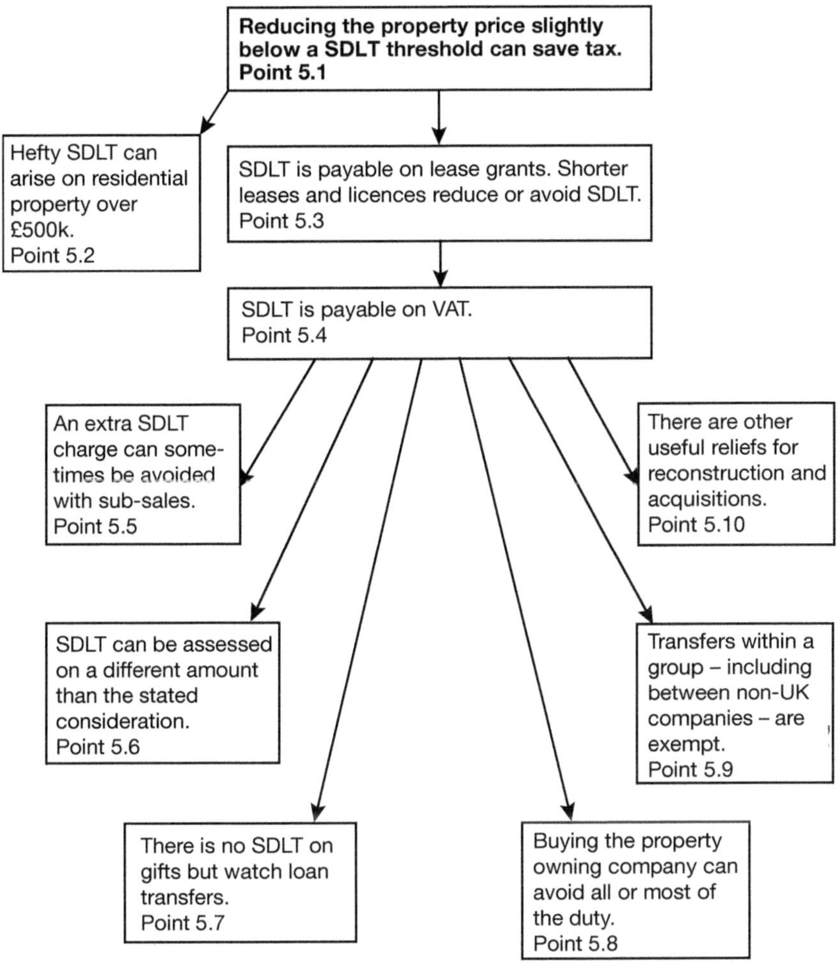

## 5 STAMP DUTY LAND TAX

**Point 5.1:** ***Stamp Duty Land Tax is chargeable on a stepped basis for both non-residential and residential property purchases, with possible additional amounts where there is contingent consideration. An extra 3% surcharge can also apply to certain residential property***

Since 1 December 2003, stamp duty land tax (SDLT), instead of stamp duty, has applied to land transactions in England, Wales and Northern Ireland. In Scotland, a separate Land and Buildings Transaction Tax is levied. A similar Land Transaction Tax replaced SDLT in Wales from 1 April 2018.

The SDLT thresholds on transfers of non-residential (or mixed non-residential/residential) freeholds and lease assignments are currently as follows:

| | |
|---|---|
| Up to £150,000 | 0% |
| The next £100,000 (the portion from £150,001 to £250,000) | 2% |
| The remaining amount (the portion above £250,000) | 5% |

Since 4 December 2014, SDLT on residential property is calculated on a 'stepped' basis. The SDLT thresholds on transfers of residential freeholds and lease assignments are currently as follows:

| **Property purchase price** | **SDLT rate** |
|---|---|
| Up to £250,000 | Zero |
| The next £675,000 (the portion from £250,001 to £925,000) | 5% |
| The next £575,000 (the portion from £925,001 to £1.5 million) | 10% |
| The remaining amount (the portion above £1.5 million) | 12% |

**Note 1** – From April 2016, the above rates apply only for purchases of an individual's main residence. If the purchase means that an individual owns more than one property (or is a purchase of residential property by a company or other entity), then an additional 3% applies to each of the rates above.

The extra 3% SDLT will not apply if the property being bought is replacing the individual's main residence and that has already been sold.

If there is a delay in selling the previous main residence and it has not been sold on the day of completion of the purchase of the new property, the higher rates will apply but a refund can be claimed if the previous main residence is sold within three years.

The additional 3% will not apply where an individual is replacing a main residence even if other rental properties are held.

There are special rules where properties are jointly owned or inherited.

**Note 2** – A 2% SDLT surcharge on purchases of residential property in England and Northern Ireland by non-residents was introduced for transactions entered into on or after 1 April 2021.

**Note 3** – A relief for first-time buyers of properties up to £625,000 (£500,000 pre 23 September 2022) applies such that there is no SDLT on the first £425,000 (£300,000 pre 23 September 2022) of the consideration and a rate of 5% applies to consideration of over £425,000 (£300,000 pre 23 September 2022) up to £625,000 (£500,000 pre 23 September 2023). There are stringent qualifying conditions including that the buyer intends to occupy the property as their only or main residence. For transactions with an effective date of on or after 1 April 2025, these thresholds will revert back to the pre-23 September 2022 levels.

Since 21 March 2012, purchases of high-value residential property by 'non-natural' persons for consideration above a certain threshold attract SDLT at 15% unless one of the reliefs is available (see Point 5.2 below). From 20 March 2014, the threshold for a high-value residential property is £500,000.

Where six or more dwellings are acquired together, these are treated as non-residential for the purposes of determining the applicable rate of SDLT. This means that the top rate of SDLT in this case would be 5%. However, note that where the purchaser is a non-natural person who does not qualify for relief (see Point 5.2 below), single dwellings with a value of over £500,000 are subject to SDLT at 15%, even if they are part of a purchase of six or more dwellings.

The above rates would apply to transfers of property and most other land transactions, eg options and waiver of rights. The grant of leases is, however, subject to a different regime, mentioned in Point 5.3 below.

A possible pitfall for buyers is to have consideration contingent on a future event. Under SDLT, that contingency will be assumed to occur, thus the SDLT is calculated on the higher amount (*FA 2003, s 51(1)*). It is, however, possible to make an application to defer the tax payable in certain circumstances (*FA 2003, s 90*). In the event that the contingency does not eventually happen, any overpaid SDLT can be recovered (*FA 2003, s 80*).

There are also various reliefs from SDLT. These are sometimes introduced by a Finance Act for a short period only, so it is important to check eligibility and the timing of a transaction to ensure a relief still applies.

A relief known as 'multiple dwellings relief' is available for residential property purchasers acquiring more than one property from the same seller. Instead of the SDLT rate being determined by the total value of the consideration paid, it is based on the average price paid for each property. Where the relief is claimed, the additional 3% SDLT will apply to the average price paid, even if one of the properties is being acquired as a main residence. The relief must be claimed in a land transaction return and will also apply to 'off-plan' dwellings in certain circumstances. Under 'multiple dwellings relief', the rate of tax on two or more residential dwellings is limited to the average price per dwelling with the charge to tax multiplied by the number of dwellings. If the average price would otherwise be charged at 0% then a minimum rate of 1% SDLT applies. Note that where the purchaser is a non-natural person who does not qualify for relief (see Point 5.2 below) in calculating the average price paid, single dwellings with a value of over £500,000 are excluded and SDLT at a rate of 15% applies to these properties. The operation of the relief is subject to consultation (see 'Recent SDLT changes relevant to individuals' above).

In 2021, HMRC launched a consultation around a potential tightening up the multiple dwellings relief rules by proposing a number of potential options, including:

- availability of the relief only where the properties are acquired either to be let out or developed with a view to sale;
- the subsidiary dwelling (eg annex) is counted as a separate dwelling only if it represents a third or more of the value of the property; and
- that relief is allowed only for purchases of three or more dwellings.

The consultation was largely driven as a result of the abuse of the rules by certain SDLT reclaim agents. No timescales have been indicated in terms of when any changes could be introduced.

Where one or more properties are transferred between the same buyer and seller or connected persons, these acquisitions may be 'linked' subject to the relief mentioned above for residential property. This means that the aggregate consideration is taken into account in calculating the SDLT. Where a property in a linked transaction is the replacement of a main residence, an apportionment can be made to reflect the normal rates of SDLT which will apply to that property (whereas the additional 3% rate will apply to other properties).

There is a specific exemption from SDLT where a house builder buys property from individuals who are selling their current residences to acquire a newly built home (*FA 2003, Sch 6A*). The subsequent purchaser from the house builder becomes liable to SDLT in the normal way.

**Point 5.2:** ***Stamp duty land tax can be as much as 15% on high-value residential properties when bought by a company or other 'non-natural person'. Furthermore, ongoing annual charges can arise.***

In March 2012, the government responded to concerns about avoidance of Stamp Duty Land Tax on expensive residential property changing hands within companies by imposing a 15% SDLT charge on properties bought for £2 million or more by 'non-natural persons'. This charge has applied to purchases with effect from 21 March 2012. From 20 March 2014, the threshold for a high value residential property is £500,000.

The expression 'non-natural persons' for this purpose is defined as companies, partnerships where one or more members is a company and collective investment schemes, whether these are UK or overseas. Trustees (other than bare trustees who hold on behalf of 'non-natural persons') will be exempt from the charge.

There are reliefs from the 15% rate of SDLT where the property is being acquired in the course of a bona fide property business including property development, dealing and letting, provided that it is not intended that the property will be occupied or available for use by a connected person. Note that where six or more dwellings are acquired (see Point 5.1 above), high-value dwellings within the 15% rate of SDLT count towards the number of dwellings, but the non-residential rates of SDLT will not apply to those dwellings. Therefore, if a transaction includes one dwelling within the 15% charge and five dwellings outside it, the five dwellings would be treated as non-residential property.

Furthermore, these high-value residential properties are excluded from the averaging relief mentioned in Point 5.1 above. So if a non-natural person buys a portfolio of properties containing both expensive and cheaper properties, any dwellings with a value of more than £500,000 would be excluded and charged at 15% (if applicable) before any averaging exercise to determine the SDLT rate on the rest of the portfolio.

An annual charge, known as 'Annual Tax on Enveloped Dwellings' ('ATED'), was introduced with effect from 1 April 2013 for non-natural persons holding residential property worth over £2 million on 1 April 2012 (or at acquisition if later). Note that the threshold after which ATED applies was reduced to £1 million for the period 1 April 2015 to 31 March 2016 and to £500,000 for periods from 1 April 2016.

The relevant ATED charges can be found on the gov.uk website and are reproduced in the table below:

| | 2022/23 | 2023/24 | 2024/25 |
|---|---|---|---|
| More than £500,000 but not more than £1m | £3,800 | £4,150 | £4,400 |
| More than £1m but not more than £2m | £7,700 | £8,450 | £9,000 |
| More than £2m but not more than £5m | £26,050 | £28,650 | £30,550 |
| More than £5m but not more than £10m | £60,900 | £67,050 | £71,500 |
| More than £10m but not more than £20m | £122,250 | £134,550 | £143,550 |
| More than £20m | £244,750 | £269,450 | £287,500 |

For 2018–19 to 2022–23, the valuation of the dwelling as at 1 April 2017 determines the band and therefore the amount of the ATED liability.

The annual charge is indexed to the Consumer Price Index ('CPI') and updated each April based on the CPI of the previous September. Similarly to the reliefs from the 15% rate of SDLT, reliefs from ATED exist where the property is held as part of certain property businesses including property development, dealing or letting, provided it is not occupied or available for use by a connected person. There are aggressive 'look-back' and 'look-forward' provisions which can apply to charge ATED for a number of years even if a non-qualifying individual occupies the dwelling for a short period of time only.

**Point 5.3:** ***SDLT is payable by tenants on lease grants. Shorter leases and licences can help to minimise the charge, as can appropriate allocation to non-rent amounts such as service fees. There is also an exemption for certain sale and leasebacks.***

SDLT must be paid by tenants entering into a new lease.

For residential property, the rate is 1% and this is applied to the present value of rents reserved under the lease over the SDLT threshold (£250,000 at the date of writing). For non-residential property, a rate of 1% is applied to the present value of rents reserved under the lease over £150,000 up to £5m and at a rate of 2% over £5m. The SDLT calculation is based on a present value formula. It is possible to access HMRC's online calculator for assistance with computing the liability (which can be found on the HMRC website at www.hmrc.gov.uk).

The rules surrounding this charge are complex, particularly in determining the SDLT where there are variable and uncertain rents. As such, any detailed discussion of the rules is outside the scope of this book. Some of the key planning pointers in this area can be summarised as follows:

(a) The consequence of the calculation is that the longer the lease and the higher the rent, the higher the SDLT charge.

(b) No SDLT is due on licences. However, where a licence is found to possess the attributes of a lease, HMRC will seek to levy a liability to SDLT.

(c) Service charges and other non-rental amounts do not figure in the calculation. Therefore, it is sensible to identify separately such amounts from the rent in any lease. Note that the amounts in question must be reasonable, or else the SDLT due is open to challenge by HMRC.

(d) A lease grant should not be subject to SDLT where it is part of a sale and leaseback to the vendor (*FA 2003, s 57A*).

**Point 5.4:** ***SDLT is payable on VAT.***

A controversial aspect of SDLT is that it is charged on the VAT-inclusive price of a property. There is thus an element of tax on tax. The position can be summarised as follows:

(a) Where the VAT exemption on a commercial property has been waived, VAT is chargeable on the sale price or, where relevant, the rent. In this case, SDLT is payable on the VAT-inclusive consideration or, with a lease grant, the present value of future VAT-inclusive rents.

(b) Similarly, where VAT must be charged – ie on the sale of new commercial property – SDLT would be computed on the price inclusive of VAT.

(c) If the sale is of a property where the exemption from VAT has not been waived at the time of completion (ie the sale is exempt), no VAT would be charged on the sale and thus would not affect the SDLT due (*FA 2003, Sch 4, para 2*).

(d) In the case of grants of leases, SDLT will only be charged on the VAT-inclusive rent figure, if VAT is chargeable at the date the lease is granted. If, at that point, there has been no election to waive the exemption, SDLT is calculated on the VAT-exclusive rent figure (*FA 2003, Sch 4, para 2*).

(e) Where a property transfer is outside the scope of VAT as a transfer of an asset as a going concern, SDLT is levied on the price exclusive of VAT.

(f) Where VAT should be charged on a barter transaction such as a sale and leaseback, SDLT can be due on the VAT element, even if the VAT amounts net off and no VAT invoices are raised.

A purchaser needs to consider the SDLT position in relation to the VAT status of the transaction and anticipate the SDLT on the VAT as an extra cost.

For further reference on the VAT position for properties, see Chapters 18 (for investors), 26 (for property dealers and developers) and 35 (for trading premises).

**Point 5.5:** ***SDLT may arise on a property transaction even where a contract of sale has not been completed. An important exception is available to enable certain sub-sales to proceed without double tax provided there has not been 'substantial performance'.***

SDLT is usually payable on completion of the property transaction.

However, SDLT can arise in relation to an uncompleted contract providing there has been 'substantial performance' (*FA 2003, s 44*).

Substantial performance can occur where the buyer becomes entitled to occupy the property, or, where relevant, to receive the rental income arising. Alternatively, there is also substantial performance when the seller receives 90% or more of the sale consideration (*FA 2003, s 44(5)*).

A commercial situation where the substantial performance rule can be particularly helpful is in the area of sub-sales. Sub-sale is the term normally applied to situations where the buyer acquires land with a view to selling-on immediately or very shortly afterwards. Normally, this would mean two occasions of charge to SDLT. However, sub-sale relief avoids the double charge (*FA 2003, Sch 2A*). If, however, the buyer completes, pays more than 90% of the purchase price, or otherwise substantially performs the contract prior to the second sale, any possibility of sub-sale relief is lost.

A condition of sub-sale relief is that the second sale completes at the same time as the first contract.

Relief may not be claimed where the sub-sale forms part of any tax avoidance arrangements. HMRC have successfully challenged avoidance schemes to exploit sub-sale relief in a number of cases and will continue to challenge users of such schemes.

**Point 5.6:** ***SDLT would normally be assessed on the consideration payable by the purchaser for the property, subject to certain exceptions where the amount may be more or less than this figure.***

For the most part, property transactions will stipulate the consideration payable and the calculation of the SDLT thereon would be relatively straightforward. There are, however, a number of exceptions.

One such situation is where there is a transfer of a property to a connected company, other than a transfer within a 75% group. In this situation, HMRC will seek to apply market value where the consideration passing is less than this figure (*FA 2003, s 53*).

A further situation arises with respect to loans. Where the consideration for the sale of property is the assumption or release of debt, the face value of the debt is treated as the consideration subject to SDLT, to the extent that it does not exceed the market value of the property (*FA 2003, Sch 4, para 8).* This could mean that SDLT is due on less than the value of the consideration, for example in a situation where the debt assumed has a higher market value than face value. This might be the case if the loan carried a particularly high interest rate.

Sometimes, properties are sold where the final consideration is not ascertainable at the outset. This may be because there is a contingency provided for or because there is some formula on which the consideration will be based.

The position with contingent consideration has already been referred to in Point 5.1 above. With regard to unascertainable consideration, the SDLT would be charged on a reasonable estimate (*FA 2003, s 51(2)*). It is possible to reclaim any overpaid SDLT, or pay over further amounts, once the actual consideration can be determined.

**Point 5.7:** ***A gift, other than a gift to an associated company, will not attract SDLT. However, if the donee agrees to take over any loan obligations, the amount of that loan will be treated as consideration subject to SDLT.***

Where there is no consideration, no SDLT arises. Typically, that would be the case where there is a gift of a property to an individual. The exception to this is where the gift is to an associated company, where market value is substituted (see Point 5.6 above).

However, if any loan is taken over by the purchaser as part of the transfer, that would be consideration and subject to SDLT.

**Point 5.8:** ***SDLT can be saved by buying the shares of the property-owning company, particularly a non-UK company, rather than the property itself.***

Whilst SDLT payable on the purchase price of a non-residential property can be up to 5%, and on a residential property, up to 15%, stamp duty on the purchase of shares in a UK company is only 0.5%. With shares in non-UK companies, no stamp duty at all is payable, even if that company is resident and active in the UK, provided the document to acquire the shares is executed outside the UK, nothing is done or to be done in the UK in relation to the share transfer (including payment of or provision of the consideration for the shares) and the company does not maintain a UK share register. Buying and selling companies is less straightforward than buying the properties that they own. A problem for the seller is tax on capital gains. Within a corporate group, the issue is highlighted in the example below.

## Example

London Limited (London) owns all the shares in Rio Limited (Rio) which two years ago bought a commercial property for £8 million. Rio financed the property purchase with £6 million external borrowings, and £2 million was lent by London. London only subscribed a nominal amount for the shares.

The property is now worth £10 million. If that property is sold to Birmingham Limited (Birmingham), Rio would make a capital gain of £2 million (ignoring indexation allowance) on which it would pay £500,000 (assuming corporation tax at 25%).

After paying off the £8 million debt, the balance of £1.50 million can be distributed to London tax-free by way of dividend. The purchaser will pay £489,500 SDLT or possibly more, if VAT is chargeable on the sale (see Point 5.4 above).

An alternative is for London to sell the shares in Rio for £2 million. Birmingham would take responsibility to procure repayment by Rio of the £8 million indebtedness, which means it is still paying £10 million.

In this case, London will have a capital gain of £2 million on the sale of the company. This would give rise to the same corporation tax liability of £500,000 for London.

The purchaser's stamp duty is limited to 0.5% of £2 million, ie £10,000, a saving of £479,500.

The problem is that the purchaser is also inheriting a future tax liability within Rio of £500,000. If the purchaser is going to be a long-term holder of that property, the cash flow benefit of avoiding stamp duty land tax now could exceed the prospect of a distant future tax liability. In that case, it could be an attractive proposition. Otherwise, the inherent tax liability could exceed the SDLT saving. The purchaser will, of course, have extra due diligence and contractual issues when buying a company, as compared to the relatively more straightforward purchase of the property.

---

Clearly, if the gain was exempt or there was only a modest gain or no gain at all, this structure would be potentially beneficial all round. Until 6 April 2019, certain gains might be exempt where the companies in question are not UK-resident (see Chapter 1) or where the substantial shareholding exemption applies (see Chapter 32). Transferring a property into a special purpose company when a sale has been contemplated is unlikely to be effective for SDLT purposes (ie the intra-group exemption would not be available – see Point 5.9 below). Furthermore, if the company itself is sold by its parent within six years of the property transfer, the disposal consideration for the parent company will increase by the gain that would have been charged had the initial property transfer not occurred intragroup (*TCGA 1992, s 179*). The seller group may be able to absorb any such gain by electing to transfer the gain into one of the retained group companies (*TCGA 1992, s 171A*) or the gain may be exempt if the substantial shareholding exemption applies (see Chapter 32).

Where the property-owning company is owned by a UK-based individual or trust keen to get direct access to the sale proceeds, the prospect of selling the company rather than the property may be relatively more attractive. The individuals or trustee shareholder cannot extract the profit of the company tax-free in the way that London Limited could in the above example. Therefore, if the company sells the property, there is the prospect of two levels of tax charge in extracting the proceeds. This would be corporation tax in the company on the gain and either income tax or CGT on extraction of profit. In addition, if the purchaser wishes to transfer the property into a new company after the acquisition, there may be a challenge from HMRC as to whether group relief is available (see Point 5.9 below).

**Point 5.9:** ***Many transactions within a group, including sales to overseas group companies, are exempt from SDLT.***

An important exemption relates to transfers of properties between group companies (*FA 2003, Sch 7, para 1*). For companies to be treated as within a group, there must be 75% common ownership (*FA 2003, Sch 7, para 1(2), (3)*).

This relief also extends to the grant of leases between group companies.

It does not matter whether or not the companies in question are UK resident. Accordingly, a UK company can transfer property to a Jersey parent, and vice versa, without an SDLT consequence.

The 75% group test requires more than simply having shares which confer 75% ownership. The test looks at the economic benefits associated with the shares, including aspects such as entitlement to dividends and assets in a winding up. This test can also take into account the rights of a lender to acquire shares (*FA 2003, Sch 7, para 1(4)–(6)*; *CTA 2010, Pt 5, Ch 6*).

The relief for intra-group transactions is subject to a number of restrictions and potential withdrawal situations.

The restriction operates where, at the time the transaction takes place, there are arrangements under which:

(a) another person can take control of the purchasing company at some stage;

(b) the purchasing company can cease to be a member of the same group as the seller; or

(c) the consideration for the sale is to be provided directly or indirectly by a third party. It is understood that HMRC do not regard normal commercial bank finance as affecting this.

(FA 2003, Sch 7, para 2)

In addition, relief is not available if the transaction is not effected for bona fide commercial reasons or forms part of arrangements of which the main purpose or one of the main purposes is the avoidance of a liability to tax (which includes stamp duty, income tax, corporation tax, capital gains tax as well as SDLT).

HMRC are increasingly focussing on the reasons behind transfers of properties where group relief is claimed and therefore it is important to be able to support and demonstrate the commercial rationale for such transfers.

Relief previously given will be withdrawn if the purchasing company ceases to be a member of the same group as the seller within three years whilst still owning the property. It will similarly be withdrawn if there are arrangements within the three years for this to happen (*FA 2003, Sch 7, para 3*). There are exceptions to this rule, such as where the purchasing company leaves the group because the seller company is wound up. It is also possible to avoid this withdrawal in some circumstances where the seller and buyer leave the group together (*FA 2003, Sch 7, para 4*).

Care is needed where, after an intra-group property transfer, the vendor company leaves the group. Whilst this in itself does not result in a clawback of relief, if, within three years from the date of that transfer, there is a change in controlling ownership, directly or indirectly, of the purchasing company, the group relief given on the intra-group transfer will be clawed back on the second event (*FA 2003, Sch 7, para 4ZA*).

**Point 5.10:** ***There are other reliefs for reconstructions and acquisitions.***

Apart from group relief, the SDLT rules also allow certain commercial transactions which do not result in a change in ownership of the property to be carried out SDLT-free.

Exemption from SDLT is available for a reconstruction (*FA 2003, Sch 7, para 7*). Typically, this occurs where property is transferred between companies, as part of a transfer of a business, where the consideration is wholly or partly the issue of non-redeemable shares to the shareholders of the target company. Where there is consideration other than the issue of these shares, this must only be the assumption of or discharge by the acquiring company of liabilities of the target company in order for the relief to be available. The shareholding of the acquiring company must be the same, or as nearly as may be the same, as that of the former company.

Acquisition relief is potentially of wider application. This reduces the rate of duty to 0.5%. This is available where a company acquires the property and related trading undertaking of the target company in consideration of the issue of non-redeemable shares or the assumption/discharge of indebtedness. Up to 10% of the nominal value of the shares can be in cash (*FA 2003, Sch 7, para 8*).

There are similar restrictions and withdrawal circumstances as for group relief (see Point 5.8 above).

*Chapter 6*

# Capital allowances on plant and machinery

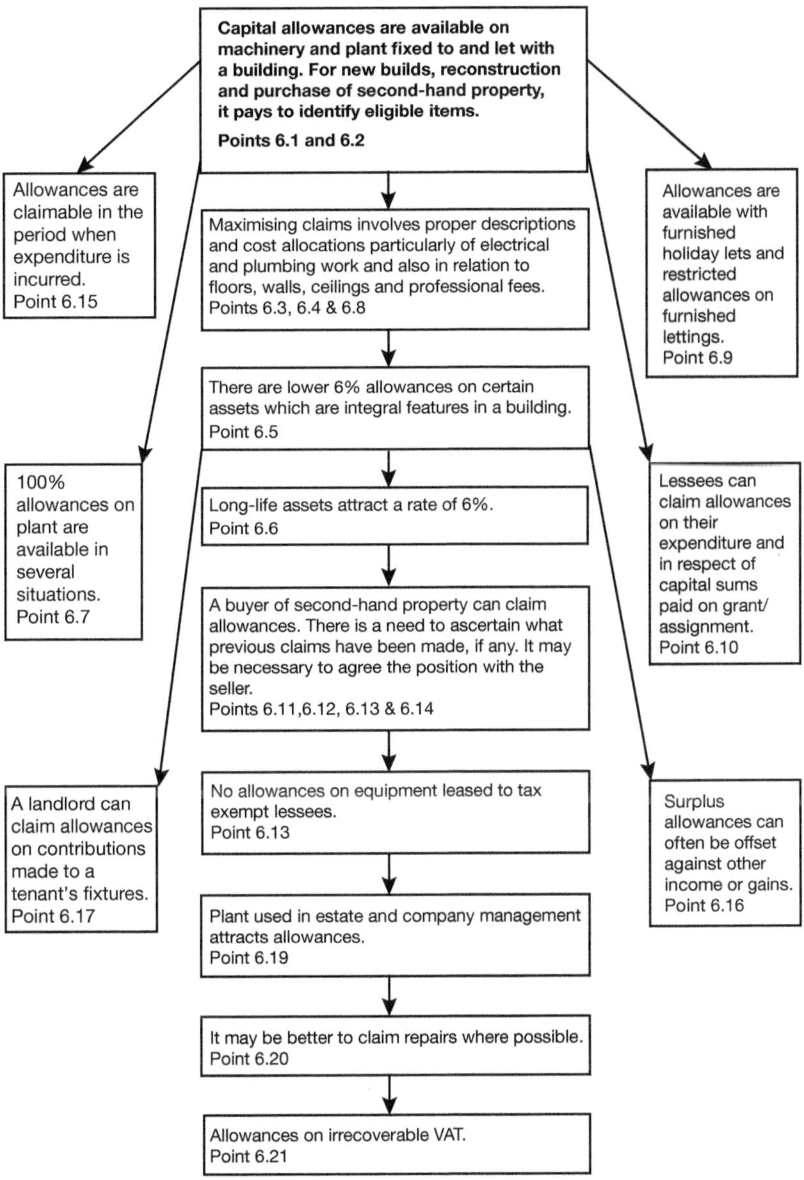

# 6 CAPITAL ALLOWANCES ON PLANT AND MACHINERY

**Point 6.1:** ***A property investor can claim capital allowances on expenditure in respect of plant and machinery that is fixed to, and let with, a building.***

The letting of property on a commercial basis is treated as a qualifying activity for capital allowance purposes (*CAA 2001, s 15(1)(b)*). So, where plant and machinery are included in a let building, the property investor can claim allowances on capital expenditure in respect of qualifying items (subject to the long funding lease rules – see Point 6.10 below). These allowances are deductible from the rental income.

Since 1 April 2012 (for companies within the charge to corporation tax) and fiscal year 2012/2013 (for other taxpayers who are subject to income tax), annual allowances at a rate of 18% per annum have been applied to the tax written-down value of the plant in each year unless the items of plant and machinery are integral features or long-life assets (see Points 6.5 and 6.6 below). Allowances for expenditure on special rate items such as thermal insulation and solar panels are also given at the rate of 6% (8% prior to April 2019).

See Point 6.15 below for a summary of the rules for identifying when expenditure is actually incurred for these purposes.

No capital allowances have historically been eligible to be claimed on plant or machinery installed in a 'dwelling house' (*CAA 2001, s 35(2)*). This restriction is confined to the residential unit. In the case of an apartment block, this should not preclude claims in respect of the common areas, eg lifts, communal corridors and plant rooms. Items installed within the demise of the individual flats would not qualify. In order to make a claim a just and reasonable apportionment of the expenditure would need to be undertaken. Structures and Buildings Allowance (SBA) are also not available for any type of residential property.

A wear-and-tear allowance was to be available instead, to provide tax relief for expenditure on furnished individual units.

The wear-and-tear allowance and the renewals allowance for property businesses has been repealed and replaced, for expenditure incurred on or after 1 April 2016 for corporation tax and on or after 6 April 2016 for income tax. The updated legislation instead allows a deduction for capital expenditure incurred by a lessor on replacing furnishings, appliances (including white goods) and kitchenware provided for the use of a lessee in a dwelling-house.

100% allowances are available in several situations (see Point 6.7 below).

**Point 6.2:** ***Whether the expenditure is on the construction of a new building, reconstruction work at an existing building or the purchase of a second-hand building, it pays to identify the items on which capital allowances could be due.***

Capital allowances are claimable on plant and machinery installed in a new building, purchased as part of the building or installed subsequently.

Where plant has become a fixture in a building and the price paid for the building includes an element in respect of the fixture, capital allowances are potentially claimable on the amount attributable to the plant (*CAA 2001, s 181(1)*). This would be the case where:

(a) a freehold is purchased;

(b) consideration is paid for the assignment of a lease; or

(c) a premium is paid on the grant of a lease.

The buyer may need to take steps to establish the seller's (or any previous owner's) capital allowance position in order to become entitled to allowances (see Point 6.12).

Although there is normally little problem in identifying items of machinery, 'plant' has proved more difficult – and further complications arise following *FA 2008* in relation to integral features (see Point 6.5 below).

The determination of which items qualified as plant has, for many years, been a matter of interpreting the decisions in a succession of tax cases. Two general principles have emerged from the cases over the years. These are:

(a) the item should perform a function in the business; and

(b) it should not be part of the setting in which the business is carried on.

For some years, the legislation has specified certain items in a building on which the related expenditure qualifies for capital allowances and some that will not (*CAA 2001, ss 21–24*). These items are summarised in Appendix I. As noted in that Appendix, expenditure on certain items of plant is, with effect from April 2008, regarded as being in respect of 'integral features' and will be part of a separate pool attracting just 6% (previously 8%) writing-down allowances.. Furthermore, some expenditure in certain buildings will be on 'long-life assets' which also attract an 6% writing-down allowance. Additionally, expenditure on thermal insulation and solar panels attracts an 6% writing-down allowance.

The legislation needs to be read in conjunction with case law where the distinction between plant and non-plant has been explored in a number of cases, as noted below.

Whilst the present legislation has resolved some of the issues, items of expenditure will continue to arise which do not fit neatly within any of the specified categories. There remain areas where it is not easy to apply the legislation in practice and where further analysis is useful to ensure that allowance claims are maximised. Some of the more typical problem areas are examined in Points 6.3 and 6.4 below.

**Point 6.3: *HMRC has often challenged allowances claimed on electrical and plumbing work. This expenditure is eligible for a lower writing down allowance, currently 6% (8% prior to 1 April 2019).***

Electrical installations and cold water systems could, in the past, attract capital allowances as plant but only if they were either provided mainly to meet the particular requirements of the qualifying activity or serve specific plant used for the purposes of the qualifying activity. An example would have been a cold water system for an industrial machine. Otherwise these items would have been regarded as part of the business's setting and hence not qualify as plant. No tax relief would have been due on this expenditure.

Since April 2008, the expenditure has qualified under the integral features rules and is, from April 2019, eligible for the 6% writing-down allowance (8% prior to April 2019) (see Point 6.5)

Where items are of sufficient nexus to the qualifying plant, they will continue to be eligible for capital allowances at the plant and machinery rate of 18%.

**Point 6.4:** ***Expenditure on certain items such as floors, walls and ceilings is not normally accepted as plant. Check whether the descriptions of these items are appropriate and also the way expenditure has been allocated to them. Some expenditure may qualify for allowances under the integral features regime. Structures and Buildings Allowance was introduced in October 2018.***

Expenditure on walls, floors or ceilings would normally be regarded as part of the setting in which the business is carried on. Even if the wall, floor or ceiling in question is part of the 'apparatus' of the trade including creating the right ambience, it is still not plant for capital allowances purposes. This was established in the cases involving Wimpy and Pizzaland Restaurants. The recent decision of the Upper Tribunal in the case of *JD Wetherspoon v Commissioners for Her Majesty's Revenue & Customs* [2012] UKUT 42 (TCC) makes the point that for decorative features to qualify as allowable they need to be exceptional and distinctive (an example of this would be in a hotel or restaurant where ambience is key to the client's enjoyment). As a result, decorative wood panelling was not considered eligible as it merely changed an un-panelled room to a panelled room.

Suspended ceilings and raised flooring can perform a function in a business. Often they provide a cover or housing for ventilation ducting, piping and IT cabling. It is advisable to ask the builder or project manager whether any proportion of the cost attributed to suspended ceilings or raised floors relates to the heating, air-conditioning, electrical or other plant installation, since that element would be allowable. An element of any three-dimensional structure such as raised floors and suspended ceilings designed to form a plenum or duct in the functioning of the heating or air-conditioning system should be part of that installation. This argument becomes even stronger if the existing flooring or ceiling has had to be modified to facilitate a new installation. Note that, since April 2008, much of this expenditure attracts a lower rate of writing-down allowances (currently 6%). (see Point 6.5 below).

However, it is important to identify all items of plant and correctly classify them. Accordingly, consider carefully whether the description of a particular item of expenditure is appropriate. For instance, expenditure on a 'mezzanine floor' has been allowed when, as a matter of fact, it was demonstrated to be a suspended demountable storage area (*Hunt v Henry Quick Ltd; King v Bridisco Ltd* [1992] STC 633).

Another example is walls that are formed by demountable partitioning. If that partitioning is actually to be moved as the requirements of the business changes, it is plant and the related expenditure will be allowable (*Jarrold v John Good & Sons Ltd* (1962) 40 TC 681). Any doors or windows that are integral with that partitioning should be similarly allowable.

In addition to description, the allocation of expenditure may merit further analysis.

Structures and buildings allowance (SBA) was introduced for qualifying expenditure incurred on or after 29 October 2018, claimable over 33 and one-third years at a rate of 3% per annum. It can be claimed by businesses that have a relevant interest in a building, as long as the first use of the building after the expenditure was incurred is on commercial activity (ie non-residential).*( CAA 2001, Pt 2A, ss 270AA–270IH).*

The rate was previously 2%, increased to 3% in April 2020. Following the rate increase, the additional amount of the 1% allowance can be claimed to cover the period between 29 October 2018 (since the introduction of SBA) until the rate increase from April 2020, subject to certain criteria being met. See further details in Chapter 7.

**Point 6.5:** ***Expenditure since April 2008 on 'integral features' must be separated from other plant and machinery, as this currently attracts a lower, 6% (8% prior to April 2019) rate of writing down allowance. This may include some items for which allowances were not previously available.***

The *Finance Act 2008* introduced a new category of certain fixtures which are considered integral to the structure of a building, referred to as 'integral features'. Expenditure on items in this category should be eligible for a lower rate of annual writing-down allowance, currently 6%.

Expenditure on the following items qualifies for the 6% rate:

- lifts, escalators and moving walkways;
- space or water heating systems;
- powered systems of ventilation, air cooling or air purification, and any floor or ceiling comprised in such systems;
- electrical systems (including lighting systems);
- cold water systems; and
- external solar shading.

Since expenditure relating to certain integral features incurred prior to the regime attracts 18% annual allowances, this suggests that buying a property company with its ongoing pool of integral features may be more beneficial than buying the property. In the first scenario, the company can carry on claiming writing-down allowances at a rate of 18% a year. If the property were acquired, only 6% allowances might be available on that expenditure. However, on a property purchase it may be possible to claim for items of integral features within a building that only qualified as such from April 2008, the cost of which was incurred by the former owner before April 2008 and so will not be within the vendor's pool.

Property transactions completed post April 2008 may also be considered where the previous owner was not within the charge to tax. In this case there would be no prior right over the integral features resulting in an unrestricted claim. In all cases the history of the property will need to be established before a claim can be made.

See Point 6.14 below for a summary of the rules for identifying when expenditure is actually incurred for these purposes.

Note that expenditure on thermal insulation (incurred from April 2008) and solar panels (from April 2012) is also treated in a similar way and added to the special rate pool eligible for 6% ( 8% prior to April 2019) allowances.

**Point 6.6:** ***In some property situations, it is also necessary to separately identify long-life machinery and plant. For accounting periods ending after 31 March 2012 for corporate tax payers and after 5 April 2012 for income tax payers, such assets only attract an 6% (8% prior to April 2019) annual writing-down allowance.***

Writing-down allowances for certain 'long-life' plant and machinery are available at a rate of 6% from April 2019 (*CAA 2001, ss 90–104*). The reduced allowance relates to items where there is a reasonable expectation of a useful economic life of at least 25 years when they are first brought into use and they cost in excess of £100,000. Typically, this will apply to specific trades such as large manufacturing trades, aircraft and shipbuilding, etc, where certain assets can be expected to be in use by the business for a long period of time without any significant upgrades or technical improvements.

These provisions do not apply where the plant and machinery in question is a fixture in a building used as a retail shop, showroom, hotel or office or for a purpose which is ancillary to any of these (*CAA 2001, s 93*).

Typical items of plant installed as fixtures of buildings would not have an expected useful life over 25 years and many of the more common commercial buildings have been excluded in any event. Where buildings are used for purposes that are not excluded – the leisure and nursing home sectors being notable examples – the category of 'long-life' assets could be relevant. Expenditure incurred on long-life assets is included in the special rate pool together with expenditure on integral features.

**Point 6.7:** ***100% capital allowances are available for the first £1,000,000 of expenditure under the annual investment allowance scheme.***

100% allowances, which provide the opportunity for a complete write-off of costs in the year in which they are incurred, can be claimed in the following situations:

(a) AIA is available for expenditure on plant or machinery on or after 1 April 2008. The maximum amount of AIA available has varied significantly over recent years. The level of AIA from 1 January 2019 was initially announced as a temporary measure up to a maximum of £1,000,000 but this has now been made permanent.

This relief can include qualifying expenditure on integral features (Point 6.5) long-life assets (Point 6.6) and also thermal insulation and solar panels. It is aimed at all sizes of businesses.

Only one annual investment allowance is available for a group of companies each year. The provisions also seek to prevent associations of companies from gaining a multiple entitlement to the allowance by fragmenting their expenditure between a number of companies.

(b) Land remediation relief is available to companies bringing derelict long-term, long-unused land back into use (see Point 4.5). 150% relief may be available in certain cases subject to meeting the criteria.

100% allowances may be available for expenditure in certain 'designated assisted areas' within enterprise zones (see Point 7.2).

(c) Capital allowances are available from 1 April 2023 for companies only in relation to qualifying new main rate plant and machinery (at 100%), described by HMRC as 'full expensing', and special rate assets (at 50%) (*F(No 2)A 2023, s 7*).

(d) Capital allowances are also available on plant and machinery for use primarily within a freeport or investment zone tax site, in respect of companies only. The plant or machinery must be new or unused and the expenditure incurred on or after the date the freeport of investment zone tax site is designated and on or before 30 September 2026 or a later date specified by regulations.

**Point 6.8:** ***Do not ignore professional fees. HMRC accept that some of these are attributable to plant and machinery installation.***

A significant element of expenditure on any building project will be professional costs. These will include fees charged by lawyers, surveyors, architects, and structural and mechanical/electrical engineers.

Professional costs relating to the acquisition of the site – particularly lawyers' and surveyors' costs – would normally be disallowed (although may form part of the base cost of the property when computing any future capital gain on sale). If any of this expenditure is in respect of related finance, it might be appropriate to have this charged separately since this could well qualify as an incidental cost of raising finance for income tax purposes or under the corporate debt rules for companies within the charge to corporation tax.

The fees of mechanical and electrical engineers are often linked to the installation of plant and these fees are part of that qualifying expenditure.

The *JD Wetherspoon* case ([2012] UKUT 42 (TCC)) provides clear guidelines on the appropriate method for the allocation of preliminaries in favour of a pro rata allocation where a detailed item by the item attribution would be disproportionately time consuming or expensive.

**Point 6.9:** ***Although no allowances are available on residential property, capital allowance claims can be made for furnished holiday lettings and, on a more restricted basis, for ordinary furnished lettings.***

As a general rule, no capital allowances are available on machinery or plant installed for use in a dwelling house (*CAA 2001, s 35*).

Landlords of furnished accommodation generally may be entitled to some deduction for their expenditure on furniture.

*Up to April 2016*, landlords were entitled to opt for tax relief in one of the following ways:

(a) on a renewals basis, ie there would be no relief for the initial cost of furniture and machinery but the future replacement cost of the items could be deducted in full;

(b) an annual deduction equivalent to 10% of the net rents in a year.

With effect from 1 April 2016, the above have been scrapped, being replaced by a new allowance called the 'replacement of domestic items relief'. This allows a deduction for the replacement of furniture and furnishings. The new item must be used in the dwelling by the tenant and that the 'old item' must no longer be usable. The new item can include furniture, furnishings (carpets, curtains, linen, etc), household appliances (eg fridges, freezers), kitchenware and televisions.

The letting of furnished holiday accommodation in the UK (see Point 10.4 for further details) is treated as a separate qualifying activity for capital allowances purposes (*CAA 2001, s 15(1)(c)*). Allowances are, therefore, available under the normal rules (*CAA 2001, s 55*) (which is subject to passing the three occupancy conditions criteria – see HMRC guidance under HS253), treating it as a separate qualifying activity from any other letting business carried on. Similarly, an EEA furnished holiday letting business is treated as a separate qualifying activity.

**Point 6.10:** ***Lessees can claim allowances in respect of fixed plant in a building even though, as a matter of law, these items belong to the freeholder.***

Lessees are entitled to allowances on fixed plant in the following circumstances:

(a) Where a lessee incurs expenditure on fixed plant for use in a qualifying activity, capital allowances can be claimed on that expenditure (*CAA 2001, s 176*).

(b) Where a lessee takes an assignment of a lease and pays a capital sum that wholly or partly represents expenditure on fixed plant, the lessee can claim allowances on that element of the payment in respect of the plant (*CAA 2001, s 181*). A claim cannot be made if anyone else has an interest in the property and has claimed allowances as a result. Thus, if a remaining sub-tenant has claimed allowances, the new landlord cannot claim for any capital sum paid in respect of the tenant's fixtures. Similarly, the lessee cannot become entitled to allowances on assets on which the freeholder is entitled to claim (*CAA 2001, s 181(2), (3)*).

The amount on which a lessee can claim allowances is restricted to the original cost of the plant, where that original cost was claimed as a capital allowance by a previous owner of the fixture (*CAA 2001, ss 185–187* – see Point 6.12 below).

(c) A lessee can claim allowances where a capital sum is paid on the grant of a lease and the sum wholly or partly includes expenditure in respect of fixed plant. However, if the lessor would otherwise have been entitled to the allowances, both the lessee and the lessor must make an election within two years of the commencement of the lease if the lessee is to claim the allowances (*CAA 2001, s 183*). If no election is made, the lessor might be entitled to the allowances.

No election is necessary if the lessor would not have been entitled to allowances (*CAA 2001, s 184*). An election cannot be made where the lessor and the lessee are connected.

(d) A lessee may be able to claim allowances as a result of the long -funding lease rules. Legislation introduced in *Finance Act 2006* aligned the treatment of finance leases (and some operating leases) to that of straightforward bank loans and outright asset purchases.

Prior to the introduction of this legislation, even though commercially the two options above are very similar, the tax treatment was different. The entitlement to capital allowances was that of the lessor in a lease arrangement, whereas funding through a bank loan entitled the purchaser (and user) of the asset to the capital allowances.

In very broad terms, for leases which meet the definition of a long funding lease and which were entered into on or after 1 April 2006, the entitlement to capital allowances is transferred from the lessor to the lessee.

A long funding lease is broadly a lease which is:

- not a short lease (a short lease is largely five years or less);
- not an excluded lease of background plant and machinery; or
- not excluded because the plant is leased with land and is of a low percentage value.

The legislation is complex and is contained within *CAA 2001, ss 70A–70YJ*.

The rules are not intended to be in point for most property investors, as mixed leases (ie where both property and plant and machinery are leased) should generally fall in either the second or third items listed above.

Where a lessee does become entitled to claim allowances in accordance with the above, the rules introduced in *Finance Act 2012* should be adhered to in order to ensure a valid claim can be made. See Point 6.12 for further details.

Background plant and machinery covers the majority of plant expected to be found within a rented property, eg air conditioning, lifts and lighting. Plant which does not fall within the category is generally that which would be found in warehouses and used for storage purposes.

**Point 6.11:** ***A buyer of second-hand property with fixtures that qualify as plant and machinery can potentially claim significant allowances. Steps should be taken to establish eligibility and the likely quantum of allowances.***

Tax relief arising from capital allowances on the purchase of a property enables the buyer to recoup a part of the cash outflow.

In some cases, 40%–50% of the purchase price of modern buildings has been attributable to fixtures and equipment eligible for allowances. Since April 2008, some of these items (5–15%) are 'integral features' (see Point 6.5 above).

The actual entitlement to allowances will be influenced by the following factors:

(a) Whether the plant allowances attach to the interest being purchased. The freeholder is normally the person owning the plant and entitled to allowances. However, in the past, an election may have been made in favour of a lessee (see (c) in Point 6.10 above). Alternatively, the allowances may arise from expenditure by the lessee, such as the retail tenant that fits out empty premises. Clearly, whether the freehold or a leasehold interest is bought, it is important to establish the capital allowances background to that interest.

(b) Whether the property is commercial or residential (see Point 6.1 above).

(c) The claims history of the previous owner or owners, and the co-operation of the seller in agreeing the capital allowance position on sale (see Point 6.12 below).

(d) For properties bought before April 2014 whether the seller, and any previous owner, has chosen not to claim allowances. In that case the buyer can still use pre-existing rules to allocate a reasonable portion of the purchase price to plant in the building (see Point 6.12).

(e) If no seller has previously been eligible to claim allowances (eg charities or property developers holding the asset as trading stock) the buyer of the property can similarly allocate a reasonable proportion of the purchase price to plant even where the property is acquired after April 2014 (see Point 6.12).

(f) Whether the plant or machinery is an integral feature, long-life asset, thermal insulation or solar panels (Points 6.5 and 6.6), and therefore subject to a reduced 6% annual allowance.

(g) Whether there could be any eligibility for an acceleration of allowances (Point 6.7 above).

(h) The long funding lease rules (Point 6.10 above).

**Point 6.12:** ***A buyer of property may not be entitled to claim allowances unless the qualifying expenditure has been established by the seller – or a previous owner – at the time of purchase.***

A property investor buying a property needs to establish what capital allowance claims the seller, or a previous owner, may have made in respect of plant in the building.

The purchaser of a property from April 2012 will find that their qualifying expenditure is treated as nil – and thus no capital allowances claimable – if a previous owner who has owned the property has claimed allowances and:

(a) the previous owner, ie the seller, has been required to bring in a disposal value but that value has not been fixed in a joint election under *CAA 2001 s 198* or *s 199* or, alternatively, by a determination from the First-tier Tribunal ('The Fixed Value requirement'); or

(b) a previous owner, other than the seller, has brought in a disposal value within two years of sale but that owner has not issued (or the buyer has not obtained) a written statement summarising the disposal value brought into account by that owner ('The Disposal Value Statement requirement').

(CAA 2001, s 187A)

Since April 2014, the seller must include the qualifying expenditure in a pool of expenditure ('The Pooling Requirement'). In these circumstances, the seller might subsequently decide to claim allowances after the sale, leaving the onus on the buyer to approach the First-tier tribunal to fix the disposal consideration.

In view of these alternative requirements, it becomes imperative for a prospective property purchaser to identify carefully the expenditure that has been brought into account by the vendor and to agree in the sale and purchase agreement the approach that will be adopted to settle the allowances available to the prospective purchaser.

Non-taxpayers (such as pension funds) acquiring property from April 2012 that intend to preserve a capital allowances entitlement for future buyers will need to obtain a commitment from the previous owner(s) regarding the disposal value to be brought into account and a written statement to confirm the amount.

If the seller, and any previous owner, were not entitled to claim allowances, the new rules noted above do not apply and the purchaser can continue to claim allowances based on an apportionment of the purchase price on a reasonable basis.

If the seller/previous owner did make a claim to allowances, the allowable expenditure claimable by the purchaser in respect of that plant cannot exceed that amount (*CAA 2001, ss 185–187*).

---

## Example 1

Kenny Ltd purchased an investment property in 1997 for £8 million. £2 million was accepted as being in respect of plant and machinery and King Ltd submitted capital allowance claims based on that figure. Rowsell Ltd bought that building for £12 million in August 2023.

The amount eligible for allowances to Rowsell Ltd will be restricted to a maximum of £2 million but no allowances will be available unless either Kenny Ltd and Rowsell Ltd jointly elect under *CAA s 198* for an agreed fixed value or Rowsell Ltd applies for this fixed value to be determined by the First-tier Tribunal.

---

## Example 2

If Kenny Ltd had sold the property to Trott Ltd in 2000, and Trott Ltd was not entitled and did not claim allowances, then Rowsell Ltd – when it buys the property in August 2023– will need to rely on Trott Ltd producing a written statement as to King Ltd's disposal value. Rowsell Ltd will be subject to a restriction of £2 million being the maximum qualifying expenditure claimable.

---

## Example 3

In Example 2, if neither Kenny Limited nor Trott Ltd claimed allowances, although eligible to do so, Rowsell Ltd cannot claim allowances, unless Trott is able to bring in qualifying expenditure into its pool.

Note that if both Kenny Ltd and Trott Ltd were ineligible to claim allowances, then a buyer from Trott Ltd could claim allowances based on a reasonable apportionment of the price paid, even where the building is acquired after March 2014.

As and when Rowsell Ltd incurs capital expenditure on new plant and machinery in the building, the maximum qualifying figure would increase accordingly, although there will also be an adjustment for any plant which is removed or disposed of.

---

**Point 6.13:** ***The buyer and seller should elect whenever possible to adopt a specific value for the plant and machinery for capital allowances purposes on the transfer of a property. Such an election can accelerate the use of allowances for the seller.***

For some years, it has been possible for both the buyer and seller to agree a transfer value for fixtures by making a joint election to HMRC within two years of the date of the transaction (*CAA 2001, s 198 or s 199 in the case of a lease*). In so doing, both the buyer and the seller have had a measure of certainty as to the tax implications of the sale and purchase as far as the capital allowances position is concerned. However, the election has been optional and, if the buyer and seller could not agree on a transfer value, it became a matter for individual negotiations with HMRC to agree the position. In accordance with rules covered by Point 6.12 above, all buyers would be well advised to settle a *s 198* election with the seller as part of any property purchase negotiation provided that the seller has claimed or pooled capital allowances. The alternative would be to involve either an application to the First-tier Tribunal to determine the amount of disposal value for this purpose or the buyer (and any successor) forfeits any capital allowance entitlement on that historic expenditure.

The value in the election cannot exceed the seller's eligible expenditure. Thus, in Example 2 in Point 6.12 above, Trott Ltd and Rowsell Ltd will be bound by the maximum of £2 million. However, they can agree and elect lower than this figure. A value specified in the election becomes the new maximum for that plant for future buyers of the property.

The election must detail the items that are the subject of the election and attribute values to them. The introduction of the integral features regime further complicates the election since some of the items included will be integral features for the purchaser, but not the vendor. Notwithstanding this, the election will need to split the elected amount between integral features and other plant.

There could be a problem for the buyer if the seller has over-claimed allowances. If HMRC have reason to reduce a seller's original capital allowances claim, they will also seek to reduce proportionately any amount that the buyer may have agreed to.

If the seller has not fully exploited the entitlement to claim allowances by omitting or overlooking a claim on some items of plant in the building, the buyer will want the seller to make a claim so that they can include the expenditure in the subsequent claim. Where a buyer and seller elect for a transfer value lower than the tax written down value of the plant and machinery, this may generate a balancing allowance in certain circumstances. This balancing allowance may be capable of being offset against other profits or group relieved as with any surplus allowances.

In view of this, there is the potential to reduce that transfer value to a nominal figure and thus get the benefit of the extra allowances arising. This is effectively accelerating the balance of allowances due on the original cost of the assets.

This planning is available whether the sale is to an unconnected party or to a fellow group company. In all cases, however, the sale must be for commercial reasons and not merely part of an arrangement to secure this tax benefit (*CAA 2001, s 197*).

**Point 6.14:** ***There remain situations where there is no restriction on the amount eligible for allowances by reference to the vendor's or previous owner's expenditure. In those instances, the amount eligible can be determined by estimating a just apportionment of the purchase price.***

As noted in Point 6.12 above, there are situations where there continue to be no restriction on the available allowances by reference to historic expenditure and disposal values. Since April 2014 this has only been the case where the seller, and any previous owner, were not entitled to claim allowances. The purchaser can claim allowances based on an apportionment of the purchase price on a reasonable basis. This could apply where a builder or property dealer has owned the property throughout the period.

As noted in Example 3 above, Rowsell Ltd would not be restricted by the quantum of historic expenditure on the allowances it could claim, if neither Kenny Ltd nor Trott Ltd were eligible to claim allowances.

The significance of there being no restriction is that it would then be open to the purchaser to value the plant and machinery bought within a building. This is an exercise that generally requires quantity surveying techniques to arrive at a hypothetical cost of that plant installed in the building on the assumption that the building was being reconstructed at the time of purchase. There is an accepted apportionment of the purchase price methodology that was agreed with the Valuation Office Agency (*CAA 2001, s 562*) to determine the qualifying plant and machinery expenditure.

---

## Example 4

In July 2022, Peaty Investments Ltd bought the freehold of an office building for £10 million. No allowances were able to be claimed by the past owners in respect of the plant therein.

A surveyor estimates that the building would now cost £6 million to construct. The cost of the plant installation, which the surveyor has identified in the building, is calculated as £2,400,000. Accordingly, 40% of the building cost would represent plant.

The land element of the purchase price is estimated at £3 million. These values would then be included in the apportionment formula to determine the value of the plant and machinery as follows:

Apportioned Value of Plant and Machinery = Purchase Price × A

(A +B+C)

A = The replacement cost of qualifying items of plant and machinery

B = The replacement cost of the building excluding qualifying items of plant and machinery

C = The bare site value

The aggregate capital allowance claim would, therefore, be £2,666,667 (ie £10 million × £2.4 million / £2.4million + £3.6 million + £3 million).

---

In practice, the plant would be itemised and the £2,666,667 apportioned accordingly.

It will be necessary to allocate the qualifying expenditure between items, qualifying for relief at 6% per annum(notably integral features – see Point 6.5 above) and other plant eligible for 18% allowances.

For large claims, HMRC involve their own District Valuer and Regional Building Surveyors to agree the estimates used.

**Point 6.15: *The allowances are claimable in the chargeable period in which expenditure is incurred.***

Capital allowances are claimable in the accounting period or the period of account when expenditure is incurred. This is the date the amount becomes unconditionally payable (*CAA 2001, s 5(1)*).

Once a trade is commenced, future expenditure is treated as incurred when there is an unconditional obligation to pay. This might be when an invoice is issued or a binding agreement signed.

On long-term construction contracts, stage payments are normally made periodically on production of an architect's certificate. When the obligation to pay becomes unconditional on the production of a certificate, expenditure is treated as incurred in a particular accounting period if the certificate is issued not more than one month after the end of the period.

Where payment is due more than four months after the obligation to pay becomes unconditional, the expenditure is treated as incurred on the date(s) it is due to be paid (*CAA 2001, s 5(5)*). The issue of an invoice or signing of a contract designed to bring forward the capital allowances claim to an earlier accounting period than would have been the case in a normal commercial transaction is countered by an anti-avoidance provision (*CAA 2001, s 5(6)*).

**Point 6.16: *Investors can use surplus allowances in a number of ways, but the rules differ depending on whether or not the claimant is a company.***

Allowances on plant used in the letting business are deductible from the rental income – see Chapter 16 for further detail on the use of any losses arising from the letting business.

A cap applies on the entitlement for individuals to offset losses and certain other deductions against general income. The restriction is the greater of £50,000 and 25% of the individual's income.

For companies, the regime for loss changed from April 2017 (see Point 16.1).

Certain complex anti-avoidance provisions are in place, aimed at capital allowance buying. These can apply in certain circumstances where a company is acquired with the objective of accessing its surplus annual allowances to shelter future taxable profits of the acquiring company/group (*FA 2013, Sch 26*).

**Point 6.17:** ***A landlord can claim allowances on contributions made to a tenant's expenditure. This might be a tax-efficient way for the landlord to offer an inducement to attract an incoming tenant.***

Capital allowances can be claimed in certain circumstances in respect of amounts contributed towards a tenant's general qualifying expenditure (*CAA 2001, s 537*).

For instance, a landlord might attract a prospective commercial tenant by offering to pay for certain fixtures. The landlord should be entitled to claim allowances on the contribution to the extent it related to items of plant.

The conditions for eligibility are:

(a) the parties cannot be connected (within the meaning *of ITA 2007, s 993* or *CTA 2010, s 1122*);

(b) the contribution must be either for the contributor's trade or other qualifying activity (eg commercial letting); and

(c) the tenant would normally have been treated as having incurred the expenditure eligible for allowances.

(CAA 2001, ss 537–540)

Where the contributor receives so-called contribution allowances and the contributor transfers the trade or land, the transferee will inherit the contributor's entitlement to annual allowances. There are no balancing adjustments (*CAA 2001, ss 538(5), 539(5), 540(5)*).

**Point 6.18:** ***No allowances will be available to lessors on fixtures which they purchase and let to a tax-exempt lessee.***

Under anti-avoidance rules, lessors cannot claim allowances on equipment which is leased to a tax-exempt lessee such as a local authority or charity (*CAA 2001, s 178*).

Although these rules are not aimed at conventional property lettings, they do apply when a third-party leases equipment to a tax-exempt occupier of a building where that equipment becomes a fixture in the building. The lessor cannot claim capital allowances on the capital expenditure it has incurred on that equipment. These provisions apply to leasing arrangements entered into after 24 July 1996.

Further, anti-avoidance legislation is in place to ensure a business entering into a sale and leaseback arrangement does not gain more tax relief as a result of the sale and leaseback than it originally claimed.

**Point 6.19:** ***Apart from plant let with a building, a property investor can claim allowances on plant and machinery used in estate management. An investment company can, in addition, claim allowances for plant used in the management of the company.***

Estate management may require the use of plant and machinery. This may, for instance, be installed as fixed plant in premises used as administrative offices.

Other items might include an information technology installation, filing cabinets and office furniture. Capital allowances can be claimed on these items and set off against the profits of the letting business.

A company with investment business can also claim allowances on plant used in the management of the company as distinct from the properties (*CAA 2001, s 253*). Such allowances can be treated as additional expenses of the business.

**Point 6.20:** ***It is worthwhile scrutinising expenditure to see whether it may strictly qualify as repairs and maintenance, since this can be fully deductible in the year it is incurred. However, from April 2023 until the end of March 2026, companies can claim 100% capital allowances on qualifying plant and machinery investments under the 'full expensing' rules.***

When an item of plant is installed or completely replaced, the related expenditure will be treated as capital and eligible for capital allowances. However, if the expenditure is in respect of the overhaul of plant or the replacement of parts, then this should qualify for a 100% deduction as repairs or maintenance.

Since April 2008, expenditure on the replacement of part of an item that qualifies as an integral feature is treated as capital expenditure if the cost is more than 50% of the cost of replacing the whole asset. Subject to this point, when reviewing a refurbishment programme it may well be sensible to consider repairing assets where this is a possibility rather than replacing them (see Point 4.1 regarding repairs as distinguished from capital expenditure).

It may be advisable to consider the exact nature of work carried out, or to be carried out, to determine whether expenditure that might appear to be capital is, in fact, revenue. For instance, if air-conditioning work involves the removal of defective ducting rather than the replacement or renewal of a whole system, this might be shown as repairs. Similarly, if heating expenditure related to the replacement of worn radiators, then it would be repairs as opposed to capital expenditure. However, if the work changes the nature of the original asset, that may not be a repair – such as in the case of plastic inner piping inserted within an old cast-iron main (*Auckland Gas Co Ltd v IRC* [2000] STC 527).

See Point 4.7 for rules which reclassify repairs as capital expenditure where there is substantial replacement of items within integral features. Note that, to obtain a deduction in a year, the relevant expenditure will need to be reflected in the profit and loss account rather than capitalised in the balance sheet. If the expenditure is capitalised, the tax treatment will follow the accounting treatment, with a deduction delayed unless and until amounts are written off as expenses through the profit and loss account.

From 1 April 2023 to 31 March 2026, companies investing in new qualifying plant and machinery assets are able to claim:

(a) a 100% first-year allowance for main pool plant and machinery assets;

(b) a 50% first-year allowance for special rate plant and machinery assets.

A few key exclusions in respect of the expensing rules apply, specifically:

(a) They are available for companies within the charge of corporation tax and corporate members within a partnership. The relief is not available to a partnership of which all members are individuals.

(b) They are only available in respect of new and unused plant and machinery (ie second-hand assets are not within scope).

(c) They are not available in respect of plant and machinery for leasing (unless the plant and machinery constitute background plant and machinery for a building).

**Point 6.21:** ***If irrecoverable VAT is incurred on a building purchase, or building/installation work, the expenditure eligible for capital allowances in relation to plant and machinery is increased accordingly.***

If a property owner cannot fully reclaim VAT on property expenditure, the irrecoverable VAT increases the related cost for direct tax purposes.

Where VAT incurred on plant expenditure is wholly or partly irrecoverable, the amount eligible for capital allowances will include the irrecoverable amount. Furthermore, if adjustments are required under the Capital Goods Scheme (CGS), resulting in changes to VAT recovery over a ten-year period, the qualifying capital allowance expenditure will vary accordingly (*CAA 2001, s 235*). See Point 35.7 for an explanation of the CGS.

*Chapter 7*

# Other allowances

**The Structures and Buildings Allowances regime was introduced for expenditure with effect from 29 October 2018.**

**Point 7.1**

↓

The Government announced the creation of Freeports specialist sites, following the UK's departure from the EU.

Point 7.2

# 7 OTHER ALLOWANCES

**Point 7.1:** ***The Structures and Buildings Allowance was introduced for expenditure with effect from 29 October 2018***

The Budget 2018 announced the introduction of Structures and Buildings Allowances (SBA) for expenditure incurred on commercial buildings or structures.

SBA can be claimed on qualifying expenditure by a sole traders, partnership or company that is carrying on a qualifying activity (see below). It applies for construction contracts entered into on or after 29 October 2018 and is available at 3% per annum over a 33 and one-third year life (2% over a 50-year life for expenditure incurred before April 2020). SBA is not available for expenditure on buildings used for residential purposes. This includes:

- a dwelling house, including a holiday home;
- residential accommodation for school pupils;
- student accommodation;
- residential accommodation for members of the armed forces;
- home or other institution providing residential accommodation apart from where personal care is provided due to old age, disability, dependence on drugs or mental disorders; and
- prison or similar establishment.

*(CA 2001, s 270CF)*

There is no definition of 'dwelling house' for this purpose so it takes its ordinary meaning. A dwelling-house is a building, or a part of a building; its distinctive characteristic is its ability to afford to those who use it the facilities required for day-to-day private domestic existence. In most cases there should be little difficulty in deciding whether or not particular premises comprise a dwelling-house, but difficult cases may need to be decided on their particular facts.

The claimant must have a relevant interest in the building and if they sell or transfer that relevant interest, then they lose entitlement to the SBA on that expenditure. Qualifying activities for the purposes of SBA are:

- a trade, profession or vocation;
- a UK or overseas property business, but excluding furnished holiday lettings;
- any concerns such as mines, quarries, etc; and
- managing investments of a company.

Businesses are permitted to claim any allowances which were missed due to it claiming 2% prior to April 2020, in the last chargeable period in which an allowance is available, ie when the period of 33 and 1/3 years ends, but only if the business which held the building in April 2020 still holds the same interest in the building at the end of the 33 and 1/3 years.

*Other allowances*

It is important that an allowance statement is prepared showing details of the building, costs and dates, without which there cannot be an SBA claim. Although these statements do not have to be submitted with a tax return, they have to be kept as evidence and in the absence of these statements, the qualifying expenditure for an SBA claim is deemed to be nil.

**Point 7.2:** ***Freeport special tax sites***

Following the UK's departure from the EU, the government announced the creation of freeports specialist sites, which are a key part of the government's economic plans.

Eight locations in England were announced as part of the March 2021 Budget statement. Following discussions with the Scottish Government, in January 2023, the UK Government announced two additional freeports in Scotland. These are the Forth Green Freeport and the Inverness and Cromarty Firth Freeport.

The 12 UK freeport locations at the time of writing are:

- Anglesey
- Celtic
- East Midlands Airport
- Felixstowe & Harwich
- Forth Green
- Humber Region
- Inverness and Cromarty Firth
- Liverpool City Region
- Plymouth & South Devon
- Solent
- Teesside
- Thames

In November 2023, it was announced that the duration of freeport tax reliefs will be extended from five to ten years, with benefits claimable until September 2031.

Businesses established in approved freeports as well as Investment Zones (see below) can benefit from full relief from stamp duty land tax and business rates, 100% first-year allowances for plant and machinery, enhanced structures and buildings allowances at a rate of 10% per annum, and employers' NICs relief for up to £25,000 per year per new, eligible employees (for up to 36 months). Freeports also have the added benefit of being customs sites and providing relief around VAT and customs.

**Point 7.3:** ***Investment zone special tax sites***

At the Spring Budget 2023, it was announced that the government intends to introduce investment zones where the tax benefits will include increased structures and buildings allowances at 10% per year. The proposed areas are listed in the Investment Zones Policy Prospectus at para 1.8 with confirmed sites in South Yorkshire focussing on advanced manufacturing and Liverpool City Region focussing on the life science, research and innovation sector.

As part of the Autumn Statement in November 2023, investment zones were confirmed for the East and West Midlands and Greater Manchester in England, and two new zones announced in the Cardiff and Newport and Wrexham and Flintshire areas within Wales.

To further boost the programme, as mentioned above, both the freeports and investment zones tax reliefs will now last for ten years instead of five years.

*Chapter 8*

# Holding investment property through a company

**Putting an investment property in a company can save considerable tax as long as the funds can be retained in the company.**

**Point 8.1**

↓

Although there is tax on extracting funds from a company, there can be an overall benefit for non-domiciliaries, non-residents and shareholders paying less than 45% tax at exit.

Point 8.2

↓

Whilst the longer-term capital gains tax cost of holding property through a company can outweigh the shorter term tax benefit, there can be a tax-efficient exit through a sale to a UK REIT.

Point 8.3

# 8 HOLDING INVESTMENT PROPERTY THROUGH A COMPANY

**Point 8.1: *Individuals can shelter investment income in a company, where the rate of corporation tax on income and capital gains can be lower.***

The main rate of corporation tax is 25%.

An individual's highest rate of income tax ('the additional rate') is 45% on taxable income over £125,140. For these taxpayers, there is a potential tax saving by holding an investment property through a company. If the rental, less expenses, amounted to, say, £200,000, there is a £40,000 saving for an additional rate taxpayer by channelling this income into a company after April 2023 (ie 45% – 25% of £200,000). The following example illustrates the effect over a five-year period:

---

## Example 1

The following example compares the retained income of an individual, paying 45% tax with a company paying corporation tax. The rental income after expenses is £200,000 per year. Interest at a rate of 2.5% is assumed and calculated on the previous year-end's balance of accumulated retained profits.

| Year 1 (commencing Apr 2023) | Individual | | Company | |
|---|---|---|---|---|
| | £ | | £ | |
| Rent | 200,000 | | 200,000 | |
| Tax | 90,000 | | 50,000 | |
| | 110,000 | 110,000 | 150,000 | 150,000 |
| Year 2 | | | | |
| Rent | 200,000 | | 200,000 | |
| Interest on retained profit | 2,750 | | 3,750 | |
| | 202,750 | | 203,750 | |
| Tax | 91,238 | | 50,938 | |
| | 111,512 | 221,512 | 152,812 | 302,812 |
| Year 3 | | | | |
| Rent | 200,000 | | 200,000 | |
| Interest on retained profit | 5,538 | | 7,570.30 | |
| | 205,538 | | 207,570.30 | |
| Tax | 92,492 | | 51,892.58 | |
| | 113,046 | 334,558 | 155,677.72 | 458,489.72 |
| Year 4 | | | | |
| Rent | 200,000 | | 200,000 | |

| Year 1 (commencing Apr 2023) | Individual | | Company | |
|---|---|---|---|---|
| | £ | | £ | |
| Interest on retained profit | 8,364 | | 11,462.24 | |
| | 208,364 | | 211,462.24 | |
| Tax | 93,764 | | 52,865.56 | |
| | 114,600 | 449,158 | 158,596.68 | 617,086.40 |
| Year 5 | | | | |
| Rent | 200,000 | | 200,000 | |
| Interest on retained profit | 11,229 | | 15,427.16 | |
| | 211,229 | | 215,427.16 | |
| Tax | 95,053 | | 53,856.79 | |
| | 116,176 | 565,334 | 161,570.37 | 778,656.77 |

As will be seen from the above example, the retained profits at the end of Year 5 are over £213,000 greater where a company is used.

There can also be a cash flow benefit in the timing of the tax payments, since individuals will often be required to make tax payments on account during the tax year. For many smaller and medium-sized companies on the other hand, tax is not due until nine months after the company's accounting year end.

The tax benefit arises where the funds are retained in the company for further investment or used to repay the principal of the property finance. As indicated in Point 8.2 below (a) a large part of the tax benefit may be clawed back if an individual is liable to higher or additional rates of income tax on the distributed income and (b) individuals who are not resident in the UK at that time may not need to pay UK tax on the distribution.

SDLT can be as high as 12% for purchases of residential property. When the property is acquired by a company, the SDLT could be 15%, see Chapter 5 on Stamp Duty Land Tax (Land and Buildings Transaction Tax applies in Scotland and Land Transaction Tax applies in Wales).

Where a residential property above a threshold value is held within a company (or other 'non-natural person'), an annual charge may be applied, referred to as the Annual Tax on Enveloped Dwellings (ATED). The threshold was reduced to £500,000 from 1 April 2016.

There is a relief from ATED for let property (as well as certain other commercial scenarios) but this relief must be claimed annually.

Since 6 April 2015, any non-UK resident (individual or company) that owns UK residential property has been potentially liable to UK capital gains tax on a gain arising when that property is sold (Point 1.2 in Chapter 1 above). From 6 April 2019, non-residents are generally liable to tax on capital gains arising from the direct or indirect disposal of interests in UK land (see Chapter 1).

**Point 8.2:** ***The realisation of income and investments locked into a company can give rise to further tax liabilities at that time. Shareholders who are not fully subject to higher or additional rate tax or who are not resident in the UK at that stage could benefit from an extraction of their profit by way of dividend. For others, a capital gains exit may be possible, taking advantage of the 20% capital gains tax rate.***

As illustrated in Example 1 in Point 8.1 above, there is greater scope for the retention of profits within a company than there is by an individual personally. However, the distribution of these profits will generate a further tax liability where the company is controlled by UK resident taxpayers (see comments on changes for non-UK resident taxpayers below).

Where a company distributes its profits by way of dividend after 5 April 2016, the individual shareholder will be assessed to tax on the net dividend without any tax credit. An additional rate income tax payer will pay 39.35% tax on those dividends, apart from the first £1,000 in 2023/24 which would be taxed at 0% (the equivalent amount was the first £2,000 in 2022/23).

---

## Example 2

Taking the situation illustrated in Example 1 in Point 8.1 above, the company's retained profits of £778,657are distributed to individuals who are 45% income taxpayers in full at the end of Year 5.

| | |
|---|---|
| Dividend received | 778,657 |
| Tax at 39.35% | 306,402 |
| Net receipt | 472,255 |

---

This is somewhat lower than the net return of £565,334 if the property had been owned directly by the shareholder. However, the position is improved for those shareholders who may not be fully subject to the highest rate of tax.

The ultimate realisation of the company-owned investment by the shareholder might be achieved by liquidating the company or by selling the shares. In the above example, if the company were to be liquidated with the reserves of £778,657 being treated as a capital gain (subject to application of the transactions in securities legislation noted below), standard rate capital gains tax of £155,731 would arise (assuming the shareholder's annual exemption and any other relief had been used elsewhere). That would result in a net return after tax of £622,926. There is, of course, an enhanced benefit if shareholders are only subject to CGT at the reduced rate of 10% (which applies where their income is below the basic rate income tax threshold).

A shareholder who is tax resident outside the UK in the year of payment may not be subject to UK tax on any dividend payment or liquidation gain made in the year of non-residence if this is part of a longer period of residence outside the UK.

From April 2019 non-UK residents have been liable to UK tax on their capital gains arising after that date on all types of UK property with an April 2019 rebasing of the base cost of property not already subject to tax. Capital gains on disposals of shares in 'property rich' companies arising after April 2019 are also generally subject to UK tax where the shareholder held at least 25% in the previous two years. A property rich company is broadly one where the UK land forms 75% of the gross assets.

There are anti-avoidance provisions that HMRC could invoke in certain situations where tax avoidance arises from 'transactions in securities' (*CTA 2010, s 733* for companies; *ITA 2007, s 682* for non-companies) or certain transactions in land (*CTA 2010, s 815* for companies; *ITA 2007, s 752* for non-companies). Advice may be necessary at the time of any realisation of proceeds on the above basis as to what grounds, if any, HMRC might have for invoking these provisions. In some cases, applying for formal clearance from HMRC may be advisable. In this connection, the related anti-avoidance rules were tightened further in the *Finance Act 2016* which may well invite more challenges from HMRC to capital treatment when accumulated profits are extracted from companies in a capital form. In view of these rules selling – rather than liquidating – a company may be preferable. This can also benefit a buyer. There are currently stamp taxes of up to 15% on a direct purchase of a residential property and up to 6% on other properties (rates vary around the United Kingdom). This is cut to 0.5% where the purchase is of shares in a UK company (see Point 5.7).

**Point 8.3:** ***Individuals and trustees who choose to own property through a company could explore selling their shares in future to a UK REIT.***

Assuming an inflation rate of 3% per year, the base cost of a property would have increased by some 34% after ten years. For example, a £1 million property bought by a company in 2012 would have a base cost of about £1.34 million in 2022. If the value of the property less selling expenses does not exceed £1.34 million at that point, no taxable gain arises.

For an individual, a taxable gain of £340,000 would have arisen.

For disposals after 5 April 2016, the standard rate of capital gains tax was reduced to 20% for additional and higher rate taxpayers (although a higher rate of 28% will continue to apply to disposals of residential property). In this example, this would give rise to a potential tax liability of £68,000 at the 20% CGT rate.

If the value of the property after ten years is £3 million, the gain to a company would be £1.66 million, but £2 million for an individual. The company would pay corporation tax on £1.66 million at 25% (assuming the post-April 2023 rate applies) which would give rise to a tax liability of £415,000. The individual would pay £400,000 on the £2 million gain, ie CGT at 20% (28% if the property is residential), assuming an additional or higher-rate taxpayer. There is also the benefit in the latter case that the proceeds are in the individual's hands. Where a company realises the gain, there is usually a further tax cost of extracting funds from the company. If the company is sold, a buyer must normally be expected to discount the price paid for the shares by at least some element of the inherent tax in the company.

The disadvantage may be avoided if, in future, the shares can be sold to a UK real estate investment trust (REIT). Gains on properties owned within a UK REIT structure will be exempt from UK tax on the gain. This extends to properties owned by companies acquired by the REIT if the owning company is a property investor and thus satisfies the property-letting business requirement of the REIT. See Chapter 14 for further comments on the REIT possibility, and the potential for the selling shareholders to roll over gains on their shares into new shares in the acquiring REIT vehicle.

A discount for any deferred tax on property capital gains may also be avoided if selling post 5 April 2019 to a non-resident collective investment vehicle that benefits from an exemption election (see Chapter 1).

*Chapter 9*

# Premiums received

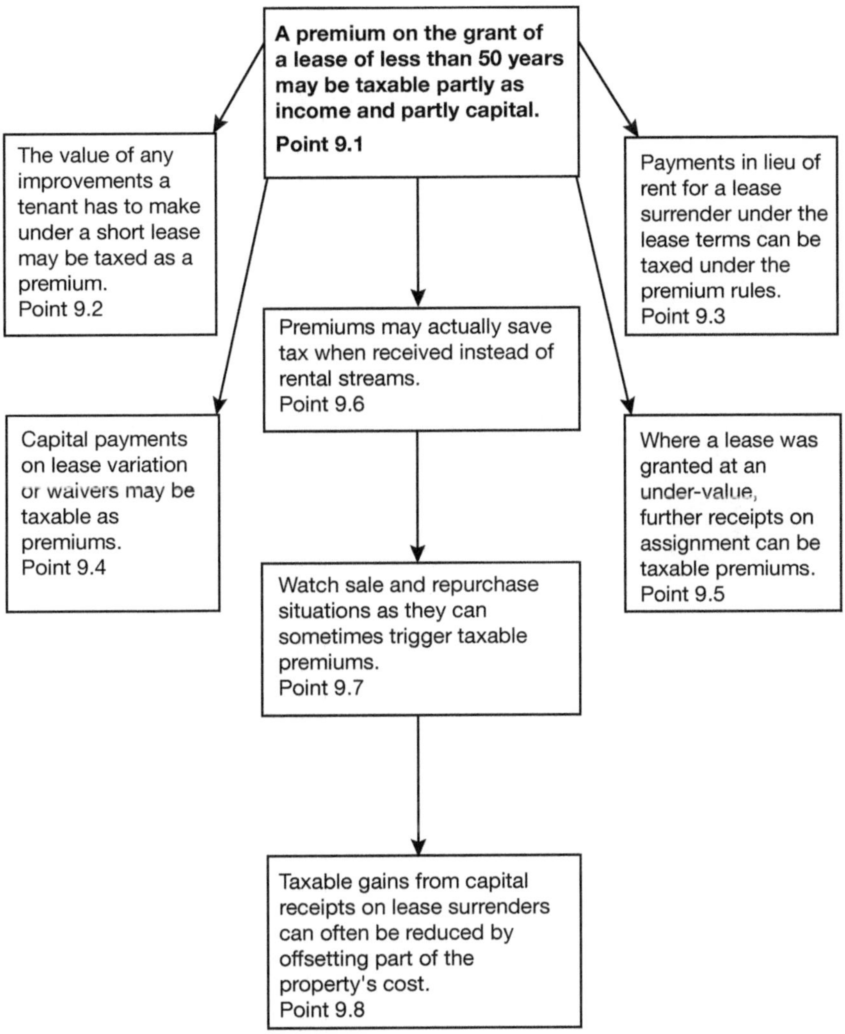

## 9 PREMIUMS RECEIVED

**Point 9.1:** ***Where a lease is granted for less than 50 years, part of any capital sum received is treated as if it were rent and taxed as income in the year of receipt. The balance of the premium will be assessed as a capital receipt for capital gains purposes.***

Part of any premium charged on the grant of a short lease of 50 years or less will be assessable as income (*CTA 2009, s 217*; *ITTOIA 2005, s 277*). The income element is determined by reducing the premium by 2% for each complete year of the lease less one. The resulting figure will be assessable to tax as additional rental income.

---

### Example 1

A 20-year lease is granted for a premium of £50,000. The property income element of this sum is:

| | £ |
|---|---|
| Premium | 50,000 |
| Less: 2% × (20 – 1) × £50,000 | (19,000) |
| Taxable as additional rent | 31,000 |

---

In the above example, £19,000 will be treated as the capital element of the receipt, representing the proceeds for the purposes of the capital gains computation.

**Point 9.2:** ***Where a tenant is required to make improvements under a lease, a notional premium can be assessed on the landlord.***

If the terms under which a lease of 50 years or less is granted impose an obligation on the tenant to undertake improvements, the landlord can be taxed as if a premium had been received (*CTA 2009, s 218; ITTOIA 2005, s 278*). This will be taxable in the manner set out in Point 9.1 above.

The premium is not based on the amount spent, but on the increase in the value of the interest held by the landlord as a result of the improvements being carried out (*CTA 2009, s 218(3); ITTOIA 2005, s 278(3)*). A charge will only arise where the obligation to carry out the work arises under the terms in the lease.

A charge under this provision is rare. The point tends to arise only where the tenant has claimed a deduction for the notional premium (see Chapter 27 in Part C).

**Point 9.3:** ***A capital payment by a tenant in lieu of rent or for the surrender of a short lease may be taxed as a premium.***

If, when a lease of 50 years or less is granted, there is provision for a future capital payment by the tenant in lieu of rent or for the surrender of the lease, the payment is a deemed premium in the hands of the landlord (*CTA 2009, ss 219–220; ITTOIA 2005, ss 279–280*). It will be assessed in the year in which it is payable by the tenant.

The income element of a receipt in lieu of rent will be computed by reference to the period for which there has been a reduction in the rent. The balance will be treated as a capital receipt subject to the rules for the taxation of capital gains.

In the case of a payment on surrender of a lease, the premium is assessed by reference to the length of time the lease had been in existence at the time of surrender.

Where there was no clause in the lease when granted providing for such a payment, no deemed premium arises. In that case, the receipt is taxable as a capital gain but with the possibility of offsetting part of the property cost.

**Point 9.4:** ***A capital payment by a tenant for the variation or waiver of a short lease could also be deemed to be a premium.***

Any payment to vary or waive the terms of a lease is treated as a lease premium. The element chargeable as income – as distinct from the capital element (see Point 9.1 above) – would be based on the duration of the lease after the waiver or variation takes effect. Periods after the waiver or variation cease to have effect are also ignored. If the relevant duration is 50 years or less, then part of the premium is taxed as rent in the year the variation or waiver takes place (*CTA 2009, s 221; ITTOIA 2005, s 281*).

---

## Example 2

A 21-year lease, when granted, contains a clause entitling the landlord to terminate the lease after 15 years should he require the property for development purposes. After 12 years, the landlord agrees to accept a sum of £50,000 from the tenant in consideration for waiving this clause.

The £50,000 will be assessed as a premium in the year of receipt. The income element will be based on the period of six years remaining after the waiver comes into effect. The amount taxable as income would, therefore, be:

| | £ |
|---|---|
| Premium | 50,000 |
| Less reduction £50,000 × 2% × (6 – 1) | (5,000) |
| Taxable as income | 45,000 |

---

The balance of £5,000 would be assessable to tax as a capital gain.

**Point 9.5: *The premium provisions only apply to a grant of a lease, although an assignment can be caught if the original grant was at an under-value.***

The assignment, as opposed to the grant, of a lease is ordinarily outside the premium provisions. There is, however, an anti-avoidance provision applying where a lease of 50 years or less had originally been granted at an under-value. Where the lease is subsequently assigned, the consideration received can be partially taxable as additional rent of the letting business (*CTA 2009, s 222; ITTOIA 2005, s 282*).

In the absence of any anti-avoidance provision, the premium rules mentioned in Point 9.1 above could be avoided by granting a short lease for a nominal premium to an associated party. The associated party could then assign the lease for full market value.

However, under *CTA 2009, s 222* and *ITTOIA 2005, s 282*, HMRC can assess the assignment consideration in this situation as a premium up to the amount of the market premium forgone on the first grant. There may also be assessments on any subsequent assignment, until HMRC have recouped tax on the deemed market value premium at the time of the original granting of the lease. The income element will be assessable as additional rental income.

---

## Example 3

Laugher Ltd granted its subsidiary Brownlee Ltd a 25-year lease of its former offices for £10,000. Brownlee Ltd then assigned this lease to a firm of solicitors for £100,000. Since the grant of the lease was at an under-value, the following corporation tax assessments would arise:

| | £ |
|---|---|
| On Laugher Ltd | |
| Premium | 10,000 |
| Less reduction (£10,000 × 2% × (25 – 1)) | (4,800) |
| Taxable as income | 5,200 |
| On Brownlee Ltd | |
| Deemed premium | 100,000 |
| Less premium paid | (10,000) |
| | 90,000 |
| Less reduction (£90,000 × 2% × (25 – 1)) | (43,200) |
| Taxable as income | 46,800 |

---

For chargeable gains purposes, Laugher Ltd will be treated as disposing of the property intra-group for a consideration giving rise to neither gain nor loss (*TCGA 1992, s 171*).

Brownlee Ltd, on the other hand, will be subject to a chargeable gain. This would not be restricted to the capital element of the receipt. No reduction is available from the £100,000 consideration for any part taxable as income (*TCGA 1992, Sch 8, para 6(2)*). There is, therefore, a significant element of double taxation on this premium.

It should be noted that the parties need not be connected or associated for this provision to apply. It is sometimes recommended that an assignee of a short lease should obtain a certificate from HMRC that the original grant was not at an under-value.

**Point 9.6:** ***There may be circumstances where a landlord might benefit from receiving a lump sum premium rather than a rental stream.***

There could be a number of situations where a one-off premium may prove more attractive from a tax viewpoint than future annual rental income. Consider the following instances:

(a) An individual or company may have a tax shelter in the year, which may not be available to carry forward against future rents. For instance, an individual might have incurred substantial trading losses or have surplus allowances. A company may be able to claim losses from a fellow subsidiary company by way of group relief. Such tax shelter can be offset against the income element of the premium arising in the year. Current or past capital losses can be offset against the capital element of the receipt.

(b) Since 5 April 2016, an individual landlord would pay up to 20% tax (assuming the landlord is an additional or higher-rate taxpayer) on the gain relating to the capital element of the premium on non-residential property (NB – the standard rate of capital gains tax on residential property is 28%).This compares with a maximum income tax rate of 45% for a rental stream receipt.

(c) A non-resident owner had traditionally been exempt from tax on the capital element of the premium (NB – tax withholding may be necessary on the income element if paid directly by a tenant to a non-resident – see Point 1.3). Note that the position on this has changed from April 2015 with regard to residential property where capital gains can be subject to tax. Additionally, under provisions having effect from April 2019, non-residents will generally be taxable on all capital gains on UK immoveable property arising after that date unless they are able to benefit from an exemption.

(d) If the building is to be sold shortly after the grant of a new short lease, any past unused losses may not be able to be offset against a capital gain. They may, as a consequence, be lost. If a premium is charged on the lease, these losses can be offset against the income element. The lease would have to reflect a suitably reduced rent payable and the sale consideration of the building would need to be correspondingly reduced, but this should also serve to diminish the chargeable capital gain arising. Accordingly, there can be an overall reduction in the tax liability without affecting the total consideration received by the landlord.

**Point 9.7:** ***A clause entitling a seller of land to buy back the property at a future date could give rise to an unexpected liability to tax under the premium provisions.***

Selling a property with the right to reacquire it in future could offer a way around the ordinary premium provisions. For this reason, a further anti-avoidance provision seeks to tax the difference between the sale price and lower purchase consideration as a deemed premium (*CTA 2009, s 224; ITTOIA 2005, s 284*). The income element is calculated under the normal premium rules and is assessable as income in the period in which the sale occurs. The term of the lease for the purposes of computing the income element is the period between sale and repurchase.

If there is no one particular date but a series of possibilities arising from the sale contract, the repurchase is treated initially as taking place at the lowest possible price under the terms of the sale, if this varies with the date. The vendor then has six years from the re-conveyance to make a claim to recover any excess tax paid, once the actual date of the re-conveyance is known.

Although an anti-avoidance provision, this could present a pitfall in an innocent transaction. The owner of land may sell a property with the right to repurchase if there is a proposed redevelopment or change of use. For this reason, careful consideration must be given to the deemed premium rules before any repurchase clauses are included in any property sale agreement.

**Point 9.8:** ***If the landlord receives a surrender payment from the tenant where there is no provision for this in the lease, the immediate taxable gain arising can be reduced by offsetting part of the base cost of the property against the receipt.***

If the terms of the lease did not provide for an early surrender payment, the receipt is assessable as a capital gain. The taxable gain is calculated under the 'part disposal rules' (*TCGA 1992, s 42*). Part of the base cost of the property can, therefore, be offset against the sum received in computing the taxable gain.

---

## Example 4

A property with a capital gains base cost of £1 million is let at a market rent. There is no provision in the lease for early surrender.

The tenant wants to relocate premises and agrees to pay the landlord a surrender premium of £300,000. Following surrender, the freehold is valued at £900,000.

£300,000 is a capital receipt against which a portion of the £1 million cost can be offset. This is determined by the fraction A/A + B, where A is the amount received and B is the value of the remaining interest. In this case, the fraction is £300,000/(£300,000 + £900,000) or one quarter. Therefore, one quarter of £1 million, ie £250,000, can be offset against the £300,000, leaving just £50,000 currently in charge to tax.

The base cost of the property for future tax purposes will be reduced by £250,000 to £750,000.

For small part disposals, a claim can be made to offset proceeds against the base cost carried forward (*TCGA 1992, s 242*). This can apply where the proceeds do not exceed £20,000 and are no more than one-fifth of the market value of the holding prior to disposal. The claim must be made by the end of the first anniversary of 31 January following the year of assessment or, for companies, within two years of the end of the accounting period in which the part disposal is made.

Where the owner is a company, indexation up to December 2017 would have accrued by reference to that lower figure. For individuals, partnerships and trusts, there is no indexation.

*Chapter 10*

# Letting as a trade

**It may be possible to characterise a residential letting activity as a trade to obtain the tax benefits of trading treatment – such as entrepreneurs' relief.**

**Point 10.1**

Commercial property might also be let in the course of a trading rather than investment activity.
Point 10.2

Where full trading status is not achievable some of the tax benefits may still be achievable by supplying the services through a separate vehicle.
Point 10.3

Holiday lettings can attract most of the tax benefits of trading treatment.
Point 10.4

# 10 LETTING AS A TRADE

**Point 10.1:** ***Residential letting is normally an investment activity. However, more favourable tax treatment as a trading activity may be available if services and facilities are provided to residents.***

The income tax treatment of letting is similar to that of a trade. However, there are a number of capital gains and inheritance tax reliefs which are available for a trading business but not for an investment activity. In view of this, the benefits of establishing trading treatment in preference to investment can be considerable. Consider the following:

(a) Substantial shareholding exemption applies to gains by companies on certain disposals of shareholdings in trading companies. Where a company owns at least 10% of the ordinary shares of a trading company, any gain on the sale of those shares is potentially free of tax. It can apply, therefore, to sales of shares in trading joint venture companies as well as subsidiaries.

    Further points on the substantial shareholding exemption are set out in Chapter 32.

    A similar relief may be available to non-residents from April 2019 when they sell an interest in shares where the value substantially derives from UK land used in a qualifying trade.

(b) Trading properties, or shares in a trading company, can be 'relevant business property' attracting 100% inheritance tax exemption (*IHTA 1984, s 105*).

(c) Gains on sales of property used for trading purposes can be deferred by rolling them over into new trading assets (see Chapter 30).

(d) Gains on the sales of a property used in a trade can be eligible for capital gains entrepreneurs' relief which reduces the capital gains tax rate for an individual or trust to 10% (see Chapter 31).

(e) The restrictions on finance cost tax relief for residential property business would not potentially apply (see Point 3.1 in Chapter 3A).

In view of the above advantages, the possibility of transforming an investment into a trading activity is often worth exploring.

There are two circumstances where a property owner might benefit from the more favourable taxation treatment as a trader. These are:

- where certain services and facilities are provided to residents; and
- where the property qualifies as a holiday letting; this is discussed in Point 10.4 below.

The dividing line between investment and trading can become blurred when services or facilities are provided, such that the letting is more like a hotel or guest house operation.

The distinction between a guest house and a pure letting has not been determined, either by legislation or in the courts, to date. Several cases have confirmed that the activity of letting accommodation and providing limited services, eg laundry, linen and cleaning, did not amount to trade (*Gittos v Barclay (Inspector of Taxes)* [1982] STC 390; *Griffiths v Jackson* [1983] STC 184 and, more recently, *Hatt v Newman* [2000] STC 113).

It is considered that, in addition to cleaning and laundry services, the provision of at least one meal would be necessary to establish a trading activity. Such a meal might be hot or cold, but should be prepared on the premises. A simple breakfast may well suffice for this purpose. However, this may need to be more than simply a welcome pack which contains certain foodstuffs. That was the conclusion in the 2015 case, *Green v Revenue and Customs Commissioners* [2015] UKFTT 334. The First-tier Tribunal were faced with a situation where a welcome pack was provided as well as provision of linen, towels, cleaning and other items. Although the issue there was inheritance tax and the availability of Business Property Relief, the decision was that the extra services provided were not significant enough to make the business any more than an investment activity.

Other tests might be the length of occupation of guests. If the right of occupation is in days or weeks, rather than months or years, it is more like a 'hostel' activity. Where longer periods are envisaged and there are multiple accommodation units, the landlord should have the right to move occupants between units at the end of any month. In that way, no occupant establishes exclusive rights over any particular units. Further, landlords should have rights of access over property at all times.

At times, it may even be beneficial to carry on a trade on a temporary basis. For instance, if a trading property is to be sold and the proceeds reinvested in a letting property, no roll-over relief would be available (see Chapter 30 in Part C for replacement of business asset, or 'roll-over', capital gains relief). However, if the new letting activity were a trading activity, at least for a short period after the reinvestment, CGT roll-over relief may be available.

There is no provision for claw-back of relief if a trading property merely ceases to be used as such – as long as the property is not a wasting asset (ie needs to be a freehold or a leasehold interest with more than 60 years to run). It must be appreciated that, if a property ceases to be used in the trading activity, then any eligibility for future roll-over relief will be affected.

As mentioned in Point 10.3 below, there may be situations where it is not possible to establish the letting as a trade despite a supply of services. In such a situation, having the services supplied through a separate vehicle might preserve some of the benefits of trading treatment.

**Point 10.2:** ***Commercial letting might also be eligible for favourable tax treatment as a trading activity, depending on the services and facilities provided to occupants.***

The possibility that residential letting may become a trade is perhaps more evident than commercial letting, because of the ready analogy of the hotel and guest house referred to in Point 10.1 above. However, in principle, certain commercial property situations can be run on trading lines and receive the benefit of the favourable tax treatments outlined in Point 10.1.

The concept of serviced offices has become quite popular. Owners of properties are offering an increasing range of services to occupants including secretarial, IT and conferencing facilities, as well as furniture, equipment, cleaning, telephone and maintenance.

As with residential situations, if occupants do not establish rights over the office units that they use and there is a frequently changing population of users, the potential to claim that a trade is carried on increases.

This opportunity may stretch to other uses of buildings such as smaller warehousing, retail or even factory units where there remains the opportunity for the owner to supply a range of services and facilities to the occupants. It might be more difficult in these situations to get a sufficiently revolving population of occupiers so that some establishment of tenant rights may be unavoidable. In that case, HMRC may consider there to be a 'hybrid' investment and trading activity.

Where services are provided which are ancillary to a letting activity, planning on the lines of Point 10.3 below might be adopted.

**Point 10.3:** ***Where extensive services are supplied, but the activity is still an investment, it may be beneficial to split out the service aspects into a separate trading vehicle.***

Where services are supplied in a situation where a landlord/tenant investment situation exists, there might be some benefit in trying to split out the trading element.

One company might, for instance, let the property under conventional letting terms. Another company – or the shareholders personally – could supply the add-on services at a price which generates an appropriate profit.

The potential advantage is that this could establish a separate business which itself could attract the benefits of trading treatment as set out in Point 10.1 above. Furthermore, insofar as the property rents are not subject to VAT, it could be charged on services supplied, which could increase opportunities for VAT recovery on costs incurred by the property owner (see Chapter 18 for a discussion on VAT).

**Point 10.4:** ***Holiday lettings, although not a trade for tax purposes, continue to attract some of the benefits of trading treatment.***

A special tax treatment applies for qualifying holiday lettings (*CTA 2009 ss 264–269A*; *ITTOIA 2005, ss 322–328B*). Although the income from such lettings is assessed as investment income, holiday lettings have enjoyed the same benefits as a trading activity (see Point 10.1 above). This also includes not being subject to the finance cost relief restrictions introduced for residential lettings (see Point 3.1 in Chapter 3A). These benefits have been subject to a number of changes in recent years but the proposed abolition of this regime has now been shelved.

To qualify as holiday lettings, the following conditions currently have to be met:

(a) The property must be let as holiday accommodation in the European Economic Area (EEA).

(b) There must be commercial letting with a view to profit.

(c) The letting must comprise furnished accommodation.

(d) The accommodation must be available for commercial letting to the public generally as holiday accommodation for periods which amount, in aggregate, to not less than 210 days.

(e) The period in which the accommodation is so let should have amounted, in aggregate, to at least 105 days (previously 70 days). The number of days should exclude periods of longer-term occupation (see (f) below). Businesses meeting this criterion in one year may elect to be treated as having met it in the two following years ('period of grace') providing certain other criteria are met.

(f) For a period comprising at least 155 days, the property must not normally be in the same occupation for a continuous period exceeding 31 days ('longer-term occupation').

It is only possible to offset losses against profits from the same furnished holiday letting business. It is no longer possible to offset such losses against other income. Furthermore, whilst UK losses can relieve profits from UK furnished holiday lettings they cannot be offset against such profits from other EEA countries. Similarly, such 'EEA' losses can only be offset against 'EEA' profits from furnished holiday lettings.

The property need not have been in an acknowledged holiday resort. The conditions could equally be satisfied by a property in the centre of a city. However, it should still, strictly, be used by holidaymakers and tourists to qualify for the special treatment.

Many people in holiday areas let their properties out during the main holiday period on a short-term basis, but during the quieter part of the year, let on a longer-term basis. These longer lettings – which may be to the same person for more than 31 days – would normally preclude a claim to CGT roll-over relief when the property is subsequently disposed of.

However, provided the letting during the main holiday period satisfies the above conditions, HMRC will regard the whole of the income derived from the property for that year as arising from commercially let furnished holiday accommodation.

The letting of holiday accommodation is subject to VAT at the standard rate, as is the sale of a new building which contains holiday accommodation. This can mean that investors buying new holiday homes to let will have to pay VAT on the purchase price and may need or choose to register for VAT in respect of their holiday letting activity. See the comments towards the end of Point 18.1 for more details.

Furnished lettings treatment also scored one advantage over trading income. As the income is technically assessable as investment income, Class 4 NICs have not been payable in respect of the activity.

Income from furnished holiday lettings counts as earnings for pension purposes.

*Chapter 11*

# Capital gains planning: properties held at 31 March 1982

**For companies, the taxable gain on a property owned at 31 March 1982 can be reduced by its value at that date where this is more favourable than original cost. For individuals, trustees and personal representatives the 31 March 1982 value will have to be adopted for disposals post-5 April 2008.**

**Point 11.1**

↓

It is sometimes favourable for companies to make an election for 31 March 1982 values to apply to all investment assets.
Point 11.2

↓

Where a company acquired an asset between 31 March 1982 and 6 April 1988 in circumstances where a roll-over or hold-over claim was made, one half of the gain at the time of transfer can be deducted from any taxable gain on sale. Individuals, trustees and personal representatives have not been able to claim this on disposals after 5 April 2008.
Point 11.3

# 11 CAPITAL GAINS PLANNING: PROPERTIES HELD AT 31 MARCH 1982

**Point 11.1:** ***For companies, the taxable gain on a property owned at 31 March 1982 can be substantially reduced by its value at that date where this is more favourable than original cost. For individuals, trustees and personal representatives the 31 March 1982 value applies for disposals post-April 2008.***

The base cost of any asset held at 31 March 1982 can be revised to its value at 31 March 1982 (*TCGA 1992, s 35*). In many cases where property was acquired before 31 March 1982, this rebasing results in a significant reduction in the gain, which would otherwise have been chargeable to tax by reference to cost.

Since 6 April 2008, the option for individuals, trustees and personal representatives to use cost as an alternative to 31 March 1982 value on the disposal of an asset held at that date has no longer been available. Only companies in charge to corporation tax will be able to use cost if it is more favourable in their calculation of capital gains in respect of disposals post-5 April 2008.

There are four situations where the rebasing will not apply, which are only likely to be relevant to companies after 5 April 2008.

These are:

(a) Where there is a gain by reference to the 1982 value but a loss compared with cost, the disposal will be treated as taking place at no gain/no loss (*TCGA 1992, s 35(4)*).

(b) Where there is a gain by reference to original cost but a loss when using the 1982 value then the disposal will be treated as taking place at no gain/no loss (*TCGA 1992, s 35(4)*).

(c) Where the overall loss by reference to cost is smaller than the loss that would arise using the 31 March 1982 value, the lower loss figure applies (*TCGA 1992, s 35(3)*).

(d) Where the company disposing of the asset did not actually own it at 31 March 1982 (*TCGA 1992, s 35(1)*). This rule is relaxed in several specific instances notably where the disposal took place between the members of a group of companies or between companies in the course of a reconstruction.

Following from (d) above, rebasing will not apply where an asset was acquired by way of gift after 31 March 1982 from someone who held it at that date and who may have claimed hold-over relief on the gift. Nor will it apply where there has been a replacement of business assets after 31 March 1982 and roll-over relief has been claimed. However, another relief may be available in these situations (see Point 11.3 below).

A claim can be made for the 31 March 1982 value to apply to all disposals. This can be particularly advantageous where either (b) or (c) above apply (see Point 11.2 below).

**Point 11.2:** ***Where use of the 31 March 1982 value would result in a loss compared with original cost, or a greater loss, it may be appropriate for a company to consider making an election for the 31 March 1982 valuation to apply. However, such an election will apply to all future disposals of assets held at 31 March 1982.***

To avoid the need to keep records in respect of the cost of, and expenditure on, assets before 31 March 1982, companies are entitled to make an election for all capital gains disposals to be computed solely by reference to their assets' 31 March 1982 values (*TCGA 1992, s 35(5)*). Where such an election is made, all pre-31 March 1982 cost figures can be disregarded. As mentioned in Point 11.1, this election was also available to non-corporate taxpayers prior to 6 April 2008. The principal advantage of this would be where (b) or (c) in Point 11.1 above applies. An election would enable a capital loss – or larger capital loss – to be available. For instance, the loss may be much lower when we compare the disposal value to original cost, or there could be a small gain. If the 1982 election is made, it would be possible to take advantage of the larger capital loss computed by reference to the 31 March 1982 'base cost'.

Making an election is not a casual matter. It is irrevocable and will apply to all future disposals of assets held at 31 March 1982.

Furthermore, individual companies within a tax group cannot make the election. It must be made by the parent company of the group and this will apply to all companies within the group at the time of the relevant disposal (*TCGA 1992, Sch 3, para 8(1), (2)*).

In view of the above, it is important to review the position for all assets before any election is made. If the historical cost for some properties (including any pre-31 March 1982 enhancement expenditure) exceeds the 31 March 1982 value, the disadvantage of making an election for such properties must be compared with the estimated benefit of the election in respect of others.

If an election is not made, the indexation allowance can be computed on the higher of original cost and the 31 March 1982 value (see Point 12.1). However, where an election is made then this allowance can only be calculated by reference to the 1982 value. It should be noted that the indexation allowance cannot create or enhance a capital loss (see Point 12.2). The indexation allowance has been frozen at December 2017 so that no additional allowance will accrue after that month.

The election for the 31 March 1982 value to apply in the case of companies must be made within two years of the end of the accounting period in which the 'first relevant disposal' takes place. The 'first relevant disposal' is the first occasion after 5 April 1988 on which an asset owned at 31 March 1982 is sold (*TCGA 1992, s 35(6)*).

**Point 11.3:** ***A special relief is available for properties that were the subject of roll-over relief or gift hold-over relief claims between 31 March 1982 and 6 April 1988. One half of the deferred gain held/rolled over can be exempt from tax. Since April 2008, this relief has been restricted to companies only.***

As mentioned in Point 11.1 above, rebasing does not apply if the asset was not owned at 31 March 1982. Whilst this seems logical, when introducing the rebasing legislation in April 1988, the government did accept that this operates unfairly in two situations:

(a) Where the property in question was acquired between 31 March 1982 and 6 April 1988, and business roll-over relief has been claimed on the basis that the proceeds of the sale of an asset owned pre-31 March 1982 were reinvested in this property (see Chapter 30 for business roll-over relief). Since the new property was not owned on 31 March 1982, tax would ordinarily be payable on any chargeable gain that arose on the property that it replaced without any relief for the pre-31 March 1982 element of the rolled-over gain.

(b) Similarly, between 31 March 1982 and 6 April 1988 there may have been a gift of an asset where the transferor and transferee elected to hold over any capital gain until the asset was sold by the transferee. Since the recipient of the asset will not have owned it on 31 March 1982, he or she could well be liable to tax on the full gain eventually arising notwithstanding the fact that some of the gain could have been referable to the period prior to 31 March 1982.

In view of the above, the government introduced a fairly arbitrary relief that can be claimed wherever situations (a) or (b) apply and there is a disposal of an asset after 5 April 1988. The relief involves the total exclusion from the final chargeable gain of one-half of the deferred gain (*TCGA 1992, Sch 4*). This relief was removed for disposals by individuals, trustees and personal representatives from 6 April 2008.

---

## Example

In December 1980, Murray Ltd acquired a freehold property for £100,000 to be used as the headquarters of its trading business. The value of the property in March 1982 was £150,000.

In December 1986, Murray Ltd sold its property realising a capital gain of £200,000. A roll-over claim was made into new premises costing £450,000.

In January 2022, when Murray Ltd sold the property, the total gain by reference to Murray Ltd's original cost plus indexation amounted to £1,500,000.

Since it did not own the asset at 31 March 1982, it could not substitute £150,000 as the market value of the asset at that date. However, by virtue of the relief in *TCGA 1992, Sch 4,* Murray Ltd is able to deduct £100,000 (ie 50% of the deferred gain of £200,000) from the gain subject to tax, thereby reducing the taxable gain to £1,400,000.

---

A claim must be made for the relief, in the case of companies, within two years of the end of the accounting period in which the relevant disposal is made (*TCGA 1992, Sch 4, para 9*).

For individuals, alone or in partnership, and trusts, the claim for relief would have to have been made no later than 31 January in the tax year following that in which the disposal takes place. Given that the last tax year for which such a claim could be made ended 5 April 2008, these claims will now be out of time.

*Chapter 12*

# Capital gains planning: the indexation allowance

**A company's gain on the sale of an asset can be reduced by indexation allowance. Individuals and trustees can only deduct indexation prior to 6 April 1998 and only where the disposal was before 6 April 2008.**
**Point 12.1**

↓

Indexation allowances cannot create or enhance a loss unless there was a previous intra-group transfer before 30 November 1993.
Point 12.2

# 12 CAPITAL GAINS PLANNING: THE INDEXATION ALLOWANCE

**Point 12.1:** ***On the sale of a property, any capital gain realised by a company is reduced by applying increases in the Retail Prices Index to the cost of the asset. Individuals and trustees ceased to be entitled to further indexation allowance from 6 April 1998 and receive no indexation allowance at all on disposals post-5 April 2008.***

The chargeable gain on the sale of an asset by a company is reduced by applying the increase in the Retail Prices Index since acquisition (or since 31 March 1982, if later) to the asset's base cost (*TCGA 1992, s 53(1)*). The Retail Prices Index increase is also applied to enhancement expenditure from the date the relevant amount became due and payable (*TCGA 1992, s 54(4)*). Following a change announced in November 2017, when a company makes a capital gain on or after 1 January 2018, the indexation allowance that is applied in order to determine the amount of the chargeable gain will only be calculated up to December 2017. For individuals and trustees, indexation allowance ceased to be available after 5 April 1998. Although any allowance accrued up to 5 April 1998 was preserved in the base cost of the property for CGT purposes, this allowance has been lost for any disposals after 5 April 2008.

For assets acquired before 31 March 1982, a corporate taxpayer can ordinarily claim an indexation allowance based on the higher of original cost and the value at 31 March 1982. For individuals, trustees and personal representatives disposing of property after 5 April 2008, the tax cost is based solely on the value at 31 March 1982 and subsequent expenditure.

---

## Example 1

Mears Ltd bought an investment property for £200,000 in March 1979. In March 1982 the property was worth £500,000. The property was sold in March 2017 for £1,500,000.

Unless an election has been made for 31 March 1982 values to apply to all Mears Ltd's pre-31 March 1982 assets (see Point 11.2), it is necessary to do two calculations:

| | [A] 1982 value as base cost | [B] Original cost |
|---|---|---|
| | £ | £ |
| Proceeds | 1,500,000 | 1,500,000 |
| Base cost | (500,000) | (200,000) |
| | 1,000,000 | 1,300,000 |
| Indexation allowance | | |
| £500,000 × 2.390 | (1,195,000) | (1,195,000) |
| Chargeable gain | NIL | £105,000 |

---

Since there is no gain in calculation [A] but a gain in calculation [B], the former calculation is adopted. Note that in both cases, however, the same indexation figure is used, which in this instance is based on the higher base cost figure of £500,000 (*TCGA 1992, s 55(2)*).

Where the company has made an election for the 31 March 1982 value to apply to all assets (see Point 11.2) this would affect the position in the above example but not the final outcome. There would only be one calculation needed, using the market value of the property at 31 March 1982 as the base cost. Note also that the March 1982 value would form the basis for the indexation allowance even if it were lower than the base cost (*TCGA 1992, s 55(2)*).

There will be situations where the use of a March 1982 valuation may not be beneficial. In the above example the value of a property might have dropped since acquisition. Even if this is not the case, substantial enhancement expenditure may have been incurred prior to 31 March 1982 which is not fully reflected in the value of the property at that date. In view of these possibilities, it could be important to consider both alternative bases for the indexation allowance and obtain a valuation of the property at 31 March 1982 to support any decision on this.

**Point 12.2: *The indexation allowance can neither create nor enhance a capital loss. However, if there was an earlier transfer between group companies, the loss may have been preserved.***

Indexation relief cannot create an allowable capital loss or increase a loss already arising by virtue of the fact that the disposal value is less than cost/31 March 1982 value (*TCGA 1992, s 53(1)*).

## Example 2

A property owned by Rose Ltd cost £1 million in 1982. In March 2017, it was sold for £1.8 million. There was an increase in the Retail Prices Index of 239% in this period. Ignoring transaction costs, the capital gains position is:

| | £ |
|---|---|
| Sales proceeds | 1,800,000 |
| Cost | 1,000,000 |
| Gain | 800,000 |
| Indexation relief – £2,390,000 but restricted to gain | 800,000 |
| Chargeable gain | NIL |

In the above example, the balance of the indexation allowance, £1,590,000, is lost. It cannot be used against other capital gains.

This restriction was introduced with effect from 30 November 1993.

If the property was acquired from a connected party before this date and if it is treated as a disposal at no gain or loss, indexation accrued up to that time is inherited intact. That indexation can be used to create or enhance a usable capital loss on the property (*TCGA 1992, s 56*).

The principal example of a 'no gain/no loss disposal' now that indexation is no longer relevant for individuals or trustees, is a transfer between two companies within a UK tax group. If this occurred before 30 November 1993, some of the effect of these provisions will have been mitigated, as the following example shows:

---

## Example 3

In Example 2 above, assume Rose Ltd has sold the property having acquired it from a fellow subsidiary, Scott Ltd, in October 1993. Indexation to October 1993 was 78.5%.

| | £ |
|---|---|
| Cost | 1,000,000 |
| Indexation relief to October 1993 | 785,000 |

In this situation, the property is treated as being transferred to X Ltd at a value which gives neither a gain nor a loss. Since Scott Ltd has a base cost of £1,785,000 (ie £1 million plus £785,000 indexation allowance), X Ltd will be treated as acquiring the property for that value and have a base cost of £1,785,000. If the property was sold for £1.7 million, it will have an allowable capital loss of £85,000 (ie £1,700,000 less £1,785,000). Thus, the full benefit of the £785,000 indexation allowance is preserved.

If the acquisition had been in December 1993 or later, no capital loss could subsequently arise as a consequence of the indexation allowance.

---

*Chapter 13*

# Capital gains planning: deferring a sale

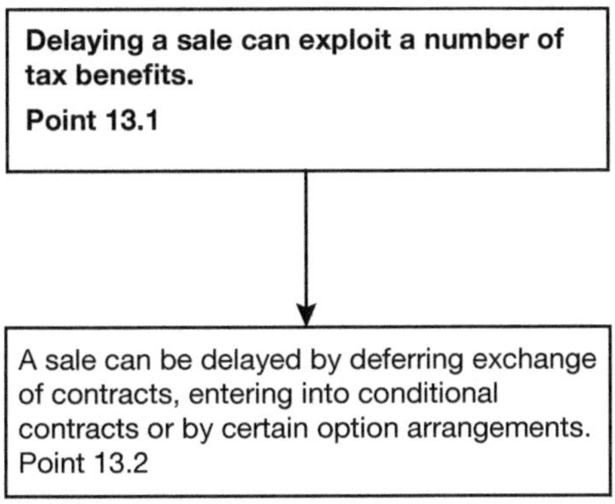

# 13 CAPITAL GAINS PLANNING: DEFERRING A SALE

**Point 13.1:** ***There are usually tax advantages to be gained from deferring a sale for capital gains purposes from one accounting period or tax year to the next. This is particularly the case if a sale is otherwise planned to take place towards the end of the year in question.***

There are several potential advantages in delaying a chargeable disposal:

(a) In the case of a corporate sale, a deferral may help ensure that any gain qualifies for substantial shareholding exemption where the minimum 12-month ownership rule must be met (see Chapter 32 for substantial shareholding relief).

(b) By pushing the gain into the following tax year, the tax on the capital gain may not be payable until one year later. This may only involve the deferral of the date of a disposal by a matter of days or weeks if it is due to take place at the end of a fiscal year or period of account. Changes affecting non-residents (not subject to corporation tax) on a disposal of UK land on or after 6 April 2019 and UK resident taxpayers (not subject to corporation tax) on a disposal of residential property on or after 6 April 2020 mean they will generally not be able to benefit from a deferral. Between 6 April 2020 and 26 October 2021, taxpayers (not subject to corporation tax) were required to report and pay CGT within 30 days of the completion date. For completions on or after 27 October 2021, thc time limit was increased to 60 days, as announced at Autumn Budget 2021.

    For non-residents (not subject to corporation tax), the disposal must be reported within 60 days regardless of whether there is tax to pay. This applies to disposals of all UK land and property by non-residents, not just residential property. For UK resident taxpayers (not subject to corporation tax), the 60-day reporting requirement only applies to disposals of residential property.

(c) In the case of a corporate sale, deferral may also help ensure that a company is not required to pay tax by quarterly instalment payments. Should a company have taxable profits above £1.5 million in two adjacent accounting periods, then it is required to pay tax on a quarterly basis. Deferring a gain until a subsequent year may assist in a company delaying falling within the regime or even avoiding it.

(d) For companies, a deferral may allow more scope to offset corporate interest in the later year.

(e) If an individual or trustee has already used the annual exemption for the tax year, there will be the opportunity of using a fresh exemption available in the following year.

(f) The deferral of a capital gain for one year may also give an opportunity to use any capital losses that arise in the following year. Capital losses can never be carried back but can be offset against gains in the same or future years. If a capital loss is anticipated but may not be realised until a succeeding year, this is added incentive to defer the gain until the same year to ensure that there will be an offset.

(g) A delay in the sale could result in an individual becoming entitled to business asset disposal relief (see Chapter 31 for an outline of business asset disposal relief).

(h) Delaying a disposal may enable a taxpayer to become resident outside the UK. With the changes to the taxation of direct and indirect sales of UK land by non-residents from 6 April 2019, the benefits are much more limited, but there could be an exemption for sales of shares in a property rich company where the investment holding has been less than 25% in the last two years.

(i) A deferral for an individual to the next year may mean that the capital gain is taxed at a lower rate (eg 10% rather than 20% for assets other than residential property and sales of carried interests post-5 April 2016) if other income and capital gains are not sufficient for this capital gain to be taxed at the higher rate.

A deferral may not always be the best outcome so it will be important to consider the implications, particularly if a gain could be sheltered by current year losses.

**Point 13.2:** ***A gain can be deferred from one accounting period or tax year to the next if either exchange of contracts is deferred or there is a conditional contract. Deferring completion will not make any difference to the date of the chargeable disposal.***

The date of disposal for capital gains tax purposes is the date when unconditional contracts are entered into (*TCGA 1992, s 28(1)*). Completion is irrelevant as far as the *date* of disposal is concerned. Interestingly, following a House of Lords' decision, it seems possible for a different person to be treated as making the disposal if that person steps into the shoes of the seller before completion. In the case in question, the benefit of a contract to sell land was transferred to an offshore trust before completion (*Jerome v Kelly* [2004] UKHL 25).

Disposals are treated as occurring after the contract date where the parties have entered into a conditional contract (*TCGA 1992, s 28(2)*). In that case, the sale is treated as taking place on the date the condition is satisfied or, if there is more than one condition, when the final condition is satisfied.

---

## Example 1

Glover Ltd contracts to sell land to Stanning Ltd on 30 December 2022, provided planning permission is granted. At that point, the contract is conditional and, in Glover Ltd's year ended 31 December 2022, there is no disposal for the purposes of corporation tax on capital gains.

The land receives planning permission in February 2023. At that point, the contract becomes unconditional, and the chargeable disposal arises in Glover Ltd's year ending 31 December 2023.

---

In recent years, parties to property transactions have used the device of cross-options with the object of deferring exchange of contracts.

---

## Example 2

Archibald grants an option to Barker under which Barker can require Archibald to sell him a site at a specific price on or after 6 April next (the call option). At the same time, Barker grants Archibald an option under which Barker can be required to purchase this land on or after 6 April next (the put option). Both Archibald and Barker are in a position to require the other party to enter into a legally binding agreement at any time on or after the following 6 April.

---

If put and call options taken together can be considered to constitute a binding contract to buy and sell at the time they are granted, no deferral is achieved. There is less exposure to an HMRC challenge, however, where the price of the put option materially differs from the price of the call option.

An alternative to cross-options is the use of a conditional contract. In a commercial context, it is common to find contracts conditional on obtaining, say, planning permission, landlord's consent to an assignment, or clearance from HMRC. A quoted company may also enter into a major contract conditional on obtaining shareholders' approval at a general meeting to be held after the end of its accounting year.

In these cases, the disposal will not take place until the condition is satisfied. For a contract to be treated as conditional, it is essential that the condition relates to an uncertain future event which is not within either party's power to bring about.

*Chapter 14*

# Capital gains planning: selling the company rather than the property and the further possibility of selling to a UK REIT

**Selling shares in a company rather than the company selling the property and distributing the proceeds will normally save tax - particularly if a favourable deal can be struck over the inherent tax on capital gains in the company.**
**Point 14.1**

↓

Selling a property investment company to a UK real estate investment trust (REIT) can provide an exit without any price reduction for the inherent tax on capital gains
Point 14.2

↓

In addition to the price benefit of selling to a REIT, a vendor can indefinitely defer any tax on the share sale by taking shares or even loan stock in the REIT.
Point 14.3

↓

Consider paying a pre-sale dividend.
Point 14.4

# 14 CAPITAL GAINS PLANNING: SELLING THE COMPANY RATHER THAN THE PROPERTY AND THE FURTHER POSSIBILITY OF SELLING TO A UK REIT

**Point 14.1:** ***Where an investment property is owned by a company, the sale of the shares in the company is usually a more tax-efficient alternative to selling the property and extracting the proceeds from the company. It also minimises stamp taxes for the purchaser.***

Where an investment property is held within a company, the shareholders could suffer two charges to tax on any appreciation of the property.

The first occasion of charge arises when the company sells the property. Corporation tax on the capital gain would be payable by the company at that stage.

The second occasion of charge arises when the shareholders extract their profit from the company. This might be as remuneration, by way of dividend, or a capital distribution on liquidation of the company. Dividends received by UK corporate shareholders are normally exempt from corporation tax (*CTA 2009, ss 931A–931W*). Where the substantial shareholdings exemption (see Chapter 32) does not apply, it could be more tax efficient for a company to extract profits by dividends rather than as a capital disposal (see Point 14.4 below).

For individuals, remuneration would be assessable to income tax on the recipient who would also suffer employee's National Insurance Contributions (NICs). Employer's NIC would also be payable by the company. For an investment company, there may well be no corporation tax relief for the remuneration paid if HMRC consider that it exceeds a reasonable expense of managing the company's affairs.

Dividends are taxable on individual or trustee recipient shareholders as income and the company will receive no tax relief for the payment. However, no NIC is payable.

On the liquidation of the company, capital distributions received by the shareholders will be assessed to tax as a capital gain in so far as they exceed the original subscription or, as the case may be, the price paid by the shareholder for the shares. The position, though, is somewhat more complicated due to revamped legislation in the *Finance Act 2016* where HMRC might attempt to argue that an income distribution arises in some circumstances, under the Targeted Anti-Avoidance Rule (TAAR).

In view of the 'double taxation' effect of extracting the proceeds of a property sale from a company, it is often preferable to sell the company itself. This assumes, of course, that the property is the sole or main asset of the company.

The purchase of a company's shares rather than the property it owns also significantly reduces stamp taxes. The buyer of property in England or Northern Ireland would have to pay up to 5% SDLT on the purchase price of non-residential property. For residential property, SDLT can be up to 12% where the value is £1.5 million or more, or indeed 15% if the buyer is itself a company or other non-natural person (see Chapter 5),with non-UK residents subject to a 2% SDLT surcharge on the acquisition of residential property in England and Northern Ireland since 1 April 2021.

A buyer of a property in Scotland will pay Land and Buildings Transaction Tax with a top rate on residential of 12% and 5% for non-residential. A buyer of a property in Wales will pay Land Transaction Tax with a top rate on residential of 12% and 6% for non-residential. Higher stamp taxes at up to 16% (from 22 December 2020) may also arise where additional residential property is acquired.

A buyer of shares, however, pays only 0.5% stamp duty on the price of the shares. In practice, this will be less than 0.5% of the value of the property if the value of the company is less than the value of the property (for instance, as a result of company indebtedness). No UK stamp duty at all may be payable if the shares are in a foreign company. See Point 5.8 for a further discussion on the stamp duty issues on selling a company. Against this must be balanced the Annual Tax on Enveloped Dwellings (ATED) that the government introduced with effect from April 2013 where companies and other non-natural persons hold certain types of high value residential property (see Chapter 5).

Sometimes a prospective purchaser will require a discount on the share price to reflect the inherent capital gain in the company. However, it then becomes a matter of the negotiating power between the parties as to whether the vendor can reduce the discount and so obtain a benefit from proceeding in this manner.

---

## Example 1

A UK resident property investment company with a March year end purchased an office building in 1970 for £500,000. All the shares in the company are owned by a UK resident husband and wife, the company had no other assets or liabilities, and any net income has been distributed.

The value of the building in March 1982 was £3 million. In April 2017, an offer of £15 million was accepted for the property. The company had no other assets and liabilities at that point.

The tax payable by the company on the prospective gain in this situation would be around £908,580 illustrated as follows:

| | £ |
|---|---|
| Proceeds | 15,000,000 |
| Value at 31 March 1982 | (3,000,000) |
| | 12,000,000 |
| Indexation allowance | |
| 3,000,000 × 2.406 | (7,218,000) |
| Chargeable gain | 4,782,000 |
| Tax at 19% (pre April 2023 rate) | 908,580 |

---

(*Note*: This example ignores transaction costs and assumes there has been no enhancement expenditure.)

If, in this example, the shareholders could persuade the prospective purchaser to buy the company instead, any sum received in excess of £14,091,420 (ie £15 million proceeds less the company's inherent tax liability) would increase the net sum due to the shareholders. This amount would be subject to capital gains tax, but would result in a much higher net return to the shareholders than the payment of a dividend or of remuneration.

Since 5 April 2016, the capital gains tax rate has been 20% (previously 28%) on non-residential property and other assets for taxpayers whose income and gains take them into the higher-rate tax bands. It remains at 10% (previously 18%) for basic-rate taxpayers. The purchaser would be saving at least £675,000 in stamp taxes by buying the shares in the company (ie 5% less 0.5% of £15 million). For residential property, the SDLT saving is potentially much greater.

It should be noted that the purchase of the company would not have increased the base cost of the property. The tax liability on the property is simply deferred until it is eventually disposed of by the company (see Point 14.2 below). As mentioned in Point 8.2, applying for clearance from HMRC may be advisable for some disposals.

**Point 14.2:** ***Selling a property investment company to a UK real estate investment trust (REIT) may present an opportunity to exit without a significant or any price reduction for the inherent corporation tax on capital gains within the company.***

An issue generally for buyers and sellers of UK resident property companies is the underlying taxable capital gains that would be crystallised within the target company when its properties are eventually sold. The tendency is for the price of such companies to be reduced to reflect a discount on the market value of the properties to account for this inherent tax.

The buyer may, therefore, be reluctant to pay £15 million for a company with £15 million worth of property where there may be potential exposure to, say, £1 million corporation tax if the properties were sold at that value. In those circumstances, the prospective buyer may only be prepared to offer, say £14 million, although a higher figure may be negotiated if the buyer has long-term plans to retain the property.

With the introduction of the real estate investment trust (REIT) in January 2007, a prospective purchaser need not face this issue, because a qualifying REIT is not liable for UK corporation tax on its capital gains on the sale of its investment properties. In passing, it should be noted that the changes in *Finance Act 2019* effective April 2019 confer a similar tax-exempt status on qualifying collective investment vehicles that elect for exempt status; further details are provided in Chapter 1.

A REIT is a property investment company or group whose shares (the shares of the parent company) are admitted to trading on a recognised stock exchange.

The stock exchange can be outside of the UK, but the company itself must be UK tax resident.

The REIT would typically hold all or most of its assets as let investment property. This is because it is a requirement of REIT status that not less than 75% of income and asset value must be derived from let property. The REIT also has a number of other conditions, including the need to distribute 90% of its net UK rental income each year to shareholders. There are also requirements in terms of its shareholders and gearing ratios. The government's intention in creating the REIT was to establish a vehicle through which institutions and the public could invest in property in a reasonably marketable and low-geared manner.

Within any group that meets the requisite REIT conditions, individual companies can generate property income and gains from selling investment property without being subject to UK tax. This will equally apply to any companies which are acquired by a qualifying UK REIT notwithstanding that there may be significant inherent chargeable gains on the target company's property assets at the time of acquisition.

*Finance Act 2019* introduces from April 2019 a further exemption for REITs making indirect disposals of qualifying property rich companies.

These changes make it easier and cheaper for companies to obtain REIT status.

**Point 14.3:** ***In addition to the price benefit of selling to a REIT, a vendor can indefinitely defer any tax on the share sale by taking shares or even loan stock in the REIT.***

With any corporate sale, there is potential for deferring tax on capital gains where the consideration received is in the form of shares or loan stock issued by the purchasing company as opposed to cash. The position is no different where the buyer is a UK REIT.

This may be an attractive proposition for any individual or family looking to exit from a corporately held property or property portfolio, using the opportunity to invest in a possibly bigger property fund where there might be lower long-term risk and higher marketability of the investment. In addition to issuing shares, some REITs may offer this option in the form of fixed-rate preference shares or indeed loan stock. They may also offer the vendors various other permutations, including taking some cash and a combination of these types of security.

The deferral of tax in any such situation is always contingent on HMRC being satisfied that the transaction is being carried out for bona fide commercial reasons and not for the avoidance of tax. It may be desirable to take advantage of the advance clearance procedure available under *TCGA 1992, s 138* and *ITA 2007, s 701*. Generally, if the reasons behind the structuring are those referred to above, or the REIT itself is keen to finance a transaction as far as possible through the use of its own paper, that would normally be sufficient to satisfy this bona fide test.

**Point 14.4:** ***Where an investment property is owned by a company, a pre-sale dividend could reduce the tax suffered by corporate shareholders on the gain on selling the company.***

Where the substantial shareholdings exemption does not apply (see Chapter 32), a capital gain may arise on the disposal of a subsidiary. This gain may be reduced or eliminated by a pre-sale dividend. Dividends received by UK companies are generally exempt from corporation tax, and a pre-sale dividend should lead to an overall reduction in corporation tax. Clearly, this is not normally appropriate for individuals, as the tax rates for income can be higher than the CGT rates.

---

## Example 2

Hill Ltd is a property investment company which is wholly owned by Jones Ltd. Jones Ltd is able to dispose of Hill Ltd and realise a gain of £10 million. As an alternative, Hill Ltd could pay out a dividend of £10 million which would not be taxable on Jones Ltd. Hill Ltd could then be disposed of without realising a gain.

This is, of course, subject to Hill Ltd having sufficient distributable reserves to pay a dividend. Additionally, anti-avoidance provisions, notably *CTA 2010, Pt 15* (transactions in securities), will need to be considered.

---

*Chapter 15*

# Enterprise Investment Scheme deferral relief and Seed EIS CGT exemption

**Any tax arising on the sale of a property investment company can be deferred indefinitely by reinvesting into the shares of a suitable unquoted trading company. There may also be opportunities under the SEIS scheme.**

**Points 15.1, 15.2 and 15.3**

# 15 ENTERPRISE INVESTMENT SCHEME DEFERRAL RELIEF AND SEED EIS CGT EXEMPTION

**Point 15.1:** ***It is possible to defer tax indefinitely on the gain on the sale of a property investment company by reinvesting the gain into a suitable unquoted trading company.***

Property investors have never been able to benefit from the capital gains roll-over relief available to traders who reinvest the proceeds of the sale of trading premises into new premises and/or other trading assets (see Chapter 30). However, individuals and trustees can defer gains by reinvesting into shares in suitable companies that qualify for the Enterprise Investment Scheme (EIS). This relief is not available to companies.

An individual or trustee that realises a gain on the sale of an asset can defer any tax on the gain by subscribing for shares in companies which satisfy conditions for the EIS (*TCGA 1992, Sch 5B*).

Income tax relief at 30% is available on the investment as well, provided, broadly that the individual is not connected with the company and holds no more than 30% of the shares. However, if the individual wishes to claim deferral relief only, these exclusions do not apply. An individual seeking to defer a capital gain can establish, or invest into, their own trading company if they wish, providing it meets the qualifying conditions.

The company must be unquoted and carry on a trade, but some trades are excluded. The excluded activities are:

(1) dealing in land, commodities, futures, shares, securities or other financial instruments;

(2) dealing in goods other than in the course of an ordinary trade of wholesale or retail distribution;

(3) banking, insurance, money-lending, debt factoring, hire purchase financing or other financial activities;

(4) leasing (including letting ships on charter) or receiving royalties or licence fees;

(5) providing legal or accountancy services;

(6) property development;

(7) farming or market gardening;

(8) holding, managing or occupying woodlands or other forestry activities;

(9) shipbuilding, producing coal or producing steel;

(10) operating or managing hotels or comparable establishments;

(11) operating or managing nursing homes or residential care homes;

(12) all energy generating activities where shares issued after April 2016 unless related to development of innovative generation technologies; and

(13) providing services to a commonly controlled company that itself carries on one of the above trades.

(*ITA 2007, s 192(1)*) A company which has been trading for more than seven years old (measured from its first commercial sale), and did not issue EIS, SEIS or VCT shares in its first seven years, is excluded unless it raises EIS/VCT money amounting to at least 50% of its five-year average turnover, and spends that money on entering a new product or geographic market within a 30-day period. Each new business activity must satisfy the 50% turnover test. A number of smaller unconnected initiatives cannot be combined in order to meet the 50% threshold.

This seven-year period is extended to 10 years if the company is a Knowledge Intensive Company (KIC). A KIC can also elect to have an initial investing period of 10 years from the date by reference to which it reaches an annual turnover of £200,000. There are additional, complex rules that have to be met to qualify as a KIC, but, broadly, a company that carries on substantial research and development to grow its business should qualify.

Since 6 April 2012, there have been additional restrictions such that the acquisition of shares or stock in a company does not, of itself, qualify as a qualifying business activity. These restrictions were extended further from 18 November 2015 to deny, as a qualifying business activity, certain other acquisitions. These rules are intended to stop EIS money being used for takeover or buyout situations where there is an existing trade.

Since 6 April 2011, it is sufficient for the company issuing the shares to have a permanent establishment in the UK (*ITA 2007, ss 180A and 191A*). It is no longer required to carry on a trade wholly or mainly in the UK. The company need not be UK resident and there have been no changes in this regard.

A further condition relates to the size of the company. To qualify for deferral relief, the company issuing the shares must not have gross assets in excess of £15 million immediately before the shares are issued, or £16 million after the shares are issued. Where the company has subsidiaries, that test is applied to the group as a whole (*TCGA 1992, Sch 5B*; *ITA 2007, s 186*). Additionally, the company must have fewer than 250 'full time equivalent' employees (500 for a KIC).

Additionally, a company must not raise more than £5m finance in any 12-month period (unless it is a KIC which can raise £10m in a 12-month period) or a total of £12m through any combination of EIS and venture capital trust investment (and other forms of state aid risk capital). For a KIC, the total State aid investment cannot exceed £20m.

Although the company must be unquoted, companies whose shares are dealt in solely on secondary markets such as the Alternative Investment Market (AIM) can qualify.

Finally, the company in question cannot be a 51% subsidiary, or otherwise be under the control, of another company (*ITA 2007, s 139*). Nor can it control another company that is itself not a 'qualifying' subsidiary (*ITA 2007, s 140*).

To qualify for the relief, the individual or trustee must subscribe in cash for shares in a qualifying company up to one year before or within three years after the disposal giving rise to the gain. The shares must be ordinary shares with no preferential rights or rights to be redeemed (*TCGA 1992, Sch 5B, para 1*). For shares issued since 6 April 2012, preferential dividend rights may be permissible provided they are not cumulative and dividends are not discretionary.

It should be noted that, unlike the relief on replacement of business assets (or 'roll-over relief') dealt with in Chapter 30, it is sufficient to reinvest only the gain to obtain full tax deferral under EIS deferral relief. For roll-over relief on replacement of business assets, the entire proceeds of sale have to be reinvested for full deferral.

There are provisions for clawback of the relief if certain things happen within three years of the issue of the shares, eg where:

(a) the acquired shares cease to be eligible shares for EIS relief (*ITA 2007, s 173*);

(b) the company ceases to be a qualifying company (*ITA 2007, s 181*); or

(c) the person holding the shares becomes resident outside the UK (unless the reason for this is a short-term working assignment abroad) (*TCGA 1992, Sch 5B, para 3*).

The relief is also clawed back if the person holding the shares or any associate receives value from the company during the four-year period which starts one year before the issue of the shares. The whole of the gain would then be brought into charge, no matter how much or little value was received, subject to the EIS *de minimis* limits on value.

Of course, the deferred gain also comes into charge whenever the shares are disposed of, unless the disposal is a transfer to the disponer's spouse at no gain, no loss. The revived gain will be subject to CGT at the rates and subject to the legislation in force at the time the gain is brought back into charge. However, gains made on or after 3 December 2014, which were eligible for business asset disposal relief when they originally occurred will be come back into charge at the business asset disposal relief rate of 10%, under current legislation.

The conditions for EIS deferral relief are restrictive. The EIS rules are complex and contain many pitfalls that can result in denial of the relief. Care is therefore required to ensure that the rules are not breached, not just when investing, but also for three years following the issue of EIS shares.

Where the investment in the company also meets the more restrictive conditions for income Enterprise Investment Scheme relief, the subscription cost of new shares acquired have attracted income tax relief under EIS at a rate of 30% since 6 April 2011 and the future growth in value can be tax free. Furthermore, the shares can be eligible for 100% business property relief for inheritance tax purposes, should there be a future gift of them or legacy on death.

In order to prevent SEIS/EIS and VCT tax reliefs being given for investments in low-risk investments, the 'risk-to-capital' condition was introduced by *Finance Act 2018* which has two parts that must be met:

(a) the investee company must have objectives to grow and develop over the long term; and

(b) the investment must carry a significant risk that the investor will lose more capital than they gain as a return.

HMRC list certain factors which will be considered to determine whether there is any capital preservation activity, for example:

- looking at whether the turnover or number of employees are expected to increase;
- whether the company has any assured income streams in place or assets being used to secure the investment or generate a low-risk income steam;
- whether the company has a founder/entrepreneur involved in the business or whether it was set up by a promoter and their associates;
- whether the investment is marketed as a short-term investment with low risk; and
- whether large amounts of money are being raised for a number of companies carrying out similar activities.

This has introduced another judgemental element to the relief.

At the same time there were positive changes announced relating to 'knowledge-intensive companies' ('KICs'). If the investee company is a KIC it can raise up to £10m in a 12-month period from SEIS, EIS and VCT rather than £5m for other qualifying companies. Additionally, the amount individuals can invest each year in EIS companies is £2m per year, provided they invest at least £1m in KICs, from 6 April 2018.

**Point 15.2:** ***Since tax year 2012–2013, it has been possible to obtain an exemption from tax on a capital gain by reinvesting the proceeds into qualifying shares issued under the Seed Enterprise Investment Scheme.***

The Seed Enterprise Investment Scheme (SEIS) started on 6 April 2012 and individuals can invest up to £200,000 per annum (£100,000 pre 6 April 2023) spread over a number of UK companies (although they must not own more than 30% of the share capital or voting rights in each company). The scheme is targeted at small companies, which undertake, or are preparing to undertake, approved trades, with less than 25 employees and gross assets of less than £350,000 (£200,000 pre 6 April 2023).

As with EIS, the SEIS shares can be eligible for 100% business property relief for inheritance tax purposes, should there be a future gift of them or legacy on death.

The maximum gain that can be held over is 50% of the relevant expenditure. Accordingly, if the full £200,000 is invested gains of £100,000 can be held over. This is in addition to income tax relief for the qualifying amount invested and an exemption from tax on capital gains on shares within the scope of SEIS.

*Chapter 16*

# Planning for losses: capital losses and surplus management expenses

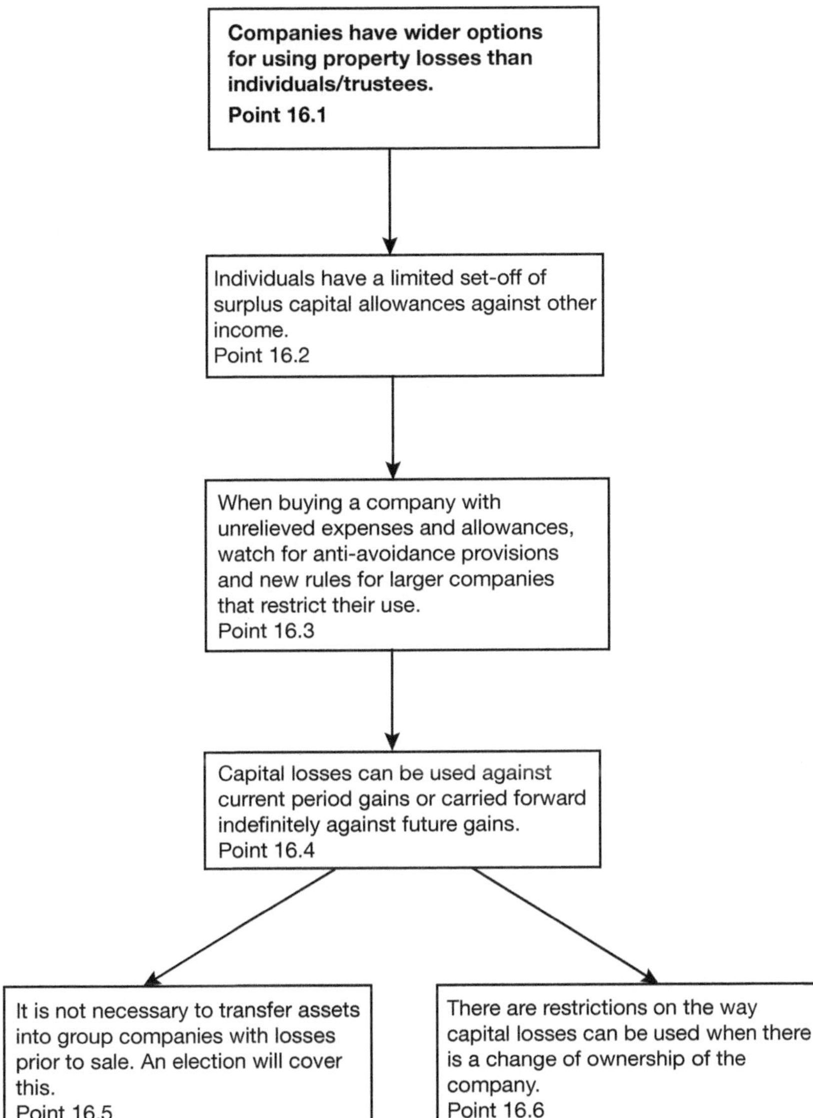

# 16 PLANNING FOR LOSSES: CAPITAL LOSSES AND SURPLUS MANAGEMENT EXPENSES

**Point 16.1***: **An excess of property expenses over rents will give rise to property losses. For taxpayers other than UK resident companies, the use of these losses is restricted to current or future property income. For a UK company, a more general offset is available for such losses.***

The income tax regime treats property investment losses differently from corporation tax. Income tax applies to individuals and trustees. UK-resident individuals and trusts are also subject to capital gains tax.

For individuals and trustees, property expenses (including finance costs, subject to certain restrictions, and capital allowances) can be deducted from rental income of the property activity. Any surplus expenses are available to carry forward against future property income (*ITA 2007, s 118*). There is no general offset against other income except for some limited scope in respect of surplus capital allowances (see Point 16.2 below). Furthermore, no successor to the property can inherit any entitlement to unrelieved expenses or allowances.

There are restrictions on the deduction of finance costs for non-corporate owners letting residential property (*ITA 2005, s 272A*). From 5 April 2020, only basic rate income tax relief is allowed.

A UK resident company is not restricted in its use of surplus property expenses in the same way as individuals. Any losses from its property rental business can be set against its total profits (including capital gains) for the period. Any excess may be surrendered as group relief. Any balance can be carried forward to the next period for set-off against total profits so long as the property rental business is still undertaken by the company (*CTA 2010, s 62*). For losses arising in respect of accounting periods commencing on or after 1 April 2017, this requires a claim to be made. Such losses are treated as UK property business losses of that accounting period and are therefore available to be offset against all profits. This treatment is only available if the letting business is carried on commercially with a reasonable expectation of profit. If, however, the letting business has ceased, any surplus expenses in the accounting period are treated as management expenses provided the company continues to be a company with investment business (*CTA 2010, s 63*).

Finance costs are treated separately with their own rules for general offset (see Point 3.16 in Chapter 3B). Furthermore, there is a category of 'management expenses' for which there is also general offset as referred to above (*CTA 2009, s 1219*).

A company can be sold, with the purchaser inheriting the entitlement to use unrelieved losses carried forward. However, there are anti-avoidance tax rules that can make it difficult for companies to use these losses under new ownership in certain circumstances (see Point 16.3 below).

Management expenses are the revenue costs of running the company as distinct from the properties. They would include:

- audit and accountancy;
- directors' fees;
- administrative salaries; and
- expenses of premises and equipment used in administration of the business.

These expenses, together with surplus finance costs, can also be offset against the company's total income and gains for the period. To the extent that there is an unrelieved surplus, they can be set off against any other group company profits for the year. Surplus management expenses can then be carried forward indefinitely against future income and gains as long as the company remains a 'company with investment business' and under the same ownership. 'A company with investment business' is any company whose business consists wholly or partly in the making of investments (*CTA 2009, s 1218*). Surplus management expenses cannot be carried back.

A company's surplus finance costs can be carried back to the previous period to reduce net finance profits or carried forward indefinitely to set against total profits (see Point 3.16 in Chapter 3B). For periods prior to 1 April 2017, the carried forward losses could only be offset against non-trading profits.

For periods after 1 April 2017, new rules were introduced for loss offset. Where profits arising after that date exceed a £5m *de minimis* figure per group per annum, the loss offset is restricted to 50% of those profits. This de minimis is adjusted for accounting periods of less than 12 months and certain restrictions depending on the other companies within the group. However, a company's carried forward losses arising after 1 April 2017 can be offset against other group companies' income and gains. There are, however, a number of detailed conditions that need to be satisfied and elections that need to be made in order to benefit from this treatment.

**Point 16.2:** ***For individuals and trusts, there is a limited offset for capital allowances against other income.***

The regime for individuals is much more restrictive than for UK companies. There is no general offset against income or gains.

Individuals and trustees can offset losses up to the amount of net capital allowances against other income (but not gains) in the year.

Where a loss arises following a claim to capital allowances, it is possible to offset that loss against general income in the same year of assessment or the next. The amount of loss relief will be restricted to the lowest of the following:

(a) the loss;

(b) the other income for the year; and

(c) the amount of capital allowances after deducting any clawback of allowances.

(*ITA 2007, ss 121–123*)

If the allowances remain unrelieved, any carry-forward is only against income from the property activity. Note that the ability for individuals to offset allowances and losses against other income is subject to a restriction, which limits the deduction to the greater of £50,000 or 25% of the individual's income (*ITA 2007, s 24A*).

HMRC treat an individual's share of a partnership's rental business as a separate business from his or her own rental business. In this regard, losses from one business cannot be offset against profits from another. This may not be the case with other joint venture structures. Therefore, where offset may be required, the legal documentation and commercial activities of a proposed joint venture should be carefully structured to avoid it becoming a partnership.

**Point 16.3:** ***The ability to deduct past unrelieved expenses and losses against all future profits can make an investment company with these losses attractive to a buyer. However, the availability of these losses can be affected by wide-ranging anti-avoidance rules and proposed new rules for larger companies.***

Anti-avoidance rules can prevent the carry forward of an investment company's losses in certain circumstances following a change in ownership. These bite where any of the following applies, as well as on a change of ownership:

(a) there is a significant increase in the company's capital;

(b) there is a major change in the nature or conduct of the business within the eight years commencing three years before the change in ownership; or

(c) the scale of activities of the company revives, having become small or negligible before the change.

(*CTA 2010, s 676AA* and *CTA 2010, s 677*)

The period referred to at (b) above applies where there is both a change in ownership and a major change in the nature or conduct of the business on or after 1 April 2017. If one of these takes place before this date the provisions of *s 676AA* are not in point and the period is six years commencing from 3 years before the change in ownership.

Broadly, a significant increase in capital arises where the value of redeemable loan stock and debt plus shares either doubles, or increases by at least £1 million (*CTA 2010, s 688*). A major change in the nature or conduct of business can include the transfer of an asset into the company from another group company (*CTA 2010, s 692*).

Where any of the above three conditions applies, none of the unused management and other expenses incurred before the date of the change of ownership are available to carry forward.

Following a change of ownership, a company's structure and activities should be monitored to ensure that the company does not fall foul of any of the above. The buyer could, for instance, plan on the basis of the losses being used, only to have HMRC seek to recover the tax relief several years later because the anti-avoidance conditions have been subsequently met.

The restriction to past losses could also apply to finance costs for which a deduction has been delayed for over 12 months since accrual. These rules are now contained in *CTA 2009, ss 372–379*. (See Point 3.17 above for the circumstances in which such late-paid interest is disallowed.)

The *Finance Act 2013* introduced additional complex anti-avoidance provisions aimed at loss and capital allowance buying. These can apply in certain circumstances where a company is acquired with the objective of accessing surplus expenses or annual capital allowances to shelter future taxable profits of the acquiring company/group (*FA 2013, Sch 26*). In addition, the *Finance Act 2015* introduced further anti-avoidance provisions to prevent companies from obtaining a corporation tax advantage by entering contrived arrangements to convert certain brought forward reliefs into more versatile current year deductions.

As mentioned in 16.1, there are also separate provisions that restrict the offset of carried forward losses to 50% of the group's profits subject to a £5m *de minimis*. These rules are also to apply to capital losses from 1 April 2020 – see 16.4 below.

## Point 16.4: *Capital losses can currently be used against current period gains or carried forward indefinitely against future gains.*

If an individual or company realises a loss on the disposal of a capital asset in a tax year or accounting period, this loss can be offset against any chargeable gain arising in the same year. Unused capital losses can be carried forward against future capital gains but never carried back, except on the taxpayer's death (when a three-year carry back is allowed) (*TCGA 1992, s 2(3)*).

Note that, where capital losses arise following a transaction with a connected person, their use is restricted. They can only be offset against gains arising on disposals to the same connected person.

In a year when a chargeable gain is likely to arise, it may be appropriate to review other assets to see whether there might be potential for realising any capital losses. The following opportunities might be available, for example:

(a) Where assets cease to have any value, a claim can be made to HMRC for any loss to be recognised in the year of claim. Such assets might include investments that have become worthless (including shares in an associated company) or possibly a property interest that has become onerous (*TCGA 1992, s 24*). Such a negligible value claim can be related back up to two years.

(b) The outright sale of any asset standing at a loss in the period in which a capital gain is likely to arise. Note, however, that the sale must be to an unconnected party. A capital loss realised on a sale to a connected party can only be offset against gains from disposals to the same person (*TCGA 1992, s 18*).

It has been possible to crystallise losses on quoted shares which are subsequently re-acquired. However, there are anti-avoidance rules for individuals to inhibit arrangements where shares are bought and sold for tax mitigation reasons (*FA 2006, s 74*).

Additionally, anti-avoidance rules exist for all taxpayers to restrict capital losses where there are arrangements which have the purpose or main purpose of securing a tax advantage (*TCGA 1992, s 16A*). Both individuals and companies can carry a capital loss forward. It is important, therefore, that details of unused capital losses are maintained with current tax information.

Where the ownership of a company changes, the future use of capital losses may be severely restricted (see Point 16.6 below). The application of these rules differs from those restricting management expenses, property losses and finance costs.

Since 1 April 2020, the proportion of annual capital gain that can be relieved by brought forward capital losses is restricted to 50%. The restriction does not apply to the first £5m of carry forward loss utilisation (whether capital or income-type losses).

Without specific rules, companies could attempt to circumvent these rules in the period prior to the legislation being enacted. As such, certain anti-forestalling provisions were brought in to ensure that where companies with accounting periods ending before 1 April 2020 were entering into arrangements (on or after 29 October 2018) whereby one of the main purposes was to secure a tax advantage, it would limit the deduction for all capital losses brought forward to 50% of the qualifying chargeable gains for the accounting period.

Where the company's accounting period straddles 1 April 2020, it has to be split into two and the restriction then applies to the period pre 1 April 2020.

**Point 16.5:** ***Within a group of companies, tax shelter may be available for capital gains by using a capital loss or surplus management expense company. It is not necessary, however, to physically transfer assets into such a company prior to sale. It is possible, instead, to make an election to transfer the gain to the appropriate company.***

An investment company can shelter chargeable gains by offsetting brought-forward capital losses (Point 16.4 above) or surplus non-trading expenses (see Point 16.1 above).

It is sufficient for the group company (X) selling the property and the company with losses (Y) to make a joint election that the property should be treated as transferred into and sold by Y. The gain is therefore treated as realised by Y and can be offset against its available losses (*TCGA 1992, s 171A*). *S 171A* enables a company to elect all or part of a gain (or loss) into another group company as opposed to deeming the property to be transferred. In most cases, this change will not impact on the tax position.

In many cases, this election will be made to use a fellow group company's losses (or gains). It might, for example, also be used to preserve losses in the actual selling company, particularly if there is a greater likelihood that these losses will be needed in future in comparison with Y's losses.

The election offers some flexibility, in that the gain or loss can be deemed to have arisen in more than one company. Accordingly, parts of the gain or loss can effectively be allocated between several companies, depending on the shelter available in those companies.

The election must be made within two years of the end of X's accounting period in which the property is sold. Elections are not restricted to onward sales to third parties. .

**Point 16.6:** ***There are restrictions on the use of losses within an acquired capital loss company.***

Anti-avoidance provisions can affect the availability of capital losses within a company. Under these provisions, where a company has become a member of a group since 1 April 1987, losses attributable to the pre-group period ('pre-entry losses') may not be offset against subsequent gains (except in certain circumstances).

These provisions were intended to stop companies sheltering capital gains by buying capital loss companies. However, they will apply in quite genuine commercial situations where groups may need to plan the matching of gains and losses more carefully.

For gains arising on or after 19 July 2011, the restrictions generally only apply to the use of losses realised prior to the loss company joining the new group. The legislation has been simplified as the targeted anti-avoidance rules in *TCGA 1992, s 184A* (see below) will still apply to situations where a company is acquired with unrealised losses as part of an avoidance scheme. In addition, since 19 July 2011, a company carrying on a business (including investment situations) can use its pre-entry losses against assets subsequently acquired and used in its business.

A pre-entry asset can also include a further asset acquired subsequently which derives its value from the first asset (*TCGA 1992, Sch 7A, para 1(8)*).

The efficacy of the arrangements put in place prior to 5 December 2005 has been successfully challenged by HMRC, thus preventing an arrangement designed to use past capital losses (*Limitgood Ltd v Revenue and Customs Commissioners*; *Prizedome Limited v Revenue and Customs Commissioners* [2009] EWCA Civ 177). HMRC have also successfully countered a similar arrangement in front of the Special Commissioners in another case (*Five Oaks Properties Limited v Revenue and Customs Commissioners* [2006] STC (SCD) 769). Since 5 December 2005, losses have not been allowed where there has been a change of ownership of a company and, broadly, there are arrangements designed to secure a tax advantage from tax losses which accrued before the change. There is, accordingly, a tax avoidance motive test which leaves little scope to defeat the rules through exploitation of any technical loophole (*TCGA 1992, ss 184A–184F*).

*Chapter 17*

# Planning for losses: transfer of investment property to a dealing company

Certain tax planning opportunities can arise where there is anticipated gain on the property.
Point 17.1

# 17 PLANNING FOR LOSSES: TRANSFER OF INVESTMENT PROPERTY TO A DEALING COMPANY

**Point 17.1:** ***Certain tax planning opportunities can arise where there is an anticipated gain on the property.***

An investment company transferring a property to a fellow group company would be treated as making a disposal at no gain, no loss for tax purposes (*TCGA 1992, s 171*). A dealing company acquiring the property will be deemed to have done so at the original base cost to the group. On appropriation to trading stock, the dealing company has a choice of two alternative values to apply on the transfer of the property into trading stock:

(a) market value (*TCGA 1992, s 161(1)*); or

(b) market value as reduced by any chargeable gain arising or increased by any chargeable loss, subject to the point below (election under *TCGA 1992, s 161(3)*).

The election possibility under option (b) can be useful where the sale of an investment property might otherwise give rise to a capital loss. Its effect is to turn the capital loss into a trading loss, which will either be realised on sale or recognised at the end of the accounting period when the property must be written down to market value to comply with generally accepted accounting practice. Since 8 March 2017, it is not possible to make an election under *TCGA 1992, s 161(3)*, if a loss would otherwise arise on an appropriation. Accordingly, such planning is no longer effective.

A tax planning opportunity can, however, arise where there is an anticipated gain on the property. It may be that there is a dealing company within the group which has brought forward trading losses arising prior to 1 April 2017 that can now only be carried forward and used against future trading profits in that company. If the property investment company were to sell the property to a third party directly, then any gain arising in that company would be taxable without any prospect of shelter from the past trading losses of the fellow group company.

If the property were transferred into the dealing company and then sold, the effect of the *s 161(3)* election would be to convert a chargeable gain into a trading profit in the transferee company. The brought-forward losses should be available to offset against this trading profit, and any tax liability that would otherwise arise could be eliminated. Note that it would be necessary to consider potential SDLT (see point 17.2 below) and VAT aspects of such a transfer.

Although references above are to group situations, the election is also relevant where a company reclassifies a property in its own accounts and can also apply to individuals, partnerships and trustees. When planning on the above lines, consideration must be given to the comments in Point 17.2 below.

Note that no similar election is available where a property is appropriated the other way, ie from trading stock to fixed assets. In this case, a taxable profit by reference to market value will arise at that point.

**Point 17.2: *The implications of decisions in Furniss v Dawson and Coates v Arndale Properties Ltd had restricted the scope of certain tax planning opportunities referred to above.***

In *Coates (Inspector of Taxes) v Arndale Properties Ltd* [1984] STC 637, there was an attempt to claim a substantial loss on an investment property as a trading loss, following its transfer from an investment company to a dealing company within the group. The property was subsequently transferred on to another group company within a short period. The House of Lords considered that the transaction was fiscally motivated and the only reason for the intra-group sale was to obtain a tax deduction. The Law Lords, accordingly confirmed the Court of Appeal's view that the dealing company had not acquired the property in question as trading stock.

Notwithstanding the *Coates v Arndale* decision, a dealing company should still be able to acquire a property as trading stock from a fellow group member, but the following points should be adhered to:

(a) The transfer of the property into the dealing company should be made as soon as a decision is made to dispose of the property. If it is left until such time as a buyer is found, HMRC could ignore the transfer to the dealing company.

(b) The transferee company should actually be an established property dealing company with a history of dealing in a similar type of property.

(c) The dealing company should carry out the necessary marketing of the property and incur any further finance charges. Any conversion or rectification of the property prior to sale should be carried out by the dealing company.

(d) The eventual sale should be to a third-party purchaser and not to another group company or connected party.

(e) For accounts purposes, the transfer consideration should be at a value which enables the dealing company to make a commercial profit. This will be adjusted in the tax computations since the figure determined in accordance with *TCGA 1992, s 161(3)* (see Point 17.1 above) will be adopted as cost for tax purposes.

The judgment of the Court of Appeal in *New Angel Court Ltd v Adam* [2004] STC 779 confirms this advice. The judges held that the fact that a group of companies wished to obtain a tax advantage was not relevant in deciding whether an asset is acquired as trading stock. What matters is whether there is a trading purpose or not. If the properties transferred to the dealing company were assets of a kind that were sold in the ordinary course of the dealing company's trade and were acquired by that company for the purposes of its trade, that was sufficient. Also, the commercial rationale for the transfer is important in the context of SDLT where the rules could deny the intra-group exemption for tax-motivated transfers (*FA 2003, Sch 7, para 2(4A)*).

*Chapter 18*

# VAT planning for property investors

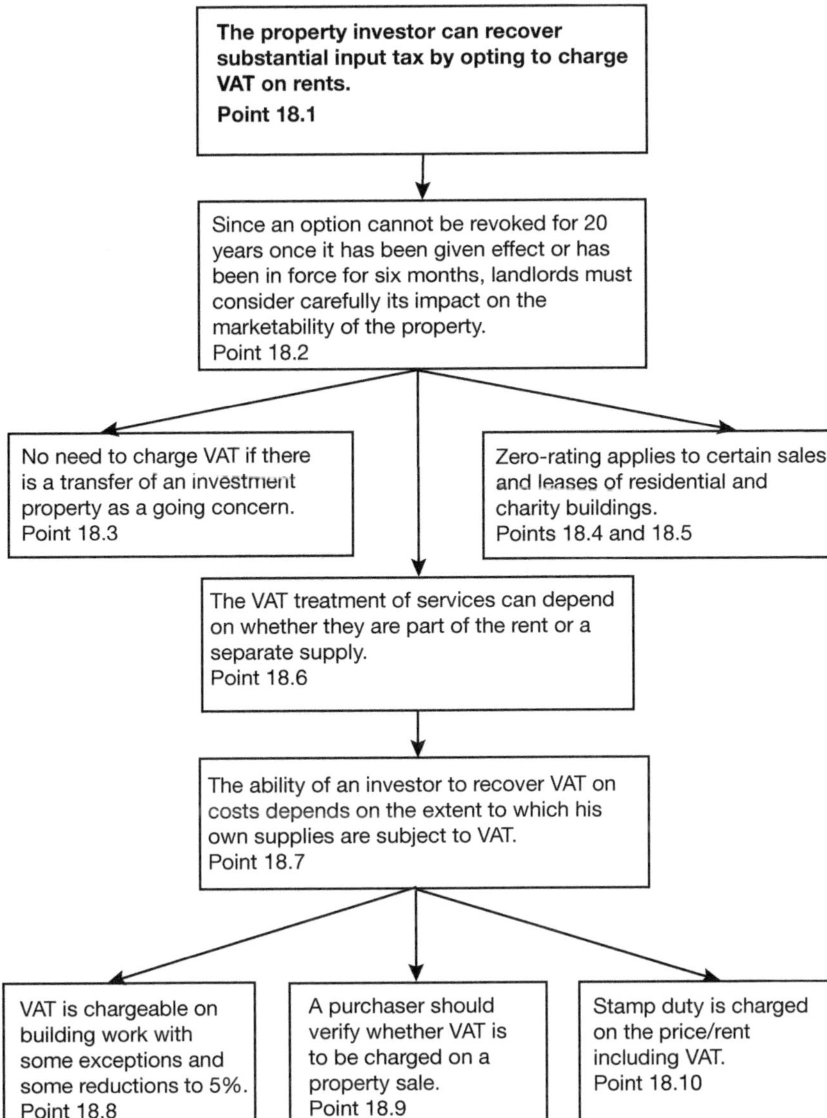

# 18 VAT PLANNING FOR PROPERTY INVESTORS

**Point 18.1:** ***The property investor can recover substantial input tax by opting to charge VAT on rents.***

The letting of property is normally an exempt supply for VAT purposes although there are exceptions in certain situations, including where leases are granted in residential property or in property for relevant residential or relevant charitable purposes where the first grant may qualify for zero-rating (see Point 18.4 below).

The implication for a property investor of having exempt supplies is that no related input tax can be recovered. Accordingly, a property investor has to bear the additional VAT cost of any refurbishment or repair work together with any ongoing professional and agents' costs, unless it can be passed on to the tenants through any service charge.

A property investor can, however, opt to tax a commercial building. In doing so, it is opting to apply VAT to future rents, grants of leases and sales in relation to that building. In that case, any input tax attributable to the taxable supply would be recoverable from HMRC.

The standard rate of VAT is 20%.

Opting to tax is a two-stage process as follows:

(1) the property investor makes the decision to opt to tax; and

(2) notifies HMRC within 30 days from the date when the decision to opt was made.

Prior to 1 September 2022 when HMRC received a VAT 1614 form (the form used to notify HMRC of the option to tax) they would send an acknowledgment letter confirming the opter's option to tax was valid. However, since 1 September 2022 acknowledgement letters have been replaced by a receipt letter, confirming an option to tax notification had been received, and recorded by HMRC.

Since 1 February 2023, HMRC have stopped issuing option to tax notification receipt letters.

Where the option to tax notification is sent by email to optiontotaxnationalunit@hmrc.gov.uk, the property investor will receive an automated response that will have the date when the notification was received by HMRC on it and which should be kept for records.

It is recommended that the following information should be included in the subject line of the email:

- Property address, including post code;
- Effective date of the option to tax notification.

Where a property investor is buying an opted property, it is always recommended that they request proof of the option to tax, as incorrectly charged VAT is not recoverable. Also, where a property is sold/purchased as a going concern proof of the option to tax should be requested.

Since HMRC's changes to the option to tax notification procedure, the evidence that can be provided now is a copy of the notification together with the automated email response.

We recommend that, when notifying an option to tax to HMRC, it is actioned via email and that an 'option to tax register' for all real estate owned by your business is maintained.

The option can be made on any building by:

- naming individual buildings;
- opting for all of the investor's buildings without naming them;
- opting for all the investor's buildings with specially named exceptions; or
- opting for all of the investor's buildings, together with any that he subsequently acquires.

Since 1 June 2008, it has also been possible to opt on a specified geographical area such as City of London, Bristol, Wales, etc.

The option can be made for any specified piece of land.

An option to tax made post-1 June 2008 applies to the land on which it is made, to any building on that land and to any building subsequently built on that land. Where an option to tax was made on a building pre-1 June 2008, it may be taken as not applying to the land or to any building subsequently built on that land if the building on which the option was made is demolished.

An option to tax applies to the whole of the building on which it is made, to any buildings which are connected internally or by covered walkways, and to the whole of an enclosed concourse or precinct.

In practice, unless there is a particularly large portfolio of properties, it is advisable to opt to tax properties or land on an individual, clearly identified basis. This avoids unintentional options and provides a clear audit trail which may be required for any subsequent disposal.

There is no requirement for the person making the option to tax to have an interest in the building or land at the time of making the option to tax.

HMRC introduced a range of certificates (VAT 1614A–1614J) which must be used for notifying an option to tax to HMRC, or advising a seller or landlord that an option to tax does not apply to a particular transaction. It is recommended that the making of an option to tax is recorded in a board minute or similar document.

There are situations in which an option, although properly made, may have no effect. These are:

- where a building or part of a building is used or is to be used as a dwelling or for a 'relevant residential purpose' (see Point 18.4 below);
- where the building or part of the building is used by a charity for its charitable activities. This does not include property used by a charity for business purposes or as an office;

- where an interest in land is granted to an individual who intends to construct a dwelling as a DIY house builder;
- where an interest in land is granted to a registered housing association for the development of residential accommodation; and
- where an existing commercial building will be converted into dwellings. From 1 June 2008, there is scope for an intermediary in a chain, where a building will ultimately be used for residential purposes, to also benefit from the exclusion from the effects of an option to tax.

The grantee must provide a certificate in order to disapply any option which has already been made by the grantor, except in the case of buildings designed as dwellings or of land acquired by a DIY house builder.

There are also provisions which disapply an option to tax from any grant of a property where there is a connection between the parties and there is an intention or expectation of exempt or non-business use by the occupier of the building. These are commonly referred to as the 'anti-avoidance' provisions and are addressed in more depth at Point 35.4. The rules are exceedingly complex, and the connection which disapplies the option to tax can arise through 'funding' of a development. So, for example, a bank providing finance for a shopping centre development and then taking a lease in a unit in the development may cause the rules to be brought into effect, thus disapplying the investor's option to tax, resulting in a consequent loss of input tax recovery.

Sometimes, HMRC must give their express permission before an option to tax can be made. This applies where there have been exempt supplies in relation to the property. Application must be made on Form VAT 1614H and will usually take some time to obtain. There are provisions set out in Notice 742A for a landlord to assume 'automatic permission', but these are tightly drawn and must be treated with great care.

The option to tax can be made at any time, subject to any requirement to obtain permission from HMRC. For an option to be effective notification must be made to HMRC within 30 days of the option being made. There are further time limits in respect of a transfer of a business as a going concern (TOGC) (see Point 18.3 below).

Where VAT has been incurred on the purchase of a property or on its refurbishment, it is advisable that any letting or grant of a lease immediately after that should be on a fully taxable basis (ie the option to tax should be made). Otherwise, there may be no immediate entitlement to recover VAT. If the letting of the property is subsequently made subject to VAT, an entitlement to recover VAT may commence under the Capital Goods Scheme. However, VAT recovery will be spread over ten years. See Point 35.7 for a discussion on the Capital Goods Scheme.

Once an option to tax has been made, it will apply to any supply involving that property unless it is disapplied by the provisions outlined above. Accordingly, the property investor must charge VAT on any future sales of the property or grants of further leases in addition to charging VAT on all future rentals.

An option can be revoked in two instances. There is a six-month 'cooling off' period after an option has been made whereby, provided that no input tax has been recovered in respect of the opted property and no supplies of the property have yet been made, the option can be revoked. In the second instance, the option can be revoked after 20 years. In certain situations an option will also be automatically revoked after the person who made it has held no interest in the property for at least six years. This automatic revocation will not apply to companies that have been affected by an option to tax within a VAT group.

In addition to those circumstances where an option to tax is disapplied from a grant because of the buyer's or tenant's intended use, the option to tax has no effect in those circumstances where the supply is otherwise subject to VAT, ie excluded from the scope of the exemption as detailed at Point 18.9 below. Notable amongst these exclusions is the supply of holiday accommodation.

Holiday accommodation is defined as any accommodation held out for holiday use or where the occupation throughout the year or use as a principal private residence is precluded by the terms of any planning or similar permission. The letting of holiday accommodation is subject to VAT at the standard rate, as is the sale of the freehold or the grant of a lease in a new building (less than three years old) comprising holiday accommodation. The sale or the grant of a lease for a premium in an old building containing holiday accommodation is, therefore, exempt from VAT. This means, for example, that the sale of a newly built holiday home is subject to VAT, but the sale of a barn converted into a holiday home is exempt – with the consequent prejudice to input tax recovery. It is however possible to opt to tax holiday accommodation.

**Point 18.2:** ***Since an option cannot be revoked for 20 years once it has been given effect or has been in force for six months, landlords must consider carefully its impact on the marketability of the property.***

As indicated in Point 18.1 above, the attraction of opting to tax rents is that the property investor can recover input tax on expenditure incurred. This also has the benefit of ensuring no irrecoverable VAT is passed to the tenants by being locked into the service charge. However, it may be important to consider the impact of opting to tax on future tenants and purchasers of the property.

Where a tenant is a VAT-registered business making fully taxable supplies, that tenant will be entitled to recover all VAT on rents charged. However, there are a number of businesses and organisations that make exempt or partly exempt supplies for VAT purposes, which will not be in a position to recover in full the VAT they incur. These include banks, buildings societies, betting shops, foreign exchange shops, and insurance brokers. National Health Service Trusts and charities may also be unable to reclaim VAT input tax, depending on how they use the premises in question.

Such prospective tenants will attempt to resist the additional rent costs arising from irrecoverable VAT if they can. If the bargaining position of the tenant is strong enough, any property investor that has opted to charge VAT may find that there is a compensating reduction in the rent charged.

Some leases may specify that VAT cannot be charged or that the rent is inclusive of any VAT. In those circumstances, any option to tax will shift the burden of tax from the tenant to the landlord, ie the landlord will be required to pay the VAT out of the rent received.

Apart from the loss of income in these situations, the property investor will also be faced with a reduced capital value of the property asset.

**Point 18.3:** ***The need to charge VAT on the sale of an opted property does not arise where it is a transfer of an investment business as a going concern.***

There is a useful relief in the VAT system which was drafted to facilitate transfers of businesses without VAT consequences, but which may be applied to certain property situations.

Certain transfers of business assets are outside the scope of VAT. Where this is relevant, VAT cannot be charged on the sale. The main advantage to the purchaser is often the cash flow saving arising from not having to pay VAT, although, as identified at Point 5.4, there will also be a saving in stamp duty land tax (SDLT), as SDLT is calculated on the VAT-inclusive selling price. The VAT-free treatment applies where there are sales of assets in connection with a TOGC. The necessary conditions for this relief are:

(a) The assets are to be used by the buyer in carrying out the same kind of business, whether or not as part of an existing business, as they were used in by the transferor.

(b) There must not be a series of immediately consecutive transfers of the business.

(c) The buyer is either already registered for VAT or immediately becomes eligible to register as a result of the transfer.

(d) If part of a business is being transferred, that part must be capable of separate operation.

(e) If the vendor has opted to tax a property which will be included in the transfer, the buyer must notify HMRC in writing, before the time of supply (ie completion or the payment of a deposit unless paid to a stakeholder), that it also has opted to tax.

(f) The buyer must warrant in writing before the time of supply that *SI 1995/1268, art 5(2B)* does not apply to him. (See below in relation to 2004 anti-avoidance legislation.)

(*Value Added Tax (Special Provisions) Order 1995, SI 1995/1268, art 5(2)*)

The above rules can benefit property investors because property investment is regarded as a business for VAT purposes. Each property within a portfolio is a part of that business capable of being operated as a separate business by the purchaser. A let or partly let property is, therefore, capable of being sold by one investor to another as the transfer of a property investment business and regarded as neither a supply of goods or services for VAT purposes,

An unlet building would not normally qualify under these rules, as the business has not been commenced; but, if the property is sold with the benefit of a prospective tenancy, ie an agreement for lease has been signed, there is scope for TOGC treatment to apply. This arrangement must not be contrived (*HMRC v Royal College of Paediatrics and Child Health and Coleridge (Theobalds Road) Ltd* ([2015] UKUT 0038 (TCC).

The situation may be different if a partly completed building is sold in the course of development to a buyer who carries on the activity. That could be treated as a sale of a property development business as a going concern (*Golden Oak Partnership v C & E Comrs* (1992) VAT decision 7212).

Where the tenant is a member of the same VAT group as the landlord, the letting is not treated as a business, as supplies between VAT group members are not recognised for VAT purposes. Prior to the decision in *Intelligent Managed Service Limited* [2015] UKUT 0341 (TCC) (IMSL), HMRC took the view that any sale where the tenant is in the same group as either the seller or the purchaser cannot be a TOGC. HMRC are now of the view that if a business is transferred to a company in a VAT group and both:

- that company intends to continue to use the transferred assets to operate the same kind of business in providing services to other group members; and
- those other group members use the services to make supplies outside of the group;

then the transfer is a TOGC at the first stage.

HMRC has also revised its policy relating to transfers out of a VAT group. Where, were it not for the VAT grouping rules, a business exists, the normal TOGC rules apply to transfers out of a VAT group.

A TOGC is not an exempt supply. It should not, therefore, give rise to any clawback of VAT input tax previously claimed by the seller. However, if the seller did not make any taxable supplies at all in relation to the property, HMRC may seek to argue that the input tax should not have been recovered in the first place.

With regard to VAT on costs relating to the transfer itself, HMRC take the following view:

- VAT incurred on services that have a direct and immediate link with the transferred part of a business should be treated as an overhead of that part of the business;
- where that part of the business makes only taxable supplies, then the VAT incurred is deductible;
- where that part of the business makes only exempt supplies, then the VAT incurred is not deductible; and
- in instances where both taxable and exempt supplies are made by that part of the business, the VAT incurred is partly deductible by reference to the partial exemption method in place.

HMRC had maintained that for a sale to qualify as a TOGC the seller must be selling the whole interest held in the property. However, following a 2012 decision of the First-tier Tribunal (*Robinson* TC02046), HMRC accept that the grant of a significant interest, where the seller retains a small reversionary interest, could qualify as a TOGC, provided all the other conditions ((a)–(e) above) are satisfied. HMRC considers that a small reversionary interest should be seen as no more than 1% of the value prior to the sale (HMRC Brief 30/12).

HMRC also accepts that in certain circumstances the surrender of a lease, with the benefits of a sub-tenancy, can qualify as a TOGC. (Business Brief 27/2014).

In 2004, anti-avoidance legislation relating to TOGCs of property was introduced. This legislation targets certain VAT avoidance schemes that used the TOGC rules to reduce the VAT cost for businesses which cannot recover all the VAT they incur. Where relevant, the legislation can both render the sale subject to VAT and block the recovery of VAT by the buyer. This anti-avoidance legislation is tied to the anti-avoidance legislation which disapplies an option to tax, and only applies to properties which fall within the CGS (see also Point 35.7).

**Point 18.4:** ***Zero-rating will apply to sales and the initial lease of certain new buildings and newly converted buildings, thus avoiding potentially irrecoverable VAT on development expenditure.***

As mentioned in Point 18.1 above, zero-rating applies in certain situations involving residential property and buildings used by charities.

Eligibility for zero-rating arises in the following cases:

(a) Where a person who has constructed a new building, which is designed for use as a dwelling, for a 'relevant residential' or a 'relevant charitable' purpose, makes their first grant of a major interest in it.

(b) There is also a similar treatment for the first grant of a major interest in a substantially reconstructed protected building (Point 18.5 below) by the person reconstructing it.

(c) Where a person who has converted a non-residential building into one which is designed as a dwelling or number of dwellings, or for a 'relevant residential purpose', makes their first grant of a major interest in it.

A major interest, for this purpose, would be a freehold sale or a grant of a lease in excess of 21 years (20 years in Scotland).

Conversion does not include simply refurbishing, altering, extending or reconstructing a building. Furthermore, grants of interests on buildings that have been converted from one type of residential use to another (for example, from a nursing home to flats) will not qualify for zero-rating and will be exempt.

Use for 'relevant residential purpose' includes use as:

(a) a home or other institution providing residential accommodation for children;

(b) a home or other institution providing residential accommodation with personal care for persons in need of such care by reason of old age, disablement, past or present dependence on alcohol or drugs or mental disorder;

(c) a hospice;

(d) residential accommodation for students or school pupils;

(e) residential accommodation for members of any of the armed forces;

(f) a monastery, nunnery or similar establishment; and

(g) an institution which is the sole or main residence of at least 90% of its residents.

Use as a hospital, prison or other similar institution, or as a hotel or similar establishment, does not constitute use for a 'relevant residential purpose'.

Use for a 'relevant charitable purpose' means use by a charity otherwise than in the course or furtherance of a business. It specifically includes, however, use of a property by a charity as a village hall or similar building providing social or recreational facilities for a local community.

Where the use is for a relevant residential or relevant charitable purpose, the supply only qualifies for zero-rating if the supply is to the user of the property (eg not to an intermediate purchaser) and the user provides a certificate confirming the use. Draft certificates are contained in Notice 708, section 18.

The VAT treatment of construction work is discussed in Point 18.8 below.

Whilst a property investor should be able to recover any input tax incurred on the development of a dwelling, or a relevant residential or relevant charitable building, any VAT on ongoing costs would not be recoverable, as it will relate to exempt supplies. The property investor can no longer recover input tax relating to future repairs or agent's costs, for example, and HMRC have challenged arrangements put in place to try and circumvent this.

It is only the consideration for the first grant of a major interest (ie a premium or the first rental payment) that is zero-rated; any subsequent rents or subsequent disposals will be exempt. This means that, for an investor, input tax on the development costs may be protected, but input tax on subsequent costs, such as repair and maintenance, may not be recoverable.

Where any property is mixed and includes residential, charitable and commercial use, then the rental income or disposal proceeds must be apportioned between the relevant parts and VAT charged accordingly.

One type of property which causes particular problems is the live/work unit as, for VAT purposes, this is seen as a mixed-use building, and rental income or disposal proceeds may have to be apportioned and treated differently for the different parts of the building.

**Point 18.5:** ***Zero-rating has been removed from situations where the property is a protected building used for relevant residential or charitable purposes.***

The 2012 Budget removed zero-rating from works of approved alterations to listed buildings for residential or charitable use from 1 October 2012, subject to certain transitional provisions. The removal of this zero-rating will also remove the ability to make zero-rated grants of leases of substantially reconstructed listed buildings which fall within Test (a) below. The transitional provisions introduced for works commenced and contracts entered into before the 2012 Budget provide that:

- Zero-rating for works of approved alterations can continue until 30 September 2015 for works where a written contract was entered into or the application for listed building consent was made before 21 March 2012;
- The application for later variations to approved alterations applied for before 21 March 2012 does not remove zero-rating to the extent the works are in accordance with a permission applied for before 21 March 2012; and
- Zero-rating for the first grant of a major interest under Test (a) below applies until 30 September 2015 where 60% of the works qualified for zero-rating or 10% of the works of substantial reconstruction were completed before 21 March 2012.

The zero-rating of construction work or the first 'supply', as discussed in Point 18.4 above, generally only applies where there is a complete construction of a new building. The requirement is, however, modified in the case of protected buildings.

As a matter of public policy, a number of buildings are protected from demolition for conservation reasons. These buildings are listed by the Department of the Environment, Food and Rural Affairs and by local authorities where they are considered to have continuing historical and architectural interest.

Where buildings and monuments are listed, building work is often prohibited insofar as it affects the façade together with any external features of architectural or historical significance. In addition to planning permission, listed building consent is often also required for specific building work and this could well vary from building to building.

If the building is used or intended to be used as a dwelling, a number of dwellings or for relevant residential or relevant charitable purpose, zero-rating will apply where the person granting a major interest in the protected building has carried out or commissioned works amounting to a 'substantial reconstruction'.

Prior to 1 October 2012 there were two separate tests for zero-rating as outlined below:

> A protected building is substantially reconstructed when major work takes place to its fabric, including the replacement of much of the internal or external structure, and either:

Test (a) at least 60% of the total cost of the reconstruction (including materials and other items to carry out the work but excluding the services of an architect, surveyor or other person acting as consultant or in a supervisory capacity) could be zero-rated as 'approved alterations'; or

Test (b) the reconstruction involves 'gutting' the building – that is no more of the original building is retained than an external wall or walls, or external walls together with other external features of architectural or historic interest.

From 1 October 2012, subject to the transitional provisions as outlined above, Test (a) has been removed and zero-rating is only available where Test (b) applies, ie the building is gutted.

Whether or not work amounts to a substantial reconstruction is clearly critical to the VAT status. If the project satisfies this test, the grant of a major interest will be zero-rated and any VAT on construction-related costs can be reclaimed. If the test is not met, the supply will be exempt and input tax recovery will be denied.

As mentioned in Point 18.4 above, only the first grant of a major interest by the person substantially reconstructing will be zero-rated. Furthermore, VAT is only recoverable on the reconstruction expenditure and not on any ongoing costs.

The question of whether a project qualifies as a substantial reconstruction under Test (a) is a difficult area for the tax specialist alone to comment on. Very often, this may be a matter which must be discussed between tax advisers, surveyors and architects at the planning stage before a project can be commenced with any certainty that zero-rating might apply.

Test (b) is more clear-cut, but in respect of both it is important to note that there are two stages to the test: the first is that, as a matter of fact, the building must be substantially reconstructed; then, secondly, either 60% of the works must qualify as approved alterations or the building must be gutted. It is not sufficient just to satisfy the 60% test.

As mentioned at Point 18.8 below, subject to its removal from 1 October 2012 and the transitional provisions, where zero-rating applied it applies to works which are both alterations to the fabric of a listed building and require – and have received – listed building consent, provided the building is to be used for a qualifying purpose. Any works which constitute reinstatement or repair and maintenance are excluded from the zero-rating and would normally be standard-rated. However, if the building in question is also being converted to form a different number of dwellings, has been empty for more than two years, or the works otherwise qualify for the reduced rate VAT, those works which are not zero-rated should qualify for the 5% rate.

It is quite possible, where a commercial listed building is being refurbished and converted in part to, say, flats, for VAT on the works to be subject to VAT at three different rates – the standard rate on the commercial element, the zero-rate for any approved alteration for the flats, and the 5% rate for the remaining works. If the works cannot be clearly measured, HMRC will accept that VAT can be charged at the appropriate rates on the basis of a fair and reasonable apportionment.

**Point 18.6:** ***Where services are provided by a landlord, they may be treated as part of the rent or as a separate supply of services. The best treatment from the landlord's viewpoint may depend on whether the rent charge is standard-rated.***

If a landlord provides services or facilities in addition to the rent, the VAT implications will have to be considered. There are two broad categories of service provision:

(a) Normal services provided under the terms of the lease for which all tenants pay in addition to the rent. Whether or not separate charges are made for these, they are regarded as further consideration for the grant of the lease. If this consideration is exempt, charges in respect of these services will be exempt. If the consideration is standard-rated, these charges will be standard-rated. Typically, such services include cleaning, maintenance, repairs, rates and insurance, but may encompass other services such as reception, light and heat or even office facilities.

(b) Services provided separately to individual tenants and for which different charges may be involved depending on usage. This may include heating, lighting, telephone and office services. The range of services will be greater for serviced offices and certain residential accommodation, possibly including receptionist, secretarial and computer facilities. As separate supplies, these are all standard-rated, but if they were provided under the terms of the lease their VAT treatment would follow that of the lease.

Where a landlord has opted to tax and is letting to commercial tenants, VAT will be charged on rents in either scenario, so the treatment is of little consequence. The landlord will still be able to fully recover input tax.

The main impact of the distinction lies where the landlord has not opted to tax. In that case, services provided in category (a) will give rise to additional exempt outputs. If the landlord is incurring VAT on supplies it receives, that VAT is irrecoverable, and may be passed on to the tenants as an increased service charge to the disadvantage of those tenants who are able to recover all their input tax.

Service charges to freehold owners are standard-rated, as they cannot be attached to any rental charge (see (a) above). However, by concession, mandatory service charges to freeholders of residential accommodation for the maintenance of common parts and similar services can be treated as exempt from VAT.

See Point 18.7 below for a further discussion on recovering input tax.

**Point 18.7:** ***If a property investor's supplies are all exempt, no input tax can be recovered. If, on the other hand, supplies are partly standard-rated and partly exempt, input tax must be attributed as far as possible to the related supply (including future supplies) and will be recoverable or irrecoverable accordingly.***

A business which has both taxable and exempt income is generally referred to as a partly exempt business and will need to consider how much input tax can be recovered.

The position on the recovery of input tax can be summarised as follows:

(a) input tax which is directly attributable to taxable supplies (taxable input tax) can be reclaimed in full;

(b) input tax which is directly attributable to exempt supplies (exempt input tax) is in principle irrecoverable; and

(c) input tax which is common to the business generally, or cannot be directly attributed to taxable or exempt supplies (residual input tax), should be apportioned between taxable and exempt supplies in order to determine the recoverable element. The apportionment must be carried out according to the standard partial exemption method (based on the value of taxable supplies compared to the value of taxable and exempt supplies) or, with HMRC's written approval, with reference to a special partial exemption method. In some circumstances, as an anti-avoidance measure, a 'use'-based apportionment may be required in place of either of the above alternatives, if the alternatives produce a result which is too favourable to the business.

A newly VAT registered business, or one which has just begun to incur exempt input tax, can itself apply a use-based partial exemption calculation for an initial period. This would be either the period up to the end of its first 'VAT year' (the registration period), or its first VAT year if exempt input tax was not incurred in the registration period.) The VAT year runs to the spring VAT return period end – ie March, April and May). This can be of particular benefit to a property investor as it allows a sensible input tax deduction to be achieved without the need to apply to HMRC for a special method in circumstances where the standard method would produce an unfavourable result. A typical example would be where an investor has acquired a mixed use property, or is carrying out some development to a mixed use property, but has not yet begun to receive taxable income.

VAT incurred prior to VAT registration can be claimed from HMRC on a business's first VAT return, to the extent that it relates to taxable or intended taxable supplies. For goods, the rules allow recovery of VAT incurred in the 4 years before the date of registration provided the goods are 'on hand' at the time of registration; but for services the limit is six months. These rules do not allow recovery of VAT incurred on a 'capital item' falling within the Capital Goods Scheme. See Point 35.7 for discussion on the Capital Goods Scheme,

Being a party exempt business does give rise to some important VAT implications for property investors. In the first place, it will be noted that inputs should be associated as far as possible with related supplies. For the property investor, this may mean looking at each property separately. If rents or premiums received in respect of a particular building are standard-rated, then all input tax relating specifically to that building, eg on repair work or management fees, should be recoverable. Similarly, if a building is generating exempt supplies, then all the related input tax is irrecoverable.

Where the option to tax rents is effective (see Point 18.1 above) input tax can be recovered, but where the rental income is exempt, either because the option to tax has not been exercised or because it is disapplied, the input tax cannot be recovered, subject to the partial exemption *de minimis* limits (see below). In a mixed-use building (such as a shop with flats above), an apportionment of input tax will be necessary in accordance with the partial exemption method applied.

For intended transactions, it is necessary to look at the nature of the anticipated income to determine the input tax recovery. HMRC accept that a taxpayer can have an intention to make taxable supplies before an option is in place, although clear documentary evidence of this intention is essential to support input tax recovery. Of course, the best documentary evidence of an intention to make taxable supplies is still a valid option to tax notification on form VAT 1614A.

For speculative property transactions, it is necessary to consider the intended nature of the anticipated supplies. If the supplies would be wholly taxable, input tax is recoverable; whereas, if the supplies would be exempt, the input tax is not recoverable. In those cases where the nature of the supply is unclear or will be a mixture of taxable and exempt elements, VAT on initial costs should be treated as residual input tax and apportioned as an overhead of the business. Once the nature of the project is determined, suitable adjustments to VAT recovery can be made.

Where input tax has been claimed in respect of intended taxable supplies, that input tax may need to be refunded to HMRC if an exempt supply takes place before taxable supplies are made. This can be the case within six years of the input tax being claimed under what are known as the 'clawback' and 'payback' rules. This may also be the case where an intention is formed to make an exempt supply. The rules also work in reverse and allow input tax to be recovered where it was originally not claimed in anticipation of exempt supplies, but is ultimately used in making taxable supplies (*VAT Regulations 1995, regs 108, 109*).

Where the first use of a property is for VAT exempt purposes, recovery of input VAT incurred may only be possible under the Capital Goods Scheme rules – ie no upfront recovery, but recovery spread over the remaining years of the relevant Capital Goods Scheme period. See point 35.7 for commentary on the Capital Goods Scheme.

There are *de minimis* limits below which there will be no restriction in VAT input recovery. In this connection, input tax which relates directly or indirectly to exempt supplies will be recoverable if it is less than £625 a month on average and it does not exceed 50% of all the input tax for that period (*VAT Regulations 1995, reg 106*).

**Point 18.8:** ***Where new property is being built for either residential, relevant residential or relevant charitable use, VAT should not be charged on most of the construction cost. Other building work will be standard-rated or may be subject to VAT at 5%.***

Certain building works in connection with new residential property, or property used for charitable purposes, will be zero-rated, as were certain works to listed buildings until 30 September 2015.

The following works qualify for zero-rating:

(a) supplies of services in the course of the construction of a building (or part of a building) designed as a dwelling or number of dwellings (*VATA 1994, Sch 8, Group 5, Item 2(a)*).

(b) supplies of services in the course of the construction of a building (or part of a building) intended for use solely for a 'relevant residential purpose' or a 'relevant charitable purpose' (*VATA 1994, Sch 8, Group 5, Item 2(a)*) to the 'user' of that building. See Point 18.4 above for relevant residential and charitable use.

(c) supplies of services to housing associations in the course of the conversion of non-residential buildings into dwellings or buildings for a relevant residential use (*VATA 1994, Sch 8, Group 5, Item 3*).

(d) 'approved alterations' to a protected building designed to remain as, or become, a dwelling or number of dwellings or intended for use solely for a 'relevant residential purpose' or 'relevant charitable purpose' after the reconstruction or alteration, *but* from 1 October 2012 only to the extent that the works are carried out by 30 September 2015 and are in accordance with a listed building consent applied for or a written contract entered into before 21 March 2012 (*VATA 1994, Sch 8, Group 6, Item 2*).

(e) supplies of services in the course of the construction of any civil engineering work necessary for the development of a permanent park for residential caravans (*VATA 1994, Sch 8, Group 5, Item 2(b)*).

In each case, the services of an architect, surveyor or any person acting as consultant or in a supervisory capacity are standard-rated, unless subsumed into a 'Design and Build' contract.

The supply of building materials in conjunction with the construction services by the person supplying those services is also zero-rated (*VATA 1994, Sch 8, Group 5, Item 4* and *Group 6, Item 3*). However, there are certain prescribed exceptions where VAT must be charged at the standard rate and cannot be recovered by the developer; these include carpeting, fitted furniture (other than kitchen furniture) and certain gas and electrical appliances.

Where the buildings are to be used for a relevant residential or relevant charitable purpose, zero-rating is only available where the supply is to the user and the user produces a certificate to the builder stating that the building is to be used for such purposes. Sample certificates are illustrated in the HMRC Notice 708 Buildings and Construction, section 18.

The question of whether or not the construction of a new building (or substantial reconstruction of a protected building) has taken place is crucial to the issue of whether VAT is charged upon the building work. HMRC have issued guidelines in their Notice 708. These can be summarised as follows:

A zero-rated building is constructed when the following applies:

(a) it is built from scratch;

(b) before work starts, any pre-existing building is demolished completely to ground level (cellars, basements and the 'slab' at ground level may be retained);

(c) it makes use of no more than a single façade (or a double façade on a corner site) of a pre-existing building, the retention of which is an explicit condition or requirement of statutory planning consent;

(d) an enlargement or extension of an existing building creates an additional dwelling or dwellings;

(e) a self-contained annexe to an existing building is built and it is intended solely for a relevant charitable purpose;

(f) a garage is built, or a building is converted into a garage, and it is constructed or converted at the same time as, and intended to be occupied with, a building designed as a dwelling or number of dwellings; or

(g) a building is built that is one of a number of buildings constructed at the same time on the same site and it is intended to be used together with those other buildings as a unit solely for a relevant residential purpose.

(HMRC VAT Notice 708, Buildings and Construction, section 3.2)

The Notice gives common examples of work that cannot be zero-rated, such as:

- a 'granny' annexe which cannot be used, or disposed of, separately from a main house;
- a detached, enclosed swimming pool in the grounds of a new house; and
- a detached building in the grounds of an existing care home which extends the facilities of the home.

There are also notes on determining the position where party walls are involved. For instance, in determining whether a building has been demolished, the retention of party walls forming part of a neighbouring property that is not being developed can be ignored. Therefore, a building is constructed when there is an infill in a row of terraced houses, provided the pre-existing house/houses is/are demolished completely (apart from the party walls at the end of the infill site) and any retained façade is retained as a condition or requirement of planning consent.

When redeveloping neighbouring houses in a terrace, the party wall between the houses being redeveloped will also need to be demolished before there is the construction of a new building for VAT purposes.

The enlargement of, or extension to, an existing building can be zero-rated to the extent that the extension or enlargement contains an additional self-contained dwelling, provided:

(a) the new dwelling is wholly within the enlargement or extension; and

(b) the new dwelling is 'designed as a dwelling'.

So, for example, a new flat built on top of an existing building can be zero-rated.

If the new dwelling is partly or wholly contained within the existing building, work cannot be zero-rated under these rules. It may be possible to reduce the rate of charge as a 'changed number of dwellings conversion' (see Notice 708, section 7, and the comment below). Also, the sale or long lease of the new dwelling may qualify for zero-rating if the existing building was a non-residential building (Notice 708, section 5).

Note that in litigation (*Astral Construction Ltd* [2015] UKUT 0021(TCC)) the Upper Tribunal accepted that the construction of a nursing home, which contained an older building (a church), which was insignificant in scale to the completed nursing home, qualified for zero-rating as the construction of a new building.

The construction of a new building as holiday accommodation will still qualify for zero-rating if the building satisfies the test to be regarded as a dwelling. The fact that it is to be used for holiday accommodation does not, on its own, detract from its status as a dwelling.

The reduced rate of VAT, currently at 5%, applies to construction works in two broad categories. The first is in respect of conversion of buildings into dwellings or other residential uses, and the second is where empty residential property is being refurbished and brought back into use. The reduced rate does not apply to any supplies of land or buildings, only to construction services.

The following supplies are chargeable at the reduced rate of 5%:

(a) converting a non-residential property into one or more single-household dwellings;

(b) converting a non-residential property into a building used solely for a 'relevant residential purpose';

(c) converting a non-residential property into a house in multiple occupation;

(d) changing the number of single-household dwellings in a building;

(e) converting a single-household dwelling or a house in multiple occupation into a building used solely for a 'relevant residential purpose';

(f) converting a house in multiple occupation into a single-household dwelling;

(g) converting a single-household dwelling into a house in multiple occupation;

(h) converting a building used for a 'relevant residential purpose' into a house in multiple occupation;

(i) renovating or altering a single-household dwelling that has not been lived in for at least two years;

(j) renovating or altering a building used solely for a 'relevant residential purpose' that has not been lived in for at least two years;

(k) renovating or altering a house in multiple occupation that has not been lived in for at least two years;

(l) constructing, renovating or converting a building into a garage as part of the conversion or renovation of a property that qualifies for the reduced rate; and

(m) building materials and certain other goods incorporated by a builder into a building in the course of supplying services under (a)–(l) above.

A single-household dwelling is a dwelling intended for occupation by a single household (ie a single individual, a couple or a family).

A house in multiple occupation is a building that contains bed-sit accommodation.

For the definition of a relevant residential building, see Point 18.4 above.

The reduced rate can also apply to certain grant-funded heating installations and energy-saving materials.

The reduced rate is wider in its application than was the zero-rate for approved alterations to listed buildings, and will apply to works of repair and maintenance as well as any alterations and extensions.

It should also be remembered that HMRC will accept a fair and reasonable apportionment of any charges between the different rates of VAT, where one project contains elements subject to VAT at different rates. However, if the builder does not agree to make an apportionment, the whole will be subject to VAT at the standard rate.

**Point 18.9:** ***Before entering into an agreement to acquire a property, a purchaser should verify whether VAT is to be charged.***

An investor negotiating the purchase of a property may need to take into account the possibility that VAT will also have to be paid on the agreed price. This is likely to be the case in three situations:

(a) Where a freehold of a partly completed commercial building or a new commercial building is acquired within three years of completion. In this case, VAT at the standard rate is chargeable by the vendor unless the 'going concern' rules apply (see Points 26.1 and 26.4).

(b) The vendor has opted to tax the building. As stated in Point 18.1 above, the option to tax can be revoked within six months of being made if it has not been given practical effect. The next opportunity to revoke the option is 20 years after the option was made. In the meantime, VAT must also be charged by the person who opted to tax his or her interest on any subsequent sales or grants of interests in the property, unless the sale is part of a transfer of a business as a going concern (see Point 18.3 above) or the option to tax is otherwise disapplied from any grant of the property (see Point 18.1 above).

(c) The grant is otherwise excluded from the scope of the exemption by *VATA 1994, Sch 9, Group 1, Item 1, (a)–(n)*. In addition to (a) above, this includes:

(i) new or partly completed civil engineering works;

(ii) a developmental lease – only certain leases granted before 1 March 1997;

(iii) a lease or licence of gaming or fishing rights;

(iv) accommodation in hotels or similar;

(v) holiday accommodation – including the freehold or leasehold in a new building (less than three years old) and the freehold or leasehold in land for the construction of holiday accommodation;

(vi) camping and seasonal caravan pitches;

(vii) facilities for parking, storing or mooring vehicles, aircraft or boats;

(viii) rights to fell timber;

(ix) rights to occupy accommodation at entertainment or sporting venues;

(x) facilities for playing sport;

(xi) option or similar rights over any of the above;

(xii) with effect from 1 October 2012, the provision of facilities for the self-storage of goods, except to 'connected' persons or to charities for non-business use; and

(xiii) with effect from 1 October 2012, the grant of facilities within premises to a person supplying hairdressing services.

If the purchaser intends to charge VAT on the letting of the property once it is acquired, there may be no serious financial consequence of having to pay VAT on the purchase (although there is likely to be a cash flow cost, and SDLT is calculated on the VAT-inclusive price). In such a case, the investor would want to give immediate notification to HMRC of making the option to tax, to ensure that it will be able to reclaim the input tax.

Where there is no intention to opt to tax or to use the property to make taxable supplies, any VAT incurred on the purchase will be irrecoverable and may represent a significant additional cost of purchasing the property.

Even where the investor is already registered for VAT and in a position to reclaim all the VAT, it could take more than four months to recover the tax from HMRC. Furthermore, if a new company is established to make the acquisition, it can frequently take more than three months to secure a VAT registration, and then a further three months to obtain and submit a VAT return. This will further delay the recovery of VAT charged on the purchase. For a £5 million purchase, therefore, the buyer will need additional funding of £1 million (based on the VAT rate of 20%) for that period, and will face an additional SDLT cost (see Chapter 5).

As mentioned above and in Point 18.3, some sales will be 'VAT Free' transfers in the course of a transfer of a business as a going concern. No VAT should be charged or paid where this applies.

If VAT is charged incorrectly, the buyer or tenant has no right to recover that VAT as input tax, and the VAT must be reclaimed from the seller or landlord. It is, therefore, critical that VAT is only paid where it is properly due – there have been many instances where VAT has been charged incorrectly, the seller has subsequently become insolvent or otherwise unable to repay the VAT, and the buyer has lost out.

**Point 18.10:** ***Stamp duty land tax is charged on the VAT-inclusive price of a property. In the case of a lease grant, extra SDLT can arise if the letting is subject to VAT.***

SDLT is a tax paid by the purchaser of a property or an incoming lessee on the grant of a new lease.

In the case of a purchase of a freehold or a lease, the SDLT is payable on the purchase price paid including any VAT which is chargeable. If no option to tax has been made on the property, or the sale qualifies as a TOGC and the sale is completed without VAT arising, there is a corresponding saving in SDLT.

With regard to grants of leases, the position is somewhat different. In these cases, the SDLT liability depends on the length of the lease and the rent passing. If the option to tax has been made in respect of the property, SDLT is assessed on the rent plus VAT.

This can be avoided if there is a specific prohibition in the lease on the landlord charging VAT.

See also Point 5.4 on SDLT and VAT.

*Part B*

# Property Dealers and Developers

*Chapter 19*

# Tax relief for reductions in property values

**Tax relief is available for a reduction in realisable value of trading stock or work-in-progress below cost.**
**Point 19.1**

↓

Unrealised profit recognised in accounts on long-term contracts may be taxed.
Point 19.2

↓

Tax relief is available for provisions and future losses reflected in the accounts.
Point 19.3

↓

On speculative developments, the inclusion of overheads in work-in-progress can delay tax relief for those costs.
Point 19.4

# 19 TAX RELIEF FOR REDUCTIONS IN PROPERTY VALUES

**Point 19.1:** ***If at the end of an accounting period the net realisable values of particular properties are lower than their cost, a provision to reduce the cost to net realisable value should be allowable for tax purposes.***

The profits of a trade for tax purposes are those which, subject to adjustments required by law, are computed in accordance with generally accepted accounting practice. This may involve UK or international financial reporting standards depending on the entity in question and the choice of accounting method (*CTA 2009, s 46*; *ITTOIA 2005, s 25*).

The proper valuation of trading stock for accounting purposes, other than long-term construction work-in-progress (see Point 19.2 below) is the lower of cost and net realisable value (ie expected saleable value less selling costs and expected cost to completion). This is a test which should be applied to each individual property rather than globally (see *IRC v Cock, Russell & Co Ltd* (1949) 29 TC 387).

Where the net realisable value of a property forming part of trading stock is below cost, the lower value should be reflected in the accounts. The reduction in value will, therefore, need to be provided for and this stock provision will reduce taxable profits accordingly.

In such instances, tax relief is effectively available on an unrealised loss. If the property subsequently recovers its value, then the loss will be reversed in a later period. In the meantime, there will have been a deferral of the earlier period's tax liability. The reversal can only bring the carrying value of the asset to cost and cannot result in any excess being taxed at that point. For accounting and tax reasons, therefore, it is important to recognise losses on trading stock as early as possible. However, where the write down of the stock gives rise to a loss carried forward, it should be noted that, for groups with profits in excess of £5m, the utilisation of brought forward losses is restricted to £5m plus 50% of the excess of current year profits (after the offset of current year reliefs) over £5m. It is, therefore, possible that a write down of the property could take place giving rise to a loss and for this write down to be subsequently reversed giving rise to a current year profit but that the loss on the write down cannot be fully offset against the profit on reversal.

The need to reverse the write-down on recovery of property values can be avoided by transferring the property to another trading company whilst the market value is still depressed. The cost of the property to the acquiring company will be that value. A commercial rationale for the transfer is important in the context of stamp duty land tax (SDLT) where the rules could deny the intra-group exemption for tax-motivated transfers (*FA 2003, Sch 7, para 2(4A)*). Going forward, that company will reflect the trading stock in its accounts at cost, so that any taxable profit is deferred until the property is actually sold at a higher market value.

**Point 19.2:** ***Unrealised profit may have to be recognised on a long-term construction project to comply with accounting standards and this profit is taxable.***

The valuation principle of 'lower of cost and net realisable value' does not necessarily apply to work-in-progress in the course of a long-term contract. 'Long-term' contracts are those which start and finish in different accounting periods.

Under UK GAAP and, in particular, Financial Reporting Standard 102 (FRS 102) – which now incorporates the former SSAP9 on stock and work in progress – an appropriate proportion of accrued profit on long-term contracts must be recognised as soon as work is sufficiently advanced for a likely profit to be determined. If at the end of an accounting period a project is, say, three-quarters complete, any projected profit on the contract should be estimated at that stage and three-quarters of this reflected in the accounts. With accounts being prepared several months after the year end, the company and its auditors will often have the benefit of hindsight in arriving at such estimates.

FRS 102 may dictate what is acceptable for the preparation of accounts, but does this mean that HMRC are entitled to tax profit on this basis?

It is an established principle of tax law that profit cannot be taxed until realised (*Willingale v International Commercial Bank Ltd* [1978] STC 75; *BSC Footwear Ltd v Ridgway* (1971) 47 TC 495). However, in HMRC's view, the valuation of long-term work-in-progress under SSAP 9 involves the recognition of profit which has been realised at the balance sheet date (following *Pearce v Woodall-Duckham Ltd* (1978) 51 TC 271). Since 6 April 1999, tax law has explicitly required the profits of a trade, profession or vocation to be computed for tax purposes in accordance with generally accepted accounting practice (GAAP) or International Financial Reporting Standards (IFRS) where appropriate, subject to any adjustment then required by tax law (eg disallowance of depreciation and so on) (*CTA 2009, s 46*; *ITTOIA 2005, s 25*). Generally, therefore, if the accounts recognise a profit, that profit is also recognised for tax purposes. By the same token, if GAAP or IFRS requires a loss to be recognised before it is incurred, that loss should also be recognised for tax. See Point 19.3 below.

**Point 19.3:** ***HMRC allow relief for anticipated losses.***

It is certainly prudent accounting practice to reflect losses in accounts as early as possible. For example, under FRS 102, a loss on a contract should be recognised in full once foreseeable and the work-in-progress valuation reduced to net realisable value for balance sheet purposes. For contracts which are likely to absorb a considerable part of the company's capacity in future periods, the work-in-progress should be further reduced for estimated administration overheads to be incurred.

In the past, HMRC believed there was a rule of tax law that neither profit nor loss could be anticipated. In their view, this overrode UK generally accepted accounting practice (GAAP) if the application of GAAP resulted in the anticipation of a profit or loss.

HMRC were forced to revise their position on this following the decision in *Herbert Smith v Honour* [1999] STC 173. This is now a leading case on the interaction between tax law and accounting practice. It concerns the allowability of a provision made where an existing contract becomes onerous. In the *Herbert Smith* case, it was a lease on vacant business premises. The judge held that:

(a) it was not open to HMRC to replace a treatment which accorded with GAAP – and indeed was the only such treatment – with one that did not; and

(b) there was no general rule of law that prohibited provisions made on the grounds of prudence, where the provision was required by GAAP.

In view of this decision, HMRC announced in a press release on 20 July 1999 that they now accept that there is no tax rule which denies provisions for anticipated losses or expenses.

This position is clearly reflected in the HMRC Business Income Manual, which states (at BIM31100):

> *Herbert Smith* establishes that where accounts are drawn up on generally accepted accountancy principles there is no overriding rule of tax law which denies relief for losses or expenses which will only be paid in the future.

Now, provisions are allowable as long as:

(a) they are in respect of allowable revenue expenditure;

(b) they are required by GAAP (or IFRS);

(c) they are estimated with sufficient accuracy; and

(d) they do not conflict with any specific tax rule as to whether the expense is allowable or governing the time at which the expenditure is allowed.

With regard to the last point, this would prevent deduction for relief, for instance, for employee or director's remuneration payable more than nine months after the year end (HMRC *Bulletin 44*, December 1999).

**Point 19.4:** ***On property developments, the inclusion of indirect expenses in the cost of work-in-progress rather than charging them to the profit and loss account may delay tax relief.***

Profits on property developments will often only be recognised when the property is sold. The proper treatment of direct costs attributable to the development is to debit them to work-in-progress. This would, therefore, include the cost of the land, plus any direct labour and material used in the construction.

With regard to indirect costs, ie overheads and finance charges, there is a choice of treatment for the developer. They can be included in work-in-progress if they specifically relate to the development. Alternatively, they can be charged directly against profit.

If overheads and interest charges are included in work-in-progress in the balance sheet, no deduction is taken for these items in the profit and loss account until that stock is actually sold. If the developer has no taxable profits during the project period then there is no tax effect, unless, in the case of a company which is a member of a group, there is potential for group relief surrender.

Groups of companies now face a restriction on the offset of carried forward losses in future to £5m plus 50% of the excess of current year taxable profits (after the offset of current year reliefs) over £5m. In this connection, only a proportion of any profits generated from 1 April 2017 can be sheltered by brought forward losses. Where this is likely to be an issue, greater consideration might be given to including expenses in work in progress where that is justifiable from an accounting perspective.

Also, as outlined in Chapter 22, companies now face an annual restriction on the deductibility of interest and other finance costs. This is broadly to a maximum of either 30% of tax-adjusted EBITDA or a group percentage of tax-adjusted EBITDA (both of which may be capped by the total worldwide net interest of the group) but subject to a *de minimis* of £2m. Where the interest costs incurred in an accounting period are less than the maximum amount allowable, it is possible to elect for the additional capacity for relief to be carried forward for up to five years by nominating a reporting company and filing a full corporate interest restriction return. Disallowed interest is carried forward for potential relief in future periods indefinitely.

The calculation of the net interest incurred under the corporate interest restriction rules appears to have been drafted on the assumption that capitalised interest is deductible in the period in which it is capitalised (which is generally the case where interest is capitalised within the cost of an investment property). However, as outlined above, where costs are capitalised as part of the cost of trading stock, tax relief is given in the period in which it is expensed in the accounts. This gives rise to a potential mismatch in the period in which tax relief is given for capitalised interest and the period in which it is taken into account for the purpose of calculating net interest incurred for the purposes of the corporate interest restriction. In order to adopt an alternative basis of calculation whereby interest capitalised as part of the cost of trading stock is taken into account for the purposes of the corporate interest restriction calculations in the same way as interest capitalised on an investment property, an irrevocable election is required. The 'effect of interest allowance (alternative calculation) election') is made in the corporate interest restriction return under *F(No 2)A 2017, Sch 5, para 16*.

*Chapter 20*

# Reclassification of trading stock as investment property

**Reclassification of trading stock as a fixed asset may crystallise taxable income – or generate an allowable loss.**
**Point 20.1**

Where a property is acquired and/or developed with the prospect of its being let for a number of years on completion, there are benefits to its being classified at the outset as an investment.
Point 20.2

# 20 RECLASSIFICATION OF TRADING STOCK AS INVESTMENT PROPERTY

**Point 20.1:** ***A reclassification of trading stock as a fixed asset or its transfer to an investment vehicle must be carefully considered, as it will result in a tax liability on any unrealised gain on the property.***

If a property trading entity were to reclassify any of its properties as investments, there would be an immediate deemed disposal under *TCGA 1992, s 161*. As a result, a taxable trading profit would arise at that time by reference to the market value of the property. The tax would become payable even though the property had not been sold and no profit realised. Therefore, any individuals, partnerships or companies who reclassify a property in this manner could face an outflow of cash to pay a tax bill without any inflow of cash from the sale proceeds of the property. A similar problem would also arise if the properties are transferred to an investment entity, including the case of a transfer between two group companies.

Where a property has been acquired as trading stock, this classification will probably not be disturbed unless there is a formal decision by the proprietors/directors to change its status at any particular time.

The courts appear reluctant to accept that a property acquired as trading stock has ceased to be trading stock merely because it has been let for a number of years rather than sold (*J & C Oliver v Farnsworth* (1956) 37 TC 51; *Speck v Morton* (1972) 48 TC 476). For the court's attitude to deemed appropriation generally, see *Taylor v Good* (1974) 49 TC 277 and *Simmons v IRC* (1980) 53 TC. In the absence of any of the following actions, trading stock should retain its existing classification:

(a) reclassification of the property in the balance sheet from trading stock to fixed assets;

(b) transfer of the property out of a trading entity into an investment entity (this will also be the case if the transfer is between two companies in the same group – *TCGA 1992, s 173*); or

(c) formal resolution or board minute that the property in question is to be held as an investment.

Before any of the above actions are taken, it is important to consider if there is likely to be a tax liability by reference to the property's market value. Timing will also be relevant in the light of the possibility of any tax shelter (eg group relief, losses in year) in the year of appropriation.

Of course, if the market value is below carrying value at the time of appropriation, this would give rise to a trading loss which can be set against other profits in the year or group relieved. Such a loss would arise in any event at the end of the accounting period (assuming the value remains depressed) by virtue of the accounting requirement to reduce carrying value to net realisable value – see Point 19.1 above. On appropriation from trading stock to investments, no election is available to defer any tax on the gain as there is with the reclassification from investments to trading stock – see Chapter 17.

**Point 20.2:** ***Where a site is acquired on which it is intended to construct a property which will be retained for investment purposes, it could save future tax if the acquisition was made by an investment company rather than by a property trading entity.***

On acquisition, the future tax position may depend on how a property is classified. If it is treated as trading stock, then on a subsequent sale or appropriation the profit will be taxed as income. Sometimes, substantial value may be added to a property during construction as a result of work carried out and increased property values. An appropriation of the property at the end of this period could be costly.

If it is recognised at the outset that any site in the process of acquisition is likely to be retained for some period, it may well be advisable to bring that property into an investment company, rather than a development company, from the start. This can have very positive advantages:

(a) It removes the problem of appropriation to investment property in future. Within property groups, there is often an incentive to classify investment properties as such, since it improves the group's balance sheet and asset backing.

(b) With an investment property, the lessor would be entitled to claim capital allowances in respect of any element of plant and machinery included in the cost and may, for non-qualifying expenditure contracted for since 29 October 2018 and subject to detailed legislation, be entitled to claim structures and buildings allowance. This would not be the case for trading stock, since any expenditure would not be 'capital expenditure' for capital allowances purposes. Once the property is appropriated, it would be possible to claim capital allowances; but, if the property has been let before that date, the company may have lost an opportunity to claim capital allowances in an earlier period.

(c) Finance costs debited to stock are not deducted until the sale of the property. In the case of investment property, costs can be deducted as incurred in line with the accounts even if capitalised (*CTA 2009, s 320*). This would not be an issue were finance costs incurred in connection with trading stock to be debited directly to the profit and loss account (see Point 19.4). However, groups with annual interest costs in excess of £2m, in particular, would need to consider the implications of the corporate interest restriction and the possible restriction of interest deductions to 30% of EBITDA. Particular care will be needed where interest is capitalised as part of the cost of trading stock as an election may be required to ensure that the interest taken into account in calculating EBITDA matches the amount treated as a loan relationship in the year for tax purposes. This area is considered in more detail in Chapter 22.

(d) Where investment property is owned by individuals or trustees, gains on sale of the property attract a relatively favourable rate of capital gains tax when compared to income. From 5 April 2016, the general capital gains tax rate reduced to 20% (previously 28%) for higher- and additional-rate taxpayers. Basic-rate taxpayers are subject to a 10% rate (previously

18%), to the extent that their combined income and gains do not make them higher-rate taxpayers. However, gains on residential properties remain subject to the former 28%/18% rates.

(e) Certain capital gains may even attract the 10% business asset disposal relief rate – see Chapter 31. Trading profits in the hands of individuals or trustees give rise to up to 45% income tax plus National Insurance Contributions at a 2% rate for amounts above the upper earnings threshold.

*Chapter 21*

# Tax planning on the transfer of trading stock

**Transfers of trading stock to an associated entity in a depressed property market may be a tax-effective way of capitalising on short-term reductions in values.**

**Point 21.1**

# 21 TAX PLANNING ON THE TRANSFER OF TRADING STOCK

**Point 21.1:** ***A transfer of a property held as trading stock must generally now be at market value. If property values are below cost, it may be worth selling to an associated entity to get relief for the reduction in value. Such a transfer will also preserve the benefit of that loss once values rise again and/or take advantage of another entity with a lower tax rate at that stage.***

When trading stock is sold, transferred or appropriated for another purpose, this must generally take place at market value. This principle, originally laid down in *Sharkey v Wernher* (1955) 36 TC 275, became enshrined in *FA 2008, Sch 15*. For disposals and acquisitions on or after 8 July 2015, *Finance (No 2) Act 2015* provides that this also takes precedence over the transfer pricing provisions which focus on transactions by large enterprises or between UK and non-UK tax residents.

*ITTOIA 2005, ss 172A–172F* for income tax and *CTA 2009, ss 156–161* for corporation tax, may indeed extend to cessations of trade where previously it has been possible to transfer stock at cost to an associated entity.

The market value requirement may present opportunities in poor market conditions. Where the value of a property has fallen below its cost price, the transfer of that property to another entity will realise the loss at that point. This loss can then be offset against other profits in that entity or offset against other income, depending on the wider ownership structure. For individuals, that may extend to general income. In a corporate group, such a loss might be offset against other companies' profits by way of group relief.

In Chapter 19, the point was made that trading stock at the year-end should be written down if its realisable value is less than cost. That would generate an allowable trading loss for tax purposes without the need for a transfer. However, an actual transfer can deliver three benefits not achieved with a simple write-down, viz:

(a) With a write-down, the entity will need to write the stock back up again should values rise. However, with an actual transfer, the cost to the transferee company is the market value at that point. If values rise, it is not required to adjust that cost figure upwards whilst it holds that stock. Accordingly, if the stock is retained for several years, the tax benefit obtained on the original reduction in value can be preserved until sold.

(b) A transfer offers the potential to move the property to an entity where there might be scope for a future lower tax charge. Consider the following possibilities:

- A partnership where the individuals currently pay income tax at 45% – as well as National Insurance contributions – might transfer to a company subject to a lower corporation tax rate.
- A company might transfer the property to a company which has trading losses carried forward which arose prior to 1 April 2017

(and which cannot, therefore, be group relieved) that can shelter future trading profits.

- The transferee might be an investor with the prospect of the future benefit from capital allowances, indexation relief (subject to the limitations introduced from December 2017) or even non-tax resident status.

(c) Capital losses previously held over as a result of a transfer from investments to stock (prior to the withdrawal of the ability to hold over such losses from 8 March 2017) may be realised as a trading loss.

Any transfer between entities will have other issues. Stamp Duty Land Tax, for instance, is potentially payable at rates of up to 5% for transfers of commercial property and up to 15% on residential property. Even transfers between group companies can be caught unless there are commercial reasons for the transfer and it is not for the avoidance of tax.

VAT could also be chargeable if there is no VAT group, which may result in a timing disadvantage and extra Stamp Duty Land Tax.

A transfer will invariably require the consent of any lenders. Such lenders may have to agree to a transfer – or novation – of the loan across to the acquiring entity, unless the transfer is accompanied by a refinancing of the property by a new lender. In both these cases, the level of finance available and therefore allowable finance costs may fall.

*Chapter 22*

# Tax relief for finance costs

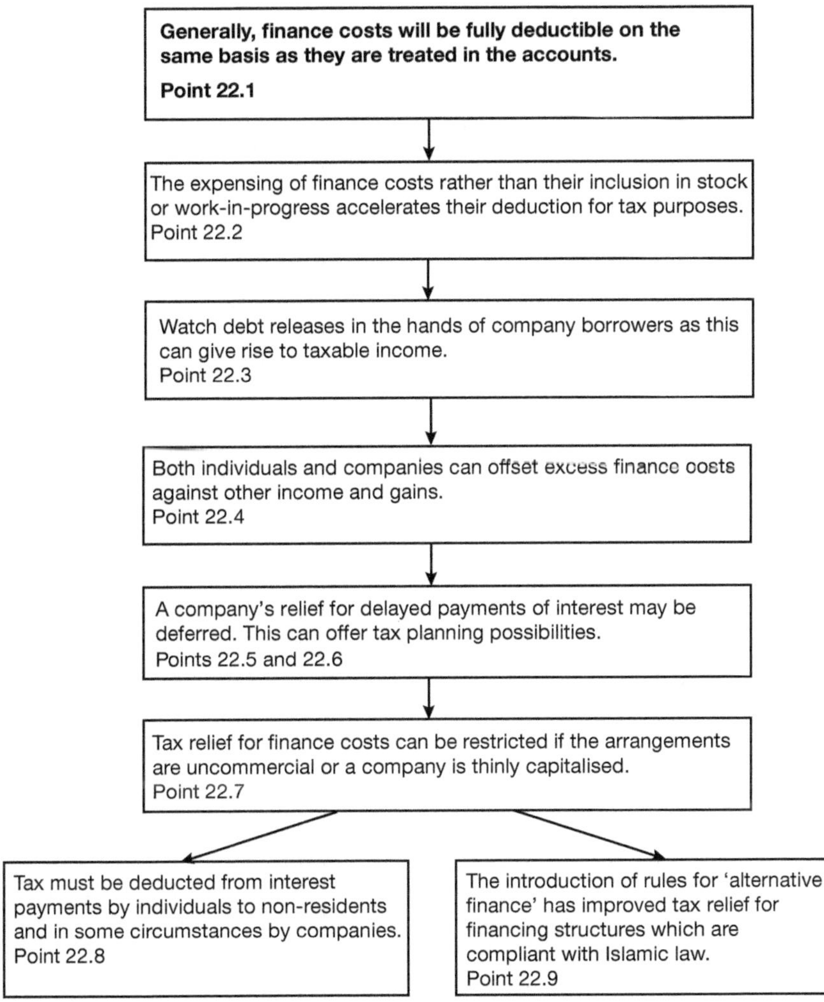

# 22 TAX RELIEF FOR FINANCE COSTS

**Point 22.1:** ***Generally, all interest and other costs incurred on property finance from third parties will be fully tax deductible on the same basis as they are treated in the accounts.***

Finance costs are, generally speaking, deductible as trading expenses from taxable trading profits on the same basis as they are reflected in the accounts.

In the context of a property trader, the differences in the treatment of companies and individuals are less significant than with investors. As a general rule, any expenses and incidental costs related to finance are going to be deductible as trading expenses. However, there are some differences, which are mentioned in Points 22.3 to 22.8 below.

Foreign companies (which are not tax resident in the UK) trading in the UK through a permanent establishment would be subject to the same rules as any UK company. Therefore, a foreign company that is trading in the UK through a permanent establishment is subject to UK corporation tax on its profits.

Also, the *Finance Act 2016* introduced provisions from 5 July 2016, under which the profits of a non-UK resident company carrying on a trade of dealing in or developing UK land will be subject to UK corporation tax. This is regardless of whether or not that company is carrying on the trade through a permanent establishment in the UK.

The general income tax principles applying to the financing costs of individuals and trustees trading in the UK are summarised at Point 3.1. The financing costs of residential property developers would seem not to be caught by these restrictions provided that no property business income is to be generated (for this purpose, revenues from the sale of residential properties would generally be regarded as trading income, rather than property business income).

The general corporation tax principles applying to the financing costs of UK companies and non-resident companies trading in land in the UK are summarised at Points 3.9 and 3.10.

**Point 22.2:** ***If finance costs are expensed to the profit and loss account, tax relief is obtained earlier than if the costs are included in stock or work-in-progress in the balance sheet.***

The normal rule provides for a deduction for any finance costs that are charged to the income statement. In such a case, costs that are included in the cost of trading stock in the balance sheet would not be allowed until the property is sold.

Under FRS 102 there is an accounting policy choice between charging financing expenses on real estate in the course of development to inventory or the income statement. Accordingly, businesses adopting FRS 102 have the opportunity of recognising the expense for tax purposes as it is incurred. Conversely, under IFRS (and FRS 101) financing expenses on real estate in the course of development must generally be booked to inventory when incurred, rather than the income statement.

There is a specific corporation tax allowance for capitalised finance costs of capital assets (see Point 3.11). This provision does not, however, help property traders and developers who include interest in the value of stock and work-in-progress in the balance sheet.

This may not be an issue where any loss crystallised by this accounting treatment of expensing costs is merely going to be carried forward. On the other hand, where the company or group has other current period taxable profits, the recognition of costs and losses in that period can shelter these. At worst, this improves cash flow although consideration will need to be given to the restrictions on the offset of brought-forward losses with effect from 1 April 2017 (see Point 22.4). At best, it may be an opportunity to use losses now in the face of a possibility that there may not be profits in the future to use these against.

**Point 22.3:** ***Watch debt releases in the hands of company borrowers, as they can be taxed.***

In the same way that costs and expenses reflected in the income statement are allowed for tax purposes, so will any credits potentially be taxed under the loan relationship rules for companies.

Distressed property situations have been resolved in the past by an arrangement between the lender and borrower under which some or all of the debt is forgiven. A credit to a company's income statement as a result of such a release typically gives rise to taxable income if the parties are not connected. This can also be the case if the credit is directly to reserves or where impaired debt is bought back by a connected company at a discount, although *Finance (No 2) Act 2015* includes a helpful corporate rescue tax exemption for distressed situations.

See Points 3.13 and 3.14 in Chapter 3B for a further discussion on debt releases, including deemed releases, together with corporate rescue and insolvency situations which do not trigger taxable debt releases.

**Point 22.4:** ***Where a borrower has raised finance for a property dealing and developing trade, surplus finance costs can reduce other income or gains chargeable to tax.***

Where funds have been borrowed for trading purposes, the related finance costs will be deductible on an accrued basis as trading expenses. The costs are part of the borrower's normal trading expenses.

For individuals (including individuals in partnerships), surplus expenses can be relieved as follows:

(a) against other income arising in the same year of assessment (*ITA 2007, s 64*). Note that offset for such losses together with certain other deductions has been capped since 5 April 2013. The annual cap is the greater of £50,000 or 25% of the individual's income;

(b) if there is still an unrelieved loss, against income of the preceding year (*ITA 2007, s 64(2)(b)*);

(c) any loss still unrelieved can be offset against any chargeable gains for the year and against chargeable gains of the previous year, if a claim for setting the loss against income of that year is possible and has been made (*ITA 2007, s 71*); and

(d) any remaining unrelieved losses can be carried forward against future trading income (*ITA 2007, s 83*).

In the first four tax years of assessment of a trading business, the possibility of offset is yet greater. The loss can be offset against other income for up to the three years preceding the year of assessment in which the loss is made (*ITA 2007, s 72*). This offset against general income is subject to the same annual cap referred to under (a) above.

There is also provision for 'terminal loss relief' where a loss is sustained in the final 12 months of trading, which supplements the reliefs mentioned above. Under the terminal loss rules, the loss can be offset against any profits from the trade in the three years ending immediately before the commencement of the 12-month period up to the date of discontinuance (*ITA 2007, s 89*).

Note that, where individuals are involved in a limited partnership or limited liability partnership, trading loss relief against other income or gains may be restricted (*ITA 2007, ss 104* and *107*).

For a company, excess financing expenses, in the form of trading losses, can be offset in the following ways:

(a) against other profits (including other income and gains) of the company in the same year (*CTA 2010, s 37(3)(a)*);

(b) surrender by way of group relief against the total taxable profit of any UK company within the same group in the same year (*CTA 2010, s 97*);

(c) carry-back up to one year against total profits of the same company (*CTA 2010, s 37(3)(b)*);

(d) carry-back up to three years as a terminal loss in the last period of trading (*CTA 2010, s 39*); and

(e) carry-forward indefinitely in the company against total profits provided the trade is continuing. For losses that arise pre 1 April 2017, it was only possible to offset the losses against future trading profits.

The use of losses brought forward after 1 April 2017 are subject to a new regime incorporating certain offset restrictions. Only 50% of group profit from this date can sheltered by carried forward losses. This is subject to a £5m profit *de minimis* below which the profit is fully offsettable.

**Point 22.5:** ***Particularly where the borrower is a close company, interest may need to be paid within 12 months of the year end to get a tax deduction in the year of accrual.***

Point 3.17 sets out the situations where the late interest rules can apply to related party financing (*CTA 2009, s 373*) and other relevant considerations.

Where these are in point, relief for accrued interest can be deferred until it is paid, if paid after 12 months from the year end. Similar provisions can apply to postpone relief for discount arising on deeply discounted securities until the debt is redeemed.

**Point 22.6:** ***The mismatch between the accruals basis of relief under the corporate debt regime and the received basis of taxation for certain lenders offers a cash flow tax planning opportunity. An individual or trust can exploit this when lending to a related UK company.***

As mentioned in Point 22.5 above, there are situations where the late interest or postponed discount rules can defer relief for finance expense payable to a related lender.

Since individuals and trustees are not subject to corporation tax, they can be regarded as related lenders where they, or their associates, lend to close companies in which they are (directly or indirectly) participators. However, a mismatch can arise because, for example, UK-resident individuals will generally suffer full UK income tax in the income tax year in which the interest is received.

In many cases, that gives rise to an opportunity to exploit a potential cash flow tax advantage. See the example at Point 3.19 in Chapter 3B for an illustration of this.

**Point 22.7:** ***Tax relief for finance costs in relation to loans directly or indirectly from connected parties may be restricted if they are non-commercial or where a borrowing company is thinly capitalised.***

See Point 3.5 (for individuals, trustees and non-resident companies) and Points 3.20 and 3.21 (for UK companies) for a discussion on the need for arm's-length terms in any borrowing arrangement, which is intended to represent a normal commercial loan, and the possibility of disallowance for companies with excessive debt to equity ratios.

Point 3.22 summarises anti-avoidance legislation that can apply where companies enter into tax-motivated financing arrangements.

**Point 22.8:** ***Individuals must generally deduct tax from interest payments to non-residents. For companies, there has been a more general requirement to deduct tax, but this is not necessary where the payee is subject to UK corporation tax on the income or is an exempt body.***

See Points 3.6 and 3.7 in Chapter 3A regarding the obligation on individuals to deduct tax on interest payments to non-residents. This also applies to trustees, although it is rare for trustees to be directly engaged in property trading as opposed to investment.

Points 3.23 to 3.28 in Chapter 3B deal with tax deduction issues for companies. As mentioned in Point 22.1 above, these will also apply to non-resident companies which are subject to corporation tax in relation to UK trading profits arising in the UK through a permanent establishment.

**Point 22.9:** ***The introduction of rules for 'alternative finance' has enabled tax relief to be obtained for costs incurred in relation to financing structures which are compliant with Islamic law.***

See Point 3.29 in Chapter 3B for an outline of the typical structures and arrangements that have been accommodated by changes in the UK tax rules. These have been consolidated into *CTA 2009* (for corporates) and *ITA 2007* (for individuals).

**Point 22.10:** ***The Corporate Interest Restriction from 1 April 2017 has a significant impact on the tax deductibility of debt.***

See Point 3.30 for a summary of the Corporate Interest Restriction provisions which can restrict the UK corporation tax relief for financing expenses of both connected and unconnected party debt.

Particular care must be taken as regard the impact on the capitalisation of interest into stock and the impact of this upon the detailed calculations of capitalised debt. Care must also be taken as regards a number of periods' worth of interest costs being amalgamated and this then exceeding the £2m threshold in a single period.

*Chapter 23*

# Acquiring a trading company with tax losses

**The acquisition of a land dealing or development company with unused past trading losses can offer future tax shelter, providing anti-avoidance provisions cannot be applied.**
**Point 23.1**

In view of the possible exposure under the anti-avoidance provisions, it is inadvisable to pay for the future benefit of a company's losses on acquisition.
Point 23.2

Once five years have elapsed from the date of purchase of a loss company, changes in the nature or conduct of the trade can occur. However, to benefit from brought-forward losses, it is still necessary to carry on the same trade.
Point 23.3

# 23 ACQUIRING A TRADING COMPANY WITH TAX LOSSES

**Point 23.1:** ***The acquisition of a land dealing or development company with unused past trading losses can offer future tax shelter, providing anti-avoidance provisions cannot be applied.***

A property dealing or developing company which has incurred trading losses would normally be able to carry forward the losses against future profits. Where a company is a member of a group and losses arising from 1 April 2017 are carried forward, the carried forward losses may also be available to surrender by way of group relief.

Once there is a change in the ownership of the company, the carry-forward of unused losses will be denied if there is a major change in the nature or conduct of the trade carried on by the company at any time within the eight-year period starting three years before and ending five years after the change in ownership. Losses carried forward will also be disallowed if a change in ownership occurs after the scale of activities becomes small or negligible and before any significant revival in the trade (*CTA 2010, s 673*). Similar rules may also apply to prevent the carry forward of losses from property letting (*CTA 2010, s 704*).

Group relief of brought forward losses is also affected by a change in ownership. Whilst brought forward losses continue to be available for surrender between companies in the acquired group, surrender to the acquiring company and/or to members of the acquiring company's group is blocked until the first accounting period commencing after the fifth anniversary of the change in ownership (*CTA 2010 Pt 14, Ch 2C*).

A change in ownership is determined by comparing the position at any two points in time within a three-year period. If, between those two points, a different person or set of persons owns more than 50% of the ordinary share capital, ownership has changed (*CTA 2010, s 719*).

The concept of a major change in the nature and conduct of a trade is potentially quite wide. Where land development becomes land dealing (or vice versa), this would probably amount to a change in the conduct of trade. Furthermore, a change from one type of building to another (eg from residential to commercial) may well come within the provisions. More narrowly, this may even occur if the change is from houses to residential flats. Another example of a situation caught by the provisions might be where a developer moves away from contract work into speculative property development.

A situation where trading activities have become small or negligible is much easier to identify although there are no definitions either in turnover or asset terms given by the legislation. It has been suggested that the reduction in activities must arise from the company's policy. If there have been attempts at maintaining activity at the normal level (as evidenced by the size of its staff and the holding of stock), but local or national economic conditions have depressed sales, it might be argued that the company's trade has not become small or negligible.

The problem with the anti-avoidance provisions arises from the uncertainty as to how wide their scope actually is. In any situation where a company can be turned around from being loss-making to profit-making, it is possible that some element in the conduct of trade has changed. However, this may well not have been the case if losses have arisen in the past from inadequate contract pricing, bad workmanship and disputes, poor financial control, or external factors such as high interest rates, market stagnation or cost escalation. HMRC have published a statement of practice with examples of situations which they would not regard as major changes in the nature or conduct of a trade (HMRC SP 10/91).

Note that it is not possible to circumvent the anti-avoidance rules by hiving down the target company's trade immediately on acquisition following the introduction of anti-avoidance rules in *Finance Act 2013*.

**Point 23.2:** ***In view of the possible exposure under the anti-avoidance provisions, it is inadvisable to pay for the future benefit of a company's losses on acquisition.***

If part of the consideration is geared to the expected use of such losses, it should only be payable as and when the Inspector has agreed to the offset of losses against future profits. In practice, this is likely to be several years after the acquisition.

**Point 23.3:** ***Once five years have elapsed from the date of purchase of a loss company, changes in the nature or conduct of the trade can occur. However, to benefit from brought-forward losses, it is still necessary to carry on the same trade.***

The real benefits from the use of a tax loss company arise from longer-term planning. As mentioned in Point 23.1 above, there is a potential disallowance of losses carried forward if there are changes in the nature or conduct of the trade within five years of the change in ownership.

Once the five years have expired, the stringent conditions of *CTA 2010, s 673* cease to be relevant. At that stage, trading reforms can be implemented which should not affect the carry-forward of past losses. It is, therefore, not uncommon for groups acquiring companies with substantial losses to delay their more radical plans for five years to ensure the continuing availability of brought-forward losses. In the interim period, trading should be carried on in a similar fashion to the pre-acquisition period.

Apart from the anti-avoidance provisions, and subject to the points raised below, the future use of trading losses arising prior to 1 April 2017 is still subject to the general rule that they can only be set against profits from the same trade (*CTA 2010, s 45*). This could be a problem if, for instance, land dealing or speculative building supersedes land development activity. Thus, in any situation where past losses are being relied on to shelter future profitable activity, it is always necessary to consider whether the new activity is a different trade to that previously carried on.

Different rules apply to trading losses arising from 1 April 2017. Provided both that the trade continues in the next accounting period and that it has not become small or negligible, trading losses can be carried forward and offset against total profits (*CTA 2010, s 45A*). Where the trade either is not continuing in the next accounting period or it has become small or negligible the carry forward of the trading losses are once again restricted to offset against future profits of the same trade.

In addition, following further anti-avoidance rules enacted in *Finance Act 2015, Sch 3* it is now possible for the use of losses to remain restricted even after a period of five years from the date of acquisition has expired. This can be the case if transactions are implemented in an attempt to enable the losses to be used in circumstances where they would not otherwise have been available. If one group company, for example, held a trading property that would realise a trading profit on sale to a third party but that company did not have trading losses brought forward, it might historically have been possible to transfer the property to a company with trading losses to enable the profit on sale to be sheltered by those losses. The utilisation of losses in this situation was blocked with effect from 18 March 2015. However, where losses have arisen since 1 April 2017 and are eligible for group relief it would no longer be necessary to transfer the property in any event as the profit on sale could be sheltered by way of group relief of the brought forward loss. These rules will also catch the transfer of an investment property which is then leased back intragroup to facilitate the use of property rental business losses.

However, assuming the new anti-avoidance rules are not engaged, once the critical five-year period for *s 673* has passed, a subsequent HMRC challenge would be restricted to denying use of pre April 2017 losses (or post April 2017 losses where the trade either ceases in the accounting period or has become small or negligible) against particular profits not arising from the same trade. Therefore, the losses could still be used in future against profits as long as the company continues the trade and it has not become small or negligible.

Notwithstanding the anti-avoidance rules, from 1 April 2017, the offset of carried forward losses by a group against profits is restricted to £5m plus 50% of the excess of profits (after the offset of current year reliefs) over £5m.

*Chapter 24*

# Selling shares in a property trading company and anti-avoidance provisions

**Sales of trading companies may be tax-free or benefit from the reduced capital gains tax rate of 10%.**

**Point 24.1**

↓

The company sale agreement should require the purchaser to ensure that the properties will be sold in the ordinary course of trade to prevent application of the anti-avoidance provisions.
Point 24.2

↓

Where vendors are relying on favourable capital gains treatment, clearance can be sought from HMRC that they will not apply certain anti-avoidance rules.
Point 24.3

# 24 SELLING SHARES IN A PROPERTY TRADING COMPANY AND ANTI-AVOIDANCE PROVISIONS

**Point 24.1:** ***For some corporate vendors, a gain on sale will be exempt from tax whereas an individual may only be subject to a 10% tax rate on his gains.***

Capital gains realised by companies selling shares in trading subsidiaries can be exempt from corporation tax providing that certain conditions are met (*TCGA 1992, Sch 7AC*).

For individuals, trustees and other taxpayers not subject to corporation tax, there is no corresponding exemption, although business asset disposal relief (BADR) may be available to reduce the rate of tax to 10% (see Chapter 31). Where such relief is not available, the normal rules of capital gains tax will apply, resulting in a 20% effective tax rate for disposals for payers of the higher or additional income tax rates.

In certain circumstances, anti-avoidance rules may come into play, even where avoidance is not a motive, or the main motive, for the transaction (see Point 24.2 below). Also sellers must be mindful of the transactions in securities provisions which enable HMRC to recharacterise a capital gain as income for tax purposes. As mentioned in Point 24.3 below, the *Finance Act 2016* strengthened HMRC's ability to assess a capital gain to income tax.

For companies, the exemption ('the substantial shareholdings exemption') applies to disposals of 'substantial shareholdings' which meet certain conditions. A 'substantial shareholding' is a holding of 10% or more.

Historically, the exemption applied where a trading company or a member of a trading group sold a 'substantial shareholding' in:

(a) a trading company; or

(b) the holding company of a trading group or subgroup; and

(c) the shareholding has been held for a continuous period of at least 12 months in the two years immediately preceding the disposal.

For disposals from 1 April 2017, the scope of the exemption was widened and now applies where a company (which need not any longer be a trading company or a member of a trading group) sells a 'substantial shareholding' in:

(a) a trading company; or

(b) the holding company of a trading group or subgroup; and

(c) the shareholding has been held for a continuous period of at least 12 months in the six years immediately preceding the disposal.

For disposals from 1 April 2017, the exemption can also apply, or partially apply, to disposals of a 'substantial shareholding' where:

(a) the shareholding has been held for a continuous period of at least 12 months in the six years immediately preceding the disposal; and

(b) the company being sold is not either a trading company or the holding company of a trading group or subgroup; and

(c) the investing company is not a disqualified listed company (which will be the case where i) any shares forming part of the ordinary share capital are listed on a recognised stock exchange; and ii) the company is not itself a qualifying institutional investor; and iii) the company is not a qualifying UK REIT).

Where these conditions are met and, immediately prior to the disposal, at least 80% of the ordinary share capital of the investing company is owned by qualifying institutional investors, the substantial shareholdings exemption is given on the entirety of the gain. Where qualifying institutional investors own less than 80% of the ordinary share capital of the investing company then, provided the qualifying institutional investors hold at least 25% of the ordinary share capital of the investing company, the substantial shareholdings exemption is given on the proportion of the gain which equates to the percentage ownership of the qualifying institutional investors.

See Chapter 32 for further points on the substantial shareholding exemption.

Where the vendor of the shares is not a company, the normal capital gains tax rules apply, unless BADR is available or the vendor belongs to a certain class of shareholder that is exempt from UK tax on gains, such as pension funds and charity trustees.

This exemption was withdrawn for non-UK residents from April 2019 for disposals of shares in 'UK property rich' companies.

From April 2019, all disposals of shares in collective investment vehicles by non UK residents will then be chargeable to UK corporation tax or UK capital gains tax irrespective of the size of holding. A collective investment vehicle for this purpose includes collective investment schemes, alternative investment vehicles, UK real estate investment trusts and similar non UK vehicles. In some circumstances, such vehicles may be able to elect for exemption from the new rules for disposals that they make themselves or which are made by their subsidiaries, including those which are UK resident. Accordingly, a disposal of shares in a UK property rich company by a member of a group which is party to such an exemption election would not be chargeable to corporation tax even if the disposal is by a UK resident.

Disposals of shares in UK property rich companies by non-residents where the shares do not represent a holding in a collective investment vehicle, by contrast, would only be chargeable to UK corporation tax or UK capital gains tax where the holding, taking into account holdings of connected shareholders and disposals made in the previous two years, is of 25% or more of the share capital.

Non-domiciled individuals used to be able to sell tax free in the UK if the company owning the property was incorporated outside the UK. However, such disposals can also be taxable under the regime from April 2019 as a disposal by the company would constitute a direct disposal and a disposal by the trust would constitute an indirect disposal for these purposes.

The position with regard to non-domiciliaries became more complicated following tax changes brought in with effect from 6 April 2008. These individuals will have to elect for the 'remittance' basis if they wish to avoid tax on gains arising and retained outside the UK. For those non-domiciliaries who have been resident in the UK for at least seven out of the last nine years, a charge is levied for this status each year.

Since 6 April 2017, individuals who have been tax resident in the UK for more than 15 out of the past 20 years will be deemed domiciled in the UK for tax purposes and hence fully within the charge to UK income tax and capital gains tax on an arising basis. Individuals who became deemed domiciled on 6 April 2017 were allowed to treat the base cost of their offshore capital assets as being the market value of those assets on 6 April 2017.

BADR applies to individuals and certain trustees, subject to qualifying conditions. The main requirements are that:

(a) the shares must be held in a trading company or the holding company of a trading group; and

(b) throughout a 'two-year qualifying period', the individual/beneficiary must:

  - be an officer or employee of the company or a company within the group (part or full time); and
  - the company is the individual's 'personal company' (ie they hold at least 5% of the ordinary shares and voting rights of the company, and are also beneficially entitled to at least 5% of the distributable profits and/or assets at winding up).

The 'two-year qualifying period' is either:

- the 24-month period immediately prior to the sale of the shares where the company continues to trade; or
- where the company ceases to trade, the 24-month period immediately prior to cessation of the trade, provided the shares are disposed of within three years of the date of cessation.

In respect of disposals made on or after 29 October 2018, a personal company means where:

- the individual holds at least 5% of the ordinary share capital of the company;
- that individual also owns at least 5% of the voting rights in the company are exercisable by the individual, and
- one of the following applies:
  - the individual is beneficially entitled to at least 5% of the profits available to shareholders and, on a winding up event, would be beneficially entitled to a minimum of 5% of available assets; or
  - where there is a disposal of the whole of the ordinary share capital of the company, the individual would be beneficially entitled to at least 5% of the proceeds.

For disposals prior to 29 October 2018 a personal company means where the individual holds at least 5% of the ordinary share capital of the company and at least 5% of the voting rights in the company.

These new tests require considerable care over the timing of a disposal. For example, a holding of shares giving an entitlement to over 5% of the voting rights but less than 5% of the profits available, assets and proceeds could have been held for many years prior to 29 October 2018. However, from that date the shares will cease to qualify. Even if the holding is increased such that the shareholder were to acquire at least 5% of the economic rights, the shares would then have to be held for 24 months from the date of that acquisition before a disposal would become qualifying for BADR again.

Shareholders whose holding is diluted below 5% after a commercial fundraising can make an election to preserve relief.

Similarly, shares which had been held for 13 months could be sold on 5 April 2019 and qualify for relief but if sold on 6 April 2019 would not qualify. Where the relief is available, the first £1 million of gains arising from the disposal of the shares will be subject to tax at a rate of 10%. In other cases, the owners may have available tax shelter through losses in the year of sale. Capital gains arising from the sale of shares in the hands of individuals, trustees and personal representatives can be subject to capital gains tax at rates of up to 20%.

Where a company is sold and the sale consideration takes the form of shares or loan notes in the buying company, it is often possible to defer any taxable gain arising. The gain on sale is rolled-over into the new shares/loans acquired, so that the gain will only crystallise when these are sold/redeemed (*TCGA 1992, s 135*).

The treatment of loan notes differs depending on whether they are qualifying corporate bonds (QCBs) or non-qualifying corporate bonds (non-QCBs). A QCB is broadly a normal commercial loan note issued by a company. Its issue in exchange for shares crystallises the chargeable gain arising in respect of the shares at that point in time but defers its being brought into charge to tax until the loan note is sold or redeemed (*TCGA 1992, s 116*).

A non-QCB is also a corporate loan note, but has one or more specified features that distinguish it from a QCB. These are: a right to subscribe for further loan notes; being capable of redemption in a foreign currency; a right to convert into shares; or entitlement to a return linked to the business's results (*TCGA 1992, s 117*). With a non-QCB, the gain in respect of the shares is not merely held over; instead, the gain does not crystallise until sale or redemption.

Where the deferred gain would have qualified for BADR at the time of the original disposal, the normal CGT deferral rules must normally be 'opted out' for BADR to be claimed, regardless of whether QCBs or non-QCBs are issued. The effect of this is to accelerate the tax charge on these loan notes to be taxed at the time of the original disposal, albeit at 10% and not 20%.

The share for share – or share for loan note – deferral relief is only available where the sale is for bona fide commercial reasons and not for the avoidance of tax. HMRC may refuse the relief where there is any indication that the tax benefits for the seller have been the driving factor for the structure of the transaction. It is advisable to obtain advance clearance from HMRC that they are satisfied that the sale is for bona fide commercial reasons and not tax driven (*TCGA 1992, s 138*).

When giving clearance under *TCGA 1992, s 138,* HMRC accept that new shares or loan stock issued by the buying company in exchange for the shares in the company acquired are treated as the same asset as the old shares. It is as if there had been a reorganisation of the target company's shares. As a result, a gain on the sale of shares can be held over or (in the case of certain loan stock) not crystallised for tax purposes until the new securities are sold or redeemed.

In the absence of HMRC clearance, any gain arising on a sale in consideration for shares or loan stock could crystallise and become taxable at that point, instead of being held over or rolled over into the new shares/securities acquired. That would mean tax would be payable on the transaction for that tax year, even though cash has not been received.

**Point 24.2:** ***When selling the shares of a dealing or development company, it is advisable to incorporate in the sale agreement the condition that the properties held by the company as trading stock are disposed of in the normal course of its trade.***

Whenever a gain is realised either directly or indirectly from property, it is necessary to consider whether a charge to tax could arise under *ITA 2007, Pt 9A* (or *CTA 2010, Pt 8ZB* for companies) to tax that gain as income. These provisions potentially apply where a profit or gain is realised from a disposal of UK land by:

(i) a person acquiring, holding or developing the land;

(ii) a person who is associated with the person acquiring, holding or developing the land; or

(iii) a person who is party to, or concerned in, an arrangement with regard to all or part of the land and which enables a profit or gain to be realised either by an indirect method or by any series of transactions.

In order for the profit or gain to be within the scope of *ITA 2007, Pt 9A* (or *CTA 2010, Pt 8ZB* for companies) the land has to fall within one of the following conditions:

(a) land, or any property deriving its value from land, is acquired and the main object, or one of the main objects, of acquiring the land is to realise a profit or gain from disposing of the land;

(b) land is held as trading stock; or

(c) land is developed with the main object, or one of the main objects, being to realise a profit or gain from disposing of all or part of the land when developed;

The sale of shares in a property dealing or developing company could give rise to a gain falling within *ITA 2007, Pt 9A* and *CTA 2010, Pt 8ZB*. There is, therefore, a possibility that the profit on sale is assessed to tax, not as a capital gain but as income in the year of sale.

There is an important exemption in *ITA 2007, s 517E* (for individuals and trustees) and *CTA 2010, s 356OC* (for companies). These sections provide that a gain will not be chargeable as income to the extent of the amount that is brought into account as income for the purposes of either income tax or corporation tax by another party. Accordingly, if a gain will be brought into account as a trading profit for corporation tax purposes by the company that is being disposed of (for example on a sale of the property) then this should mean that any gain on the sale of the shares should not also be at risk of being charged to tax as income.

These provisions were enacted by *FA 2016* and apply to disposals with effect from 5 July 2016.

The predecessor legislation was applied in the case of *Chilcott v IRC* [1982] STC 1 where the taxpayer sold shares in a property company on the specific condition that the land stock should be sold in the normal course of its trading. The legislation in force at the time (*ICTA 1988, s 776)* was held not to apply in that case by virtue of *s 776(10)* (the predecessor to what is now *ITA 2007, s 517E* for individuals and *CTA 2010, s 356OC* for companies).

Since the sale of any property-owning company is potentially a situation within *ITA 2007, Pt 9A* or *CTA 2010, Pt 8ZB*, it is advisable to incorporate the condition in the sale contract that the stock will be sold in the normal course of trade. This would help the vendor rely on the exemption in *ITA 2007, s 517E* and *CTA 2010, s 356OC*, as well as forming the basis of any damages claim if the purchaser ignored the undertaking and a liability under *ITA 2007, Pt 9A* or *CTA 2010, Pt 8ZB* consequently arose for the vendor.

**Point 24.3:** ***Notwithstanding the position under ITA 2007, Pt 9A and CTA 2010, Pt 8ZB, before any sale of shares, formal clearance should be obtained from HMRC that the anti-avoidance rules relating to transactions in securities will not apply.***

Where shareholders realise gains on the sale of a company, the possibility that the gains will be charged to tax as income cannot be ruled out. In *IRC v Wiggins* [1979] STC 244, it was established that the anti-avoidance provisions of *CTA 2010, s 733* (for corporation tax) or *ITA 2007, s 682* (for income tax) may apply. These sections, which seek to tax gains from certain 'transactions in securities' to income tax in prescribed situations, may well apply if the proceeds of sale reflect the value of underlying stock. By selling the company, the shareholders have effectively avoided the additional tax that would have become payable if the stock had been realised and the proceeds distributed.

There is, however, a formal clearance procedure under which confirmation of the *CTA 2010, s 733* and *ITA 2007, s 682* position can be obtained in advance (*CTA 2010, s 748*; *ITA 2007, ss 701–702*). HMRC are required to respond within 30 days to any application for formal clearance, which is normally in the form that they either are or are not satisfied that the anti-avoidance provisions should be applied.

If complete information is supplied with a clearance application, and clearance is formally given, the transaction can proceed without fear of any liability under these anti-avoidance sections. For this reason, an application for clearance is a common procedure in advance of many share sales.

As mentioned, HMRC are reluctant to give clearance where they consider that the sale is a device to extract tax-free funds. Sales where vendor shareholders retain shares through the buying company after the sale normally attract extra scrutiny from HMRC.

This clearance is separate from the clearance, mentioned in Point 24.1 above, in respect of share for share and share for loan note sales, although requests for the two clearances may be submitted in a single application to HMRC.

A sale involving the issue of shares or loan notes in the buying company normally proceeds after obtaining clearances under both *CTA 2010, s 748* or *ITA 2007, s 701* and *TCGA 1992, s 138*. It is possible for a transaction to receive clearance under one head but for clearance to be refused for the other.

*FA 2016* extended the potential situations where HMRC might treat as income what might otherwise have been a realisation of a capital gain. Targeted situations can include the winding up of companies with accumulated cash representing undistributed income and also 'phoenixing' – where shareholders liquidate or sell a company to extract cash profits, only to then start up the same or a similar business within two years. This is likely to be of particular relevance to property businesses where it is common to undertake property transactions using a single purpose vehicle. This increases the risk that a subsequent project undertaken in this way would be seen as 'starting up' a similar business to that carried on by the previous project vehicle which has since been wound up.

*Chapter 25*

# Construction Industry Scheme

**Any individual, company or partnership involved in construction work needs to consider the tax deduction requirements of the Construction Industry Scheme.**
**Point 25.1**

↓

The compliance obligations should ideally be set out in the agreement between the parties.
Point 25.2

↓

There is a need to determine whether a sub-contractor might be regarded as an employee, in which case PAYE and NIC issues could arise.
Point 25.3

↓

A developer undertaking sub-contract work may need to register with HMRC for gross payment status to avoid cash flow problems.
Point 25.4

# 25 CONSTRUCTION INDUSTRY SCHEME

**Point 25.1:** ***Any individual, partnership or company that carries out or engages in construction work needs to consider the implications of the Construction Industry Scheme. Failure to withhold tax from payments where required under the scheme could result in a contractor being liable to account for the tax.***

The Construction Industry Scheme (CIS) is designed to minimise tax evasion in the building industry. It does this by putting the onus on a 'contractor' to withhold one of two prescribed rates on account of income tax from payments to a 'sub-contractor' in respect of any works of construction carried out – unless the sub-contractor has successfully registered for gross payment status with HMRC and the contractor has verified that status. The tax deduction is not applied to payments in respect of materials and VAT.

A 'contractor' for these purposes is a person carrying on a business which includes 'construction operations'. 'Construction operations' can cover a wide range of activities including maintenance and repairs *(FA 2004, s 74)*. Guidance on the scope of work that can be caught within the ambit of the CIS is summarised in Appendix II. The definition of a contractor is not solely limited to persons carrying on a business which includes 'construction operations'. Businesses whose annual expenditure on 'construction operations' exceeds a certain minimum level are 'deemed contractors' under these rules and must operate CIS when making payments to subcontractors. Since 6 April 2021, this limit is £3m per annum which must be applied over a rolling 12-month period (previously £1m per annum averaged over three years).

The prescribed rates of tax withholding are 20% for standard rated sub-contractors and 30% for unmatched sub-contractors, ie unknown to HMRC as working in the construction industry.

Any contractor who fails to fulfil this obligation could be liable to HMRC for the amount of tax which should have been deducted. A genuine belief that the sub-contractor in question has properly accounted for receipts to HMRC and paid any related income or corporation tax will not necessarily prevent the contractor from still being liable for the withholding tax. However, HMRC should take any such payments into account to avoid double taxation (see Point 25.3).

A contractor must also consider whether an individual sub-contractor would be regarded as self-employed for tax purposes rather than as an employee (see Point 25.3). If satisfied the sub-contractor is not an employee, contractors must now verify their payment status by contacting HMRC using information provided by the sub-contractor. This can only be done by using the free HMRC online service or commercial third-party CIS software. HMRC provide a verification number and a payment status, gross or under deduction rate (20% or 30%) which a contractor should use until HMRC instructs otherwise or there is a gap between payments of more than two years. HMRC annually check gross payment sub-contractors' compliance and as a result have moved many on to deduction. Contractors receive a letter giving at least 30 days' notice of this change. HMRC are actively pursuing this policy and are generally taking a strict line. Contractors must provide sub-contractors on deduction with a statement that includes the amount deducted and the relevant unique verification number provided by HMRC.

CIS returns should be made monthly and show the sub-contractor's details and the amounts paid and deducted. Additionally, the return includes a declaration that employment status has been considered (see Point 25.4) and that all sub-contractors have been verified.

HMRC may charge penalties for late returns, incorrect returns, failures to provide statements to sub-contractors or failure to provide records to HMRC.

**Point 25.2:** ***It is advisable for there to be a contractual requirement for a sub-contractor to provide the information required for verification as a pre-condition to the making of any payment.***

The necessary information includes the sub-contractor's name, unique taxpayer reference, National Insurance number or company registration number. Additionally, for individuals it would be advisable to include a contractual requirement for sub-contractors to provide information required to establish their employment status.

As mentioned above, the contractor can be liable for tax and fines if these procedures are not followed.

**Point 25.3:** ***Contractors must also distinguish between self-employed individuals and those that HMRC regard as employees. For these latter persons, PAYE and NICs may apply to payments.***

According to the legislation, the onus is on the contractor to first determine whether the subcontractor is employed or not, and secondly to establish if any CIS withholdings are due. If the subcontractor is deemed to be employed by the contractor, they should be put on payroll and income tax and NIC deducted accordingly via the PAYE process.

On the other hand, if they are found to be self-employed, the CIS rules should be in point and the contractor must then verify the payment status of the subcontractor, with a view to determining if any tax deductions should be made.

Often, individuals are treated as self-employed by the person for whom they work when, in fact, they have many of the characteristics of employees. In those cases, HMRC will try to re-categorise the individual as an employee and collect back tax and National Insurance from the 'employer' going back up to six years for tax and National Insurance Contributions.

Typically, the self-employed deal with a number of non-associated customers, have their own premises and have their own resources of finance, staff and tools etc. Where those features are missing, HMRC will look for an employer/employee relationship for tax purposes, whether or not that is the case under employment law. Pointers for them include:

(a) Whether an individual works virtually full-time for the engager or is otherwise economically dependent on the engager.

(b) Does the individual have his own business premises?

(c) Does the individual have his own staff?

(d) Is the individual at risk for his time and capital?

Where the answer to the first question above is yes, and the answer to the remaining questions is no, there is a strong presumption in favour of an employer/employee relationship. If agreement cannot be reached with HMRC, the parties have to contemplate the time, expense and uncertainty of a hearing before the Appeals' Tribunals, and beyond that, the courts. Any Tribunal will look at the facts and circumstances of each case. The factors mentioned above and others (which can be found on HMRC website at https://www.gov.uk/employment-status/worker) will be persuasive but not decisive in the decision. It is important to remember also that what the parties may agree among themselves (eg the contract may state that the worker is self-employed and responsible for his or her own tax, etc) will be of little weight if the facts point the other way.

Prior to April 2014 there was legislation in existence which was known as the 'agency legislation'. Essentially where an agency engaged an individual personally to work for another party and the individual was under 'direction, supervision or control' (DSC), the agency was responsible for operating PAYE/NIC on payments made to the individual. However, agencies would fall outside of this requirement if the individual did not have to provide services personally. In view of this, agency contracts would often include a 'substitution clause' thus avoiding this legislation and the requirement for the agency to deduct PAYE/NIC. To counter this avoidance, the 'agency legislation' was revised as set out below. This legislation takes precedence over the CIS rules.

From 6 April 2014, an individual is treated as an employee for PAYE/NIC purposes if their work is undertaken and subject to (or to a right of) DSC by any party. If the answer to this question is yes then PAYE/NIC is due and the engagement is one of employment.

What then needs to be considered is: who is the intermediary; and who has to deduct the PAYE/NIC? A simple scenario would be where an end client engages with an agency (or intermediary) for the supply of services from an individual. As only one intermediary is involved, the intermediary is responsible for the PAYE/NIC.

It becomes more complicated if a supply chain is in existence, ie possibly more than one entity could be regarded as an intermediary. Regardless of where the intermediaries are based (onshore or offshore) HMRC will look to the intermediary 'closest' to the end user (ie the entity contracting directly with the end client) to operate PAYE/NIC.

It is clear that when an entity is engaging individuals and they are the entity 'closest' to the end user in the supply chain, it is that entity's obligation to understand the supply chain and know if PAYE/NIC has been deducted and paid over to HMRC. However, any entity in the supply chain could be regarded for the purposes of the legislation as an intermediary and therefore all entities should properly understand where they sit in that chain.

There is also a question as to whether a Personal Service Company (PSC) – typically an individual providing services through their own limited company – could be regarded as an intermediary. However, HMRC has stated that they do not expect the majority of PSCs to be regarded as such. This is on the basis that any payments made to the individual (generally a director shareholder of the PSC) will either be liable to PAYE/NIC as salary paid; a deemed payment via IR35; or dividends to the shareholder director which are not liable to PAYE/NIC,

To ensure that HMRC are aware of all engagements involving self-employed individuals quarterly reporting requirements were introduced from April 2015 for any intermediary caught by the legislation that does not operate PAYE/NIC on payments made to these individuals. Although the reporting requirement does not apply in cases where the intermediary has operated PAYE on payments made to the workers, there is no exclusion for subcontractors within CIS. Therefore, the intermediary still has to submit a quarterly report even if payments to all workers have already been included in monthly CIS returns.

Where an intermediary does not believe that the individual is subject to (or the right of) DSC, the reporting intermediary may then have to consider operating CIS on the payments if within the scope of the scheme and also make quarterly returns as the payments have not been subject to PAYE/NIC.

A different situation prevails if the individual worker is engaged indirectly through the medium of a service company or partnership ('the intermediary'), ie where the contract for the individual's services is concluded between the client and the intermediary that retains the individual's services. In such circumstances, if the facts are that the individual would be treated as an employee of the client if he or she had contracted directly with that client, then the 'IR35 rules' come into play. Under these rules (contained in *ITEPA 2003, Pt 2, Ch 8*), the intermediary will be liable for PAYE and National Insurance as if the payment from the client to the intermediary for the individual's services had been made by the intermediary to the worker as employment income, whether or not any such payment has been made (often, using the example of a service company, the individual will draw a small salary from the intermediary and receive the rest of the payment as a dividend).

If IR35 applies and the Construction Industry Scheme applies to payments by the client to the intermediary, the intermediary is treated as having received the payment gross (ie without taking any tax deduction into account) when the amount of the deemed payment under the IR35 rules is calculated. However, by concession, a company may set CIS deductions against IR35 tax and NIC due providing it makes a formal claim for a CIS deduction repayment by 31 January following the tax year.

Further legislation came into existence on 6 April 2017 called Off payroll working in the Public Sector. Where an individual provides their personal services through an intermediary, usually a PSC, to a Public Sector entity this entity has to determine if the individual would have been their employee had the PSC not existed. If the decision is yes and the Public Sector entity pays the PSC the Public Sector has to deduct PAYE/NIC on the invoice submitted. If the Public Sector does not pay the PSC because another intermediary or agency is the fee payer, the Public Sector must notify the fee payer of their decision on the employment status of the worker. The fee payer is then responsible for deducting PAYE/NIC.

If the worker is self-employed then the invoice can be paid gross. This legislation takes precedence over CIS.

It was announced that from April 2021 the same changes as above for the public sector will also be implemented for the private sector. However, the Chancellor's mini-budget in September 2022 confirmed that the new IR35 rules will be scrapped from April 2023 and from this date, the onus of determining IR35 status will be back on the contractor for both the public and private sectors. Under the managed service company (MSC) legislation, subject to a number of conditions, the IR35 rules do not apply. If the MSC rules apply, HMRC may transfer any PAYE/NIC debt to other parties. HMRC have said that normally it will not attempt to transfer the debt to a client. However, if the client knows the worker has come from an MSC, has encouraged the worker to provide his services through an MSC or has promoted the MSC then HMRC may seek to transfer the debt.

Since April 2021, HMRC has had the power to amend unsupported CIS deductions on a real time basis via real time information (RTI) employer payment summary (EPS) returns. This measure was introduced because as CIS deductions were being made against PAYE liabilities in some cases by non-CIS employers and subcontractor employers that were not companies, which exceeded the sums recorded as having been withheld from particular subcontractors in contractor returns.

This measure allows HMRC to amend unsupported deductions in real time in cases where there is evidence of incorrect deductions being made, by allowing the CIS deductions figure claimed in the subcontractor employer's EPS return to be corrected, in the absence of satisfactory supporting evidence.

According to HMRC, it will only take this step where subcontractors refuse to make corrections when they are directed to do so, however claimants will be given the opportunity to explain genuine errors.

**Point 25.4:** ***If a developer undertakes contract work, gross payment status may be essential to avoid a cash flow problem.***

Where the developer is potentially a sub-contractor and where work is being carried out for a 'contractor' (which may include persons outside the construction industry – see Point 34.1) gross payment status may be essential.

In the absence of gross payment status a withholding on payments must be applied and this will represent a payment on account of the developer's PAYE/NIC or final tax liability. In the meantime, the developer is faced with a loss of cash flow.

This means, currently, for instance, a 20% or 30% withholding of tax potentially leaves the developer with insufficient cash to pay for materials, staff, its own sub-contractors and income tax payments on account. However, sub-contractor companies – but not individuals or partnerships – may reduce their monthly payments to HMRC or PAYE/NIC and CIS deductions by the amount withheld. Consequently, subject, of course, to the relative amounts, fewer cash-flow difficulties arise for companies. If the subcontractor is paid net of 20% or 30% tax, the withholding is applied only to the labour element, excluding the cost of materials and VAT. Following an amendment to the legislation, with effect from 6 April 2021, any materials costs must have been incurred by the subcontractor in order to be disregarded.

Since 6 April 2021, penalties for false statements or documents submitted for the purpose of becoming registered for gross payment status have been in place. A maximum penalty of £3,000 may be charged, which can include the applicant, but also any person HMRC believes has exercised influence and control over a false CIS registration application. A developer anticipating the possibility of sub-contractor status on future projects should obtain and maintain gross payment status. HMRC reviews the compliance record of every gross payment sub-contractor every year. Results show that about one third of all sub-contractors fail the compliance test which, until recently, was carried out completely automatically. Many recover their gross payment status on appeal but not all, and these cannot reapply for a year. However, because of the First-tier Tribunal decisions noted below, which were won by the appellant in respect of the intended withdrawal of gross payment status, HMRC now exercise their discretion and write to subcontractors who could lose their gross payment status, to request details of why the failures occurred. If they can prove 'reasonable excuse' then gross payment status is not withdrawn and the appeal process does not have to be followed.

In the first of these Tribunal decisions, *John Scofield v HMRC* (TC 01068), the judge determined that HMRC were permitted to exercise discretion and indeed should have done so before issuing the withdrawal notice. In *Alan Kincaid t/a A K Construction v HMRC* (TC01090), the Tribunal accepted that reasonable excuse existed for two surcharges paid late. As the appellant also agreed a time to pay arrangement with HMRC, even though it was after the tax was due, the Tribunal agreed he was acting to address his problems. The Tribunal agreed the sub-contractor was behaving responsibly in relation to his tax affairs during the period in question. Therefore, it was reasonable to conclude there were no expectations of future compliance failures. These cases are welcomed on the basis that legislation can be challenged if the sub-contractor can demonstrate they acted responsibly.

Sub-contractors must fully comply with all their tax obligations to ensure they do not fail the scheduled review.

In this connection, sub-contractor status may not always be obvious. One relaxation in the rules is that payments from developers to tenants for fit out works are not caught by the scheme.

Gross payment status involves a detailed application procedure and is only issued to those individuals, partnerships and companies that meet the criteria.

In that connection, there are three tests to satisfy before HMRC will grant gross payment status. These are:

(a) The business test – essentially that the company is carrying on a construction business in the UK or providing workers for such a business. It also has to have its business bank account in the UK.

(b) The turnover test – income net of VAT and materials must be at least £30,000 per year in the case of sole traders. For companies and partnerships, it is £30,000 multiplied by the number of directors or partners, as the case may be. For larger businesses, there is the alternative test of a minimum of £100,000 turnover.

(c) The compliance test – to satisfy this the tax affairs of the business must be up to date for the preceding 12 months.

As part of the Autumn Statement on 22 November 2023, it was announced that VAT compliance will be included in the statutory compliance obligations for subcontractors applying for gross payment status from 6 April 2024.

In response to HMRC consultation, further changes are to be introduced to remove the majority of payments from landlords to tenants from the scope of CIS. This will result in subcontractor registrations not being required. Other changes have been introduced, such as the reduction from 12 months to six months for the review following GPS being granted, and the move to digital applications for CIS registrations. Assuming the platform is safe and secure, this should be more effective and allow HMRC to be chased for a response.

Notwithstanding the fact that the provisions were introduced to deal with small firms and individuals, it is also necessary for large firms to be able to demonstrate to HMRC a history of regular compliance with their corporation tax returns and payments.

Where gross payment status cannot be obtained, all contracts which might result in the development entity becoming a sub-contractor should be approached with caution. An unexpected withholding could well upset cash and profit budgets on a job.

*Chapter 26*

# VAT points for property developers

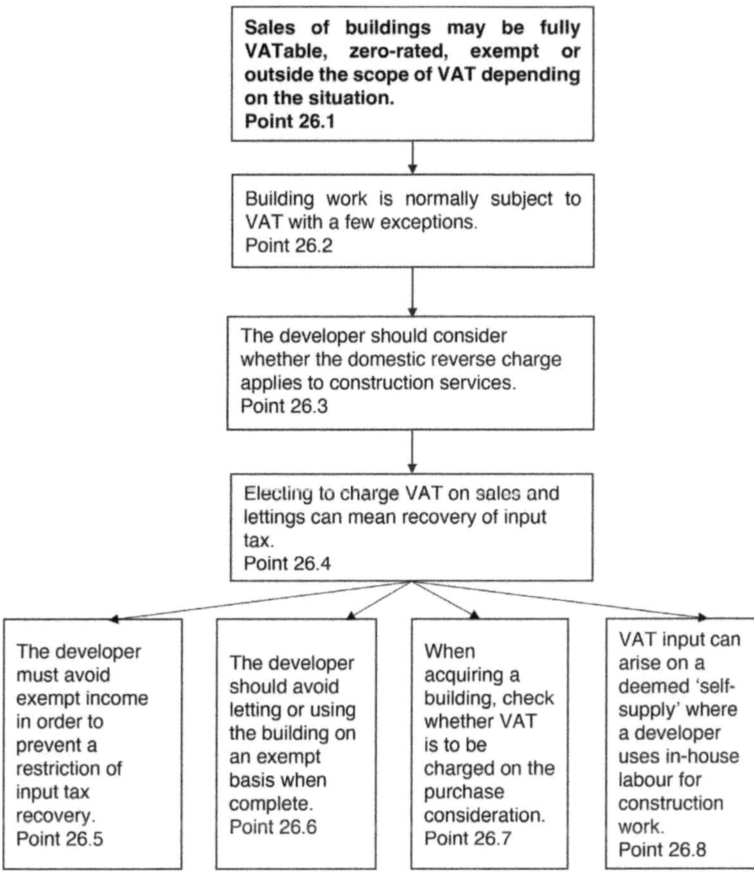

# 26 VAT POINTS FOR PROPERTY DEVELOPERS

**Point 26.1:** ***Sales of commercial buildings within three years of completion are VAT standard-rated supplies. Sales of new properties for residential or charitable use may be zero-rated. Any other sales would be exempt supplies, subject to the option to tax, unless outside the scope of VAT because of the 'going concern' rules.***

There are several possible VAT situations in connection with property-related supplies. These can be summarised as follows:

*Zero-rated*

(1) The sale by the developer of the freehold of a new building which is designed as a dwelling or where the purchaser is to use the property for a relevant residential or charitable purpose (a qualifying building) (see Point 18.4 for 'relevant' residential or charitable use). Also, zero-rated is the first sale of a renovated building that has not been used for any residential purpose for at least ten years, and is to be used as a dwelling. The sale of a qualifying building, which incorporates an insignificant part of a former building, could be zero-rated but this will be fact-specific (see *Astral Construction Ltd* [2015] UKUT 0021 (TCC)).

(2) The sale by the developer of the freehold of a building (or part of a building) which is designed as a dwelling or is to be used as in (1) above which is not new but is a substantially reconstructed protected building (see Point 18.5).

(3) The grant by the developer of a lease of more than 21 years (not less than 20 years in Scotland) in a building which is either new or a substantially reconstructed protected building where the design or use is as in (1) above (but see Point 18.5 for situations where this zero-rating has been removed or is subject to transitional rules). Only the initial consideration will be treated as the zero-rated output. This may be a premium payable on grant or the first rent payment if there is no premium.

(4) The grant of a lease of over 21 years (not less than 20 years in Scotland) or a freehold interest by a person converting a building from a non-residential building (or a non-residential part of a building) into a dwelling or dwellings or a property intended solely for a relevant residential use. Note that HMRC maintain that to qualify for zero-rating, the newly created dwelling must contain no part of any former dwelling.

*Standard-rated*

(5) The sale of a freehold of a non-residential building within three years of its completion.

(6) The sale of a freehold non-residential building more than three years after its completion if the developer has opted to tax that building. In the absence of such an option, any such sale would constitute an exempt supply (see (9) below, and Point 18.1 for the option to tax).

(7) The grant of a lease of a non-residential building by a developer who has opted to tax, as in (6), in respect of the building. In this situation, VAT must be added to any premiums and rents charged.

(8) The assignment or surrender of a lease of a commercial building by a person who has opted to tax the building.

*Exempt*

(9) All freehold sales, assignments, surrenders, grants of leases and licences other than the specified situations in (1) to (8) or (10) or listed at Point 18.9(c).

*Outside the scope of VAT*

(10) Sales of properties where there is a transfer of the business as a going concern (see Point 18.3).

The recovery of input tax, which could be substantial where there are major construction, refurbishment or repair works, may only be possible if property sales or grants are either zero-rated or standard-rated for VAT purposes. The developer's strategy should be to avoid exempt supplies. This may involve opting to tax lettings or sales, as discussed in Point 26.3 below. Alternatively, a sale which is outside the scope of VAT, such as in (10) above, may avoid irrecoverable VAT.

**Point 26.2:** ***Building work is subject to VAT at the standard rate with a few exceptions. These include the new construction of a building for residential or charitable use or the conversion, and in some circumstances the refurbishment, of a building for residential use.***

See Point 18.8 for a discussion of standard-rated and zero-rated building work, as well as the reduced 5% rate applying to certain conversions and refurbishments.

As a reminder, the 5% rate applies to the following supplies:

(a) converting a non-residential property into one or more single-household dwellings;

(b) converting a non-residential property into a building used solely for a 'relevant residential purpose';

(c) converting a non-residential property into a house in multiple occupation;

(d) changing the number of single-household dwellings in a building or part of a building;

(e) converting a single-household dwelling or a house in multiple occupation into a building used solely for a 'relevant residential purpose';

(f) converting a house in multiple occupation into a single-household dwelling;

(g) converting a single-household dwelling into a house in multiple occupation;

(h) converting a building used for a 'relevant residential purpose' into a house in multiple occupation;

(i) renovating or altering a single-household dwelling that has not been lived in for at least two years;

(j) renovating or altering a building used solely for a 'relevant residential purpose' that has not been lived in for at least two years;

(k) renovating or altering a house in multiple occupation that has not been lived in for at least two years;

(l) constructing, renovating or converting a building into a garage as part of the conversion or renovation of a property that qualifies for the reduced rate; and

(m) building materials and certain other goods incorporated by a builder into a building in the course of supplying services under (a)–(l) above.

A single-household dwelling is a dwelling intended for occupation by a single household (ie a single individual, a couple or a family).

A house in multiple occupation is a building that contains bed-sit accommodation.

For the definition of a relevant residential building, see Point 18.4 above.

The reduced rate can also apply to certain grant-funded heating installations and energy-saving materials.

**Point 26.3:** ***The developer should consider whether the domestic reverse charge applies to construction services.***

The domestic reverse charge for building work was introduced on 1 March 2021. Its purpose is to counter fraud in the construction industry (*VATA 1994, s 55A*).

Where a VAT-registered business supplies certain construction services to another VAT-registered business for onward sale, it is required to not charge VAT and issues a VAT invoice referencing reverse charge.

The recipient must account, as output tax, for the VAT due on that supply through its VAT return, instead of paying the VAT amount to the supplier. The recipient may recover that VAT amount as input tax, subject to the normal rules. The input tax will normally be recoverable in full, so that the reverse charge itself has no net effect.

The domestic reverse charge applies to supplies of 'specified services' between VAT-registered businesses where the recipient then makes an onward supply of those specified services. Specified services are generally services that are defined as construction operations for purposes of the Construction Industry Scheme (CIS).

Therefore, among those included within the scope of the rules are construction, alteration, repair, extension, painting, and decorating, plus the demolition of buildings, civil engineering and the installation of heating, lighting, and air-conditioning.

The domestic reverse charge applies if the following conditions are met.

(1) a supplier who is (or should be) registered for VAT makes a supply of building work at the reduced or standard rate;

(2) the customer is (or should be) 'registered' as a CIS contractor, and the payment for the supply is a CIS contract payment.;

(3) the customer is (or should be) registered for VAT and is acting in a business capacity; and

(4) the customer has not notified the supplier that it is an 'end user' or 'intermediary supplier.

When goods are supplied with construction services this is a single supply for VAT purposes and the domestic reverse charge applies to the full value of the invoice. However, there are exceptions to this rule as outlined below:

- Where the reverse charge element is 5% or less, the whole supply can continue to follow normal rules. However, where specified services have been provided between two parties, then subsequent services on the same site by the same supplier may also be covered by the domestic reverse charge, if both parties agree.
- If one supplier enters into two separate contracts and one of the contracts is within the scope of the Construction Industry Scheme, and the contracts are linked and both contracts will be carried out on the same site, the domestic reverse charge will apply to both contracts (subject to the 5% disregard rule above) as they comprise a single supply for VAT purposes.
- When a customer places a single supply and fix order within the scope of the Construction Industry Scheme with a supplier, the reverse charge will apply to the full value of the order even if the supplier issues separate invoices for the supply and fix elements.

The domestic reverse charge will apply to specified services unless:

- the services are supplied to an end user, such as the property owner, or directly to a developer that sells or lets a newly completed building;
- the services are supplied to an intermediary supplier, such as a company that is part of the same corporate group as the end user, or the services are supplied to a landlord for onward supply to a tenant or vice versa. The recipient is not VAT registered or required to be VAT registered;
- the recipient is not registered for the CIS; or
- the supplies are zero-rated.

An end user is a person who receives the specified services for any purpose other than making an onward supply of those services.

For the reverse charge not to apply to end users and intermediary supplies, they should notify the supplier or building contractor in writing that they are an end user or intermediary supplier.

### Invoicing

It is a legal requirement that suppliers include a statement on their invoices stating that the reverse charge applies. The following are examples of wording that meet the legal requirement, reverse charge:

- 'VAT Act 1994 Section 55A applies'.
- 'S55A VATA 94 applies'.
- 'Customer to pay the VAT to HMRC'.

The above is an overview of the domestic reverse charge; more detailed information can be found in HMRC's guidance 'VAT domestic reverse charge technical guide' at: www.gov.uk/guidance/vat-reverse-charge-technical-guide#how-to-account-for-the-reverse-charge.

**Point 26.4:** ***The developer should consider whether to opt to tax in situations where the sale or letting of a commercial property might otherwise be an exempt supply. This would give the developer the opportunity to recover any VAT incurred.***

The situations where a supply in connection with a commercial property is exempt for VAT purposes are highlighted in Point 26.1 above. In these situations, a developer can opt to tax in respect of any specific property, although if the building is a dwelling or used for relevant residential or charitable purposes (see Point 18.4) or where the option to tax is otherwise disapplied (see Point 18.1) the option to tax may have no effect.

The advantage for a property developer in making standard-rated as opposed to exempt supplies is that input tax incurred will be recoverable. Given that substantial VAT is likely to be involved in any construction or refurbishment project, this represents an important opportunity to recover this VAT. The VAT could not be recovered if the supplies in relation to a building remain exempt. Irrecoverable VAT could also arise on the deemed 'self-supplies' of construction services, as discussed in Point 26.7 below.

The discussion in Point 18.1, regarding the option to tax in relation to a property investor, is also relevant to a property developer, as is the cautionary message in Point 18.2. The option, once made, can only be revoked within six months of its being made, provided no input tax has been reclaimed and no supplies of the property have been made, or once 20 years have expired after making the option. Subject to that, it applies to all future supplies of the property. Thus, if a letting is taxable, so will be any subsequent lease grants. If the person making the option owns the freehold, then VAT would also have to be charged on any sale of a freehold, unless the 'going concern' rules apply (see Point 26.6 below). Furthermore, SDLT is also chargeable on the VAT element of the sale consideration or lease premium (see Point 5.4).

**Point 26.5:** ***Any exempt income during or after the development period can prejudice the entitlement to VAT recovery.***

VAT recovery will also be affected if the developer has exempt income during the period of construction or refurbishment. This might arise, for instance, if the person constructing it uses a site on an exempt basis in this period. This could happen with any exempt or partially exempt organisation, such as a charity, hospital, educational establishment or financial institution.

Alternatively, the site may be let on an exempt basis to users during the construction period.

Strictly, if there are only exempt supplies in a period, none of the VAT incurred during that period is recoverable. However, HMRC can agree a reasonable level of VAT recovery, taking into account prospective taxable supplies (*VAT Regulations 1995, reg 102*). As far as possible, it is advisable to establish a basis for recovery with HMRC at the outset. Otherwise, the developer may be budgeting for a higher level of VAT recovery than HMRC are prepared to allow. See Point 18.7 for a discussion on VAT recovery in respect of speculative and intended property developments and reference to the ability to apply a 'use based' calculation to some initial VAT recovery.

The developer should also be prepared for an impact on the VAT recovery if there is a subsequent change in plan that affects the anticipated periods of exempt and taxable supplies, either under the Capital Goods Scheme rules (see Chapter 35) or under the clawback rules (see comments at 18.7 and 26.6 below).

**Point 26.6:** ***The developer should try to avoid exempt letting or exempt use of the property at the outset.***

If a developer's first lease grant is on a VAT-exempt basis, any VAT reclaimed on the construction or refurbishment work can be clawed back by HMRC (VAT Registration 108). For that reason, the developer should ensure, where possible, that the initial lease grant is either zero rated, in the case of residential or charitable property (see Point 26.1 above), or opt to tax in the case of commercial property.

If the exempt letting is only temporary and the developer can demonstrate a definite intention to grant taxable interests or standard-rate rents, some recovery of VAT input tax is still possible and any adjustment to input tax recovery may arise under the 'clawback' rule in Regulation 108. (Refer to the HMRC Information Sheet 07/08 for commentary on HMRC's view.) The approach could involve agreeing with HMRC an appropriate basis for apportioning the VAT incurred between taxable and exempt supplies (see also *C & E Comrs v Briararch Ltd; C & E Comrs v Curtis Henderson Ltd* [1992] STC 732). There will, inevitably, be some loss of VAT in that situation, but note also the comments in 18.7.

**Point 26.7:** ***When acquiring a building, check whether VAT is to be charged on the purchase consideration.***

The question of VAT becoming chargeable on the purchase price is discussed in Point 18.9, and reference should be made to that section.

There is the possibility that a property sale is outside the scope of VAT if it is in connection with the transfer of a business as a going concern (TOGC). This topic is dealt with in Point 18.3 in relation to property investors. In some cases, the sale of a partially completed new development to a developer who carries on the project can be treated as a TOGC (*Golden Oak Partnership v C & E Comrs* (1992) VAT decision 7212).

As far as the seller is concerned, a TOGC does not create the same problem with VAT input recovery that an exempt supply would and any obligations for adjustment to input tax recovery either under the Capital Goods Scheme ('CGS') (see Point 35.7) or the clawback rules (Point 26.6) will pass to the buyer. The buyer, in turn, avoids having to pay VAT. However, this treatment is not optional.

Where VAT is chargeable on a sale, this will also result in an increased stamp duty land tax liability for the purchaser (see Point 18.10).

**Point 26.8:** ***When using in-house labour to construct a property, there is a deemed VAT charge on the self-supply of construction services. Normally this is recoverable, except where the building is wholly or partially let or occupied on an exempt basis.***

Where any construction work is undertaken in-house by a developer (or a member of the developer's VAT group), there is a deemed self-supply of construction services, unless the open-market value of the services is less than £100,000. VAT is charged on the market value of these services.

This represents a potential pitfall for the developer who enlarges or extends a building and grants a lease without electing to charge VAT on any rents or premiums due.

*Part C*

# Trading Premises

*Chapter 27*

# Premium relief on the acquisition of a short lease

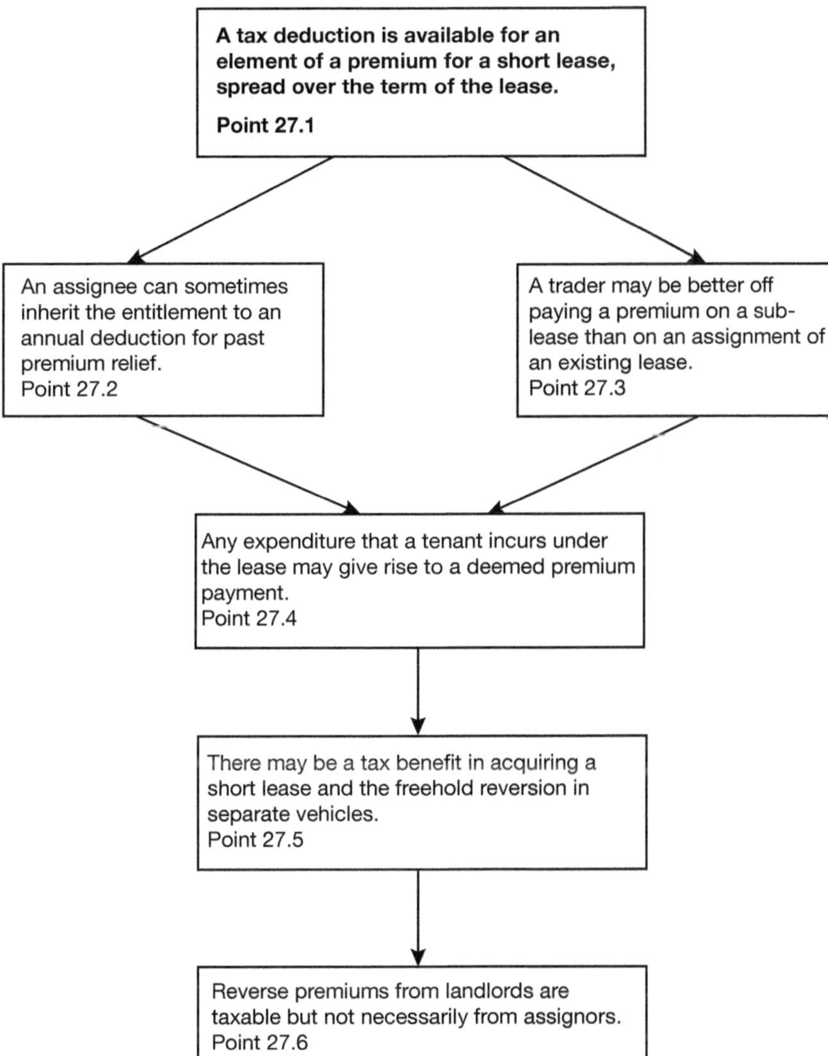

# 27 PREMIUM RELIEF ON THE ACQUISITION OF A SHORT LEASE

**Point 27.1:** ***Where a trader pays a premium on the grant of a short lease for business premises, an annual tax deduction can currently be claimed against trading income in respect of the 'income element'.***

On the grant of a lease of less than 50 years, the recipient of any premium paid will be assessed to tax on part of the total amount as if it were income rather than capital (see Chapter 9 in Part A). Where the premium is paid by a trader (including property rental businesses), an annual deduction can be claimed for this 'income element' spread over the life of the lease (*CTA 2009, s 66* for corporation tax; *ITTOIA 2005, ss 60, 61* for income tax).

The 'income element' is the total premium reduced by 2% for each year of the lease except the first.

---

## Example 1

A trader pays a £100,000 premium on the grant of a 20-year lease. The income element is £62,000 (£100,000 less 2% × (20 – 1) × £100,000). The annual deduction against the trader's profits will be this amount spread over the life of the lease, i.e. £3,100.

---

It will be noted that, whereas the recipient of a premium will be assessed to tax on the whole sum in the year of receipt, the lessee's relief must be spread over the full term.

**Point 27.2:** ***Premium relief is not limited to tenants paying a premium on the grant of a lease. An assignee of a lease can continue claiming the annual deduction which would have been available to the assignor, providing the property continues to be used for trading purposes.***

The annual premium deduction referred to in Point 27.1 above is available to any trader occupying the property for the duration of the lease. Thus, another trader taking an assignment of the lease will inherit the previous leaseholder's entitlement to a tax deduction, assuming the property is used for trading purposes. This will also be the case if the previous tenant was not entitled to a deduction. As long as, on the original grant of the lease, a premium was partly assessable as income (whether or not it was actually chargeable), a deduction will be available during the life of the lease to any successor in title using the property for trading purposes.

The relief gives rise to the practical problem of determining whether any premium was originally paid and to what extent it was assessable on the landlord. These are matters which should be ascertained, as far as possible, at the time of grant or assignment. Generally, details of any premium paid originally should be shown on the lease agreement or gleaned from Land Registry documents.

**Point 27.3:** ***In view of premium relief, a trader may be better off paying a premium on the grant of a sub-lease rather than on an assignment of the existing lease. There could well be situations where the assignor would be amenable to such an arrangement.***

---

## Example 2

A five-year lease is to be assigned for £100,000. No relief would be available on the expenditure of £100,000, except insofar as it formed part of the base cost of the lease for capital gains tax purposes. This would be depreciated to zero over its life. If, as an alternative, a sub-lease is granted for four years and eleven months on the payment of a premium of £105,000, £98,700 would be treated as the revenue element (i.e. £105,000 less 2% × (4 – 1) × 105,000). The trader would, therefore, be entitled to a monthly deduction of £1,673 over the 59 months of the lease.

---

Property vendors might be reluctant to enter into such an arrangement as it would involve them being taxed as a deemed recipient of rental income rather than as capital on part of their receipt. However, it may be a useful arrangement for, say, a pension fund that would be exempt from tax. Certain other vendors may also be prepared to enter into the arrangement if they have losses available to offset against any taxable profit arising.

A disadvantage from the grantor's point of view is that it leaves behind a residual interest (in this case, one month). For this reason it might be appropriate to offer somewhat more than the assignment price to compensate for this as in the example. Alternatively, the residual interest might be assigned to the lessee or an associate for a nominal sum at a later stage.

Another point to factor in to this planning is SDLT. The amount of SDLT payable will differ depending on whether a lease grant or lease assignment route is chosen. See Chapter 5 for further details on SDLT.

**Point 27.4:** ***A premium may not just be a cash payment to the landlord. Any expenditure which the tenant is obliged to incur under the terms of granting a lease could give rise to a premium relief deduction for the tenant.***

Where the terms under which the lease is granted impose an obligation to carry out any improvements, a deemed premium will arise. The measure of the premium is not the cost of the work, but the increase in the value of the recipient's interest as a direct result of the work. This amount would be taxable on the landlord in accordance with the premium rules and there would be the corresponding deduction for the tenant if occupied for the purpose of a trade.

This point could easily be overlooked by a tenant who might be faced with a disallowance of the expense of any improvement work. Clearly, there is a practical problem of determining the increase in the landlord's interest. However, as long as the situation is identified, it should be possible to liaise with the landlord or HMRC to ensure the appropriate relief is obtained.

**Point 27.5:** ***The availability of annual deductions for premiums paid does offer some scope for tax relief on the acquisition of long leasehold and freehold property. This can be achieved by acquiring a short lease and the reversionary interest separately.***

A trader, anticipating the acquisition of freehold or long leasehold premises, might take advantage of premium relief by carrying out the transaction in two stages:

(a) taking a grant of a short lease on the payment of a full market premium; and

(b) purchasing the residuary interest through a separate entity.

If we take the example of the proposed acquisition of a freehold for £1 million, a five-year lease could perhaps be granted for £250,000. The freehold could then be conveyed to, say, another group company for £750,000. Using the formula referred to in Point 27.1 above, the deemed income element would be £230,000, which would be allowable as a trading expense at a rate of £46,000 per year for five years to the leaseholder.

The arrangement has disadvantages from the view point of tax on capital gains. The short lease is a wasting asset for capital gains purposes and, after five years, no part of the £250,000 paid would be reflected in the base cost of the freehold. Accordingly, the capital gains cost on the property would be £750,000 rather than £1 million. Historically, a further consideration has been that companies within the charge to corporation tax have an entitlement to claim an indexation allowance calculated by reference to the retail prices index and applied to the base cost. As the retail prices index for this purpose were frozen with effect from December 2017, this is no longer a consideration for new transactions but would still be relevant to future disposals of properties where leases were granted at a premium in the past. In these circumstances, indexation allowance would only be calculated on £750,000 in the example.

Many trading companies may not be affected by the possibility of extra tax on capital gains. In practice, this can often be deferred indefinitely by claiming relief for replacement of business assets (see Chapter 30).

A further capital gains disadvantage can arise here from the fact that the company owning the freehold will not be occupying it for trading purposes. Thus, the property will not technically be an asset qualifying under the capital gains roll-over provisions. However, relief is nevertheless available in the following situations:

(a) a property is owned by an individual and occupied by his family trading company (*TCGA 1992, s 157*);

(b) a property is owned by a partner and used by the partnership (*TCGA 1992, s 152* – see Statement of Practice D11); or

(c) a property is held by a property holding company within a group and occupied by a fellow group company (*TCGA 1992, s 175*).

In the above situations, therefore, the availability of roll-over relief need not be jeopardised by this arrangement. Accordingly, this type of planning could provide the opportunity for short-term revenue deductions for a trading entity, whereas the extra tax on capital gains might be deferred indefinitely.

**Point 27.6:** ***Premiums received by tenants from landlords as inducements to enter into a lease ('reverse premiums') are taxable. Tax can be deferred depending on the accounting policy adopted or if the receipt is a contribution to fixtures and fittings. Inducement payments from assignors should not be taxable.***

Where a tenant receives a payment from a prospective landlord as an inducement to enter into a lease, this is taxable as part of the profits of the tenant (*CTA 2009, s 250; ITTOIA 2005, s 101*).

In taxing the receipt, HMRC will follow the tenant's accounting treatment for the item, assuming it is in accordance with generally accepted accounting practice. If this involves bringing the receipt into the balance sheet and then crediting it to the profit and loss account over, say, the five years to the first rent review (as would be the case under historic UK Generally Accepted Accounting Practice) or over, say, the lease term (as is the case under Financial Reporting Standard 102) only the amount so credited each year is taxable.

An alternative treatment is available if the receipt is a contribution toward fixtures and fittings. Where these are eligible for capital allowances as plant or machinery (see Chapter 6), the allowances are restricted to the expenditure net of the contribution. That means that the contribution is effectively brought into taxable profit over a period through capital allowances at a rate of 18% each year on a reducing balance basis. After eight years, around 80% of the amount would have been brought into tax with most of the remaining 20% taking a further 14 years or so to be subject to tax. If the contribution is in respect of 'integral features' or 'long-life assets' (see Points 6.5 and 6.6), the annual writing-down allowance is at the lower rate of 6% (8% prior to April 2019) and the process is extended accordingly.

Whilst there is specific legislation with regard to inducement payments given to existing tenants by landlords, there are no rules for similar payments from assignors of leases – unless either the assignors are connected with the landlord (see HMRC *Bulletin 44*, December 1999) or acting on the directions of the landlord. These receipts are capital in nature and, in the absence of special rules, are not taxable as income. Since an asset (ie the lease) is only owned as a consequence of receiving the amount, there is no capital sum derived from an asset or its disposal and, as a consequence, the capital gain is not taxable. Therefore, as long as it is a pure inducement payment, an amount paid to a prospective tenant to take an assignment of a lease should not be taxable on the tenant.

What needs to be avoided, as far as the tenant is concerned, where the payment is on an assignment, is any reference to the assignor's contributing to the new tenant's fit-out. In that situation, there would be effective taxation of the receipt through disallowance of capital allowances on the related element of expenditure.

*Chapter 28*

# Tax relief for finance costs

**Generally, finance costs will be fully deductible on the same basis as they are treated in the accounts.**
**Point 28.1**

Companies should try and get professional fees on property projects allocated as far as reasonable to the funding aspects. These and other finance costs will be allowable even if capitalised in the accounts.
Points 28.2 and 28.3

Watch debt releases in the hands of company borrowers as this can give rise to taxable income.
Point 28.4

Individuals and companies can offset excess finance costs against other income and gains.
Point 28.5

A company's relief for delayed payments of interest may be deferred. This can offer tax planning possibilities.
Point 28.6

Tax relief for finance costs can be restricted if the arrangements are uncommercial or a company is thinly capitalised.
Point 28.7

Tax must be deducted from interest payments by individuals to non-residents and in some circumstances by companies.
Point 28.8

The introduction of rules for 'alternative finance' has improved tax relief for financing structures which are compliant with Islamic law.
Point 28.9

# 28 TAX RELIEF FOR FINANCE COSTS

**Point 28.1:** ***A trader that obtains conventional finance from an unconnected lender for property investment is entitled to a tax deduction for the related finance costs. The deduction for the interest and other costs is normally given on the same basis as they are treated in the accounts.***

Finance costs are, generally speaking, deductible from taxable trading profits on the same basis as they are reflected in the accounts.

The treatment differs depending on whether or not the borrower is a company. If it is, there are a range of deductions permissible as set out below. For an individual or trustee, the deduction is limited to finance costs of a revenue nature. However, in principle, 'capital' costs such as legal, accounting and bank fees relating to the borrowing may be allowable as incidental costs of obtaining finance. There are also differences as mentioned in Points 28.2 to 28.8 below.

Foreign companies would generally be subject to the same rules as a UK company with regards to UK property.

The general income tax principles applying to the financing costs of individuals and trustees are summarised at Point 3.1. The measures which begin to cap the availability of relief for non-corporate owned residential property businesses from 6 April 2017 (and now restricted to basic rate tax reduction) would not be in point here.

The general corporation tax principles applying to the financing costs of UK and non-resident companies are summarised at Points 3.9 and 3.10. This commentary includes measures intended to modernise and simplify the loan relationships rules included in the *Finance (No 2) Act 2015*.

**Point 28.2:** ***For UK corporate borrowers funding purchases of property or related capital projects, fees should be allocated as far as reasonable to the funding.***

The purchase of trading premises – or, indeed, any capital asset – gives rise to costs that may not be deductible from taxable profit. Such costs may be of a capital nature, ie they relate to an item which confers a benefit for far longer than just the current accounting period. As such, they cannot be expensed for tax purposes against the profits of this or any other year.

Where a property attracts an element of capital allowances (see Chapter 29), the professional costs might be apportioned wholly or partly over the relevant aspects of the property and included in the related capital allowance claim. At best, however, this will only confer a deduction which must be spread over a number of years.

If the fees relate to the funding, then they are part of the finance costs for which a deduction can be claimed. It is, therefore, worthwhile liaising with professionals supplying their services in relation to a property acquisition, reconstruction or refurbishment to ensure they allocate an appropriate portion of their fees to the related funding exercise.

**Point 28.3:** ***If a UK company capitalises interest in the balance sheet, tax relief can still be claimed in that year where the finance is in respect of capital assets.***

The normal rule provides for a deduction for any finance costs which are charged to the income statement.

Where interest is included in the value of a fixed asset in the balance sheet, a deduction can be claimed for tax purposes (*CTA 2009, s 320*). This would include, therefore, interest on finance for purchases and development of trading premises. See Point 3.11 for further commentary on this.

**Point 28.4:** ***Watch debt releases, as they can give rise to a tax liability in the hands of a corporate borrower.***

In the same way that costs and expenses reflected in the income statement are normally allowed for tax purposes, so will any credits potentially be taxed under the loan relationship rules for companies.

Distressed property situations have been resolved in the past by an arrangement between the lender and borrower under which some or all of the debt is forgiven. A credit to a company's income statement as a result of such a release typically gives rise to taxable income if the parties are not connected. This can also be the case if the credit is directly to reserves or where impaired debt is bought back by a connected company at a discount, although the legislation includes a helpful corporate rescue exemption for distressed situations.

See Points 3.13 and 3.14 in Chapter 3B for a further discussion on debt releases, including deemed releases, together with corporate rescue and insolvency situations which do not trigger taxable debt releases.

**Point 28.5:** ***Where a borrower has raised finance for a property used in a trade, excess finance costs can reduce other income or gains chargeable to tax.***

Where funds have been borrowed for trading purposes, the related finance costs will usually be deductible on an accruals basis as trading expenses. The costs are part of the borrower's normal trading expenses.

For individuals (including individuals in partnerships), surplus expenses can be relieved as follows:

(a) against other income arising in the same year of assessment (*ITA 2007, s 64*). Note that offset for such losses together with certain other deductions .being capped as the greater of £50,000 or 25% of the individual's income;

(b) if there is still an unrelieved loss, against income of the preceding year (*ITA 2007, s 64(2)(b)*);

(c) any loss still unrelieved can be offset against any chargeable gains for the year and against chargeable gains of the previous year, if a claim for setting the loss against income of that year is possible and has been made (*ITA 2007, s 71*); and

(d) any remaining unrelieved losses can be carried forward against future trading income (*ITA 2007, s 83*).

In the first four tax years of assessment of a trading business, the possibility of offset is yet greater. The loss can be offset against income for up to three years preceding the year of assessment in which the loss is made. This offset against general income is subject to the same annual cap referred to under (a) above (*ITA 2007, s 72*).

Note that, where individuals are involved in limited partnerships or limited liability partnerships, loss relief against other income or gains may be restricted (*ITA 2007, ss 104* and *107*).

There is also provision for 'terminal loss relief' where a loss is sustained in the final 12 months of trading, which supplements the reliefs mentioned above. Under the terminal loss rules, the loss can be offset against any profits from the trade in the three years ending immediately before the commencement of the 12-month period up to the date of discontinuance (*ITA 2007, s 89*).

For a company, expenses can be offset in the following ways:

(a) against other profits (including other income and gains) of the company in the same year (*CTA 2010, s 37(3)(a)*);

(b) surrender by way of group relief against the total taxable profit of any UK company within the same group in the same year (*CTA 2010, s 97*);

(c) carry-back up to one year against total profits of the same company (*CTA 2010, s 37(3)(b)*);

(d) carry-back up to three years as a terminal loss in the last period of trading (*CTA 2010, s 39*);

(e) carry-forward indefinitely in the company against total profits from the same trade . For losses that arose pre-1 April 2017 and were carried forward, the loss relief was only available against profits of the same trade.

For losses that accrue after 1 April 2017, only 50% of group profit can be sheltered by carried forward losses. This is subject to a £5m profit *de minimis* below which the profit would be fully offsettable. This £5m threshold applies on a group basis.

**Point 28.6:** ***Particularly where the borrower is a close company, interest may need to be paid within 12 months of the year end to get a tax deduction in the year of accrual.***

Point 3.17 sets out the situations where the late interest rules can apply to related party financing (*CTA 2009, s 373*) and other relevant considerations. Where these are in point, relief for accrued interest can be deferred until it is paid, if after 12 months from the year end. Similar provisions can apply to postpone relief for discount arising on deeply discounted securities until the debt is redeemed.

Since individuals and trustees are not subject to corporation tax, they can be regarded as related lenders where they, or their associates, lend to close companies in which they are (directly or indirectly) participators. However, a mismatch can arise because, for example, UK-resident individuals will generally suffer full UK income tax in the income tax year in which the interest is received.

In many cases, that gives rise to an opportunity to exploit a potential cash flow tax advantage. See the example at Point 3.19 in Chapter 3B for an illustration of this.

**Point 28.7:** ***Finance costs are allowable on funds borrowed from associated and connected persons. This includes lenders based overseas. However, transfer pricing rules will restrict deductibility where loans are not commercial or borrowed by companies that are thinly capitalised.***

See Point 3.5 (for individuals, trustees and non-resident companies) and Points 3.20 and 3.21 (for UK companies) for a discussion on the need for arm's-length terms in any borrowing arrangement, which is intended to represent a normal commercial loan, and the possibility of disallowance for companies with excessive debt-to-equity ratios.

Point 3.22 summarises anti-avoidance legislation that can apply where companies enter into tax-motivated financing arrangements, including the introduction of a general anti-abuse rule in *Finance Act 2013*.

**Point 28.8:** ***For payments of interest to anyone other than a UK bank, it is always advisable to check whether there is an obligation to deduct tax.***

HMRC can collect tax from borrowers who make payments of interest in a number of situations.

There is a different regime for individuals, on the one hand, and UK companies on the other. See Points 3.6 and 3.7 in Chapter 3A regarding the obligation on individuals (including individuals in partnerships) to deduct tax on interest payments to non-residents. This also relates to trustees, although it is rare for trustees to be directly involved in trading activities.

Points 3.23 to 3.28 in Chapter 3B deal with the tax deduction issues for companies.

**Point 28.9:** ***The introduction of rules for 'alternative finance' has enabled tax relief to be obtained for costs incurred in relation to financing structures which are compliant with Islamic law.***

See Point 3.29 in Chapter 3B for an outline of the typical structures and arrangements that have been accommodated by changes in the UK tax rules.

These have been consolidated into *CTA 2009* (for corporates) and *ITA 2007* (for individuals).

**Point 28.10:** ***The Corporate Interest Restriction from 1 April 2017 has a significant impact on the tax deductibility of debt.***

See Point 3.30 for a summary of the Corporate Interest Restriction provisions which can restrict the UK corporation tax relief for financing expenses of both connected and unconnected party debt.

# Chapter 29

# Capital allowances on plant and machinery

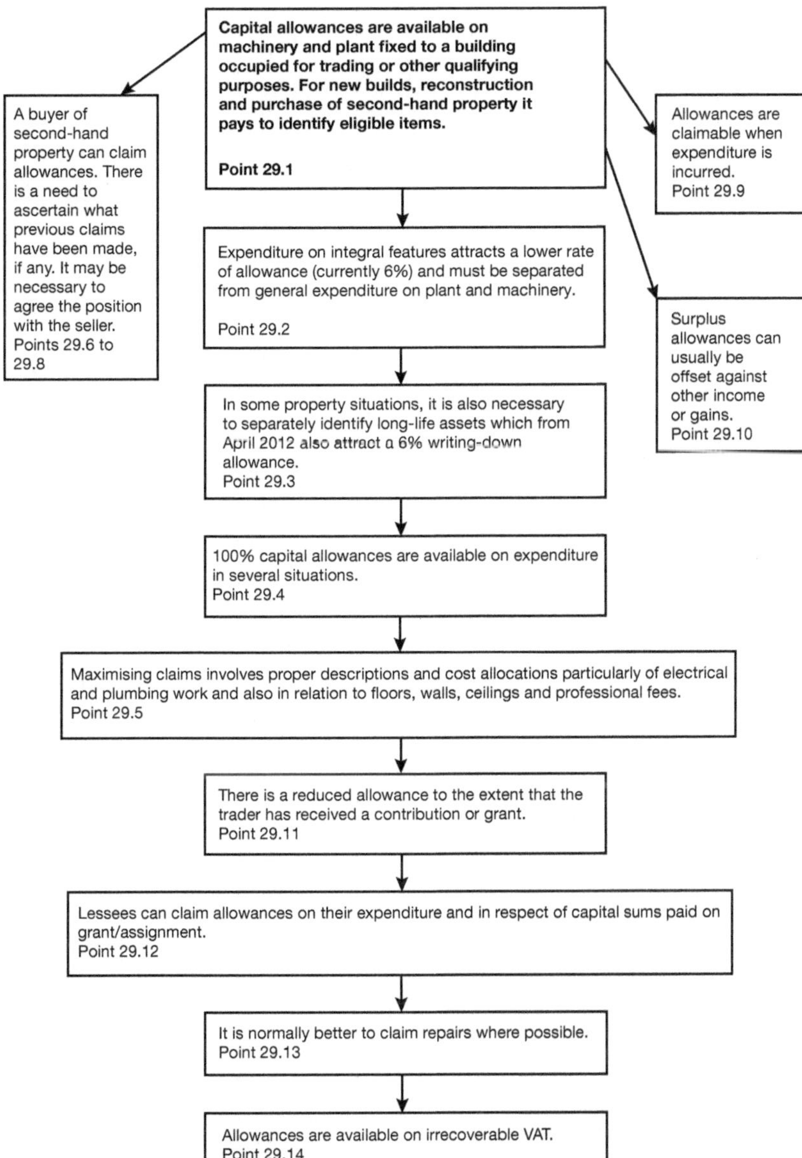

# 29 CAPITAL ALLOWANCES ON PLANT AND MACHINERY

**Point 29.1:** ***A trader can claim capital allowances on expenditure in respect of plant and machinery that is fixed to a building occupied for trading purposes.***

Capital allowances are available on capital expenditure incurred by a person carrying on a 'qualifying activity' on plant and machinery acquired for that purpose (*CAA 2001, s 11*). A trade is a qualifying activity (*CAA 2001, s 15(1)(a)*).

For accounting periods ending after 31 March 2012 for corporate taxpayers and after 5 April 2012 for individuals and others subject to income tax, annual allowances at a rate of 18% can be applied to the tax written-down value of the plant unless the items of plant and machinery are integral features or long-life assets (see Points 29.2 and 29.3 below).

Expenditure on the separate categories of 'integral features' and long-life assets within a building attract a reduced annual writing-down allowance of 6% (8% prior to April 2019 – see Points 29.2 and 29.3 below).

First-year allowances have been largely replaced from April 2008 by the annual investment allowance (AIA).

With the AIA amount having gone through several changes over the years, the standard AIA, previously set at £200,000, was temporarily increased to £1 million from January 2019 and was due to revert back to its level of £200,000 after March 2023.

However, to support businesses to invest in the UK, the government permanently increased the AIA level to £1 million from 1 April 2023.

**Point 29.2:** ***Expenditure on 'integral features' is separated from other plant and machinery, as this attracts a lower rate of annual allowance. For accounting periods after 1 April 2019 for corporate tax payers and after 6 April 2019 for income tax payers, the rate is 6% (8% prior to these dates). The category of integral features may include some items for which allowances were not previously available.***

From April 2008, a new category of plant was introduced for certain fixtures which are considered to be integral to the structure of a building. Initially, a 10% rate of annual writing-down allowance applied, but this fell to 8% from April 2012 and reduced to 6% from April 2019.

There is a short but specific list of items that are eligible for this lower allowance (see Point 6.5). This covers some of the more significant areas of plant expenditure within a construction or refurbishment project.

Under this new category, there is expenditure which previously was not eligible for writing-down allowances as plant or machinery. The items eligible for this allowance are:

(a) lifts, escalators and moving walkways;

(b) space or water heating systems;

(c) powered systems of ventilation, air cooling or air purification, and any floor or ceiling comprised in such systems;

(d) electrical systems (including lighting systems);

(e) cold water systems; and

(f) external solar shading.

The current rate of 6% applies for accounting periods commencing after 1 April 2019 for corporate tax payers, and after 6 April 2019 for income tax payers..

A taxpayer may have incurred some expenditure relating to integral features prior to the current regime where this expenditure is within a pool attracting allowances at the 18% rate applying from April 2012. For certain transactions, therefore, buying a property company with its ongoing plant and machinery pool may be more beneficial than buying the property if there was significant spend on, say, air conditioning, which previously qualified as plant and machinery but now qualifies as an integral feature. However, where there is substantial expenditure on, say, general electrical systems, it may be more beneficial to purchase the property itself. Electrical systems, for instance, now qualify as an integral feature where previously they were ineligible for capital allowances, although for property acquired on or after 1 April 2014 for corporation tax and 6 April 2014 for income tax there may be a restriction imposed if the vendor had not included the plant in their capital allowance calculations (see Point 6.12 for further details of the *Finance Act 2012* changes).

See Point 29.11 below for a summary of the rules for identifying when expenditure is actually incurred for these purposes.

**Point 29.3:** ***In some property situations, it is also necessary to separately identify long-life machinery, and plant which also attract an 6% allowance.***

Writing-down allowances for certain 'long-life' plant and machinery are currently available at a rate which is 6% from April 2019 (previously 8%).

The reduced allowance relates to items where there is a reasonable expectation of a useful economic life of at least 25 years when they are first brought into use and cost in excess of £100,000. These provisions do not apply where the plant and machinery in question is a fixture in a building used as a retail shop, showroom, hotel or office or for a purpose which is ancillary to any of these (*CAA 2001, s 93*).

Typical items of plant installed as fixtures of buildings would not have an expected useful life over 25 years and many of the more common commercial buildings have been excluded in any event. Where buildings are used for purposes that are not excluded – the leisure and nursing home sectors being notable examples – the category of 'long-life' assets could be relevant. Expenditure on 'long-life' assets is included in the special rate pool with expenditure on integral features together with expenditure on thermal insulation and solar panels.

**Point 29.4:** ***100% capital allowances are available for certain expenditure of up to £1,000,000 under the annual investment allowance scheme.***

100% allowances, which provide the opportunity for a complete write-off of costs in the year in which they are incurred, can be claimed in the following situations:

(a) The first £1,000,000 of expenditure on plant and machinery incurred by a business under the annual investment allowance (AIA) scheme. This relief can include qualifying expenditure on integral features (Point 29.2) and long-life assets (Point 29.3). It is aimed at all sizes of businesses (*CAA 2001, s 51A*).

Only one AIA is available for a group of companies each year. The provisions also seek to prevent associations of companies from gaining a multiple entitlement to the allowance by fragmenting their expenditure between a number of companies.

(b) Land remediation relief is available to companies bringing derelict long-term unused land (see Point 4.5), back into use. A similar relief exists for contaminated land. Note that it may be possible to achieve a 150% deduction for this type of expenditure.

(c) Full expensing for companies – for qualifying expenditure incurred on or after 1 April 2023 and before 1 April 2026, companies can claim:

- a 100% first-year allowance for main rate expenditure – (full expensing); and
- a 50% first-year allowance for special rate expenditure.

**Point 29.5:** ***Whether the expenditure is on the construction of a new building, reconstruction work at an existing building or the purchase of a second-hand building, it pays to identify the items on which capital allowances could be due.***

See Points 6.1 to 6.4 in Part A for a discussion of what constitutes plant and machinery in a building. Appendix I lists some of the more common items within a building and the extent to which they qualify for allowances. Note that expenditure on some of the items of plant listed have, since April 2008, been regarded as integral features and part of a separate pool attracting a lower rate of writing-down allowances (see Point 29.2 above). Furthermore, some expenditure in certain buildings is treated as 'long-life assets' which also attract a reduced rate of writing-down allowance (see Point 29.3 above). This expenditure will go into the special rate pool together with expenditure on integral features, thermal insulation and solar panels.

The above legislation, in specifying which items constitute plant, needs to be read in conjunction with case law where the distinction between plant and non-plant has been explored in a number of cases (see Points 6.3 and 6.4 in Part A).

In the past, there has been much debate over what expenditure does qualify as plant. Electrical and water installations can be problematic with HMRC seeking to disallow normal services to the building. This issue has been alleviated as a result of the integral features regime (see Points 6.3, 6.4 and 6.5 in Part A).

Expenditure on items such as floors, walls and ceilings have, in the past, been disallowed, since these items are normally associated with the setting of the business rather than apparatus used in the trade. However, sometimes allowances are lost because of inappropriate description or allocation of the amounts involved. As mentioned above, the integral features category of expenditure introduced in April 2008 also provides opportunities to claim allowances (see further Points 6.4 and 6.5).

Finally, an element of professional fees should be allowed (see Point 6.8).

As mentioned in Point 29.6 below, the introduction in *Finance Act 2012* of rules on capital allowance claims on property acquisitions from April 2012 where a claim has been made by a previous owner makes claims more complex for the new owner.

**Point 29.6:** ***A buyer of second-hand property with fixtures that qualify as plant and machinery can potentially claim significant allowances. Steps should be taken to establish eligibility and the likely quantum of allowances.***

Tax relief arising from capital allowances on the purchase of a property enables the buyer to recoup a part of the cash outflow. A buyer will, in many cases, need the co-operation of the seller in identifying details of past expenditure and verifying the amount available for allowances going forward. See Point 6.12 in Chapter 6 for a further discussion on these rules.

Since April 2008, some items of expenditure relate to 'integral features' (see Point 29.2 above) attracting writing-down allowances at a lower rate of 6% (8% prior to April 2019). The actual entitlement to allowances will be influenced by the following factors:

(a) Whether the plant allowances attach to the interest being purchased. The freeholder is normally the person owning the plant and entitled to allowances. However, in the past, an election may have been made in favour of a long lessee (see Point 6.10). Alternatively, the allowances may arise from expenditure by the lessee, such as the retail tenant that fits out empty premises. Clearly, whether the freehold or a leasehold interest is bought, it is important to establish the capital allowances background to that interest.

    Note that lessees can claim allowances in respect of fixed plant in a building even though as a matter of law these items belong to the freeholder (see Point 6.10).

(b) For properties bought on or after 1 April 2012 (for corporation tax purposes) or 6 April 2012 (for income tax purposes) what was the vendor's claims history, and is the vendor looking to do a deal on the allowances (see Point 6.12).

(c) Whether the plant or machinery is an integral feature or long-life asset (see Points 6.5 and 6.6) or otherwise subject to a reduced 6% annual allowance – see Point 29.3 above.

(d) Whether there might be eligibility for 100% allowances on any expenditure (see Point 29.4 above).

(e) The long funding lease legislation introduced in *FA 2006* (see Point 6.10).

**Point 29.7:** ***The buyer and seller should elect, whenever possible, to fix the value of the plant and machinery for capital allowances purposes on the transfer of a property.***

See Point 6.13 in Part A for a discussion on this point.

**Point 29.8:** ***There remain situations where there is no restriction on the amount eligible for allowances by reference to the vendor's or previous owner's expenditure. In those instances, the amount eligible can be determined by estimating a just and reasonable apportionment of the purchase price.***

See Point 6.14 for details of these situations.

**Point 29.9:** ***The allowances are claimable in the chargeable period in which expenditure is incurred.***

Capital allowances are claimable when expenditure is incurred.

Once a trade is commenced, future expenditure is treated as incurred when there is an unconditional obligation to pay (*CAA 2001, s 5(1)*). This might be when an invoice is issued or a binding agreement signed.

On long-term construction contracts, stage payments are normally made periodically on production of an architect's certificate. When the obligation to pay becomes unconditional on the production of a certificate, expenditure is treated as incurred in an accounting period or period of account if the certificate is issued not more than one month after the end of the period.

Where payment is due more than four months after the obligation to pay becomes unconditional, the expenditure is treated as incurred on the date(s) it is due to be paid (*CAA 2001, s 5(5)*). The issue of an invoice or signing of a contract designed to bring forward the capital allowances claim to an earlier accounting period or period of account than would have been the case in a normal commercial transaction is countered by an anti-avoidance provision (*CAA 2001, s 5(6)*).

**Point 29.10:** ***Traders can use surplus allowances in a number of ways, but the rules differ depending on whether or not the claimant is a company.***

Where capital allowances exceed income, individuals and companies can use the resulting trading loss in a number of ways. These have already been set out in Chapter 28 in relation to finance costs, and reference can be made to Point 28.5 on this. As mentioned, the government introduced a cap on the amount of such deductions against an individual's general income from 6 April 2013. For companies, the offset of carried forward losses is set to be restricted to 50% of profits after 1 April 2017, subject to a *de minimis* per group of £2m profits.

**Point 29.11:** ***If a trader receives a contribution towards capital expenditure, capital allowances will usually be restricted.***

A capital contribution or grant that a trader gets toward the installation of plant or machinery will normally restrict the amount eligible for capital allowances accordingly (*CAA 2001, s 532*).

Where the contribution toward a prospective tenant's capital allowances expenditure is agreed by a landlord as an inducement for the tenant to enter into a lease ie a rent free period, this may result in a more favourable treatment than a pure inducement payment (see Point 27.6). On the other hand, where the payer is not the landlord – for instance, the assignor of the lease – a pure inducement payment unattached to any specific works/assets may well not give rise to any tax liability in the trader's hands and thus be a better proposition for the tenant than a contribution toward fit-out (which would be deductible from the capital allowances identified).

**Point 29.12:** ***Lessees can claim allowances in respect of fixed plant in a building even though, as a matter of law, these items belong to the freeholder.***

Lessees are entitled to allowances on fixed plant in the following circumstances:

(a) Where a lessee incurs expenditure on fixed plant for use in a trade (or other qualifying activity), capital allowances can be claimed on that expenditure (*CAA 2001, s 176*).

(b) Where a lessee takes an assignment of a lease and pays a capital sum that wholly or partly represents expenditure on fixed plant, the lessee can claim allowances on that element of the payment in respect of the plant (*CAA 2001, s 181*). A claim can only be made if either no one has previously been entitled to claim the allowance, or the receipt is brought into the vendor's capital allowances computation. The new lessee's expenditure for capital allowance purposes cannot include items which belong to a sub-tenant, nor can the lessee become entitled to allowances on assets on which the freeholder is entitled to claim.

(c) A lessee can claim allowances where a capital sum is paid on the grant of a lease and the sum wholly or partly includes expenditure in respect of fixed plant (*CAA 2001, s 184*). However, if the lessor would otherwise have been entitled to the allowances, both the lessee and the lessor must make an election within two years of the commencement of the lease if the lessee is to claim the allowances (*CAA 2001, s 183*). If no election is made, the lessor might be entitled to the allowances.

No election is necessary if the lessor would not have been entitled to allowances. An election cannot be made where the lessor and the lessee are connected, or the sole or main object would be the obtaining of allowances.

(d) A lessee may be able to claim allowances where the long funding lease rules apply (Point 6.10).

Where a lessee does become entitled to claim allowances in accordance with (b) and (c) above, the rules introduced in *Finance Act 2012* should be adhered to in order to ensure a valid claim can be made. See Point 6.12 for further details.

**Point 29.13:** ***It is worthwhile scrutinising expenditure to see whether it may strictly qualify as repairs and maintenance, since this can be fully deductible in the year it is incurred.***

When an item of plant is installed or completely replaced, the related expenditure will be treated as capital and eligible for capital allowances. However, if the expenditure is in respect of the overhaul of plant or the replacement of parts, then this should qualify for a full deduction as repairs or maintenance at the point it is expensed.

It may be advisable to consider the exact nature of work carried out, or to be carried out, to determine whether expenditure that might appear to be capital is, in fact, revenue. For instance, if air-conditioning work involves the removal of defective ducting, rather than the replacement or renewal of a whole system, that might be shown as repairs. Similarly, if heating expenditure related to the replacement of worn radiators, then it would be repairs as opposed to capital expenditure. However, if the work changes the nature of the original asset, that would not be a repair – such as in the case of plastic inner piping inserted within an old cast-iron main (*Auckland Gas Co Ltd v IRC* [2000] STC 527).

Since April 2008, expenditure on the replacement of part of an item of plant that qualifies as an integral feature is treated as capital expenditure if the cost is more than 50% of the cost of replacing the whole asset (see Point 4.7). Subject to this point, when reviewing a refurbishment programme, it may well be sensible to consider repairing assets where this is a possibility rather than replacing them (see Point 4.1 regarding repairs as distinguished from capital expenditure).

Note that, to obtain a deduction in a year, the relevant expenditure will need to be reflected in the profit and loss account rather than capitalised in the balance sheet. If the expenditure is capitalised, the tax treatment will follow the accounting treatment, with a deduction delayed unless and until amounts are written off as expenses through the profit and loss account.

However, as mentioned above, full expensing for companies is available between 1 April 2023 until 1 31 March 2026.

**Point 29.14:** ***If irrecoverable VAT is incurred on a building purchase, or building/installation work, the expenditure eligible for capital allowances in relation to plant and machinery is increased accordingly.***

If a trader cannot fully reclaim VAT on property expenditure, the irrecoverable VAT increases the related cost for direct tax purposes.

Where VAT incurred on plant expenditure is wholly or partly irrecoverable, the amount eligible for capital allowances will include the irrecoverable amount. Furthermore, if adjustments are required under the Capital Goods Scheme ('CGS'), resulting in changes to VAT recovery over a ten-year period, the qualifying capital allowance expenditure will vary accordingly (*CAA 2001, s 235*).

See Chapter 35 for further points on VAT and Point 35.7 for an explanation of the CGS.

*Chapter 30*

# Capital gains planning: replacement of business assets ('roll-over') relief

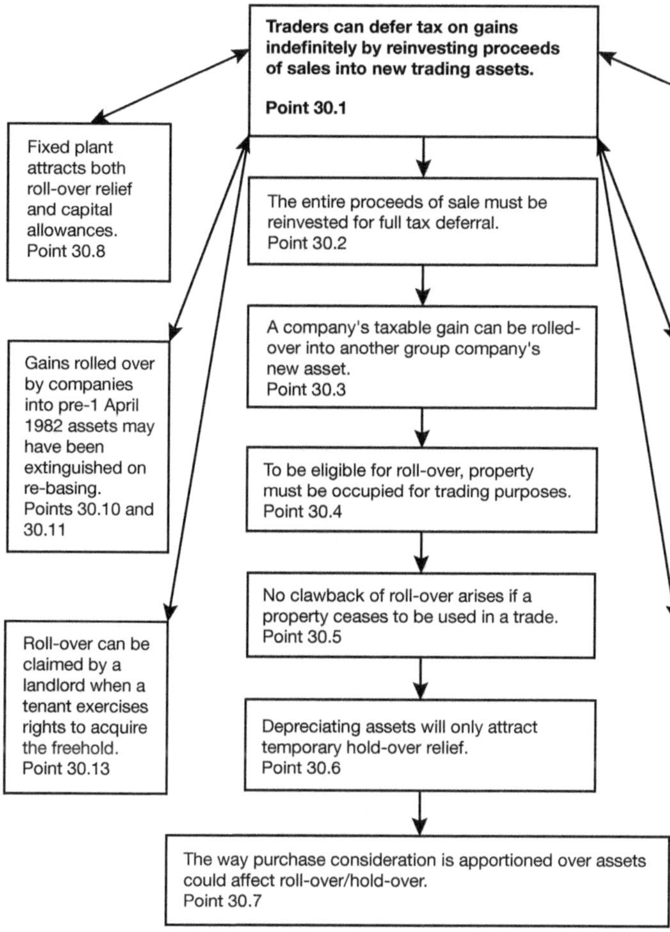

# 30 CAPITAL GAINS PLANNING: REPLACEMENT OF BUSINESS ASSETS ('ROLL-OVER') RELIEF

**Point 30.1:** ***A trader can defer indefinitely any tax arising on the sale of a property that has been used for the purposes of a trade by reinvesting the proceeds of disposal into appropriate assets during the requisite time period.***

A claim can be made to defer tax on capital gains where business assets are sold and replaced by new assets (*TCGA 1992, s 152*). The effect of the claim is to reduce the base cost of the 'new' assets for capital gains purposes by the gain on disposal of the old assets (*TCGA 1992, s 152(1)(b)*).

---

## Example 1

Freehold trading premises are sold for £1 million, realising a chargeable gain of £300,000. New freehold trading premises are acquired for £1.5 million. The gain on the old property can be 'rolled over' into the new asset, reducing the base cost for capital gains purposes to £1.2 million.

---

On the disposal of the second asset, there may be a further claim for roll-over relief. There is, therefore, the opportunity of indefinite deferral of tax on capital gains. In this way, the relief is invaluable for traders who are ploughing back capital gains on the sale of properties used to finance further expansion.

The 'old' and 'new' assets must be within the following categories:

(a) land and buildings;

(b) fixed plant and machinery;

(c) goodwill (but see below);

(d) ships, aircraft and hovercraft;

(e) satellites, space stations and spacecraft;

(f) milk and potato quotas (but see below); and

(g) ewe and suckler cow premium quotas (but see below).

(*TCGA 1992, s 155*)

Since 1 April 2002, companies have not been able to roll-over capital gains against the acquisition on or after that date of the following new assets:

(a) goodwill;

(b) milk and potato quotas; and

(c) ewe and suckler-cow premium quotas.

This is because these assets qualify as intangible property, for which a new tax regime applied from that date. Companies disposing of intangible property are able to claim reinvestment relief (similar to roll-over relief) against the acquisition of other intangible property. Special transitional rules apply to disposals of goodwill acquired before 1 April 2002 (*FA 2002, Sch 29, para 131*).

There was no change at all to the roll-over rules for non-corporate taxpayers, to whom the intangible property regime does not apply (*FA 2002, Sch 29, para 1*).

The reinvestment must take place within a four-year period commencing up to 12 months before the date of sale and ending three years after (*TCGA 1992, s 152(3)*). HMRC are entitled to extend the deadlines where appropriate (proviso to *TCGA 1992, s 152(3)*). If there are particular reasons for delays in selling or acquiring assets, there may well be valid grounds for asking the Inspector for a time extension.

It is not necessary for an asset in one particular class to be replaced by an asset in the same class. An individual trader could sell some business premises and reinvest the proceeds in fixed plant for inclusion in another property.

It is also not necessary for the proceeds to be reinvested in an asset in the same trade. A sale of factory premises followed by a purchase of a retail shop would potentially attract the relief. All trades carried on by an individual or company are treated as the same trade (*TCGA 1992, s 152*).

**Point 30.2:** ***To obtain full deferral, the entire proceeds of sale of an asset must be reinvested. However, partial relief is available if proceeds at least equal to the base cost plus indexation allowance (for companies) on the 'old' asset are used to fund the 'new' asset(s).***

Where all the proceeds of the sale of an asset are used to purchase the new asset, full roll-over is potentially available. If the extent of reinvestment in new assets over the four-year period amounts to less than the proceeds of sale, part of the gain will crystallise (*TCGA 1992, s 153*).

The part of the gain not deferred will be equivalent to the amount of unreinvested proceeds.

---

## Example 2

A freehold property is sold by Jones Ltd for £3 million, realising a chargeable gain after indexation of £1.5 million. A smaller property is acquired for £2.5 million. Since £500,000 of the proceeds have not been reinvested, tax on this amount of the gain will crystallise. £1 million of the gain can be rolled over.

---

No deferral is available unless the reinvested amount is more than the indexed base cost of the asset. Therefore, if, in the above example, the new property cost just £1.5 million, none of the taxable gain could be deferred.

**Point 30.3:** ***Within a group of companies, it does not matter if one company makes the disposal and a completely separate company within the group makes the acquisition. The first company is entitled to roll over the gain, which is carried forward in the second company.***

All companies within a tax group are treated as carrying on a single trade for capital gains roll-over purposes. Therefore, the gains in one group member can be rolled over against the cost of a qualifying asset acquired by another (*TCGA 1992, s 175(2A)*).

---

## Example 3

Group member Mills Ltd, an importer of catering equipment, sells one of its warehouses for £1 million, realising a chargeable gain of £500,000. Fellow group member Dujardin Ltd, a hotel operator, acquires a freehold hotel two years later for £2 million. The gain of £500,000 on Mills Ltd's disposal can be rolled over against Dujardin Ltd's hotel acquisition, reducing the base cost for tax purposes to £1.5 million.

---

All UK-resident companies which are under the common 75% ownership of a principal company are within a tax group for capital gains purposes. This also includes the UK branches and permanent establishments of non-resident companies (*TCGA 1992, s 175(1A)*).

Where a non-trading group company holds properties that are used and occupied for trading purposes by other group companies within the definition of a group, these properties are treated as group assets eligible for business roll-over relief (*TCGA 1992, s 175(20)*).

Roll-over relief is also extended to an individual owning assets that are used and occupied by his or her personal company, ie a company in which the shareholder has at least 5% of the voting rights (*TCGA 1992, s 157*).

**Point 30.4:** ***The 'old' and 'new' assets must actually be used for trading purposes to be eligible for relief.***

For business roll-over relief purposes, both the old and new assets must be used for the purposes of a trade. Land must be occupied by the taxpayer as well as used for trading purposes (*TCGA 1992, s 155*).

The definition of trade includes professions and vocations. It should be noted that furnished holiday lettings currently qualify as a trade for this purpose. It was originally proposed that such businesses would no longer qualify for this favourable treatment. However the government has decided to retain the relief although it has tightened the qualifying conditions. Chapter 10 provides further details of these.

The old asset must have been used for trading purposes throughout the period of ownership. If this is not the case, only a portion of the gain may be eligible for roll-over (*TCGA 1992, s 152(7)*).

---

## Example 4

A freehold building was occupied as the business premises of Clarke & Co from January 2009 to December 2021. In January 2018, new trading premises were acquired and occupied immediately. The old building is let to a tenant until the end of December 2022, when it is sold.

As the old asset was used and occupied for trading purposes for nine out of the ten years of ownership, 9/10 of the gain is eligible for roll-over.

---

For a property bought before 31 March 1982, only the period of ownership after 31 March 1982 can be considered in determining the proportion attributable to business use (*TCGA 1992, s 152(9)*).

An apportionment must similarly be made if part of the property has not been occupied for trading purposes. From that perspective, it may be better to try and maximise the use of the property for the purposes of a trade, eg by using areas for storage.

Where the old asset has only partly been used for trading purposes, the roll-over relief is calculated on the basis that two separate assets are sold. Only the proceeds apportioned to the part used in the trade need be reinvested to obtain roll-over relief in respect of the qualifying element of the gain (*TCGA 1992, s 152(6)*).

---

## Example 5

Clancy Ltd bought a freehold office building, with four equal-sized floors, in 2006 for £900,000. Three of the four floors have been occupied by Clancy Ltd and used for trading purposes. The fourth floor has been let to a tenant. In 2018, the building was sold for £1.5 million. The indexation allowance is £200,000.

| | Total | Trading element 75% | Non-trading element 25% |
|---|---|---|---|
| Proceeds | £1,500,000 | £1,125,000 | £375,000 |
| Cost | (900,000) | (675,000) | (225,000) |
| Indexation | (200,000) | (150,000) | (50,000) |
| Gain | £400,000 | £300,000 | £100,000 |

No business roll-over will be available on the non-trading element of the gain, ie £100,000.

With regard to the remaining £300,000, roll-over relief will be fully available if proceeds of £1,125,000 are reinvested in new assets. The minimum reinvestment below which any roll-over would not be achieved is £825,000 (ie £1,125,000 less £300,000 – see Point 30.2 above).

---

The new property (or other specified asset) should be a trading asset immediately on acquisition. If the property has to be substantially refurbished before occupation, this, strictly speaking, would not satisfy the roll-over conditions. However, HMRC have published a concession under which roll-over is allowed in such circumstances providing the following conditions are met:

(a) the owner proposes to incur capital expenditure for the purpose of enhancing the new asset's value;

(b) any work arising from such expenditure begins as soon as possible after acquisition and is completed within a reasonable time;

(c) on completion of the work, the asset is taken into use for the purposes of the trade and no other purpose;

(d) the asset is not let or used for any non-trading purpose in the period between acquisition and the time it is taken into use for the purposes of a trade; and

(e) if a building is being constructed on land, the expenditure on both the land and the building will qualify if the building is to be used in the trade on completion.

(HMRC Extra-Statutory Concession D24)

It is worth noting the comments in the HMRC Manuals (CG60810) which confirm HMRC's continued application of ESC D24:

> This interpretation of the statutory wording "which on the acquisition are taken into use" in TCGA92/152(1) was given judicial approval by Sir Richard Scott in Steibelt v Paling [1999] STC 594 when he commented "*I regard D24 as being a very sensible attempt by the Revenue to indicate how it believes the language of the 1992 Act in this regard should be applied.*" Accordingly, HMRC will continue to draw on the interpretation as set out in ESC D24 where appropriate, whilst acknowledging Sir Richard's Scott's conclusion that ESC D24 is not strictly a concession.

**Point 30.5:** ***Relief in respect of an 'old' asset will not be clawed back if a 'new' asset ceases to be used for trading purposes (unless it is a depreciating asset – see Point 30.6 below). Future roll-over relief will, however, be affected.***

The roll-over on the first asset will still be effective even if the replacement asset subsequently ceases to be used for the purposes of a trade. There will be no clawback of relief at that stage. The second property will, however, only be eligible for restricted roll-over relief on its sale (see Point 30.4 above).

There are two exceptions to this point:

(a) if the 'new' asset is a depreciating asset, tax will crystallise on the cessation of use for trading purposes (see Point 30.6 below); and

(b) if the new asset is bought wholly or partly for the purpose of realising a gain on disposal (*TCGA 1992, s 152(5)*), no roll-over would be available.

**Point 30.6:** ***If the new assets are 'depreciating' assets, then only temporary 'hold-over' relief is available unless there is a subsequent further reinvestment into non-depreciating assets.***

The general rule in capital gains roll-over situations is that the cost of the new asset for tax purposes is reduced by the gain arising on the old asset. This gain will not crystallise until the new asset is sold and, at that stage, a further claim to roll-over may be made. On this basis, tax could be deferred indefinitely.

The rule does not apply, however, where the new assets are 'depreciating assets'. The relief then becomes a temporary 'hold-over' of the chargeable gain (*TCGA 1992, s 154*).

A 'depreciating asset' for this purpose is one that is, or would become, a wasting asset at any time within ten years of its acquisition (*TCGA 1992, s 154(7)*). A wasting asset, by definition, has an anticipated life not exceeding 50 years (*TCGA 1992, s 44*). Therefore, a lease with not more than 60 years to run would be treated as a depreciating asset, as would a building built on land held under a lease of less than 60 years (HMRC *Tax Bulletin 7*, May 1993).

Other replacement assets, including fixed plant (other than plant forming a building fixture – see Point 30.8 below) ships or aircraft, would often also be 'depreciating assets'.

The held-over tax charge will crystallise ten years after the acquisition of a depreciating asset at the latest. It may crystallise earlier, however, if the asset is sold or ceases to be used for the purpose of the trade (*TCGA 1992, s 154(2)*).

On the acquisition of a depreciating asset, there is merely an opportunity to hold-over a gain for a period ending with the earliest of the events mentioned above. If there is an acquisition of a non-depreciating asset within the four-year reinvestment period mentioned in Point 30.1 above, then this asset can be substituted by making a variation of the original roll-over claim before the depreciating asset is sold or ceases to be used (*TCGA 1992, s 154(4), (5)*). The deferral of the original gain (or part of the gain) indefinitely will then be a possibility.

---

## Example 6

The proceeds of the sale of a building in February 2023 were reinvested, in March 2023, in a lease of new business premises with 55 years remaining. As a 55-year lease is a depreciating asset, the original gain will crystallise and tax will become payable at the earliest of the following:

(1) the ten-year anniversary of the acquisition (ie March 2033);

(2) disposal of the lease; and

(3) the building ceasing to be used for the purposes of the trade.

If, before February 2026 – assuming the 55-year lease is still owned and the building still occupied – a new freehold is purchased, this freehold can be substituted for the short lease, providing the cost would have been sufficient for a roll-over claim on the original disposal.

Note that the new freehold must be acquired before any of the above events. Thus, if there are plans to move out of the leasehold premises or sell them, the freehold must first be bought (ie contracts must be exchanged) to avoid any crystallisation of tax.

---

In view of the above, it is important to be constantly aware of hold-over claims that have been made involving acquisitions of depreciating assets. If non-depreciating trading assets are acquired subsequently within the requisite period, the claim should be amended as far as possible to include these.

It should also be remembered that the crystallisation of the tax charge on cessation of use only applies to depreciating assets. If a freehold or long leasehold property is vacated and subsequently let to a tenant, the original roll-over is not affected. The crystallisation of the tax charge also does not apply to assets which subsequently become depreciating assets. A gain rolled into a lease exceeding 60 years would, therefore, be extinguished if the lease were to be held until expiry.

**Point 30.7:** ***In view of the position regarding depreciating assets, the allocation of consideration on the purchase of business premises may be important.***

Where new premises are acquired which are subject to a short lease, it has often been advantageous to allocate expenditure, as far as possible, to goodwill. However, as explained in Point 30.1 above, goodwill has ceased to be an eligible asset for corporate taxpayers since 1 April 2002. Expenditure allocated to goodwill since that date would not be eligible for roll-over relief in the hands of a UK corporation tax payer, although it is still eligible for other taxpayers.

Although fixed plant itself is a depreciating asset (when it does not form part of a building), there may be a benefit in attributing a reasonable value to this item (see Point 30.8 below).

**Point 30.8:** ***When purchasing property, the allocation of part of the consideration to fixed plant and equipment could be eligible for both capital allowances and capital gains roll-over relief.***

The element of expenditure attributable to fixed plant in a building should be separated in order to formulate a capital allowances claim (see Point 29.1).

Such expenditure will attract roll-over relief if the plant or machinery becomes part of a building (HMRC *Tax Bulletin* 7, May 1993). This would apply to items such as air conditioning, sanitary fittings and lift systems.

If the plant or machinery is fixed but does not form part of a building, then the items will be depreciating assets eligible for hold-over relief. This might include certain partitioning or floor coverings.

Expenditure allocated to elements of plant in a purchased building can, therefore, help to defer a tax liability on a capital gain as well as being eligible for capital allowances.

**Point 30.9:** ***For business properties held at 6 April 1988 by companies where there may have been an earlier roll-over claim, one half of the deferred gain could be exempt from tax altogether.***

As explained in Point 11.3, there is a special relief where the following applies:

(a) a gain arose on an 'old' asset, acquired before 31 March 1982 and sold before 6 April 1988, which was rolled over into a 'new' asset; and

(b) the 'new' asset, which was acquired after 31 March 1982, was still held at 6 April 1988.

In this situation, 50% of the rolled-over gain on the disposal of the new asset will fall out of charge to tax (*TCGA 1992, Sch 4*).

Since 6 April 2008, this relief has only been available for companies within the charge to corporation tax. Individuals, trustees and personal representatives ceased to benefit from that date.

---

## Example 7

Hinch Ltd bought a factory in 1981, which was sold in 1986 for £1 million. The gain on sale after indexation amounted to £580,000.

In 1987, Hinch Ltd bought a warehouse for £2 million and made a claim to roll over the gain on the factory into that acquisition.

In 2019, the warehouse is sold for £4 million.

The capital gain on the warehouse, ignoring indexation allowance, would be:

| | £ | £ |
|---|---|---|
| Sale proceeds | | 4,000,000 |
| Less: Cost | 2,000,000 | |
| Less: Rolled-over gain | (580,000) | |
| | 1,420,000 | (1,420,000) |
| | | 2,580,000 |

| | £ | £ |
|---|---|---|
| Less: *TCGA 1992, Sch 4* relief | | (290,000) |
| (50% of £580,000) | | |
| Taxable gain before indexation | | 2,290,000 |

A company within the charge to corporation tax must claim the relief within two years of the end of the accounting period in which the relevant disposal was made. Disposals for this purpose will also include any roll-over situations. For instance, if the property in question is sold and the proceeds are reinvested under the roll-over rules in a further acquisition, the relief will crystallise at that time and should be claimed in respect of that roll-over situation. The effect of this will be that the relief will reduce the deferred gain that is carried over to the new asset.

**Point 30.10:** ***Gains on assets sold before 1 April 1982 which have been rolled over into new assets may not be subject to tax at all.***

As a result of the rebasing provisions in *FA 1988*, an asset disposed of after 5 April 1988 which was owned on 31 March 1982 can be treated as having an uplifted base cost, for the purposes of tax on capital gains, equal to its value at 31 March 1982 (see Chapter 11).

Consider the position where a business property was sold before 31 March 1982 and the proceeds of sale re-invested in a new business asset acquired on or before 31 March 1982. Ordinarily, the original cost of the new asset would be reduced by the 'rolled-over' gain to arrive at the base cost for future capital gains purposes. However, under the rebasing provisions, if the new asset is sold after 6 April 1988, the market value of the new asset can, for corporates, and must, for individuals, be substituted for its original adjusted base cost.

As will be seen, in this situation the rolled-over gain should drop out of charge altogether and no tax would be payable on the gain realised before 31 March 1982.

## Example 8

A property was sold in 1980, realising a gain of £200,000. The proceeds were reinvested in a further freehold property acquired in 1981 for £1 million. That property was valued at £1.5 million on 31 March 1982 and was sold in July 2018.

On claiming roll-over relief, the base cost of the second property was reduced by £200,000 to £800,000. However, since the property was sold after 6 April 1988, the value at 31 March 1982 can be used as the base cost. This was £1.5 million. Accordingly, the £200,000 deferred gain from 1981 will never be taxed.

**Point 30.11: *There may be cases where a gain after 31 March 1982 is not subject to tax at all, having been rolled over into an asset acquired before 1 April 1982.***

As mentioned in Point 30.1 above, a gain can be rolled over into an asset acquired up to 12 months before the 'old' asset was sold. There may be instances, therefore, where a property has been sold after 31 March 1982 but the proceeds deemed to have been re-invested in a property or other business asset acquired before 31 March 1982. Accordingly, any rolled-over capital gain would fall out of charge.

---

## Example 9

Taking a similar situation to Example 8 in Point 30.10 above, assume the property was sold in January 1983. The new property was bought one year earlier, in January 1982. On the basis of the same figures quoted there, the £200,000 would similarly never be taxed in this situation. The base cost of the property acquired in January 1982 would become its market value at 31 March 1982.

---

**Point 30.12: *Where land is disposed of to an authority with compulsory purchase powers, a landlord can defer any tax on the gain arising by reinvesting the proceeds into new property.***

Roll-over relief is available where land is acquired by an authority with compulsory purchase powers (*TCGA 1992, s 247*). This might be, for example, a local authority or regional development agency. Note that it is sufficient for the authority to have compulsory purchase powers. It does not need to formally exercise them.

The rules for this relief operate in a similar way to those referred to above in this chapter for replacement of business assets. The reinvestment cannot be into a property used as a dwelling house if part or all of the gain arising to the landowner on a disposal of that dwelling house within six years would not be a chargeable gain by virtue of the relief from capital gains tax for the disposal of a private residence (*TCGA 1992, s 248*).

The owner should not have been marketing the property or otherwise advertising the property for sale prior to the sale to the authority in question.

The relief is available to landlords as well as owners occupying their properties for trading purposes.

Owners occupying their properties for trading purposes can reinvest the proceeds of disposal into any of the categories of permitted expenditure for roll-over relief outlined in Point 30.1 above by applying the general rules for roll-over relief claims and, in addition, can also apply the proceeds towards reinvestment in non-trading land including investment property. Landlords are restricted in their reinvestment to other land, including interests in land and rights over land, such as replacement investment property.

**Point 30.13:** ***Roll-over relief can also be claimed by a property owner where a tenant exercises the right to acquire the freehold reversion or extension of the lease.***

The roll-over relief available to property owners whose property is compulsorily purchased (Point 30.12 above) has been extended to situations where the tenant exercises rights under the *Leasehold Reform Act 1967*, the *Housing Acts 1985* to *1996* or the *Housing and Urban Development Act 1993* (HMRC Statement of Practice SP 13/93 and RI 205, June 1999). As with the relief for landlords considered in Point 30.12 above, the reinvestment of proceeds is restricted to reinvestment in other land; interests in land or rights over land. The land in which the reinvestment takes place must not be the same land as that which gave rise to the disposal. Accordingly, for the purposes of the relief, the proceeds of disposal from a leasehold flat cannot be applied in the refurbishment of other flats in the same building but must be applied in respect of another property.

**Point 30.14:** ***Roll-over relief may be available where compensation is received on the destruction of a property.***

Where a capital sum is recovered following the destruction of a property and that is applied on the replacement of the asset (eg through an insurance claim), a form of roll-over may be claimed. This would mean that no gain – or loss – would arise on the receipt of the capital sum on the deemed 'disposal' of the old asset. Instead, the gain would be deducted from the cost of the new asset for future capital gains purposes (*TCGA 1992, s 23*).

The compensation must be wholly applied in the purchase of a replacement asset within one year of its receipt, although that period may be extended by HMRC.

Roll-over can extend to situations where the property has been damaged but not completely destroyed. The receipt of compensation will not trigger a capital gain if the amount is wholly applied in restoring the asset – although, if any non-invested amount is relatively small, that may be ignored.

*Chapter 31*

# Capital gains tax planning: Business asset disposal relief and investors' reliefs for individuals and trusts

Business Asset Disposal Relief (BADR) also means a 10% rate of CGT on certain gains on the disposal of business assets up to a lifetime limit of £1m.
Point 31.1

BADR also means a 10% rate of CGT on certain gains on the disposal of shares in personal trading companies up to a lifetime limit of £1m.
Point 31.2

Investor's relief also means a 10% rate of CGT on certain gains on the disposal of investments in the shares of trading companies up to a lifetime limit of £10m.
Point 31.3

It may be possible to split ownership of businesses to take advantage of other family member's lifetime relief entitlement.
Point 31.4

The timing of sale can be important in view of the ownership periods and also, for BADR, time the limit of three years once a business has ceased.
Point 31.5

A gain on the sale of a property used in a business can qualify for BADR.
Point 31.6

BADR is restricted where rent is charged for use of the property.
Point 31.7

# 31 CAPITAL GAINS TAX PLANNING: BUSINESS ASSET DISPOSAL RELIEF AND INVESTORS' RELIEFS FOR INDIVIDUALS AND TRUSTS

**Point 31.1:** ***In certain situations, there are reliefs which allow a capital gains rate of 10% on certain gains on the disposal of business assets of up to £1 million.***

Between 23 June 2010 and 6 April 2016, the normal rate of capital gains tax was 28% which applied to chargeable gains to the extent a taxpayer's income and gains were chargeable to the higher rate. An 18% rate applied to gains where the taxpayer's income was fully within the basic rate band.

From 6 April 2016, these rates were reduced to 20% and 10% respectively (although the previous rates continue for chargeable gains on the disposal of residential property and certain carried interest gains).

A special rate of 10% is available where the circumstances of the gain qualify the taxpayer for business asset disposal relief (BADR). As noted at Point 31.2 below, in the case of a qualifying sale of shares, BADR applies where the person realising the gain is an employee or director of the company being sold.

BADR is currently restricted to £1 million of qualifying gains over the lifetime of a taxpayer.

As further outlined in Point 31.6 below, the relief will be available in respect of gains on property disposals where the disposal is, or is associated with, a qualifying business disposal by an individual or trust (*TCGA 1992, s 169H*).

Qualifying disposals in relation to an individual are:

(a) all or part of an individual's business;

(b) all or part of an individual's interest in a trading partnership;

(c) disposals of property previously used in a qualifying business within three years of cessation;

(d) certain disposals of shares in a trading company; and

(e) associated disposals linked to a material disposal of qualifying shares or of a qualifying interest in a trading partnership.

(*TCGA 1992, s 169I*)

'Business' for the purposes of BADR is defined as a trade, profession or vocation conducted on a commercial basis and with a view to the realisation of profits (*TCGA 1992, s 169S(1)*). This currently includes furnished holiday lettings (see Point 10.4). 'Associated disposals' arise in relation to a property which is owned directly by an individual and let to a partnership or company that he or she is involved in for the purposes of the business carried on by the partnership/company (see Point 31.6 below). Note that, if any rent has been charged since 6 April 2008, this can impact on the entitlement to BADR (see Point 31.7 below).

Historically, for the disposal of interests in businesses, including interests in trading partnerships, and the disposal of assets used in a business, an additional qualifying condition has been that the business had been carried on for at least 12 months at the date of the disposal. In the case of associated disposals, the asset needed to have been used in the business for at least 12 months.

From 6 April 2019, this period was extended to 24 months.

Trust gains can also attract BADR. The conditions are that:

(a) the trustees make a disposal of business assets; and

(b) an individual has an interest in possession in the trust's business assets.

(*TCGA 1992, s 169J*)

The same holding periods which apply for assets held by individuals outlined above also apply to trust assets.

The overall £1 million limit for the relief applies to the trust and the individual jointly. It is not possible to get extra relief by splitting out some of an individual's ownership of a business or company into a trust.

Other conditions, such as the need for the disposal of an asset to be associated with a disposal of a business (see Point 31.6 below), apply equally to trusts as for individuals.

**Point 31.2:** ***In certain situations, there are reliefs which allow a capital gains rate of 10% on gains on shares in personal trading companies owning property up to £1 million.***

As noted at Point 31.1 above, certain disposals of shares in trading companies are included in the list of qualifying disposals for individuals. BADR is available for certain investments by an individual in a personal trading company.

The main requirements are that:

(a) the shares must be held in a trading company or the holding company of a trading group; and

(b) throughout a 'two-year qualifying period', the individual/beneficiary must:

- be an officer or employee of the company or a company within the group (part or full time); and
- the company is the individual's 'personal company' (ie they hold at least 5% of the ordinary shares and voting rights of the company, and are also beneficially entitled to at least 5% of the distributable profits and / or assets at winding up).

The 'two-year qualifying period' is either:

- the 24-month period immediately prior to the sale of the shares where the company continues to trade; or
- where the company ceases to trade, the 24-month period immediately prior to cessation of the trade, provided the shares are disposed of within three years of the date of cessation.

In respect of disposals made on or after 29 October 2018, a personal company means where:

- the individual holds at least 5% of the ordinary share capital of the company;
- that individual also owns at least 5% of the voting rights in the company are exercisable by the individual; and
- one of the following applies:
  - (a) The individual is beneficially entitled to at least 5% of the profits available to shareholders and, on a winding up event, would be beneficially entitled to a minimum of 5% of available assets; or
  - (b) where there is a disposal of the whole of the ordinary share capital of the company, the individual would be beneficially entitled to at least 5% of the proceeds

(*TCGA 1992, ss 169I(6)* and *169S(3)*)

For disposals prior to 29 October 2018 a personal company meant where the individual holds at least 5% of the ordinary share capital of the company and at least 5% of the voting rights in the company.

These new tests require considerable care over the timing of a disposal. For example, a holding of shares giving an entitlement to over 5% of the voting rights but less than 5% of the profits available, assets and proceeds could have been held for many years prior to 29 October 2018. However, from that date the shares will cease to qualify. Even if the holding is increased such that the shareholder were to acquire at least 5% of the economic rights, the shares would then have to be held for 24 months from the date of that acquisition before a disposal would become qualifying for BADR again.

Shareholders whose holding is diluted below 5% after a commercial fundraising can make an election to preserve relief.

Where the company carries on a significant proportion of non-trading activity, there is a danger that it will no longer be a trading company and hence the relief would not apply. Therefore, care should be taken to ensure that the company does not have significant levels of non-trading assets or activity. Additionally, if retained cash balances are high, a review should be undertaken to ensure that there are business reasons for their retention.

From 6 April 2016, a further relief, known as 'investors' relief' was introduced for similar disposals by taxpayers who are not employed by the company in question (see Point 31.3 below). BADR and investors' relief will be available either for capital gains on the disposal of property trading and development companies or trading companies which hold premises used in their trade. They are separate reliefs and independent reliefs each with their own lifetime limits (£1m for BADR and £10m for investors' relief) and so the current maximum benefit to a taxpayer across both reliefs is, therefore, £1,100,000 (ie 20% – 10% × £11 million ). In some circumstances, a share might potentially qualify for both reliefs.

As noted in Point 31.1 above, trust gains can also attract BADR. Where the business asset in question is a shareholding in a company, the individual entitled to the interest in possession must meet the requirements relating to a personal company as set out above.

The same holding periods which apply for assets held by individuals outlined above also apply to trust assets which are, therefore, similarly extended to 24 months for disposals which take place on or after 6 April 2019.

The overall £1 million limit for the relief applies to the trust and the individual jointly. It is not possible to get extra relief by splitting out some of an individual's ownership of a company into a trust.

**Point 31.3:** ***In certain situations, there are reliefs which allow a capital gains rate of 10% on gains on investments in the shares of trading companies owning property up to £10 million.***

As noted at Point 31.2 above, in order to qualify for BADR, shareholders in a company who qualify under the shareholding test should be an officer or employee of the company, or fellow group company. A similar relief, investors' relief, was introduced by *FA 2016*, for disposals of shares in unlisted trading companies or in the holding companies of unlisted trading groups. The legislation for this is set out at *TCGA 1992, Ch 5, Pt V*. Although similar to BADR, there are a number of key differences which are set out below:

(a) Neither the investor nor anyone connected with him may be a relevant employee of the company throughout the period for which the shares have been held. An individual is a relevant employee if they are either an officer or employee of the company issuing the shares or any connected company (*TCGA 1992, s 169VW*). An unremunerated director will not, however, be a relevant employee provided that they (or anyone connected with them) were not previously either connected with the company or involved in carrying on the trade of the company (either in whole or in part) or the trade of a connected company.

(b) The qualifying shares must be ordinary shares acquired on an issue by way of subscription by the investor, which are fully paid up in cash and which have been held continuously since acquisition (*TCGA 1992, s 169VU*). If an investor later transfers shares that they have subscribed for to their spouse or civil partner then the shares will continue to qualify provided that the investor was living together with his/her spouse or civil partner at the time the shares were transferred.

(c) The share issue must have been subscribed for at arm's length and for commercial reasons and cannot have been as part of a scheme or arrangement with a purpose of tax avoidance *(TCGA 1992, s 169VU)*.

(d) The shares must have been issued on or after 17 March 2016 and held for at least three years. For shares issued between 17 March 2016 and 5 April 2016, this is extended to at least three years from 6 April 2016 *(TCGA 1992, s 169VB)*.

(e) There is no minimum qualifying percentage holding; and

(f) The company must have been an unlisted trading company or the holding company of an unlisted trading group when the shares were issued *(TCGA 1992, s 169VB)*. Shares listed on AIM are considered to be unlisted for this purpose.

In view of the requirement that the shares must have been held for a period of three years, the first possible disposal of shares which will qualify for investors' relief cannot occur until 6 April 2019. If the investor receives value from the company at any time in the four year period up to the 3rd anniversary of the date of issue of the shares then the shares will be disqualified from qualifying for investors relief *(TCGA 1992, Sch 7ZB)*. Receipts of value for this purpose include, among other things:

(i) the repayment, redemption or repurchase of share capital and securities, including any payment to the investor for giving up a right in relation to the share capital or in relation to any security, either by the company or any person connected with it;

(ii) the advancement of loans to the investor not repaid in full prior to the issue of the shares;

(iii) the disposal of assets to the investor for consideration of less than the full market value of the assets;

(iv) the acquisition of assets from the investor for consideration in excess of the full market value of the assets;

(v) the waiver of debts owed by the investor or the discharge of liabilities of the investor owed to third parties; or

(vi) the making of any payment to the investor other than a qualifying payment. Qualifying payments include the payment of remuneration, interest representing a reasonable commercial return, the payment of dividends, the payment of commercial rent and payments for goods, services or assets which are not in excess of market value.

**Point 31.4:** ***Although BADR and investors' reliefs are each restricted to their own lifetime limits, it is possible to split the ownership in a qualifying business or company between a spouse and other family members, to use the lifetime limits of these other investors.***

As mentioned above, BADR and investors' reliefs are limited to £1m and £10m of gains respectively (their own individual limits). Where gains exceed these respective limits, the benefit is increased where the investment is spread between, say, members of a family.

---

Example 1

In July 2022, Mr Reed disposes of shares in a company for £44 million, realising a capital gain of £30 million. The shares qualify for investors' relief. He makes his maximum claim for investors' relief. His tax liability is £5 million (10% × £10 million + 20% × £20 million).

If his son and daughter had equally invested in the company and met the investors' relief conditions, each shareholder would have a tax liability of £1 million on their £10 million capital gain. Total tax liabilities for all the shareholders would, therefore, be £3 million, saving the family £2 million in tax.

---

Where an existing qualifying investment in a trading business or company would realise a gain in excess of the lifetime limit, the investment could be transferred to a spouse or civil partner at no gain, no loss, or to a child and a gift hold-over election made. Provided the transferee qualifies for BADR (including the minimum holding period of two years), their lifetime limits can be used to reduce the overall tax liability.

All individuals would need to satisfy the qualifying conditions in Point 31.1 above, in terms of ownership of the assets and involvement in the businesses.

**Point 31.5:** ***The timing of any sale can be important. BADR, for instance, requires an individual to hold a qualifying asset/shares throughout the qualifying period and the asset/shares must be sold within three years of cessation of a business.***

BADR requires the shareholder to hold the qualifying asset for two years. Similarly, investors' relief requires the shareholder to have held the shares for three years. Therefore, the date of acquisition and the date of sale are important. Where a shareholder wishes to benefit from these reliefs a delay may be beneficial.

Where a business ceases, a qualifying asset can be sold at or after the time the business ceases. However, in order for BADR to be available, that must be no later than three years after the date of cessation.

**Point 31.6:** ***Where property is used by an individual in his or her business, including a qualifying partnership or personal company, it may qualify for BADR.***

Subject to the restriction in Point 31.7 below, assets used in a qualifying partnership or personal company can qualify for BADR if they have been used by that partnership or company for at least two years prior to the disposal of the qualifying partnership or company. Such disposals are termed 'associated disposals'. The one-year period of ownership will continue to apply in the case of disposals of property used in a qualifying business within three years of cessation where the business ceased prior to 29 October 2018.

For disposals of assets acquired from 13 June 2016, the asset also needs to have been owned throughout the period of three years up to the date of disposal. This new condition has created uncertainty in relation to some disposals, particularly those involving land, where an interest in property was owned prior to 13 June 2016 and is subsequently enhanced.

---

## Example 2

Philip acquired a one third share in land together with his brother, Spencer, and his father Andrew on 1 June 2016. The land is provided rent free to an accounting partnership operated by Philip and Spencer but is not a partnership asset. Andrew died on 1 June 2017 leaving his share of the land to Philip. Philip's share in the land was sold on 2 June 2018 on Philip's retirement from farming to pursue a new career in computer programming. At that date, Philip will have owned the land for less than three years but part of his interest was acquired prior to 13 June 2016.

In these circumstances it is unclear whether Philip will be entitled to BADR on the gain relating to all of his interest in the land, including the one third share inherited from his father, or just on the gain attributable to the share of the land acquired on 1 June 2016 or whether no entitlement to BADR arises due to the original interest becoming tainted by the later inheritance.

---

In addition, to qualify as 'associated disposals', the disposal of assets needs to occur as part of the withdrawal of the individual from participation in the business carried on by the partnership/company. HMRC will generally accept that a disposal within three years of the disposal of the shares or partnership interest is part of the withdrawal from participation in the business provided the assets have not been used for any purpose other than for the purpose of the business during that period. No relief is available once the three-year period has expired. It is important to ensure that sufficient time is given for the disposal to take place, as delays may cause the three-year window to be exceeded.

The disposal of the qualifying partnership or company must also be a 'material' disposal. The disposal must be of an interest of at least 5% of the partnership assets or 5% of the shares in order for assets owned independently and used for the purposes of the business of the partnership/company to qualify.

This restriction created hardship in certain circumstances and has been relaxed for interests in partnerships following *FA 2016*. Accordingly, disposals of assets used by a partnership will now qualify for BADR where there is an interest in the partnership of less than 5% provided an interest of at least 5% was held for a continuous period of at least three years in the eight years up to the date of disposal (*TCGA 1992, s 169K*).

Where rent is charged for the use of a property by the qualifying business, BADR can be restricted on the disposal of the property.

The restriction will depend on the level of rent paid, so that a full market rent would prevent the relief being claimed. Where a below-market rent is charged, this is compared with the market rent and used to calculate the restriction.

---

## Example 3

The market rent for a property occupied by Satch Ltd is £1,000 per month. However, the company pays only £250 per month. Assuming a gain of £1 million is realised on the qualifying disposal of the property, only £750,000 (ie 75% of £1,000,000) would qualify for BADR.

---

In evaluating this restriction, consideration will need to be given to the rent paid over the whole of the ownership period of the asset. Periods prior to 6 April 2008 are ignored.

In any event, subject to being able to service interest payments on loans used to acquire the property, consideration should be given to reducing the rent charged and thereby reduce the restriction if it is anticipated that this relief is to be claimed.

The use of rent as a profit extraction method, means of servicing debt and reward for use of an asset should all be carefully weighed against the benefit of entrepreneurs' relief.

Rent is defined as consideration given for the use of an asset (*TCGA 1992, s 169S(5)*). Thus, this restriction may not apply if, instead of rent, a property-owning partner merely extracts additional profit to reflect the provision of the asset.

*Chapter 32*

# Capital gains planning for companies: exemption for sales of substantial shareholdings

**Companies can enjoy complete exemption from tax in respect of gains on sales of shareholdings of 10% or more in trading companies.**
**Point 32.1**

↓

Companies held by qualifying institutional investors can enjoy complete exemption from tax in respect of gains on sales of substantial shareholdings in other companies.
Point 32.2

↓

Losses on the sale of substantial shareholdings are disregarded. Therefore, an asset sale might be preferable where a capital loss is likely to arise.
Point 32.3

↓

Since sales of shares in investment companies and assets generally will not be exempt from tax, maximisation of past and current capital losses to carry forward may still be useful.
Point 32.4

# 32 CAPITAL GAINS PLANNING FOR COMPANIES: EXEMPTION FOR SALES OF SUBSTANTIAL SHAREHOLDINGS

**Point 32.1:** ***Companies can enjoy complete exemption from tax in respect of gains on sales of substantial shareholdings in trading companies.***

Sales of certain shareholdings by UK companies are exempt from tax. These rules (*TCGA 1992, Sch 7AC*) mean that a corporate shareholding in an associated or subsidiary company can be sold free of tax, providing that the related conditions are satisfied.

For disposals from 1 April 2017, the scope of the exemption has been widened and now applies where a company (which need not any longer be a trading company or a member of a trading group) sells a holding where the following conditions are satisfied:

(a) The company being sold must be a trading company or the holding company of a trading group or subgroup. This requires that the activities of the company should not include to any substantial extent non-trading activities (*TCGA 1992, Sch 7AC, paras 20, 21*). This is generally interpreted as meaning that non-trading activities should not exceed 20% of the total activities. However, the company being sold is no longer required to be a trading company (or the holding company of a trading group or subgroup) immediately following the disposal unless the disposal is being made to a connected person (*TCGA 1992, Sch 7AC, para 19*).

(b) The company making the disposal must have held a 'substantial shareholding' in the company being sold for a continuous period of at least 12 months in the six years immediately preceding the disposal (*TCGA 1992, Sch 7AC, para 7*). It is no longer required that the disposal is being made out of a 'substantial shareholding' at the time of disposal. This enables disposals of holdings of less than 10% to qualify for the relief where disposals of a 'substantial shareholding' are made in stages.

---

## Example 1

Agbeze Ltd is a group holding company. In January 2014, it sold 95% of its shares in a trading subsidiary, Neville Ltd, to Housby Ltd, a third party. Agbeze Ltd retained a holding of 5% in Neville Ltd which was sold in September 2018 to Housby Ltd.

The disposal in January 2014 would have qualified as a disposal of substantial shareholding under the legislation in force up to 31 March 2017. Had the old rules remained in force, the disposal in September 2018 would not have qualified as a disposal of a substantial shareholding as it would have represented a disposal out of a holding of less than 10%.

However, under the legislation in force from 1 April 2017, the disposal in September 2018 would now qualify as a disposal of a substantial shareholding because Tracey Ltd had a 'substantial shareholding' in Neville Limited for a continuous period of 12 months in the period from October 2012 to September 2018 (from October 2012 until December 2013).

---

Clearly, where a property disposal is contemplated out of a group, but there is the prospect of selling the company along with its trading activity, this should be considered in view of the potential tax exemption on the sale of shares. Under the historic rules, this also required an undertaking from the purchaser that they would continue the trade in order that the company being sold could be a trading company immediately after the disposal. As this is no longer a requirement, such an undertaking would not now be necessary.

The historic requirement for the company exiting the group to be a trading company immediately after the disposal could not, in principle, be met where the disposal arose as a consequence of a winding up or dissolution of a trading subsidiary. In these circumstances, the disposal was still treated as qualifying provided that there was a time in the two years prior to the winding up or dissolution when a disposal of the company would have qualified (*TCGA 1992 Sch 7AC, para 3(2)*). This would no longer be relevant as it is not now required that the company being disposed of should be a trading company immediately after disposal.

Historically, the selling company/group also needed to carry on trading after the sale and this requirement was similarly relaxed in circumstances where the selling company was wound up or dissolved as soon as was reasonably practicable in the circumstances (*TCGA 1992, Sch 7AC, para 3(3)*). This relaxation was relevant where a non-trading holding company disposed of its sole trading subsidiary. Again, under the rules which have applied since 1 April 2017 this is no longer relevant as the selling company is not required to be a trading company or the holding company of a trading group.

Although some of the historic problems with the exemption have been removed as a result of the new rules which apply from 1 April 2017, some issues remain. The company being disposed of is still required to be a trading company at the time of the disposal. This can be problematic where a trading company sells its trade and assets and is then subsequently liquidated as the company is no longer a trading company at the time of disposal. It can also be problematic where a holding company sells its sole trading subsidiary and is then liquidated itself.

The legislation effecting the relaxation to the historic rules that resolved some of these types of issues is now technically deficient as it now refers in several places to legislation which has been repealed. However, the legislation remains sufficiently similar to suggest that the historic relaxations would continue to apply in these circumstances provided there was a time in the previous two years when the disposal would have qualified had it taken place at that time. Accordingly, the liquidation of a company which has sold its trade and assets or the liquidation of a holding company which has sold its only trading subsidiary should still qualify as a disposal of a substantial shareholding provided that the liquidation happens within two years of the sale of the trade.

Where a trading group carries on multiple trading activities, separating the activities out individually into special purpose subsidiaries offers the opportunity to sell on those companies – together with their businesses and assets – tax free under the substantial shareholding exemption.

A strategy of selling a company may be attractive to a purchaser, as he or she may reduce their exposure to SDLT on the purchase (See Point 14.1 above).

**Point 32.2:** ***Companies held by qualifying institutional investors can enjoy complete exemption from tax in respect of gains on sales of substantial shareholdings in other companies.***

For disposals from 1 April 2017, the exemption can also apply, or partially apply, to disposals of a 'substantial shareholding' held by qualifying institutional investors where the following conditions are met:

(a) The shareholding must have been held for a continuous period of at least 12 months in the six years immediately preceding the disposal (*TCGA 1992, Sch 7AC, paras 3A and 7*). As outlined in Example 1 above, this enables disposals of less than 10% to qualify for the exemption in some circumstances.

(b) The company being sold must not be either a trading company or the holding company of a trading group or subgroup (*TCGA 1992, Sch 7AC, paras 3A and 19*).

(c) The investing company is not a disqualified listed company (*TCGA 1992, Sch 7AC, para 3A)*. A disqualified listed company for this purpose is one where i) any of the shares forming part of the ordinary share capital are listed on a recognised stock exchange; and ii) the company is not itself a qualifying institutional investor; and iii) the company is not a qualifying UK REIT).

The term 'qualifying institutional investor' is defined by *TCGA 1992, Sch 7AC, para 30A* and includes pension schemes, charities, life assurance businesses, investment trusts and authorised investment funds.

Where these conditions are met and, immediately prior to the disposal, at least 80% of the ordinary share capital of the investing company is owned by qualifying institutional investors, the substantial shareholdings exemption is given on the entirety of the gain. Where qualifying institutional investors own less than 80% of the ordinary share capital of the investing company then, provided the qualifying institutional investors hold at least 25% of the ordinary share capital of the investing company, the substantial shareholdings exemption is given on the proportion of the gain which equates to the percentage ownership of the qualifying institutional investors.

As the rules for qualifying institutional investors do not require the company being sold to be a trading company, from 1 April 2017 gains on disposals of shares in property investment companies can potentially qualify for the substantial shareholdings exemption where the shares are held by qualifying institutional investors.

**Point 32.3:** ***Losses on the sale of substantial shareholdings are disregarded. Therefore, an asset sale might be preferable where a capital loss is likely to arise.***

The relief mentioned in Points 32.1 and 32.2 above, which exempts gains on the sale of substantial shareholdings, equally disregards losses, which would not, therefore, be available for tax shelter elsewhere. Accordingly, where there is a property sale and a capital loss is likely to arise, alternative planning to that suggested in Point 32.1 should be adopted. Indeed, if a company sale is being contemplated where a property sale could give rise to a loss, consideration might be given to selling the property separately and then transferring the shares. An election can be made by the selling company's group to use that loss against gains which arise elsewhere in the group (see Point 16.5).

**Point 32.4:** ***Since sales of shares in investment companies and assets generally will not be exempt from tax, maximisation of past and current capital losses to carry forward may still be useful.***

Notwithstanding the relief for substantial shareholdings, groups will still find situations where sales are subject to tax and a gain arises. Apart from sales of assets and businesses out of companies, this will be the case for disposals of:

(i) any shares of companies where the holding is below the 10% threshold and where a 10% stake was not held for 12 months within the previous six years;

(ii) shares in investment companies where the holding of qualifying institutional investors is below 80%; and

(iii) any shares which have not been held for the requisite period.

Given these potential situations, capital losses remain relevant to many groups, and opportunities to crystallise capital losses should be exploited. This might include making negligible value claims in situations where the loss would be allowable.

**Point 32.5:** ***Companies eligible for the substantial shareholdings exemption can transfer properties into a trading subsidiary and claim an exemption on the disposal of shares, without realising a gain on the property.***

A company which transfers a property within a capital gains group is treated as making a no gain/no loss disposal. *TCGA 1992, s 179* deems the subsidiary company to have disposed of and reacquired the property at market value on transfer if the subsidiary is sold within six years of the property transfer.

The gain arising under *s 179* can normally be added to the consideration received by the company disposing of its subsidiary. Where the disposal is eligible for the substantial shareholdings exemption, such a gain is exempt.

It should be noted that an SDLT exit charge could still arise if there is a share disposal within three years of the property transfer.

## Example 2

Ransley Ltd is a group holding company. In May 2023, it transferred an office block to one of its trading subsidiaries, Skelton Ltd. Skelton Ltd occupies the office block. The gain at the time of transfer would have been £2 million, but as the transfer was within a capital gains group, no gain arose.

In June 2023, Skelton Ltd was sold. The £2 million gain will be added to the consideration received by Ransley Ltd for the Skelton Ltd shares. Providing the substantial shareholdings exemption applies, no taxable gain will arise.

As it is leaving the group within three years of the property transfer, Skelton Ltd will become liable to SDLT on the value of the office block at the date of transfer.

*Chapter 33*

# Tax-free statutory compensation

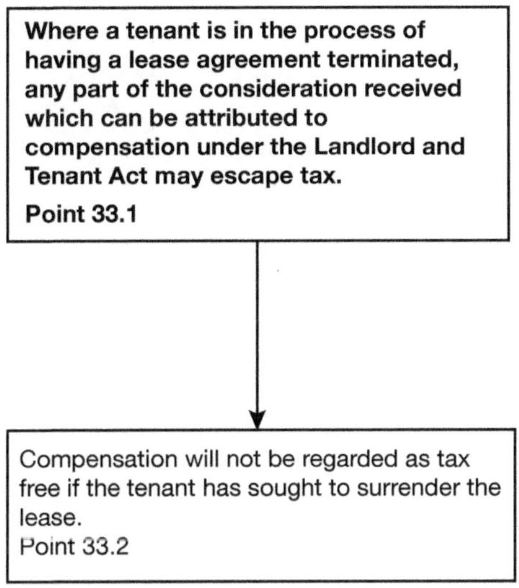

# 33 TAX-FREE STATUTORY COMPENSATION

**Point 33.1:** ***Where a tenant is in the process of having a lease agreement terminated, any part of the consideration received which can be attributed to compensation under the Landlord and Tenant Act may escape tax.***

Where a landlord gives notice to a tenant under the *Landlord and Tenant Act 1954* that the lease is to be terminated and not renewed, there are statutory provisions for a compensation payment to be made to the tenant. This is, generally speaking, twice the rateable value of the property.

It has been established, following the case of *Drummond (Inspector of Taxes) v Austin Brown* [1984] STC 321 that statutory compensation payments cannot be subject to tax on capital gains, since the payment arises by virtue of a right incorporated in the legislation rather than a disposal of an asset. This reinforces the principle already established in the case of statutory compensation for disturbance on surrender of an agricultural lease (*Davis (Inspector of Taxes) v Powell* (1977) 51 TC 492). In that case, it was similarly established that compensation under the *Agricultural Holdings Act 1948* was not subject to tax on capital gains. Since the payment is of a capital nature, there should not be an alternative assessment on it as income.

The exemption for such payments means that, where a landlord wishes to terminate a lease, the tenant may well be in a position to minimise the tax liability on any compensation made by ensuring as much as possible is statutory compensation under the *Landlord and Tenant Act 1954* or the *Agricultural Holdings Act 1948*.

No exemption is available if the tenant receives a capital sum for surrendering the 'fag end' of his lease.

HMRC have published an 'interpretation' in this area (RI 145, see *Tax Bulletin 22*, April 1996). This followed two further unsuccessful attempts to tax compensation received by outgoing tenants (*Davis v Henderson* [1995] STC (SCD) 308, and *Pritchard v Purves* [1995] STC (SCD) 316).

HMRC now accept that, where a tenant enters into an agreement to surrender a lease after receiving a genuine notice to quit from the landlord, any statutory compensation paid under the surrender agreement will not be chargeable to CGT.

All other amounts under the agreement will be taxable.

**Point 33.2:** ***Compensation will not be regarded as tax-free if the tenant has sought to surrender the lease.***

The HMRC interpretation referred to above only covers surrenders agreed as a result of a unilateral and unsolicited notice to quit. If there is evidence that the tenant has sought to surrender the lease and a notice to quit is then issued, HMRC will seek to tax the full amount received by the tenant.

*Chapter 34*

# Construction Industry Scheme

**A trader that commissions construction or refurbishment work may need to satisfy the obligations of the Construction Industry Scheme.**

**Point 34.1**

# 34 CONSTRUCTION INDUSTRY SCHEME

**Point 34.1:** ***A trader who commissions construction or refurbishment work on properties may well need to follow the procedures required under the Construction Industry Scheme if the work is not on a property used in the trade.***

As already mentioned, there are certain requirements imposed on a 'contractor' within the meaning of the Construction Industry Scheme (CIS) (see Point 25.1).

Up to 5 April 2021, the average annual expenditure on 'construction operations' in the three years ending with the last accounting date of the business exceeds £1 million. From 6 April 2021, this limit was increased to £3m per annum, with the test applied over a rolling 12-month period.

(*FA 2004, s 59(1)(l)*) and *FA 2021, Sch 6, paras* 2, 3).

HMRC guidelines as to what constitutes 'construction operations' are set out in Appendix II.

The important point about this aspect of the definition of 'contractor' is that the legislation is not confined merely to property developers or builders. Commercial organisations owning property for trading as well as investment purposes spend substantial amounts annually on construction operations.

The Construction Industry Scheme does not need to be applied to work on properties used 100% in the company's trade. If letting of any of the property to third parties takes place the exemption will not apply. This is a helpful exemption, for instance, for retailers or hoteliers constructing or refurbishing their premises. However, where these businesses also own other property, the construction operations can still be caught. The obligations of a 'contractor' have already been set out under Point 25.1. It is important to recognise that failure to operate the scheme would result in the contractor remaining liable to pay to HMRC tax which should have been withheld. In this connection, the contractor must ensure that all payments to sub-contractors without a verified gross payment status are made net of tax at the prescribed rate of tax and the appropriate returns made to HMRC.

Where tax withholding is required, the current prescribed rate is 20% for standard rated sub-contractors (ie known to HMRC) and 30% for unmatched sub-contractors (ie not known to HMRC as working in the construction industry).

*Chapter 35*

# VAT and trading premises

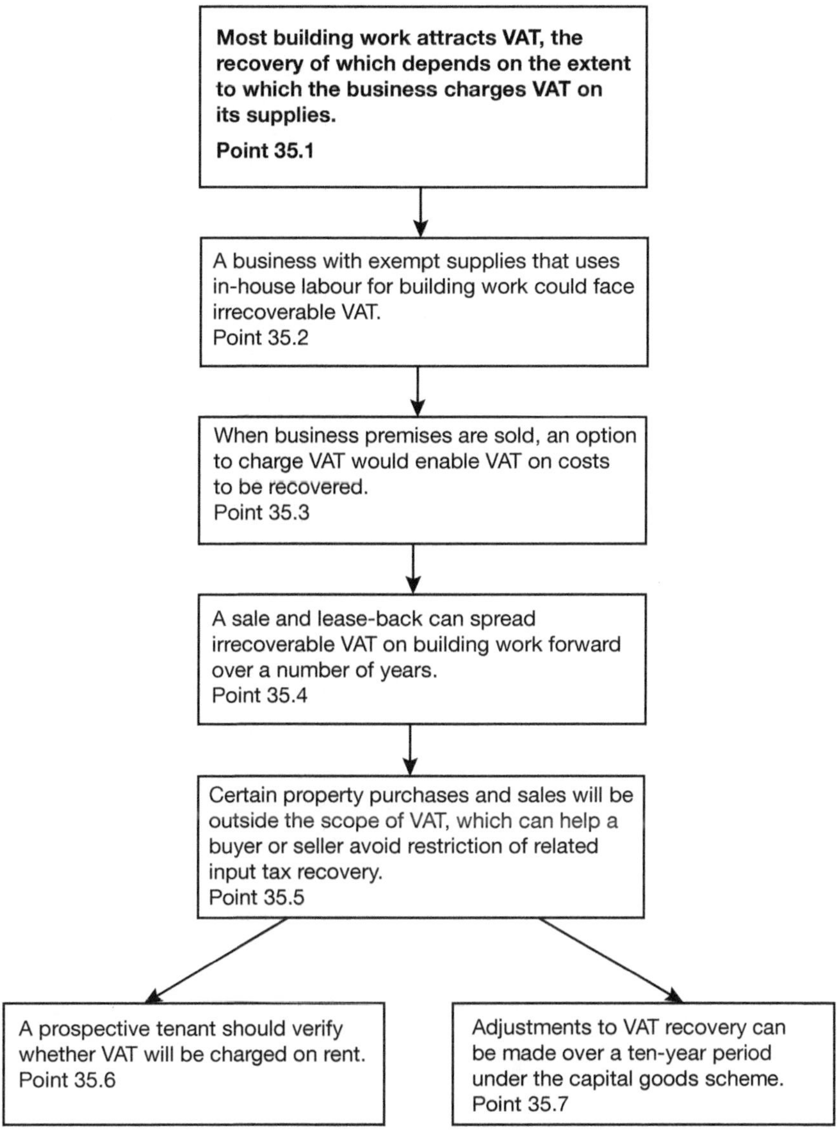

# 35 VAT AND TRADING PREMISES

**Point 35.1:** ***Most building work is subject to VAT at the standard rate. Where a business is wholly or partially exempt, part or all of this input VAT will be irrecoverable.***

The position regarding the taxability of building work has already been discussed in relation to property investors (see Point 18.8) and for property developers/dealers (see Point 26.2).

The reader will note from the discussion under the above points that all building work on business premises will be subject to standard-rated VAT, except for some instances where they are for relevant residential or relevant charitable use. This is regardless of whether building work is on new or existing buildings.

The standard rate of VAT is 20%.

For the VAT-registered business with fully taxable supplies, all of the deductible input tax can be recovered from HMRC. However, those businesses which make wholly or partly exempt supplies will be unable to recover all of their input VAT. This VAT will, therefore, represent an additional cost of the building work to a number of businesses, such as insurance brokers, bookmakers, hospitals, banks and building societies.

It is not necessary for a business to opt to tax a building to recover input tax on that building if it is used wholly for the business's own purposes. The input tax recovery is determined by the use made of the building i.e. if the business is fully taxable, the VAT should be recoverable. If the business is to let part of the building to tenants, then making an option to tax may be necessary to protect any input tax incurred on the building (see Point 18.1).

**Point 35.2:** ***A business with exempt supplies could face irrecoverable VAT on a deemed supply of construction services when it uses in-house labour to build, extend or alter a building.***

Where a business carries out any construction work using in-house labour, there is a deemed self-supply of construction services, unless the open market value (OMV) of those services is less than £100,000. Where the value of the services is £100,000 or more, VAT is chargeable on the market value of this supply.

A deemed self-supply arises with the construction of a new building, or the extension, enlargement or alteration work which results in an increase in the floor area by more than 10%. The VAT is declared as output tax and then recovered according to the business's input tax recovery position. For the exempt or partially exempt business, there is likely to be irrecoverable VAT unless the building itself is used wholly for taxable supplies.

The tax point for the charge is the date on which the work is completed or, if earlier, the date on which the new parts of the building are occupied.

Any input VAT arising from these self-supply rules is subject to adjustment under the Capital Goods Scheme (CGS) (see Point 35.7 below) if there is a change in the use of the building.

**Point 35.3:** ***Where a business sells a property, consideration might be given to opting to tax the building to charge VAT on the sale.***

The sale of business premises will generally constitute an exempt supply for VAT purposes, unless the property was completed in the previous three years or the sale forms part of a transfer of the business as a going concern (see Points 35.4 and 35.5 below). This could mean that, if any significant building work is carried out prior to sale, some or all of the related input tax could be attributed to the sale of the property. On this basis, the input tax could be irrecoverable regardless of the status of other supplies by the business.

In every case where a business is faced with an exempt supply and the possibility of suffering irrecoverable input tax, consideration might be given to opting to tax in respect of that sale (see Points 18.1 and 26.3). This would mean that VAT at the standard rate would have to be added to the sale price. This, in turn, would mean that any input tax incurred on the property and related selling costs (ie legal fees, estate agents, commissions, etc) that are attributable to the sale would be recoverable.

This is also relevant to the Capital Goods Scheme (CGS), where an exempt sale within ten years will result in repayment to HMRC of a proportion of the VAT claimed on the property, even if the property was used for trading purposes (see Point 35.7 below for an illustration of the CGS).

There is a discussion on the option to tax in Points 18.1 and 26.3.

A separate consideration of the VAT position may be necessary if the sale of the premises is part of a sale and lease-back deal (see Point 35.4 below) or of the sale of the business as a going concern (see Point 35.5 below).

**Point 35.4:** ***If a business constructs a new building for its own use and then sells the freehold as part of a sale and lease-back transaction within three years of completion, VAT must be charged on the property. This minimises or avoids irrecoverable input tax on building work.***

It will be noted from Point 26.1 that the freehold sale of a building within three years of its completion represents a standard-rated supply, unless the 'going concern' rules mentioned in Point 35.5 below apply. This will need to be borne in mind by any business that constructs its own premises, buys premises from a developer or has them built by a builder and refinances the cost by way of a sale and lease-back deal.

In the absence of a sale and lease-back arrangement, if the business makes largely exempt supplies, any input tax incurred on building supplies would be wholly or partly irrecoverable. The mechanism of the CGS would be relevant to dictate the manner in which the business has to adjust any VAT recovery over a ten-year period (see Point 35.7 below).

If the property is sold and leased-back, VAT may have to be charged on the sale price. If VAT is charged, there should be a full recovery of any VAT incurred on the building expenditure or purchase price.

The entity that purchases the building will itself be keen to recover the VAT element of the cost. It will probably achieve this by opting to tax the building, leading to VAT on the rentals charged to the vendor under the lease-back arrangement. For the exempt or partially exempt business, this can result in the spreading forward over a number of years of the irrecoverable VAT that would normally arise on the construction or purchase.

However, it should be noted that the option to tax is disapplied under certain circumstances, which will affect some sale and lease-back arrangements. Broadly, the option to tax is disapplied from any grant of a property where the property falls within the CGS, where the occupier's use of the property will not be 80% or more for taxable purposes, and there is a connection between the occupier and the developer or anyone providing finance for the development. This ultimately means that the VAT that is chargeable on the sale (or development) of the building will represent a cost to the landlord, as his or her rental income will revert back to being exempt from VAT.

A good illustration of these rules can be found in the case of *Winterthur Life* (VTD 15785) where an insurance business acquired a property through its pension scheme. This was held to be a connected supply to a mainly exempt business and the anti-avoidance provisions disapplied the option to tax, resulting in the loss of input tax to the pension scheme, even though the transaction was on wholly commercial terms.

This is a particularly complex area of VAT, and specialist advice should always be sought in advance.

**Point 35.5:** ***The transfer of property as part of the sale of the business may be treated as neither a supply of goods, nor services, rather than either an exempt or standard-rated supply.***

Where a business is sold as a going concern, the transaction, together with the related transfer of assets and liabilities, is outside the scope of VAT (*VAT (Special Provisions) Order 1995, art 5*). This is also the case for the sale of part of the business and can apply to a property investment business (see Point 18.3) and to a property occupied by the business being sold. However, the following conditions must be met before this treatment applies:

(a) The business (or the part of the business which is being transferred) must be a going concern at the time of transfer.

(b) The assets, including any property transferred, must be for use by the new owner in carrying on the same kind of business as that carried on by the former owner. It does not matter whether this will be a new business which the transferee will be carrying on or whether he or she will carry it on as part of the existing business.

(c) There must not be a series of immediately consecutive transfers of the business.

(d) If only part of the business is being transferred, the part must be capable of being operated separately from any other businesses the transferee carries on.

(e) The new owner must already be registered or, at the time of transfer, become liable to be registered.

(f) If the vendor has opted to tax the building, the new owner must notify HMRC, before the time of supply, that it, too, has opted to tax. This is strictly interpreted.

(g) The new owner is required to make a declaration to the vendor, before the time of supply, stating that anti-avoidance legislation (see Point 18.3) does not apply to the transaction.

Where these conditions are satisfied, the transfer of a property as part of a sale of a business will not be deemed to be a supply for VAT purposes. Accordingly, provided that the underlying business makes taxable supplies, no restriction on the recovery of input tax will arise, which might otherwise be the case if a transfer of land represented an exempt supply. The time of supply is the date any payment is made to the vendor or the vendor's agent. A payment to someone acting as a stakeholder will not create a time of supply and this usually arises on completion, but care must always be taken, and best advice is that any option to tax is resolved prior to exchange. Auctions can create particular problems, as the auctioneers historically took deposits on the day of the auction as agent for the seller. Consequently, where property is to be bought at an auction, the option to tax should be made and notified to HMRC before the auction date, unless it is clear that the auctioneer will hold any deposit as a stakeholder (*Higher Education Statistics Agency Ltd v Customs and Excise Comrs* [2000] STC 332 and *Clark Hill Limited v HMRC* [2018] UKFTT TC06368).

HMRC had maintained that for a sale to qualify as a TOGC the seller must be selling the whole interest held in the property. However, following a 2012 decision of the First-tier Tribunal (*Robinson* TC02046), HMRC accepted that the grant of a significant interest, where the seller retains a small reversionary interest, could qualify as a TOGC, provided all the other conditions ((a)–(f) above) are satisfied. HMRC considers that a small reversionary interest should be seen as no more than 1% of the value prior to the sale (HMRC Brief 30/12).

It should be recognised that any obligations under the Capital Goods Scheme (see Point 35.7 below) or under the clawback rules in *reg 108* of the *VAT Regulations 1995* (see Point 18.7) transfer to the buyer when a property is transferred as part of a TOGC.

**Point 35.6: *When a tenancy is being entered into, the tenant should verify whether VAT is to be charged on the rents.***

As noted in Point 18.1, many investors will be considering whether to charge VAT on property lettings so that they themselves can recover any input tax on, say, construction and refurbishment.

For an exempt or partly exempt business, any VAT charged on the rents clearly constitutes an additional expense and should be resisted if possible. This may, in some cases, mean agreeing to a slightly higher rent so that the impact of the additional cost can be split between the parties. Note that, where VAT is charged on the rent, this will also increase the SDLT payable on the grant of the lease (see Points 5.2 and 5.3 on SDLT on lease grants and SDLT and VAT respectively).

There may be cases where even a fully taxable business may wish to resist VAT on rents charged, possibly for cash flow reasons or because there is an intention to sub-let part of the property. If, by the nature of the location or the type of building, the premises would attract exempt or partly exempt tenants, the landlord by opting to tax will make the rent more expensive for such tenants by up to the amount of VAT – plus an additional SDLT cost.

Ultimately, this will be a bargaining point between landlord and tenant in future. However, in certain situations, the landlord will have no choice. If a landlord has already made an option to tax on the property, any future lettings or assignments must be taxable, subject to the disapplication provisions outlined at Point 18.1. Furthermore, if the premises are part of a complex or precinct, an option would have to cover all units within that complex or precinct.

**Point 35.7:** ***Where the proportion of a business's exempt outputs changes, this can result in an adjustment to the VAT reclaimable on premises under the Capital Goods Scheme. A substantial clawback of VAT can arise on a sale within ten years from purchase if the option to tax is not made prior to any sale.***

Under the Capital Goods Scheme (CGS), there is a potential annual adjustment over a ten-year period in respect of VAT claimed on expenditure on premises (*VAT Regulations 1995, regs 112–116*).

The CGS applies to capital assets held by a business and does not normally apply to property held as trading stock, although, if trading stock is let, HMRC may take the view that it should be subject to the CGS.

As far as trading premises, including let premises, are concerned, the scheme applies to the capital expenditure as set out below:

The CGS rules were substantially amended with effect from 1 January 2011, although the old rules apply to expenditure incurred before 1 January 2011.

For expenditure incurred from 1 January 2011, the CGS rules apply to:

(a) land;

(b) a building or part of a building;

(c) a civil engineering work or part of a civil engineering work;

where the expenditure incurred was £250,000 or more and was in respect of:

(i) acquisition;

(ii) construction;

(iii) refurbishment;

(iv) fitting out;

(v) alteration; or

(vi) extension (including the construction of an annex).

Note that the expenditure in the different categories above is not aggregated for CGS purposes.

For expenditure incurred before 1 January 2011 the rules applied in the following circumstances:

(a) A building (or parts of buildings or a civil engineering work) where the cost subject to VAT to the buyer was £250,000 or more.

(b) A building or part of a building in respect of which the owner has been subject to a self-supply charge on change of use from residential or charitable purposes, and the value of the self-supply was £250,000 or more. Such a self-supply charge is made (under *VATA 1994, Sch 10, para 37*) where the owner acquired his or her interest in the building by means of a zero-rated supply, on the grounds that the building was to be used solely for a residential or charitable purpose; and, within ten years from the date of completion of the building, it begins to be used for some other purpose.

(c) A building or part of a building in respect of which the owner was subject before 2 March 1997 to the former developer's self-supply charge, and the value of that self-supply was £250,000 or more. The developer's self-supply charge was made under *VATA 1994, Sch 10, paras5–6* in specified circumstances where a developer either granted an exempt interest in the building or occupied it himself at a time when he was not a fully taxable person.

(d) A building which was constructed by the owner and first brought into use by him after 31 March 1990 if the value of all taxable supplies relating to the land and taxable supplies of goods or services (other than zero-rated supplies) made to him after that date in connection with the construction is £250,000 or more.

(e) A building which the owner alters (including constructing an extension or annexe) where additional floor area of 10% or more is created and the value of all taxable supplies (other than zero-rated supplies) of goods or services made to him after that date in connection with the alteration is £250,000 or more.

(f) Civil engineering work constructed by the owner and first brought into use by him after 2 July 1997 if the aggregate value of taxable supplies to the owner after that date relating to the land (other than zero-rated supplies) made to him in connection with the construction of the work is £250,000 or more.

(g) A building which the owner refurbishes or fits out where the value of capital expenditure on the taxable supplies of services and goods affixed to the building made to the owner in connection with the refurbishment after 2 July 1997 is £250,000 or more.

The adjustment is calculated by comparing the initial input tax recovery percentage to the input tax recovery percentage in the second and subsequent years, and applying the difference to one-tenth of the input tax incurred in each of those years. If the building is sold or otherwise disposed of, or the VAT registration is cancelled, there is a closing adjustment treating the remaining intervals in accordance with the nature of the disposal or deemed disposal in the case of cancellation of a VAT registration.

If there are subsequent developments to the building complex, parallel adjustments can arise.

An illustration how this operates is given in the simple example below:

---

## Example

A building is purchased by an insurance company for £10 million plus £2 million VAT (using the VAT rate of 20%).

In the first three years, it is used as a branch office by the company whose recovery rate was 10%, 25% and 10% in each of those years. At the beginning of Year 4, the building is sold and the insurance company exercises the option to tax the sale. The position in each year will be:

| Year | Partial exemption recovery rate | Capital goods calculation | Input tax recovered/ (repaid) |
|---|---|---|---|
| | | | £ |
| 1 | 10% | £2,000,000 × 10% | 200,000 |
| 2 | 25% | £2,000,000 × 15% × 1/10 | 30,000 |
| 3 | 10% | £2,000,000 × 0% × 1/10 | 0 |
| 4 | 100% | £2,000,000 × 90% × 7/10 | 1,260,000 |
| | | | 1,490,000 |

---

In Year 1, the company recovers 10% of the VAT incurred. In subsequent years, there are adjustments between that figure and the actual recovery percentage for the year in question, depending on whether the proportion of taxable supplies increases or decreases.

In Year 4, because there is a taxable sale of the property, it is assumed that the property in Years 4–10 is used in a fully taxable way. Accordingly, in a closing adjustment representing use for those seven years, the company can recover the input tax incurred (£2 million) divided by the adjustment period (ten years) times the difference between the subsequent use percentage (100%) and the input tax initially recovered (10%) times the number of years remaining (7). Thus 2,000,000/10 × 90% × 7 years = £1,260,000.

There is a potential pitfall in the CGS for the trader that sells premises without opting to tax. If, in the above example, the property were sold on an exempt basis at the beginning of Year 4, there is a negative adjustment for the last seven years.

The presumption is that, for those seven years, the property is used in a totally exempt way. Therefore, instead of being able to recover an additional amount of input VAT of £1,260,000 making a total of £1,490,000, the company must actually pay back to HMRC £140,000 (£2,000,000/10 × 10% × 7). This reduces the overall VAT recovered to £90,000 (£200,000 + £30,000 – £140,000).

If the VAT recovery in the two situations is compared, the benefit of opting to tax the property is evident. Taxing the sale of the property yielded a further £1,260,000 in respect of Years 4–7, whereas not opting led to a repayment to HMRC of £140,000.

In the second situation, a large proportion of the VAT was irrecoverable.

This problem is not just confined to partially taxable businesses. If a fully taxable business were to sell premises in the same manner, it would still be required to repay a large amount of VAT if it does not opt to tax the property prior to the sale.

*Part D*

# Private Residences

*Chapter 36*

# The capital gains tax, ATED and SDLT regimes for residential property

**Whether or not a property is classed as 'residential' can significantly impact the tax position in relation to the purchase, sale or even the ongoing ownership of a property. This is particularly the case where the owner is tax resident outside the UK.**
**Point 36.1**

↓

Non-residents are liable to tax when they sell residential property.
Point 36.2

↓

Owning a property through a vehicle regarded as a 'non-natural person' can significantly increase tax exposure.
Point 36.3

↓

Relief from ATED is available where the property is used, or let, commercially. The relief must be claimed annually.
Point 36.4

↓

Where a property is acquired by a non-natural person in certain situations, there can be a 15% rate of SDLT charged when a property costing more than £500,000 is first acquired by the purchasing vehicle. As with ATED, a relief is available for certain situations.
Point 36.2

# 36 THE CAPITAL GAINS TAX, ATED AND SDLT REGIMES FOR RESIDENTIAL PROPERTY

**Point 36.1***: Whether or not a property is classed as 'residential' can significantly impact the tax position in relation to the purchase, sale or even the ongoing ownership of a property. This is particularly the case where the owner is tax resident outside the UK.***

In recent years, there have been moves to extract additional taxation from the ownership of residential property. This additional taxation has impacted in several ways:

- As noted in Chapter 5, rates of Stamp Duty Land Tax (SDLT) in respect of residential property purchases differ from commercial property. Currently, whereas the maximum SDLT rate for commercial property is 5%, for residential property it can rise to 15% for any element of the price paid over £1.5 million including the 3% surcharge that now applies to purchases by companies or of second homes by individuals. The 15% rate can also apply where a non-natural person (see Point 36.3 below) buys the property for more than £500,000.
- An acquisition of a dwelling in England or Northern Ireland by a non-resident buyer on or after 1 April 2021 could be subject to a 2% SDLT surcharge in addition to the normal and higher rates of SDLT, up to a maximum of 17%. As explained in Point 36.3 below, where the property is owned by a non-natural person, an annual charge known as the Annual Tax on Enveloped Dwellings (ATED) can arise, depending on the value of the property.
- Capital gains tax or income tax will now arise on most gains on the sale of residential property. There was formerly a capital gains tax exemption for non-resident owners but, as explained in Points 36.2 to 36.4 below, this has largely disappeared. With regard to properties occupied as a main residence, the general capital gains exemption and related rules have largely been retained, but the availability of the exemption has been curtailed for certain individuals spending much of their time outside the UK (see Point 36.2).

This begs the question of what constitutes 'residential' as opposed to 'non-residential' property.

The usual meaning of residential property in the various taxing acts has been adapted further for these recent tax measures. In general, residential property means:

(a) a building that is used or suitable for use as a dwelling or is in the process of being constructed or adapted for such use; and

(b) land that forms part of the garden or grounds of such a building; or

(c) land that subsists for the benefit of such a building.

(*Finance Act 2003, s 116(1)*)

HMRC's SDLT manuals contain guidance on whether a property may be seen as being residential or not including the points set out below:

- If a building is not in use at the effective date but its last use was as a dwelling, it will be taken to be 'suitable for use as a dwelling' and treated as residential property, unless evidence is produced to the contrary.
- A property with a long history of non-residential use, and which does not have permission to be occupied as a residence, is unlikely to be viewed by HMRC as a dwelling, or suitable for use as a dwelling. HMRC may take a contrary view where, for example, a property's last use was as an office but before the property is sold planning permission is granted for use as a dwelling, provided that, at the effective date of the transaction, the property is otherwise suitable for use as a dwelling or is being adapted for such use.
- Undeveloped land is essentially non-residential but may be residential property if, at the effective date, a residential building is being built on it.
- Where, at the effective date, an existing building is being adapted or marketed for, or restored to, domestic use, it is treated as residential property.

(HMRC SDLT Manual 00360 to 00400)

There are certain specific types of dwellings which are deemed to be dwellings for SDLT (other than for the purposes of the 3% SDLT surcharge on additional residential property and the 2% surcharge for non-resident transactions) – but not ATED purposes. These are:

(a) residential accommodation for school pupils;

(b) certain residential accommodation for students;

(c) residential accommodation for members of the armed forces; and

(d) an institution that is the sole or main residence of at least 90% of its residents and does not fall within any of paragraphs (a) to (f) below.

On the other hand, a building used for any of the following purposes is not regarded as a dwelling–

(a) a home or other institution providing residential accommodation for children;

(b) a hall of residence for students in further or higher education;

(c) a home or other institution providing residential accommodation with personal care for persons in need of personal care by reason of old age, disablement, past or present dependence on alcohol or drugs or past or present mental disorder;

(d) a hospital or hospice;

(e) a prison or similar establishment; and

(f) a hotel or inn or similar establishment.

**Point 36.2:** ***Non-residents are liable to tax when they sell residential property.***

Prior to 5 April 2015, non-UK tax residents were not liable to tax on any capital gains made on any assets, unless they were used in a trade carried on in the UK or were residential property held by a 'non-natural person' and subject to the ATED-related capital gains tax charge (see Point 1.2 in Chapter 1). That general exemption disappeared from that date and non-residents can now be liable for capital gains tax when they sell – or make a deemed sale of – residential property for a gain (*TCGA 1992, s 14D*).

Even where a UK property might qualify as a non-UK resident's main residence, exemption from capital gains tax is only available for any year if the individual (or his spouse/civil partner) spent at least 90 midnights in that property – or in aggregate in all their UK properties – in that year.

Note that widely held/non-close investment vehicles are not subject to this charge – a measure designed to exclude institutional investors being subject to capital gains tax (*TCGA 1992, s 14F* and *Sch C1*).

There is an extended meaning of residential property for the new CGT rules for non-residents. Property and land that has at any time in the relevant ownership period consisted of or included a dwelling would be included in the definition.

For capital gains tax purposes, none of the buildings deemed to be residential for SDLT as listed in (a)–(d) in Point 36.1 are treated as dwellings for capital gains tax. There are, however, further detailed conditions that need to be satisfied for student accommodation/halls of residence to not be treated as dwellings. In addition, the 90% condition in (1)(d) is relaxed.

A building that is used only partly as a dwelling may nevertheless be suitable for use wholly as a dwelling. Its overall suitability will be judged from the facilities available at the effective date. For example, if two rooms of a house were in use as a doctor's surgery and waiting room, HMRC would treat this property as suitable for use as a dwelling.

For individuals, the capital gains tax rate applicable will be 18% or 28% depending on the amount of gain. The reduction in the capital gains tax rates from 6 April 2016 (to 10% and 20% respectively) do not apply to gains on residential property.

The rate payable by trustees is 28%. The amount subject to tax is the gain accruing post-5 April 2015. There are alternative methods of computation of the gain (*TCGA 1992, Sch 4ZZB*).

Since 6 April 2019, corporation tax rather than CGT is chargeable on gains from UK property or land for all non-resident companies.

**Point 36.3:** ***Owning a property through a vehicle regarded as a 'non-natural person' can significantly increase tax exposure.***

Since 2013, there has been an annual tax charge for residential properties above a certain value which are owned by non-natural persons. The particular aim was to extract tax where residential properties were owned by companies (most typically overseas registered companies) such that when the property changed hands through the sale of the company, no SDLT or stamp duty was due.

Broadly, a non-natural person is:

- a company;
- a partnership where one or more members is a company; or
- a collective investment scheme, eg a unit trust.

The annual tax in question is known as the Annual Tax on Enveloped Dwellings ('ATED'). The rates of ATED applicable from 1 April 2018 are:

| **Property value** | **Annual charge in 2023–2024** |
|---|---|
| £500,000-£1,000,000 | £4,150 |
| £1,000,001–£2,000,000 | £8,450 |
| £2,000,001–£5,000,000 | £28,650 |
| £5,000,001–£10,000,000 | £67,050 |
| £10,000,001–£20,000,000 | £134,550 |
| £20,000,001+ | £269,450 |

Where a new property is constructed, the relevant valuation date is generally the date that the building is complete and becomes liable to council tax.

The property must be revalued every five years in line with the ATED legislation. If a property is acquired on or before 1 April 2022, 1 April 2022 must be used as the revaluation date.

**Point 36.4:** ***Relief from ATED is available where the property is used, or let, commercially. The relief must be claimed annually.***

Relief from ATED is available where the dwelling is used exclusively for one or more of the following businesses:

(a) for the purposes of a property rental, property development or property trading business provided the dwelling is not occupied by a non-qualifying individual. 'Non-qualifying individual' has a wide definition but is broadly a person connected with the owner of the property or a relative of a connected person;

(b) made available to the public as part of a trade carried on on a commercial basis with a view to profit (eg a stately home);

(c) held via re-possession by the mortgage lender following default on the loan;

(d) for housing one or more employees (and their families if necessary);

(e) as a farmhouse and forms part of land that is occupied for the purposes of a qualifying farming trade; and

(f) held by a profit-making registered provider of social housing.

An ATED return is required to be submitted annually to HMRC in order to claim relief. Note that failure to file the return will give rise to penalties even where no ATED is due as indicated by two cases which have recently come before the courts (*Lucas Properties Ltd* v *HMRC*; *Monaco Group of Companies Ltd* v *HMRC*).

**Point 36.5*: Where a property is acquired by a non-natural person in situations where there would be an on-going liability to ATED, there is also a 15% rate of SDLT charged when a property costing more than £500,000 is first acquired by the purchasing vehicle. As with ATED, a relief is available for certain situations.***

Relief from the 15% rate of SDLT is available where the property is acquired exclusively for one or more of the following:

(a) for the purposes of a property rental, property development or property trading business provided it is not intended for a non-qualifying individual to be permitted to occupy the dwelling. 'Non-qualifying individual' has a wide definition but is broadly the purchaser or a connected person or a relative of a connected person;

(b) made available to the public as part of a trade carried on on a commercial basis with a view to profit (eg a stately home);

(c) via re-possession by the mortgage lender following default on the loan;

(d) for the intention of housing one or more employees (and their families if necessary); and

(e) to be used as a farmhouse and forms part of land that is occupied for the purposes of a qualifying farming trade.

Relief must be claimed on the land transaction return.

Note that relief from the 15% may be withdrawn within three years following the acquisition where the conditions for the relief are no longer satisfied.

*Chapter 37*

# Motive for acquisition of a residence

Exemption from capital gains tax is available on the sale of a 'main residence' unless the property was acquired wholly or partly for the purpose of realising a gain. A seller may have to show that the reason for buying a property was to occupy it as a residence.
Point 37.1

# 37 MOTIVE FOR ACQUISITION OF A RESIDENCE

**Point 37.1:** ***Exemption from capital gains tax is available to a UK resident disposing of his/her main residence unless the property was acquired wholly or partly for the purpose of realising a gain. Where circumstances suggest that this might have been the case, a taxpayer may have to show that the reason for buying a property was to occupy it as a residence.***

Normally, a gain realised by an individual on a dwelling house which was occupied as a main residence is exempt from capital gains tax. However, a gain on a main residence which was bought wholly or partly with the objective of realising a gain on sale is excluded from the exemption (*TCGA 1992, s 224(3)*).

This can give rise to some cause for concern. A house purchaser often expects that the property value will increase over a period of time and there is an anticipation of gain on a future sale. Many individuals and couples acquire properties which they know they will be selling in, say, two or three years' time to buy larger properties.

The exclusion of the main residence exemption is clearly not aimed at normal home purchases and sales. The fact that the house has been purchased because it may have been a 'bargain' or was expected to appreciate in value does not itself prevent the exemption from applying. However, if there is a purchase and sale within a relatively short period of time, the point could be raised in a Tax Inspector's mind that the principal reason for buying was to realise a quick profit. Similarly, if HMRC consider that the property was acquired to trade then they might seek to treat the gain arising as trading profit subject to income tax and not capital gains tax.

Where a residence is purchased and sold at a profit within a short period, it may be necessary to demonstrate the following facts to the Inspector:

(a) That the intention was to occupy the property as a main residence. This might be evidenced by reasons as to why the house and location, together with any local amenities, were particularly desirable. It may also be useful to give positive reasons for leaving the previous residence.

(b) That the property was actually occupied as a main residence. Whilst intention to occupy will help refute any contention that the property was bought with the objective of selling at a profit, no exemption will be available unless the property is actually occupied as a main residence (*Goodwin v Curtis* [1998] STC 475). Apart from the family's furniture being moved there, it should also be seen that the family slept in the house; cooked and entertained there; received mail there; the address is used for local amenity purposes eg with libraries; and the occupants are registered there in the electoral register.

(c) The intention to sell should have arisen after the property was acquired. It may be necessary to demonstrate special reasons for a short-term sale such as financial problems, job requirements, problems with neighbours or any other reasons why the location or house may have become unsuitable.

(d) The timing of any advertising of the property for sale or its placement with estate agents should be consistent with the facts referred to in (a), (b) and (c) above.

There have been several cases recently where taxpayers' claims for main residence relief have failed. Whilst there were differing circumstances in each case, a common thread was that there was insufficient evidence of the property in question actually becoming the individual's home at any point. In the cases of *Anthony Metcalf* (TC753) and *Malcolm Springthorpe* (TC832), for instance, the courts referred to the low level of power consumption in electricity bills in reaching the conclusion that there was insufficient occupation to be eligible for the exemption.

The First-tier Tribunal followed the above decisions in *MJ Harte* (TC01951) when it considered the appellant had not demonstrated that the short period of occupation of a property had any degree of permanence or expectation of continuance. In particular, there had been no notifications of change of address to either the bank or the council and within either days or weeks of acquiring the property the appellant had obtained a valuation with a view to selling. On those facts, the Tribunal found that there was no degree of permanence and no expectation of continuity. It therefore found that, at best, the appellant had temporary occupation of the property in question, which did not amount to residence.

There have been subsequent cases where the Tribunal has similarly ruled in favour of HMRC. On the other hand, in the recent case of *David Morgan* (TC2596), the FTT ruled that the taxpayer's property had been his main residence after only a short period of occupation. In that case, Mr Morgan has acquired the property when engaged to be married with a view to it becoming his family home. Although he left the property a few months later, shortly after his engagement broke up, the FTT considered that he had demonstrated a clear intention for it to be his main residence.

A further case where HMRC successfully refused a main residence exemption was the 2016 case of *M Kothari* (TC 4915). Again, the FTT were not convinced that occupation of the property had the necessary degree of permanence or continuity to be a main residence. The recent case of *HMRC v Desmond Higgins* [2018] UKUT 0280 (TCC) on the scenario of off-plan purchases should be considered when there is an extended delay before residency is taken. This may substantially reduce the availability of the relief.

The main residence exemption is a valuable one. Care should be taken to ensure that the status of main residence is established beyond all reasonable doubt and, if an early sale is found to be necessary, it can be properly related to the facts above.

Note that, from 6 April 2015, individuals and certain companies which are non-UK resident as well as non-resident personal representatives, partners, trustees and foundations can be liable to CGT on gains accruing from that date on disposal of a UK residential property interest, even where the property is the individual's main residence (see Point 36.2). Non-UK residents will find it harder to treat a UK property as his or her main residence for the purpose of this exemption. The ability to elect the property as a main residence has, since 5 April 2015, been subject to quite restrictive conditions (see Point 38.5).

The Court of Appeal has ruled that the 'period of ownership' for private residence relief begins when the property purchase is completed, not from exchange. In the case of *Higgins v Revenue and Customs Commissioners* [2019] EWCA Civ 1860, it was held that a contract to acquire the property did not amount to possession. This decision reversed the decision of the Upper Tier Tribunal where it was decided that the period of ownership commenced when the contract to acquire the property was entered into.

In the case of *Gerald and Sarah Lee v* HMRC [2022] TC 8502, the FTT decided in favour of the Lees.

In October 2010, the Lees bought a property and soon after had it demolished without ever living in it. They built a new house on the land that was completed in March 2013 and which they lived in as their home until it was sold in May 2014. They made a gain from the sale of more than £550,000. They claimed PRR for the whole gain. HMRC said that Lees' home only existed for part of the period of ownership (March 2013 to May 2014) whereas the gain accrued over the whole period from October 2010.

HMRC's view was that PRR was limited to the period from March 2013. HMRC appealed to the Upper Tribunal.

The arguments put forward from both sides were unchanged and centred on their respective interpretations of the law regarding the meaning of 'period of ownership' for PRR purposes.

HMRC added two new analogies to its original argument to support its view:

(1) The PRR rules are clear that if a person buys a lease on a property and later purchases the freehold, the 'period of ownership' starts with the date of the lease purchase.

(2) If Lees and the FTT were correct that ownership for PRR purposes commenced when the new property was completed, it would mean that legislation passed in 2020 (the subject of extensive discussion and a Court of Appeal ruling which confirmed ownership for off-plan homes starts when the contract to buy the plot is signed) would have been unnecessary.

The Upper Tribunal found conflicting evidence supporting both sides, but eventually ruled in the Lees' favour. The Upper Tribunal ruled that the whole capital gain qualified for private residence relief (PRR) and so was not taxable.

*Chapter 38*

# Main residence election where more than one property is owned

**When more than one residence is owned, it is important to consider making an election as to which one is to be treated as the main residence for CGT purposes.**

**Point 38.1**

↓

Where more than one property is owned, the advantage of making a main residence election for one is that it can at any time subsequently be varied in favour of the other.
Point 38.2

↓

A main residence election could be of crucial importance if an individual both owns and rents accommodation.
Point 38.3

↓

During periods of overseas absence or other absence, an election in respect of the property which would otherwise have been the UK residence could be useful in establishing a continuous period of eligibility for capital gains tax exemption for that property.
Point 38.4

# 38 MAIN RESIDENCE ELECTION WHERE MORE THAN ONE PROPERTY IS OWNED

**Point 38.1:** ***When more than one residence is owned, it is important to consider making an election as to which one is to be treated as the main residence for capital gains tax purposes.***

The capital gains tax (CGT) exemption available for the main residence may require particular consideration where more than one property is owned.

If a family has more than one home, it is a question of fact which of the two is an individual's or family's main residence. Relevant factors are:

(a) where the family lives for the greater part of an average week;

(b) in which property is the main furniture kept and used;

(c) which address is used for correspondence; and

(d) which address appears on the electoral list.

It is possible to pre-empt any question of fact by making a specific election that one or other of the properties shall be treated as the main residence (*TCGA 1992, s 222(5)(a)*). An election is advisable where substantial appreciation is anticipated in respect of one of the properties and there may be doubt as to whether this would ordinarily be regarded as the main residence.

The main residence exemption is also available to trustees who hold property which is occupied as their main residence by a person who is entitled to do so under the terms of the trust. An election for the main residence exemption, if required, must be made jointly by the trustees and the person occupying the property (*TCGA 1992 s 225*).

An example might be where two properties are owned, one in the centre of a town and the other in the country. The town property may be used as a matter of convenience for a working couple where business commitments prevent them from returning to the country. The country home is used as the normal residence at weekends, holidays and all other times when business pressures are not too heavy. In such circumstances, HMRC may well treat the country property as the main residence as a matter of fact. However, if the town property has a higher inherent capital gain, an election to treat that as the main residence should be beneficial.

No election can be made unless the property in question is occupied as a residence (although not necessarily as a main residence). Thus it cannot be claimed in respect of a property which is let or used for other purposes. However, it may be claimed on a property which is available for use, occasionally occupied and is furnished for occupation.

Where a property has been treated at some time as a main residence, the last nine months of ownership (18 months prior to 6 April 2020) are automatically always deemed to be a period of main residence as well (*TCGA 1992, s 223(1)*). (This period was the last 36 months of ownership for disposals before 6 April 2014 – although this 36-month period will continue to apply in a limited number of situations such as a long-term resident in a care home.) Therefore, when two residences are owned, it is generally beneficial for a property to cease to be treated as a main residence within nine months of sale and another residence to be so treated. This may mean varying the election on the first property and substituting the other residence as the main residence (see Point 38.2 below).

As a result of this specific allowance in the legislation, it is possible in that particular nine-month period effectively to enjoy the main residence exemption in respect of two properties at the same time.

An election must be made within two years of the date when it is necessary to decide the issue. Therefore, if a taxpayer wants a property to be treated as a main residence an election must be filed with HMRC within two years of the date of acquiring (whether by buying or renting) a second residence (*TCGA 1992, s 222(5)(a)* and *Griffin v Craig-Harvey* [1994] STC 54). However, once an election has been made, it can be varied (see Point 38.2 below).

The main residence position for any taxpayer with more than one property should be kept under review in the two-year period when an election can be made in relation to changes in use of the property and movements in their market values. The making of a timely election can maximise the exemption for the property with the largest prospective gain. Also, by taking advantage of the exempt period in the last nine months of ownership, there is the opportunity to reduce the prospective taxable gain on another property owned at the same time.

**Point 38.2: *Where more than one property is owned, the advantage of making a main residence election for one is that it can at any time subsequently be varied in favour of the other.***

As mentioned in Point 38.1 above, a main residence election must be made within two years of an acquisition of a second property (*Griffin v Craig-Harvey* [1994] STC 54). If it is not made within that period, the taxpayer cannot choose which property should be treated as his main residence. Instead, it will depend on the facts.

Once made, an election can be varied. The election can be effective from up to two years before the date of variation (*TCGA 1992, s 222(5)(a)*).

---

Example

Mr and Mrs Durant have lived in a cottage in the Cotswolds since 2000. On 1 June 2019, they bought a flat in North London for occasional use to spend some time near children living in London.

The Cotswold property remains the main residence as a matter of fact. If, therefore, no main residence election is made by 31 May 2021 in favour of the London property, only the Cotswold property can attract exemption whilst the two properties are owned.

If the Cotswold and London properties were both sold in, say, June 2022 at a profit, the gain on the Cotswold property only would be exempt from tax. The gain on the London flat would be fully chargeable.

In the above example, if Mr and Mrs Durant were able to make an election for the London flat to be their main residence shortly before selling it, part of the gain on that flat could be exempt from tax as well – because the last nine months of ownership of a main residence are always exempt (see Point 41.1). However, they could not make the election for the London flat, because the two-year time limit had expired on 31 May 2021.

The way for Mr and Mrs Durant to have got the best of both worlds here would have been to make the election for the London property to be the main residence, and to do this within the two-year period, ie by 31 May 2021.

Electing on this basis would mean that Mr and Mrs Durant could then give notice to HMRC of a variation to that election, say, one week later, enabling the London property to be treated as a main residence from two years previous to that election. That would mean the last nine months that the London property is owned are exempt – which would be half of the whole period of ownership in this example, with the loss of only one week's exemption on the Cotswold house. (See Chapter 41 for the exemption in the last nine months.)

---

Therefore, the making of an election in the first place allows for greater flexibility – particularly enhancing the possibility of exploiting the automatic exemption for the last nine months of ownership referred to in Point 38.1 above.

**Point 38.3:** ***A main residence election could be of crucial importance if an individual both owns and rents accommodation.***

As stated in Point 38.1 above, in the absence of any election, it will be a matter of fact which of two (or more) properties is the main residence for CGT purposes. Whether such a property is owned by the taxpayer or occupied under lease is irrelevant to this issue. However, occupation under licence is ignored.

Accordingly, a person who rents a second residence could find that it is that property which is treated as the main residence. The CGT exemption in that situation would be of no benefit and, on the sale of the other property, a CGT liability will arise.

An election for the owned property to be treated as the main residence would avoid this problem and is important in this situation.

Note, however, that the day count test (see Point 38.5 below) may catch out UK residents who rent a home in the UK and own an overseas home (or holiday home) but do not spend 90 days there in a tax year and therefore will not be able to make a main residence election for the overseas home.

HMRC recognise the potential inequity of treating rented accommodation as a main residence for CGT purposes where another property is owned and also occupied. By way of concession, HMRC are prepared to extend the two-year time limit for making such an election (HMRC Extra-Statutory Concession D21). This applies where the taxpayer's interest in one of the properties has 'no more than a negligible value in the open market'. If a taxpayer in this case has been unaware of his entitlement to make an election, HMRC will accept a late election providing it is made within a reasonable period after the person first became aware of the possibility of making the election. It will be treated as effective from the date the nominated residence was acquired.

***Point 38.4:* During periods of overseas absence or other absence, an election in respect of the property which would otherwise have been the UK residence could be useful in establishing a continuous period of eligibility for capital gains tax exemption for that property.**

As will be noted in Chapter 42, some periods of absence from a property are ignored when determining if the CGT exemption is restricted (*TCGA 1992, s 223(3)*). The potential problem is that the absences are only ignored providing there is no other main residence eligible for relief (*TCGA 1992, s 223(3A and 3B)*).Therefore, following from Point 38.2 above, if there is the possibility that another property may be treated as the main residence, an election should be made for the principal UK property to be so treated.

See also Point 42.2 on this point.

For individuals living outside the UK, the issues referred to in Point 38.5 below will be relevant.

***Point 38.5*: There are conditions to satisfy before an individual who is non-UK resident or based outside the UK can treat a property as a main residence.**

Main residence treatment – or an election for such treatment – is available in respect of a residential property for a tax year if the person making the disposal has been either tax resident in the country where the property is located; or has spent at least 90 days in that property in the tax year (the day count test *s 222C* inserted by *FA 2015, Sch 9 para 3*). The 90-day requirement is reduced *pro rata* where the property was only owned for part of a tax year. For a day to count, the individual must either be present at the property 'at the end of the day' or he must be there at some point during the day and the next day he stays there 'overnight' ('at the end of the day' and 'overnight' are not defined). For the purposes of the day count test, occupation by one spouse counts as occupation by the other, although double-counting is not permitted if both are there on the same day. This is helpful for those for whom 90 days in the UK would be enough to make them UK resident under the statutory residence test, eg a couple (where either or both are non-resident) could each spend separately, say, 50 days in the property and claim the relief. A full discussion of the statutory residence test is, however, beyond the scope of this book.

If the individual has more than one residence in the UK, then for one of these to be treated as a main residence, the 90 days can be spread over all those properties. So spending 40 days in one property and, say, 50 in another means that the 90-day test is satisfied in the year in question, enabling one or other of these properties to qualify as a main residence.

The test is only applied from 5 April 2015. Years from 5 April 2015 where this test is not satisfied may require a *pro rata* adjustment to the capital gains exemption calculation.

*Chapter 39*

# Land and buildings included with a residence – maximising the exemption

**The main residence exemption includes land used as grounds or for garden purposes where the total area, except in certain cases, does not exceed half a hectare. It may also extend to other properties enjoyed with the house.**
**Point 39.1**

↓

An area of over half a hectare may be permitted within the exemption if that larger area is required for the reasonable enjoyment of the residence.
Point 39.2

↓

A main residence exemption may not be available on the disposal of any part of the grounds that has been retained after the sale of the house. The land should be sold at the same time as the house.
Point 39.3

# 39 LAND AND BUILDINGS INCLUDED WITH A RESIDENCE – MAXIMISING THE EXEMPTION

**Point 39.1:** ***The main residence exemption includes land used as grounds or for garden purposes where the total area, except in certain cases, does not exceed half a hectare. It may extend to other properties enjoyed with the house.***

The main residence exemption extends to land that is occupied and enjoyed with the house as garden or grounds (*TCGA 1992, s 222(1)(b)*).

The exemption provides for a permitted area not exceeding a half of a hectare (approximately one-and-a-quarter acres, or 5,000 square metres). This includes the area occupied by the house. In certain circumstances, a larger area may be allowed by HMRC (see Point 39.2 below).

If the land is not enjoyed and occupied as garden or grounds, then it will not be covered by the exemption. Therefore, any area devoted to farming, grazing or stables may well not qualify, whether or not the total area is less than half a hectare.

Any land that is physically separated from the house by a road, fence or other houses, can qualify for exemption. However, it is still necessary to satisfy the requirement that it is enjoyed as garden or grounds with the house.

The main residence exemption can extend to other properties within the grounds that are used in conjunction with the house. There have been a number of cases to determine whether separate buildings form part of one dwelling for the purposes of the main residence exemption. As a result of these, two principal tests have been established for the separate building to qualify with the main part of the dwelling, namely:

(a) The building must be used in conjunction with the enjoyment of the main dwelling to form part of one residence. Thus a cottage to house a caretaker and another for a gardener were held to be occupied for the benefit of the main house. This was sufficient for them to be included with the house and thus form part of the main residence (*Batey (Inspector of Taxes) v Wakefield* [1981] STC 521 and *Williams (Inspector of Taxes) v Merrylees* [1987] STC 445).

(b) The building must be adjacent or at least quite close to the main house. For this reason, a cottage on the opposite side of a large estate to the main house has been considered not to be part of the main residence (*Lewis (Inspector of Taxes) v Rook* [1992] STC 171). See also *Markey (Inspector of Taxes) v Sanders* [1987] STC 256. This test was also used to deny the exemption on additional flats in a block used by a family as additional space to the main accommodation in the block (*Honour (Inspector of Taxes) v Norris* [1992] STC 304).

**Point 39.2:** ***An area of over half a hectare may be permitted within the exemption if that larger area is required for the reasonable enjoyment of the residence.***

HMRC can allow the permitted area qualifying for the exemption to exceed a half hectare. However, whereas for areas of less than this it is sufficient to show that the land was part of the garden or grounds of the house, there is a stricter test for larger areas. HMRC must be satisfied that the extra area is required for the reasonable enjoyment of the property, given the size and character of the house (*TCGA 1992, s 222(3)*).

It is not sufficient for this purpose that the property owner has his or her own special requirements. For instance, an individual may use extra grounds to keep horses or vintage cars. That does not mean that area is necessary for the reasonable enjoyment of the property, as other occupiers may not have this requirement (*Longson v Baker (Inspector of Taxes)* [2001] STC 6).

Where the grounds exceed half a hectare, it may be crucial that the land is bought and sold with the house. If it is bought or sold separately, this would indicate that a previous or subsequent owner did not 'require' this land for the 'reasonable enjoyment' of the residence.

**Point 39.3:** ***The main residence exemption may not be available on the disposal of any part of the grounds that has been retained after the sale of the house. In view of this, it is advisable to sell the land before, or at the same time as, the sale of the house.***

In Point 39.2 above, it was mentioned that land greater than half a hectare would normally have to be bought and sold with the house to satisfy the requisite test. Although this is not essential for the general exemption for land, it should be noted that a problem could arise in relation to any part of the land retained after sale of the house.

At the time when land is sold, it must have been owned and used for enjoyment with the house. This condition cannot have been met where any portion of the land had been kept after the sale of the house. Accordingly, the gain on such land will not, strictly, come within the main residence exemption (*Varty v Lynes* [1976] STC 508). This is the case even if the original total area was less than half a hectare.

The above technically applies regardless of whether the gap between the sale of the house and the land was several years or one day. Furthermore, no exemption at all is available for the remaining land, notwithstanding the fact that it may have been occupied with the house for most of the period of ownership. Nor is the deemed final nine months of residence (see Point 38) applied in the case of the land only.

HMRC have stated in the past that they would not seek to assess tax on land sold in such circumstances unless it had development value. However, HMRC varied their view in August 1994 when they stated that no relief is due on the sale of a garden which takes place after a sale of the house (HMRC Capital Gains Manual, CG64377–64387).

Where the land is over half a hectare, the exemption may be restricted whether it is sold before, at the same time as or after the house is sold. As stated above, once land can be shown to be separable from the main residence, it must weaken the argument that the land is required for the reasonable enjoyment of the dwelling house.

*Chapter 40*

# Converting, reconstructing or refurbishing a main residence

**If construction, refurbishment or improvement work is carried out on a main residence to enhance its value on sale, part or all of the gain arising may not be eligible for the capital gains tax exemption.**

**Point 40.1**

↓

Where an opportunity arises to commercially develop a main residence, it might be appropriate to transfer the property to a company or partnership before any work is carried out. This could help ensure that the gain to the date of transfer will be exempt from tax.
Point 40.2

↓

The profit on the sale of a main residence following reconstruction, conversion and refurbishment could be taxable as income.
Point 40.3

# 40 CONVERTING, RECONSTRUCTING OR REFURBISHING A MAIN RESIDENCE

**Point 40.1:** ***If any construction, refurbishment or improvement work is carried out on a main residence to enhance its value on sale, part or all of the gain arising may not be eligible for the capital gains tax exemption.***

Gains attributable to expenditure incurred wholly or partly for the purpose of realising a gain on the sale of the property are excluded from the main residence CGT exemption (*TCGA 1992, s 224(3)*). Therefore, any development and building profit arising from applying for planning permission and incurring construction costs could be fully assessable to CGT. The related provision is also sufficiently wide to catch any improvements that increase the value of the property on sale. This includes the acquisition of the freehold reversion by a leaseholder. Note that simply incurring expenditure on planning permission, or having a restricted covenant released, will not itself result in any loss of the exemption (HMRC Capital Gains Manual CG65243).

To some extent, there are similar considerations here to those mentioned in Chapter 37. Improvements may well be carried out with the expectation that the value of the house will be increased as a result. Any such expenditure could, technically, result in a restriction of the exemption. Accordingly, it may be necessary to demonstrate, where appropriate, that the whole or main objective of any work done was to improve the amenities of the property for the owner's benefit and not to realise a profit.

If the property is sold shortly after any work is carried out, this must add support to a possible argument that the expenditure was incurred with a profit motive. Where this inference is incorrect, the taxpayer may have to be prepared to present to HMRC evidence that the intention to sell arose after the work commenced. In this connection, any special reasons for an unexpected sale might need to be put to HMRC, for example financial problems, job requirements or problems with neighbours.

**Point 40.2:** ***Where an opportunity arises to commercially develop a main residence, it might be appropriate to transfer the property to a company or partnership before any work is carried out. This could help ensure that the gain to the date of transfer will be exempt from tax.***

The legislation does not specify how a gain arising in the circumstances of Point 40.1 above should be computed. HMRC's approach is to calculate the non-exempt gain as if the property was acquired for its unenhanced value at the date of the actual disposal (see HMRC Capital Gains Manual CG65270–65271). This will be based on the hypothetical value of the property as if no enhancement expenditure had been incurred. To achieve some measure of certainty in this situation, the property could be transferred at full market value to a property dealing/developing company or partnership prior to carrying out any work. That would crystallise the exempt gain at that point in time. As mentioned in Point 40.1 above, HMRC do not apply any restriction if the only expenditure incurred is obtaining planning permission or removing restrictive covenants. If there is a proposed change of use of the property and it is likely that planning permission will be successfully obtained, the transfer value of the property after planning permission could reflect some development value. In that way, the exempt gain could reflect part of that development value.

Any tax saving should be balanced against a potential Stamp Duty Land Tax (SDLT) charge. In the case of a UK company buying residential property for development, SDLT rates of up to 15% could be payable. On the other hand, the SDLT cost of transferring to a partnership may be minimal if the ownership is effectively in the same hands.

The further gain on the property in the hands of a company or partnership would almost certainly be taxable. This would most likely be as trading income (under *ITTOIA 2005, s 5* for income tax payers, or under *CTA 2009, s 201* for companies within charge to corporation tax) but possibly as unearned income (*ITA 2007, s 755*) – see Point 40.3 below.

**Point 40.3:** ***The profit on the sale of a main residence following reconstruction, conversion and refurbishment could be taxable as income.***

Apart from capital gains treatment, profits from land transactions can also be taxed as income. In certain circumstances, the profit could be assessed as trading income or as unearned income (under *ITA 2007, s 755*).

An isolated transaction can constitute an adventure in the nature of a trade for tax purposes. When an Inspector considers that this is the case, some or all of the profit arising is potentially assessable as trading income.

It is rare for an individual to be treated as trading in a property that has been used as a main residence. However, this cannot be ruled out where a person has a history of property dealing or developing. In this case, HMRC would treat the property as appropriated to trading stock when it appeared that steps were taken to exploit it commercially. The capital gain up to that date should be covered by the main residence exemption. The gain after that date would be taxable as trading income.

Trading treatment can sometimes be more beneficial than taxation as a capital gain. Financing costs, for instance, can be deducted. Furthermore, if a spouse with no other income is actively involved as a partner or employee in relation to the development, any profit share or reasonable wages paid to him or her can use up personal allowances or lower tax rate bands. Note that, if this is merely used as a way to divert income to a spouse to reduce tax, HMRC use anti-avoidance rules relating to settlements to counter this (*ITTOIA 2005, s 624*). HMRC sometimes seek to tax a gain as unearned income in the following situations:

(a) land, or any property deriving its value from land, is acquired with the object of realising gain from disposing of the land;

(b) land is held as trading stock; or

(c) land is developed with the sole or main object of realising a gain from disposing of the land when developed.

(*ITA 2007, s 756*, formerly *ICTA 1988, s 776*)

Although these provisions are quite wide-ranging, they are generally used as an anti-avoidance measure. In this connection, the following should be noted:

(a) they do not apply where the property being developed was a main residence at the time of the intention to develop (*ITA 2007, s 767*); and

(b) they cannot apply where the proper treatment of the transaction was as an adventure in the nature of trade. Unearned income treatment can only apply where the gain is otherwise of a capital nature (*ITA 2007, s 772(1)*).

*Chapter 41*

# Main residence: taking advantage of the exemption for the last nine months of ownership

**Since the last 9 months of ownership of a main residence will always qualify for exemption even if it has not been occupied as such in that period, two properties may qualify at the same time.**

**Point 41.1**

↓

A main residence election can help two properties to benefit from the capital gains tax exemption in the last 9 months of ownership where one of the properties is not occupied as a main residence.
Point 41.2

# 41 MAIN RESIDENCE: TAKING ADVANTAGE OF THE EXEMPTION FOR THE LAST NINE MONTHS OF OWNERSHIP

**Point 41.1:** ***Since the last nine months of ownership of a main residence will always qualify for exemption, even if it has not been occupied as such in that period, two properties may qualify at the same time.***

Normally, if a property has not been occupied as a main residence throughout the period of ownership, there will be a restriction on the amount of gain eligible for exemption. The gain attributable to the period of main residence will be calculated on a time apportionment basis, and that element of the overall gain treated as exempt. The balance would be a chargeable capital gain.

This calculation proceeds subject to the important proviso that the last nine months of ownership (the last 18 months for disposals before 6 April 2020) are always regarded as a period of main residence, regardless of whether or not the property is occupied as such in that period, but provided the property has been a main residence at some point (*TCGA 1992, s 223(1) and s 223(2)*). Where the individual making the disposal or their spouse is disabled or a long-term resident in a care home, the final 36 months is regarded as a period of main residence (*TCGA 1992, s 225E*).

If the property has been an elected or was an actual main residence before April 2015, this can be taken into account on a future disposal by a non-resident (see Point 38.1 above). The final nine months of ownership will still be exempt.

---

Example

Mr and Mrs Triggs bought a London property in 2011 which they occupied as a residence until 2016. At that time, whilst retaining the house in London, they bought a flat in Bournemouth to be near an ageing parent. The house was subsequently let until 2021 when it was sold.

Out of the ten years' ownership, Mr and Mrs Triggs only occupied the house as a residence for five years. However, as the last nine months of ownership are treated as a period of main residence, 57.5% of the gain is exempt (ie 69 months out of 120) rather than just 50%.

---

In this example, the Bournemouth flat is also a main residence for a period and will similarly benefit from this last nine months of its ownership being treated as a period of main residence. The example in Point 38.2 illustrates how the main residence election can be used in conjunction with this nine -month rule to increase the gains exempt from capital gains tax where more than one property is owned.

**Point 41.2:** ***If a second property is used as a residence, but has not been used as a main residence at any stage, a main residence election can help both properties to benefit from the CGT exemption in the last nine months of ownership of one of the properties.***

As explained in Chapter 38, a main residence election can ensure that more than one property is eligible for capital gains tax exemption at the same time. This can be particularly used to exploit the advantage of the last nine months as a period automatically included in the qualifying period. This would be relevant where one of the properties would not normally be treated as a main residence.

See Points 38.1 and 38.2 for further explanation of this.

As noted in Point 38.5, since April 2015 it has become much more difficult for a non-UK resident to make a valid election for a UK property to be their main residence.

*Chapter 42*

# Temporary absences: preserving the exemption

**A taxpayer who spends a long period living away from his main residence can still be entitled to the full capital gains exemption if he subsequently resumes occupation of that residence.**
**Point 42.1**

An election may have to be considered where another property is occupied during this same period.
Point 42.2

# 42 TEMPORARY ABSENCES: PRESERVING THE EXEMPTION

**Point 42.1***: **A taxpayer who, in certain circumstances, spends a lengthy period living away from his main residence can still be entitled to the full capital gains exemption if he subsequently resumes occupation of that residence.***

A period of absence from a main residence would normally result in the *pro rata* restriction of the main residence exemption referred to in Point 41.1. However, following the rebasing of capital gains at 31 March 1982 (see Chapter 11), periods of absence before 31 March 1982 can be ignored (*TCGA 1992, s 223(7)*).

There are also three situations where periods of absence are ignored, providing the property is occupied as a main residence at some stage before and after the period in question. The three situations are:

(1) A period of absence of up to three years, for whatever reason. The absence may be in the UK or abroad. In arriving at the period of three years, all shorter periods of absence are aggregated during the total period of ownership.

(2) Any period of absence, regardless of length, provided that, throughout the whole period, the individual was required to perform the duties of an employment outside the UK.

(3) Any period of absence up to four years during which the requirements of an individual's employment prevented him from living in the house. As with (1) above, the period of four years may be made up of shorter periods aggregated during the period of ownership.

(*TCGA 1992, s 223(3)*)

The property need not have been left vacant during the period. Even if it had been let, the house can still be treated as a main residence.

As mentioned, it is fundamental that the property in question is the individual's main residence at some time both before and after the period of absence. It can be crucial, therefore, that the individual does re-occupy the property at some time after the above periods have come to an end, at least for a short period.

---

## Example

Langrid buys a house in July 2005 for £180,000. After living there for three years, in July 2008 he and his family are sent abroad by his employer.

On his return in June 2022, it was valued at £600,000.

Langrid sold the house in July 2022, without resuming occupation. The CGT position in 2022/23 would be:

| | | £ |
|---|---|---|
| Sale proceeds | | 600,000 |
| Cost – July 2005 | | (180,000) |
| Total gain | | 420,000 |
| Exempt | | |
| Occupation as main residence | 36 months | |
| Last 9 months | 9 months | |
| | 45 months | |
| Total ownership | 204 months | |
| Exempt 45/204 × £420,000 | | (92,647) |
| Gain before annual exemption | | 327,353 |
| Annual exemption – 2022/23 | | (6,000) |
| Chargeable gain | | 321,353 |
| Tax at 28% | | 89,978.84 |

If Langrid had resumed ownership for a short period, the entire gain would have been exempt.

---

There are circumstances where HMRC do not require a taxpayer to re-occupy the property. This applies in situations (2) and (3) above, where the taxpayer is unable to re-occupy the residence because the terms of his employment require him to work elsewhere (*TCGA 1992, s 223(3A and 3B)*).

***Point 42.2*: Notwithstanding the permitted period of absence above, an election may have to be considered where another property is occupied during this same period.**

The provisions regarding the permitted periods of absence in Point 42.1 above only apply where there is no other residence eligible for relief (*TCGA 1992, s 223(3B)*). Whilst the objective may have been to prevent two properties being eligible for relief at the same time, it also creates a pitfall where long-term absences are involved.

A family having to live away from their usual home for an extended period will need residential accommodation elsewhere. Whether this is within the UK or abroad, this accommodation must, by definition, be the taxpayer's only or main residence during that period and is eligible for the exemption.

It would make a nonsense of the permitted period of absence provision if HMRC did not overlook at least certain types of accommodation. This might include hotel suites, company-owned property, rented houses or apartments. However, there could be a problem if another property is acquired for occupation during the period. Accordingly, where a second property is bought, it may be advisable to elect to treat the first property as a main residence (see Chapter 38).

If a second residence is acquired and the first property temporarily let, HMRC may not accept a main residence election in respect of the let property. In this case, the message must be that buying a second residence during a period of absence could well prejudice the availability of a full capital gains tax exemption on the first house particularly if it is let during the period of absence.

Anyone living outside the UK will also need to bear in mind the conditions required for a valid main residence election introduced from 5 April 2015 (see Point 38.5).

*Chapter 43*

# Taking advantage of the exemption on let property

**From 1 April 2020, lettings relief is not available if the whole property is let out.**
**Point 43.1**

# 43 TAKING ADVANTAGE OF THE EXEMPTION ON LET PROPERTY

**Point 43.1:** ***From 1 April 2020, lettings relief is not available if the whole property is let out.***

Let property, which was the owner's residence at some time during the period of ownership, attracts an additional capital gains exemption on disposal. The extra exemption is the lowest of £40,000, the gain attributable to the let period, and the main residence exemption in respect of this disposal (*TCGA 1992, s 223(4)*).

Whilst lettings relief can be given in addition to PPR relief, from 1 April 2020, lettings relief is not available if the whole property is let out. It is only available where there is a tenant in another part of the same house whilst the other part of the property continues to be occupied by the owner.

Lettings relief is capped at the lower of the PPR exempt gain, and £40,000. Note that lettings relief cannot turn a gain into a loss.

---

## Example

Andrew sells a house in November 2022 and realises a gain (before any reliefs of £300,000). He has lived in the house as his principal private residence throughout his period of ownership. However, throughout that period 50% of the floor area of the house was let out.

Andrew's chargeable gain for 2022/23 in respect of the house will be as follows:

| | |
|---|---|
| Gain before reliefs | 300,000 |
| Less: Main residence relief (50%) | (150,000) |
| Less: letting relief–lower of: | |
| • Main residence relief | 150,000 |
| • Gain attributable to letting | 150,000 |
| • £40,000 | (40,000) |
| Chargeable gain | £110,000 |

---

To obtain some capital gains tax exemption, it is not necessary to occupy the property as a main residence. Even where there is occasional occupation in a period, provided it is, in fact, occupied as a residence, an election can be made for a property to be treated as a main residence (see Chapter 38). Anyone living outside the UK will have to satisfy the conditions introduced from 5 April 2015 before a valid election can be made (see Point 38.5).

In view of the potential capital gains tax exemptions, the occupation of a property to take advantage of a main residence election could well prove worthwhile if at all practical. This may be the case where the property has already been owned for some years and substantial appreciation in its value has already taken place.

As discussed in Chapter 44, periods prior to 31 March 1982 are ignored in determining the appropriate period of exemption. Thus, in the above example, if the period of occupation had been in 1981, this would have been ignored. The last nine months would still be exempt.

*Chapter 44*

# Main residences: periods before 31 March 1982

**Periods before 31 March 1982 are ignored for the purposes of the main residence exemption. This could be helpful where absences or letting have taken place before that date.**

**Point 44.1**

↓

Where the owner occupied the property as a main residence before 31 March 1982 but not since, the last nine months should still be exempt.
Point 44.2

# 44 MAIN RESIDENCES: PERIODS BEFORE 31 MARCH 1982

**Point 44.1:** ***Periods before 31 March 1982 are ignored for the purposes of the main residence exemption. This could be helpful where absences or letting have taken place before that date.***

In Chapter 11, the effects of the rebasing provisions were discussed for assets owned at 31 March 1982. It is possible to calculate a gain by reference to the 31 March 1982 market value of a property instead of cost for capital gains purposes. For disposals after 5 April 2008, gains by non-corporates may only be calculated using the 31 March 1982 value, rather than cost, for assets held at that date.

As far as main residences are concerned, it will be noted from Chapters 41, 42 and 43 that a gain on a main residence may not be totally exempt where there have been periods during which the property has not been occupied as a main residence. This may also be the case where a taxpayer owns more than one residence, since he can only elect for one to be treated as a main residence at any time (see Chapter 38).

In conjunction with the introduction of the rebasing provisions, the main residence exemption was amended so that periods prior to 31 March 1982 are ignored in determining the amount of exemption. Clearly, this would be beneficial where there has been a period of letting or absence from a property which only occurred before 31 March 1982.

---

## Example 1

Mr and Mrs Bolt bought a holiday cottage as residential investment in 1970. It was let until March 1982. They subsequently occupied it until 2023 when the property was sold.

The entire gain on the property would be exempt. The period of letting occurred prior to 31 March 1982 and is, therefore, ignored.

---

**Point 44.2:** ***Where the owner occupied the property as a main residence before 31 March 1982 but not since, the last nine months should still be exempt.***

Following on from the point in Point 44.1 above, where a property had only been occupied as a main residence before 31 March 1982, none of that period can qualify for exemption. This raises the question, however, of whether a taxpayer would still be entitled to have the last nine months of ownership treated as a period of qualifying residence.

It does appear that entitlement to the main residence exemption in the first instance arises where there has been, at any stage, occupation of the property as such. The restriction of the period of ownership to that period after 31 March 1982 seems to be relevant only for the purposes of determining the fraction to be applied in computing the extent of the exemption (*TCGA 1992, s 223(7)*). For the purposes of this fraction, however, the last nine months of ownership are always assumed to be a period of occupation of a main residence (*TCGA 1992, s 223(2)*).

*Chapter 45*

# Rent a room: income tax exemption on part letting of a main residence

| |
|---|
| **There is exemption from income tax where part of a home is let and the annual gross receipts do not exceed £7,500.**<br><br>**Point 45.1** |

# 45 RENT A ROOM: INCOME TAX EXEMPTION ON PART LETTING OF A MAIN RESIDENCE

**Point 45.1:** ***There is exemption from income tax where part of a home is let and the annual gross receipts do not exceed £7,500 from 6 April 2016 unless there is shared occupancy (previously £4,250).***

The government introduced the 'rent a room' relief in 1992. This applies where an individual or individuals let furnished rooms within their main residence (*ITTOIA 2005, ss 784–802*).

The relief applies where the 'relevant sums' received from the accommodation do not exceed £7,500 from 5 April 2016 – previously £4,250) (*ITTOIA 2005, s 789*). The receipts are fully exempt from tax.

Relevant sums include charges for items such as meals, cleaning, laundry and similar items in addition to rent (*ITTOIA 2005, s 786*). Expenses and capital allowances cannot be deducted.

Where the property is owned by more than one person, the relief is halved (*ITTOIA 2005, s 789*) regardless of the number of owners. Therefore, a husband and wife owning the property would each be entitled to earn £3,750. If four friends own a property which is their main residence, each would also have an exemption of £3,750. In that case, total exemptions would be £15,000.

If the receipts exceed the exemption, the individual can elect to be taxed on the excess without any deduction for expenses or capital allowances (*ITTOIA 2005, s 795*).

Rent a room relief applies in respect of furnished accommodation. Relief is only available in respect of accommodation let in the individual's main residence. If more than one property is owned, it is a question of fact which is the main residence. No election is possible, unlike the position for capital gains tax.

If a taxpayer makes a loss in a year which can be offset against other income, it may not be beneficial to claim the rent a room exemption. The individual can opt out of the exemption for that year by notifying HMRC on or before the first anniversary of the 31 January next following the year of assessment, ie 22 months after the year end (*ITTOIA 2005, s 799*).

HMRC accept that the letting of accommodation which is an integral part of a main residence will not affect the capital gains exemption available on the sale of the property. However, if it is self-contained and the owner lives in the residence at the same time, the taxpayer may have to rely on letting relief for capital gains tax exemption (see Chapter 43).

*Chapter 46*

# Expense deductions for business use of home

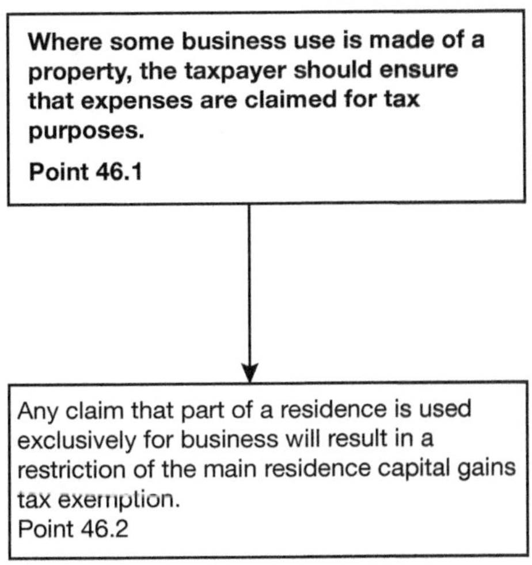

# 46 EXPENSE DEDUCTIONS FOR BUSINESS USE OF HOME

**Point 46.1:** ***Where some business use is made of a property, the taxpayer should ensure that expenses are claimed for tax purposes.***

Many individuals use their properties, to a greater or lesser extent, for the purposes of a trade or employment carried on by them. This could well mean that there is an entitlement to claim related household expenses for tax purposes.

A person carrying on a trade, profession or vocation can deduct any expenses that are wholly and exclusively incurred for the purposes of the trade etc (*ITTOIA 2005, s 34*). This could include heating, lighting and power costs resulting directly from his use of the property for business purposes. Often, this can be estimated based on the amount of time spent on business activities in the home and the space occupied.

In addition, where an individual exclusively uses part of the premises for business purposes (eg where it is used as a doctor's surgery or as a self-contained office) it may also be possible to claim an appropriate portion of other expenses, such as rent, repairs, insurance, interest charges and council tax. Strictly, such expenses are deductible only if they are exclusive to the business area being used. In practice, HMRC does allow *pro rata* expense claims, provided an area is exclusively used for business. However, the possible restriction in the capital gains tax exemption should be noted (see Point 46.2 below). HMRC may also be prepared to accept apportioned sums in respect of heating, lighting and council tax (rates in Northern Ireland) where business use of a room or rooms is not exclusive, as will usually be the case (Business Income Manual BIM47815). Alternatively, sole traders and partnerships where proprietors work at least 25 hours a month at home can claim a monthly flat rate to cover household running expenses such as heat, light, power. The flat rate does not include telephone and broadband/internet. The business proportion of these bills may be claimed by working out actual costs. The current starting rate for flat rate expenses are listed at www.gov.uk/simpler-income-tax-simplified-expenses/overview.

An employee may similarly be entitled to deductions where an area is occupied exclusively for his work. However, the employee has the additional burden of showing that the expense was necessarily as well as wholly and exclusively incurred. Thus, an employee or director who chooses to do certain work at home rather than at the office would probably not satisfy the 'necessarily' test, although it is common in practice for HMRC to require only the 'wholly' and 'exclusively' tests to be met. On the other hand, a travelling salesman or area manager who is required to use his home as a base may well need to use a room in his home as an office. Where rooms are not used exclusively for the purpose of the employment, HMRC are prepared to accept the extra cost of heating and lighting the room(s) while in use for business. However, in contrast with the position for the self-employed (see above) no deduction may be claimed for council tax (see Employment Income Manual EIM32810).

Even where an employee cannot make a claim for a deduction of expenses paid, this will not prevent employers making a tax/NIC-free payment to the employee covering unreceipted expenses for working at home. The guideline 'home working allowance' is £6 per week (£4 prior to 6 April 2020). Greater amounts may be paid if the employer provides evidence to justify them (*ITEPA 2003, s 316A*).

**Point 46.2:** ***Any claim that part of a residence is used exclusively for business will result in a restriction of the main residence exemption.***

If part of the house is used exclusively for business purposes, then it is not covered by the main residence exemption (*TCGA 1992, s 224(1)*). Examples are doctors and dentists who have used two or three rooms within their house for the purposes of a surgery and waiting room. However, many individuals do set aside part of their house as a study or office, either informally or as a formal business address. In other cases, garages or sheds within a garden area are converted into workshops for trading purposes.

If a claim is made that a particular room is being set aside wholly for business purposes, then it will be necessary to estimate the portion of the gain attributable to that room. This will be excluded from the main residence exemption. If one room in a ten-room house is being so used, then it may be reasonable to assume the figure is 10%, although it could be higher or lower depending on the size of the room in question relative to the rest of the house. In addition, it may be possible to claim a portion of the interest paid on the loan to purchase the property.

A higher rate taxpayer may be better off with the income tax relief than the capital gains exemption.

---

## Example

Between April 2006 and April 2016, an individual, who was paying tax at the marginal rate of 40% up to 5 April 2010, 50% from 6 April 2010 to 5 April 2013 and 45% thereafter, agreed with HMRC that part of his house was used exclusively for business purposes. His bills for utilities, insurance, repairs and maintenance plus interest charges averaged £20,000 per year, and 10% of this was allowed as trading expense.

The house cost £300,000 in April 2006 and was sold for £600,000 on 1 April 2016.

**Income tax saving over ten years**:

20006/07 to 2015/16

| | £ |
|---|---|
| 4 × 10% × £20,000 × 40% = | 3,200 |
| 3 × 10% × £20,000 × 50% = | 3,000 |
| 3 × 10% × £20,000 × 45% = | 2,700 |
| | 8,900 |

| | £ | |
|---|---|---|
| **Capital gains position** | | |
| Sale proceeds | 600,000 | |
| Cost | 300,000 | |
| Gain | 300,000 | |
| | *Non-business* | *Business* |
| Exempt – 90% (non-business) | 270,000 | |
| Chargeable – 10% business | | 30,000 |
| Annual exemption | | (11,100) |
| Chargeable gain | | 18,900 |
| Extra capital gains tax payable at 28% | | 5,292 |

As mentioned in Point 46.1 above, even if part of a house is exclusively used for business, the allowance of certain expenses on a *pro rata* basis may be more a matter of HMRC practice specific to the circumstances of the case.

# Appendices

*Appendix 1*

# Items of Expenditure on Buildings and Structures Qualifying and Non-Qualifying as Plant/Integral Features (CAA 2001, Part 2, Chapter 3)

[*Note*: Since April 2008, a category of 'integral fixtures' in a building has attracted a lower rate of annual writing-down allowance. Details of the assets in this category are set out in II below. Some of these items formerly were included with the qualifying items in I below. Other items now attract allowances where they would not have been available pre April 2008. See Point 6.5 in Chapter 6 for further commentary on this.]

**I. Qualifying expenditure – items which become part of a building (s 23, List C). [This expenditure attracts 18% annual writing-down allowances].**

(1) Machinery (including devices for motive power) not within any other item in this list.

(2) [Electrical system (including lighting systems) and cold water, gas and sewerage systems provided mainly:

- (a) to meet the particular requirements of the qualifying activity; or
- (b) to serve particular machinery or plant used for the purposes of the qualifying activity.] [Note that, since April 2008, these items have been moved to the category of 'integral features' – see II below.]

(3) [Space or water heating systems; powered systems of ventilation, air cooling or air purification; and any ceiling or floor comprised in such systems]. [*Note that, since April 2008, these items have been moved to the category of 'integral features' – see II below.]*

(4) Manufacturing or processing equipment; storage equipment (including cold rooms); display equipment; and counters, checkouts and similar equipment.

(5) Cookers, washing machines, dishwashers, refrigerators and similar equipment; washbasins, sinks, baths, showers, sanitary ware and similar equipment; and furniture and fittings.

(6) [Lifts, hoists, escalators and moving walkways.] [*Note that, since April 2008, these items have been moved to the category of 'integral features' – see II below.]*

(7) Sound insulation provided mainly to meet the particular requirements of the qualifying activity.

(8) Computer, telecommunication and surveillance systems (including their wiring and other links).

(9) Refrigeration or cooling equipment.

(10) Fire alarm systems; sprinkler and other equipment for extinguishing or containing fire.

(11) Burglar alarm systems.

(12) Strong rooms in bank or building society premises; safes.

(13) Partition walls, where moveable and intended to be moved in the course of the qualifying activity.

(14) Decorative assets provided for the enjoyment of the public in the hotel, restaurant or similar trades.

(15) Advertising hoarding; signs, displays and other similar assets.

(16) Swimming pools (including diving boards, slides and structures on which such boards or slides are mounted).

(17) Any glasshouse constructed so that the required environment (namely air, heat, light, irrigation and temperature) for the growing of plants is provided automatically by means of devices forming an integral part of its structure.

(18) Cold stores.

(19) Caravans provided mainly for holiday lettings.

(20) Buildings provided for testing aircraft engines run within the buildings.

(21) Moveable buildings intended to be moved in the course of the qualifying activity.

(22) The alteration of land for the purpose only of installing plant or machinery.

(23) The provision of dry docks.

(24) The provision of any jetty or similar structure provided mainly to carry plant or machinery.

(25) The provision of pipelines or underground ducts or tunnels with a primary purpose of carrying utility conduits.

(26) The provision of towers to support floodlights.

(27) The provision of:

(a) any reservoir incorporated into a water-treatment works; or

(b) any service reservoir of treated water for supply within any housing estate or other particular locality.

(28) The provision of:

(a) silos provided for temporary storage; or

(b) storage tanks.

(29) The provision of slurry pits or silage clamps.

(30) The provision of fish tanks or fish ponds.

(31) The provision of rails, sleepers and ballast for a railway or tramway.

(32) The provision of structures and other assets for providing the setting for any ride at an amusement park or exhibition.

(33) The provision of fixed zoo cages. *Note:*

Items 1 to 16 do not include any asset whose principal purpose is to insulate or enclose the interior of a building or to provide for an interior wall, floor or ceiling which (in each case) is intended to remain permanently in place.

**II. Expenditure qualifying under the 'integral features' category – CAA 2001, s 33A. [This expenditure attracts 6% annual writing-down allowances with effect from corporation tax accounting periods ending on or after 31 March 2019, and income tax chargeable periods ending on or after 6 April 2019.]**

(1) Lifts, escalators and moving walkways.

(2) Space or water heating systems.

(3) Powered systems of ventilation, air cooling or air purification, and any floor or ceiling comprised in such systems.

(4) Electrical systems (including lighting systems).

(5) Cold water systems.

(6) External solar shading.

(7) Thermal insulation.

**III. Non-qualifying expenditure – assets treated as buildings (section 21, List A)**

(1) Walls, floors, ceilings, doors, gates, shutters, windows and stairs.

(2) Mains services and systems, for water, electricity and gas.

(3) Waste disposal systems.

(4) Sewerage and drainage systems.

(5) Shafts or other structures in which lifts, hoists, escalators and moving walkways are installed.

(6) Fire safety systems.

**IV. Non-qualifying expenditure – structures and other assets (section 22, List B)**

(1) A tunnel, bridge, viaduct, aqueduct, embankment or cutting.

(2) A way, hard standing (such as a pavement), road, railway, tramway, a park for vehicles or containers, or an airstrip or runway.

(3) An inland navigation, including a canal or basin or a navigable river.

(4) A dam, reservoir or barrage, including any sluices, gates, generators and other equipment associated with the dam, reservoir or barrage.

(5) A dock, harbour, wharf, pier, marina or jetty or any other structure in or at which vessels may be kept, or merchandise or passengers may be shipped or unshipped.

(6) A dyke, sea wall, weir or drainage ditch.

(7) Any structure not within items (1) to (6) other than:

- (a) a structure (but not a building) within the definition of an industrial building for the purpose of industrial buildings allowances;
- (b) a structure in use for the purposes of an undertaking for the extraction, production, processing or distribution of gas; and
- (c) a structure in use for the purposes of a trade which consists in the provision of telecommunications, television or radio services.

*Appendix II*

# Construction operations for the purposes of the Construction Industry Scheme

The following list produced by HM Revenue and Customs gives guidance on which types of construction work are within the scheme and which are not. Where a contract relates to a number of operations, some of which appear in the 'Operations excluded' column, the contract as a whole will be one relating to construction operations, and the deduction scheme should be operated for all payments under the contract.

**Planning**

| Operations included | Operations excluded |
|---|---|
| None | Professional work (including the ancillary work of engineers, draughtsmen, scientists and technicians) of architects, surveyors or consultants in building, engineering, decoration (interior or exterior) or landscaping. |

**Site preparation**

| Operations included | Operations excluded |
|---|---|
| Demolition of buildings, structures, tree-felling, etc. Preparation of site and site clearance, earth-moving on the site, excavation, tunnelling, boring. | Delivery of materials.<br>Transport of spoil from site. |

**Construction**

| Operations included | Operations excluded |
|---|---|
| Preparation and laying of foundations and piling. | Manufacture or off-site fabrication of components or equipment, materials, plant or machinery and delivery of these to the site. For example traditional building materials prefabricated beams and panels and ready mixed concrete. |

| Operations included | Operations excluded |
| --- | --- |
| Actual construction, alteration or repair of a permanent or temporary building or civil, chemical or other industrial engineering work or industrial plant or structure. For example: storage tanks, silos, pylons, cranes or derricks and pumps. | |
| Construction of site facilities. | Manufacture and delivery of pre-fabricated site facilities. Running of site facilities such as canteens, hostels, offices, toilets and medical centres or the supply of security guards. |
| Installation of power lines, pipelines, gas mains, sewers, drainage, cable television and telecommunications distribution systems. | Installation or replacement of telecommunication or computer wiring through pre-existing ducting in buildings. |
| Installation of closed circuit television for purposes other than security (such as traffic management). | |
| Installation of public services. | |
| Construction, repair and resurfacing of roads and bridges, including white-lining. | Delivery of road-making materials. Setting out traffic cones. |
| Provision of temporary and permanent roadways and other access works such as drives. | |
| Erection or dismantling of scaffolding falsework and formwork. | Hire of scaffolding equipment (without labour). |
| Plant hire with operator for use on site. | Delivery, repair or maintenance of construction plant or hire equipment with an operator. For example concrete mixers, pumps and skips. |
| Installation of fire protection systems designed specifically to protect the fabric of the building (such as sprinkler systems, fireproof cladding) rather than a fire warning (alarm) system. | Installation of fire alarms, security systems including burglar alarms, closed-circuit television as part of a security system, and public address systems. |
| Installation of pre-fabricated component or equipment under 'supply and fix' arrangements. | |

| Operations included | Operations excluded |
| --- | --- |
| Transportation of materials on site. | Transport of materials from site to site on the public highway. |
| | Assembly of temporary stages and exhibition stands, including lighting. |
| Internal cleaning of buildings and structures carried out in the course of, or on completion of, their construction, alteration, extension, repair or restoration. | External cleaning (other than painting or decorating) of buildings and structures. |
| Work done on installations (such as rigs, pipelines, construction platforms) maintained or intended to be established for underwater exploration for, or exploitation of, minerals where the work is on land or in UK territorial waters up to the 12 mile limit. | Drilling for, or extraction of, oil or natural gas. Extraction of minerals, boring or construction of underground works for this purpose. |
| Installation of systems of heating, lighting, air conditioning, ventilation, power supply and distribution, drainage, sanitation, water supply and distribution, and fire protection works. | Manufacture, delivery, repair or maintenance of these items. Replacement of system parts not involving other construction operations (eg taps or a radiator). |
| Installation of lifts, plant, or machinery needed by the specification of a building under construction or alteration. | Servicing, repair or maintenance of these items. Stairlifts requiring no alteration or repair to the building. |
| Construction and repair of industrial plant. | |
| Site restoration and landscaping. | Tree planting and felling in the ordinary course of forestry or estate management. |
| Installation, structural repair and painting of lamp standards, traffic lights, parking meters and street furniture. | Manufacture and delivery of lamp standards. Routine maintenance such as cleaning and general replacement. |
| Construction of concrete and marble floors. Fitting of eye bolts, whether internal or external. | Manufacture off-site and delivery of flooring materials. |

| **Operations included** | **Operations excluded** |
|---|---|
| Installation and repair to: glazing, doors and rolling grills or security shutters, kitchens and bathrooms, shop-fittings including fixed furniture (except seating and freestanding display cabinets). | Manufacture and delivery of: glazing materials, computer and instrumentation systems, thermal insulation materials, heating and ventilation systems, doors and rolling grills, painting or decorating materials. |
| Painting and decorating the internal or external surfaces of any building or structure. | Manufacture, delivery and installation of seating, blinds and louvred shutters. |
| | Manufacture, installation and repair of artistic works (for example, sculptures and murals) which are wholly decorative in nature (not functional items caught by the Scheme which incidentally have artistic merit). |
| | Manufacture and installation of solar, blackout or anti-shatter film. |
| | Signwriting and erecting, installation and repair of signboards and advertisements. |
| Fitting of: floor coverings, such as vinyl, linoleum (but not carpet) and laminated wooden flooring, pigeon mesh, TV aerials and satellite receivers. | |
| Installation of refrigeration units. | |
| *But only where these finishing operations render complete a building or structure that has been constructed or altered.* | |

# Index

*All references are to Point numbers*